U0581320

FORT OSWEGO

FORT NIAGARA

RT DETROIT

FORT SANDUSKY

FORT DUQUESNE

FORT CUMBERLAND

Albany

Falmouth (Portland)

Portsmouth

Boston

Newport
New London

New York

Philadelphia

Baltimore

St. Augustine

SEA INDUSTRIES:

fishing

whaling

FOREST INDUSTRIES:

lumber and timber

shipbuilding

naval stores

GENERAL INDUSTRIES:

ironworks

rum distilleries

Post Roads

0   50   100   150   200 Miles

Highlights of American History

美国历史风云

范咏涛 编著

Sichuan University Press
四川大学出版社

责任编辑：敬铃凌
责任校对：夏　宇
封面设计：米茄设计工作室
责任印制：李　平

图书在版编目(CIP)数据

美国历史风云 / 范咏涛编著. —成都：四川大学
出版社，2010.7
（美国视野）
ISBN 978-7-5614-4967-7

Ⅰ.①美… Ⅱ.①范… Ⅲ.①英语-听说教学-高等
学校-教材②英语-阅读教学-高等学校-教材③美国-
历史　Ⅳ.①H319：K

中国版本图书馆 CIP 数据核字（2010）第 154083 号

书　名	美国历史风云
	Meiguo Lishi Fengyun
编　著	范咏涛
出　版	四川大学出版社
地　址	成都市一环路南一段24号 (610065)
发　行	四川大学出版社
书　号	ISBN 978-7-5614-4967-7
印　刷	郫县犀浦印刷厂
成品尺寸	210 mm×285 mm
印　张	19.25
字　数	565 千字
版　次	2010 年 10 月第 1 版
印　次	2010 年 10 月第 1 次印刷
印　数	0 001～3 000 册
定　价	48.00 元

◆读者邮购本书,请与本社发行科
　联系。电 话:85408408/85401670/
　85408023　邮政编码:610065

◆本社图书如有印装质量问题,请
　寄回出版社调换。

◆网址:www.scupress.com.cn

版权所有◆侵权必究

前　言

　　《美国历史风云》是为我国高等院校英语专业一、二年级学生准备的一本把阅读、听力、历史与文化知识融为一体的新型教材，它与已经先期出版的《美国文化风云人物》组成一套体系，其首要目标是按照《高等学校英语专业英语教学大纲》的要求，帮助低年级学生从"读"和"听"两个方面打好扎实的英语语言基本功，同时拓宽他们的文化知识领域。

　　本书既可以作为专业技能必修课"阅读"课程的教材，也可以作为专业知识选修课"美国历史"、"美国社会与文化"等课程的教材。同时，本书也适合有一定英语基础并且对美国历史感兴趣的其他专业的学生以及其他有意提高英语水平的人士阅读和使用。

本书的两大特点

　　本书的第一个特点就是它是一本难度适中的有声读物。对于英语词汇量有限的大多数学生来说，要发展阅读技能，培养阅读兴趣，所选用的阅读材料难度一定不要过高，否则只会适得其反。另外，掌握语言的诀窍在于首先要掌握它的"声音"。对于仍然处于基础学习阶段的学生来说，对英语"声音"的接触、模仿、训练自然是越多越好。充分了解有声读物的性质与特点并加以充分利用，是打好语言基础和培养语感的最佳途径。

　　本书的第二个特点就是它围绕美国历史这个主题为学习者提供了丰富的知识。母语学习的实践告诉我们，在发展阅读技能和吸取知识两个方面，比较深入地阅读一本书往往比阅读零散而内容不相干的文章的效果更好一些。另外，语言学习也不应该与语言所代表的文化分隔开来。我们要真正掌握英语，就必须对英语文化背景知识有最起码的了解。第二次世界大战以后，美国逐渐成为一个世界超级强国，而它的历史与文化一直就成为各国英语学习者讨论和研究的热门话题。尽管囿于篇幅，本书不是一部完整的美国历史，但它展现出的美国两百多年历史画卷中最重要的事件和人物，是非常值得每一个英语学习者了解和学习的。

关于英语阅读课程

　　英语阅读课程既要培养学习者的英语阅读理解能力，也应激发学习者通过阅读吸收英语文化和科技知识的兴趣。在近年来的阅读课教学上，编者认为有两个倾向需要注意。

　　第一是阅读题材过于广泛的倾向。从阅读的目标看，一个人的阅读范围当然是越广越好。然而，对大多数英语水平有限的学生来说，过分广泛的题材只会对他们英语阅读技能的发展造成更大的障碍。翻开近年来我国学生使用的一些英语阅读教材，我们发现几乎每一个单元都涉及社会或科技方面的一个新领域，而每一个领域的新概念和新词汇对学生的阅读和理解都是一个巨大的挑战。这种挑战迫使学生在阅读过程中始终处于一种艰难挣扎的状态，因而很难体会到阅读给人带来的精神愉悦，很难产生对英语阅读发自内心的兴趣。另外，由于文章内容不停地从一个领域转到另一个领域，生词和难词的重复率也很低，许多刚接触到的词语也很快就会被忘掉。

　　第二是阅读训练考试化的倾向。考试是检验学习效果的重要手段，但它永远只能是学习的副产物，永远不应该对正常的学习形成干扰。我们从一些英语阅读教材中看到，在一篇长度仅为一两页的文章后面，常常紧跟着五六页的以测试为目的的各种练习。这样的课程设计给学习者一个强烈的信号：只有完成了这些习题才达到了学习的目标。在实际的教学中我们不难发现，面对一篇文章，许多学生首先选择去读练习题，然后在读文章的过程中对号入座，以求用最快的方法得到习题答案。把这种原本为考试设计的练习推广到正常的阅读实践中，其负面影响是显而易见的：学习者既不愿意用"心"去阅读，也无法培养出真正的阅读兴趣。

对使用本书的建议

本书由 16 个教学单元组成，每个单元有 4 篇文章。如果把此书作为阅读课程的主要教材，建议每周学习一个单元，全书内容在一个学期内完成；如果作为阅读课程的辅助教材，可以考虑每两周学习一个单元，全书内容在两个学期内完成。

编者给教师的其他建议如下：

1. 教师尽可能要求学生在上新课之前听录音预习课文。

2. 对于不能在课堂内完成的文章，教师应要求学生在课外学习，培养学生的自学能力。

3. 每篇文章后面的问题既可以安排在课堂上讨论，也可以作为书面作业要求学生在课内或课外完成，其目的是检验学生的理解能力和归纳能力。书面作业一是不要用所谓的"标准答案"来束缚学生的思想，二是要求学生注意文字的正式性和准确性。

4. 鼓励学生演唱一些课文后面附加的美国历史歌曲。唱英语歌曲是掌握正确的英语语音语调、克服地方口音的最好方法。教师应该要求学生在课堂上或课外活动中唱这些歌曲。

把阅读、听力，以及系统的文化和历史知识等内容有机地融合在一起编写基础英语教材是一种新的尝试。由于这是一项新的工作，加之编者水平有限，本书一定存在不少缺点或疏漏之处。本书编者诚恳欢迎使用本书的教师和学生提出批评与建议（E-mail: yongtaofan@ hotmail. com）。同时，编者对《美国之音》为本书提供全部基础资料表示最衷心的感谢。

范咏涛

2010 年 10 月于成都

Contents

Unit 1　The New World

1　The First People That Arrived in the New World

最早来到新大陆的人们

当波澜壮阔的美国历史画卷随着意大利人克里斯托弗·哥伦布 1492 年远航的风帆涂涂展开之际，地球上恐怕没有任何人能够预见到一个崭新而伟大的文明——美利坚文明——将在今后的数百年中迅速崛起，为已经延续大约五千年的人类文明史增添了辉煌的一页。

如果从 1776 年《独立宣言》发布之日算起，美国的历史仅有 200 多年；即使从 1607 年第一批英国移民在弗吉尼亚詹姆斯敦安营扎寨算起，美国的历史也只有区区 400 年。然而，在这样一个位于大西洋沿岸一片狭长地带的年轻国度里，诞生了世界上第一部成文宪法，产生了世界上第一位民选总统，美国也因此被称为全世界的"共和国之祖国"。在一段用历史眼光看起来极其短暂的时间里，美国飞快地发展成为一个举足轻重、影响深远的世界大国，它在政治、经济、科技、文化等领域所取得的成就举世瞩目。因此，学习、了解和研究美国的历史，其重要性不言而喻。

与世界上其他国家截然不同的是，美国几乎是一个百分之百的移民国家。欧洲人——主要是英格兰人——是现在称为美国这块土地上的最初移民。然而，这并不是全部的事实。在欧洲人到达之前，早已有人捷足先登，在整个美洲大陆创建了独特而丰富多彩的文化和文明。现在，让我们在科学家和历史学家的指引下，去了解那些最早在新大陆定居的人类。

Scientists and history experts say the first people ever to come to the **Western Hemisphere** arrived between 15,000 and 35,000 years ago. They may have come in several different groups. No one is really sure who they were or where they lived before. Experts say the best possible answer about where they came from is northern Asia. Most experts believe they crossed to the Western Hemisphere from the part of Russia now called **Siberia**. The first people came to the **New World** in a time of fierce cold. Much of the Northern part of the world was covered in ice. Because of this, the oceans were hundreds of meters lower than they are now. Scientists believe this made it possible to walk across the area that is now the **Bering Sea**.

For a moment, let us follow a family group as it begins to cross the area that is now the Bering Sea. The time is more than 20,000 years ago.

The hunter watched the small group of animals. It had been several days since he had last killed an animal for food. The hunter's family had not much left to eat. It was the responsibility of the men to provide the food. Today they must get meat or their families would not survive. The **fierce cold** added to the **sharp hunger** that the hunter felt. He was dressed from head to foot in heavy animal skins to protect against the cold.

The hunter was several kilometers from the animals. The animals had moved slowly during the night toward the rising sun. They had been moving in this direction for several days. They were also looking for food. The hunter knew there was not much for them to eat in this area. He knew the animals would keep moving. The hunter's people had always followed animals for food. But they had never followed them this far toward the rising sun. The hunter looked behind him. He could see the women and children far behind. He picked up his weapon and moved forward.

Later, the men killed two animals. It was enough to feed all their people for perhaps two days. That night as they cooked the meat, the hunter thought about turning back to the land behind them. The hunter knew that area well. But the hunting had been poor for a long time. This was the first group of animals they had been able **to follow any length of time**. It was not a large group of animals but there were enough to follow. He decided that in the morning they could continue toward the rising sun. They would stay with this herd of animals. He knew his family had little choice: Follow them and live; or go back and perhaps die from a lack of food.

This is just a story. But it could be true. Scientists believe such hunters followed animals east across what is now the Bering Sea. It is only about 80 kilometers from Siberia to what is now the American state of **Alaska**. Eighty kilometers would not be a long trip for ancient people following animal herds. Scientists have done new **genetic tests** on large populations of people. They show that about 95 percent of all native peoples in the Western Hemisphere came from the same family group. The scientists say this family may have crossed into the west about 20,000 years ago. This family group would have grown and divided during the next several thousand years. **Over time**, they would have spread out and explored most of the land that is North, Central and South America.

Many of those early peoples stayed in the far northern parts of the American continents. They were already used to living in the extreme cold. They knew how to survive. Today members of a tribe called the **Yuit** still live near the Bering Sea in

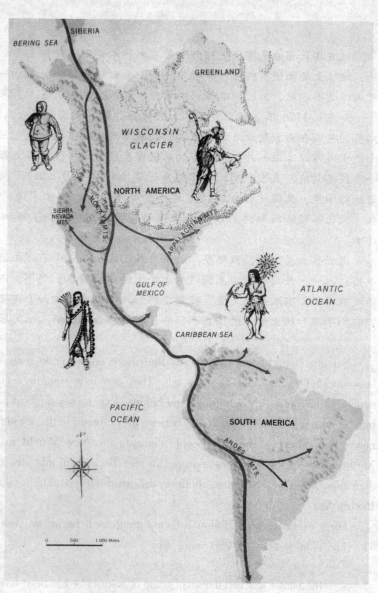

Migration of Indians to the Americas

Alaska. Other tribes live in the **Arctic Circles** of northern Canada. These include several different tribes of the **Inuit**. Many of these people of the far North still hunt wild animals for much of their food.

The early settlers in North America were not able to immediately travel south. Huge amounts of ice stopped them. Experts believe the early settlers lived in the far north for about 2,000 years before they began to move south. One expert says it could have taken only 500 years for the early Indians to settle all of the Western Hemisphere from southern Canada to the end of South America.

Scientists say it is more likely that the movement took several thousand years. But in time these people spread out over the Western Hemisphere. They became thousands of different tribes with many languages, from the Inuit in the far north, to the **Yahgan** people near the end of South America. One group was the **Maya of Mexico**. They learned to read and write their language and build huge stone buildings that can still be seen today. The **Inca of Peru** also built stone buildings that are extremely beautiful. Some Indians still live much the same as they always have. An example is the **Bora** tribe that lives deep in the **Amazon area of South America**. Other native peoples settled across the land that would later become the United States.

The earliest evidence of the existence of ancient Indians in North America was found in 1926. A worker found the bones of an animal sticking out of the ground. The bones were much larger than normal. Experts were called. The experts learned that the bones were from an animal that is no longer found in North America. The experts also found the **stone points** of weapons that were used to kill this animal. Since then experts have found many similar areas with animal bones and weapon points. The experts believe most of these finds are between 10,000 and 11,500 years old.

The experts agree that these stone weapon points are very similar to weapons that have been found in the far northern parts of Siberia. They say this helps prove the idea that the first settlers in North America came from North Eastern Asia. Near the small town of Clovis in the western state of New Mexico, experts found a new kind of stone weapon point. They named it the Clovis point. These points have been made very sharp by cutting away some of the stone from the sides. Experts say this kind of stone point is only found in America. The earliest ones were made about 11,500 years ago. Experts say at the time, this kind of stone point was the most modern weapon of its time. They were a great improvement over the older kind of stone point.

Many of the larger animals that were hunted by the early Indians began to die off with the end of the **ice age**. The Indians were forced to hunt smaller animals. In a period of several thousand years, the first peoples moved and settled across the land that would become the United States. Some settled in the forest land of the east, like the **Iroquois**. Some lived in the Southern desert like the **Apache**. Some settled in the open country of middle America like the **Lakota**. And others settled in the American northwest like the **Nez Perce**. These tribes and several hundred others had lived in the western part of the world many thousands of years before the first Europeans arrived. **Christopher Columbus** landed on the island of **San Salvador** in 1492. People in Europe did not know at that time that this land existed.

When Columbus landed, several million people lived in the area between the far north of North America to the end of land in South America. These included large groups and small. Most had their own culture, language and religion. Many were extremely fierce. Some were very peaceful. Some were hunters. Others were farmers. Some built huge cities of stone. Others lived in simple homes made from animal skins or wood from trees. Their ways of living would change forever when European explorers found their land.

Words, Expressions and Notes

Western Hemisphere 西半球

Siberia *n.* 西伯利亚

New World 新大陆，即美洲。此说法与欧洲大陆（Old World）相对应。

Bering Sea 白令海

fierce cold 严寒

sharp hunger 剧烈的饥饿

to follow any length of time 尾随相当长一段时间

Alaska *n.* 阿拉斯加

genetic tests 遗传测试

over time 随着时间的推移

Yuit 居住在西伯利亚地区的印第安部落

Arctic Circles 北极圈

Inuit 因纽特族，居住在北美洲北端育空地区的印第安部落

Yahgan 雅甘人，居住在南美洲最南端的印第安部落

Maya of Mexico 墨西哥马雅人，中美洲印第安人一族，曾拥有高度文明（大约公元 300 年至 900 年），以金字塔、庙宇、雕塑以及数学和天文学闻名。

Inca of Peru 秘鲁印加人，南美洲印第安人部落，曾建有印加帝国（The Inca Empire），于 16 世纪初期被西班牙人征服。

Bora 博拉人，居住在南美洲印第安人部落

Amazon area of South America 南美洲亚马逊河流域

stone points （早期人类作为武器用的）尖状石头

ice age 冰河时期

Iroquois 易洛魁人，居住在美国东北部地区的印第安部落

Apache 阿帕切人，居住在美国西南部地区的印第安部落

Lakota 拉科塔人，居住在美国中部大平原地区的印第安人，又称"苏人"（the Sioux）

Nez Perce 内兹佩尔塞人，居住在美国西北地区的印第安部落

Christopher Columbus 克里斯托弗·哥伦布（1451—1506），因于 1492 年发现新大陆而闻名。

San Salvador 圣萨尔瓦多岛，哥伦布最早在美洲登陆之处

Questions for Comprehension and Discussion

1. When did the first people arrive in the New World?

2. Where did they come from and why did they come?

3. How long did it take for the first peoples to spread out over the Western Hemisphere?

4. What was the group of people that created their own language and built good stone buildings in the land now called Mexico?

5. What can we learn from ancient stone weapon points that have been found in North America?

2 Early European Explorations

早期欧洲人的探险活动

1095 年 11 月，罗马教皇乌尔班二世发表讲话，发起十字军东征运动。西欧各国迅速集结兵力投入战争，并在最初取得一连串的胜利。1099 年，十字军洗劫圣城耶路撒冷，屠杀了 1 万穆斯林和犹太居民。两大宗教之间的战争持续了近两百年，最后穆斯林国家还是逐步收复了失去的土地和城市。

尽管从军事的角度看十字军东征是失败的，但它却在客观上开阔了欧洲人的眼界，极大地刺激了商业的发展，激发了欧洲国家中产阶级对财富的追求。在这样的背景下，欧洲从 15 世纪开始进入地理大发现时代（The Age of Discovery），而与之结伴而行的便是欧洲的殖民主义。

葡萄牙和西班牙两个国家是早期地理探索和殖民活动的急先锋。在众多的远航探索者中，代表西班牙的意大利人哥伦布的发现彻底改变了世界——尽管他自己从未见过未来美国的主要陆地。我们能否设想：一个没有西红柿的意大利，一个没有土豆的爱尔兰或者俄罗斯，或是一个没有可可粉的瑞士会是什么样子？在哥伦布发现美洲大陆之前，这些农作物在美洲之外毫不为世人所知。在带回农作物的同时，哥伦布给美洲带去了马匹，而这种美洲原本没有的动物从根本上改变了北美大平原上印第安人的传统生活方式，加速了美洲野牛等野生动物的灭绝。更为可怕的是，被哥伦布带去美洲大陆的还有天花、麻疹、流感等疾病，而正是这些疾病在哥伦布到达美洲后的 10 年之内导致了大约 300 万土著人的死亡。

早期欧洲殖民者在美洲探险的同时，对土著印第安人采取欺骗、威吓、抢劫、杀戮等各种手段，不择手段地掠夺金银财宝，干下许多罪恶勾当，在西方近代历史上写下了十分不光彩的一页。

The first Europeans arrived about 2,000 years ago in the area now called North America. A **Norse** explorer, Leif Erickson, sailed his boat from **Greenland** around the northeastern coast of the continent. He returned home to Greenland to tell others about the new country. He called it "Vinland." A few **settlements** were created following his explorations. Experts digging in eastern Canada thirty years ago found a village of houses just like those found in Greenland, Iceland, and Norway. But the **Norsemen** did not develop any permanent settlements in North America.

About 1000, Europe was beginning a period of great change. One reason was the religious wars known as the **Crusades**. These wars were efforts by Europeans who were mainly **Roman Catholic Christians**. They wanted to force **Muslims** out of what is now the Middle East. The Crusades began at the end of the 11th century. They continued for about 200 years. The presence of European armies in the Middle East increased trade which was controlled by businessmen in **Venice** and other Italian **city-states**. The businessmen were earning large profits by transporting and supplying the **warring** armies. When the European crusaders returned home, they brought with them some new and useful products. The products included spices, perfumes, silk cloth, steel products and drugs. Such products became highly valued all over Europe. Increased trade resulted which led to the growth of towns. It also created a large number of rich European businessmen. The European nations were growing. They developed armies and

5

governments. These had to be paid for by taxes from the people. By the 15th century, European countries were ready to explore new parts of the world.

The first explorers were the **Portuguese**. By 1400, they wanted to control the Eastern spice trade. European businessmen did not want to continue paying **Venetian** and **Arab** traders for their costly spices. They wanted to set up trade themselves. If they could sail to Asia directly for these products, the resulting trade would bring huge profits. The leader of Portugal's exploration efforts was Prince Henry, a son of King John I. He was interested in sea travel and exploration. So he became known as Henry the Navigator. Prince Henry brought experts to his country and studied the sciences involved in exploration. He built an **observatory** to study the stars. Portuguese sea captains led their ships around the west coast of Africa hoping to find a path to India and East Asia. They finally found the end of the African continent, the area called the **Cape of Good Hope**.

It took the Portuguese only about 50 years to take control of the spice trade. They established trading colonies in Africa, the **Persian Gulf**, India and China. Improvements in technology helped them succeed. One improvement was a new kind of ship. It could sail more easily through ocean storms and winds. Other inventions like the **compass** permitted them to sail out of sight of land. The Portuguese also armed their ships with modern **cannon**. They used these weapons to battle Muslim and East Asian traders.

The other European nations would not permit Portugal to control this trade for long, however. Spain's **Queen Isabella and King Ferdinand** agreed to provide ships, crew and supplies for an exploration by an Italian seaman, Christopher Columbus. Columbus thought the shortest way to reach the East was to sail west across the Atlantic Ocean. He was right. But he also was wrong. He believed the world was much smaller than it is. He did not imagine the existence of other lands and another huge ocean area between Europe and East Asia.

Columbus and a crew of 88 men left Spain on August 3rd, 1492 in three ships. On October 12th, they stood on land again on an island that Columbus named San Salvador. He explored it, and the nearby islands of what is now known as **Cuba** and **Hispaniola**. He believed they were part of the coast of East Asia, which was called the **Indies**. He called the people he found there Indians. Columbus left about forty men on the island to build a fort from the wood of one of the ships. He returned to Spain with captured natives, birds, plants, and gold. Columbus was considered a national hero when he reached Spain in March, 1493.

Columbus returned across the Atlantic Ocean to the **Caribbean** area five months later. This time, he had many more men and all the animals and equipment needed to start a colony on Hispaniola. He found that the protective fort built by his men had been destroyed by fire. Columbus did not find any of his men. Seven months later, Columbus sent five ships back to Spain. They carried Indians to be sold as slaves. Columbus also sailed back to Spain leaving behind some settlers who were not happy with conditions. Christopher Columbus made another trip in 1498, with six ships. This time he saw the coast of South America. The settlers were so unhappy with conditions in the new colony, Columbus was sent back to Spain as a prisoner. Spain's rulers pardoned him. In 1502, Columbus made his final

Christopher Columbus

voyage to what some were calling the New World. He stayed on the island of **Jamaica** until he returned home in 1504.

During all of his trips, Columbus explored islands and waterways, searching for a passage to the Indies. He never found it. He also did not find spices or great amounts of gold. Yet he always believed that he had found the Indies. He refused to recognize that it was really a new world. Evidence of this was all around him—strange plants that were not known in either Europe or Asia and a different people who did not understand any language spoken in the East. Columbus's voyages, however, opened up the New World. Others later explored all of North America.

You may be wondering about the name of this new land. If Christopher Columbus was the first European to attempt to settle the New World, why is it called "America"? The answer lies with the name of an Italian explorer, **Amerigo Vespucci**. He visited the coast of South America in 1499. He wrote stories about his experiences that were widely read in Europe. In 1507, a German mapmaker read Vespucci's stories. He decided that the writer had discovered the New World and suggested that it be called America in his honor. So it was.

Spanish explorers sought to find gold and power in the New World. They also wanted to expand belief in what they considered to be the true religion, **Christianity**. The first of these Spanish explorers was **Juan Ponce de León**. He landed on North America in 1513. He explored the eastern coast of what is now the southern state of **Florida**. He was searching for a special kind of water that people in Europe believed existed. They believed that this water could make old people young again. Ponce de León never found it.

Also in 1513, **Vasco Núñez de Balboa** crossed the **Isthmus of Panama** and reached the Pacific Ocean. In 1519, **Hernán Cortés** landed an army in Mexico and destroyed the Empire of the Aztec Indians. That same year **Ferdinand Magellan** began his three-year voyage around the world. And in the 1530s, **Francisco Pizarro** destroyed the Inca Indian Empire in Peru.

Ten years later, **Francisco Vásquez de Coronado** had marched as far north as the Central American state of Kansas and west to the **Grand Canyon**. About the same time, **Hernan de Soto** reached the Mississippi River. Fifty years after Columbus first landed in San Salvador, Spain claimed a huge area of America. The riches of these new lands made Spain the greatest power in Europe. But other nations refused to accept Spain's claim to rights in the New World. Explorers from England, France and Holland also were traveling to North America.

Words, Expressions and Notes

Norse *a.* 古代斯堪的纳维亚人的

Greenland *n.* （丹麦）格陵兰岛

settlement *n.* 居留地

Norseman *n.* 古代斯堪的纳维亚人（又称"北欧海盗"）

Crusades 十字军东征

Roman Catholic Christians 罗马天主教徒

Muslims *n.* 穆斯林，伊斯兰教信徒

Venice *n.* 威尼斯

city-states *n.* 城邦

warring *a.* 交战的

Portuguese *n.* 葡萄牙人

Venetian *a.* 威尼斯的

Arab *a.* 阿拉伯的

observatory *n.* 天文台

Cape of Good Hope 好望角

Persian Gulf 波斯湾

compass *n.* 罗盘，指南针

cannon *n.* 大炮

Queen Isabella and King Ferdinand 伊莎贝拉女王与其夫斐迪南德国王，二人共同统治西班牙，曾资助哥伦布航海探险。

Cuba *n.* 古巴

Hispaniola *n.* 伊斯帕尼奥拉岛，即海地岛（Haiti），

位于拉丁美洲西印度群岛中部。

Indies *n.* 东印度群岛

Caribbean *a.* 加勒比海的

Jamaica *n.* 牙买加

Amerigo Vespucci 阿美利哥·韦斯普奇（1454—1512），意大利商人和航海家，确认新发现的大西洋以西的陆地不是亚洲的一部分而是新大陆。

Christianity *n.* 基督教

Juan Ponce de León 庞塞·德莱昂（1460—1521），西班牙探险家，曾任波多黎各总督。

Florida 佛罗里达（美国州名）

Vasco Núñez de Balboa 瓦斯科·努捏斯·德巴尔波（1475—1519），西班牙探险家

Isthmus of Panama 巴拿马地峡

Hernán Cortés 赫尔南·科特斯（1485—1547），西班牙探险家，1521年率军队征服墨西哥阿兹特克帝国（the Aztec Empire）。

Ferdinand Magellan 费迪南德·麦哲伦（1480—1521），葡萄牙航海家，1519年率西班牙船队作首次环球航行。

Francisco Pizarro 佛朗西斯科·皮萨罗（1475？—1541），西班牙冒险家，征服秘鲁印加帝国，发现太平洋。

Francisco Vásquez de Coronado 弗朗西斯科·瓦斯科·德·科洛纳多（1510—1554），西班牙征服者，到美国西南部地区探险的第一个西方人

Grand Canyon 大峡谷，即科罗拉多河峡谷，位于美国亚利桑那州西北部，世界地理奇观之一。

Hernan de Soto 赫尔南·德·索托（大约1496—1542），西班牙探险家，第一个发现密西西比河的欧洲人

Questions for Comprehension and Discussion

1. What were the major results of the Crusades—the religious wars between Roman Catholic Christians and the Muslims?
2. Who were the first to explore new parts of the world in the 15th century?
3. Why was Christopher Columbus both right and wrong when he planned to sail across the Atlantic Ocean to reach the East?
4. Why did Columbus call the native people he found in the New World "Indians"?
5. Why was the New World named "America"?

3 English Settlements in North America

英国在北美洲的殖民开拓

与葡萄牙和西班牙相比，英国在新大陆的殖民冒险活动上是一个迟到者，但从一开始它就显示出一些不同的特点和做法。

早期的葡萄牙、西班牙殖民者无不以攻城掠寨、攫取黄金白银作为首要目标，他们把主要精力放在贵金属开采和对殖民地的控制上，因而不重视建立稳定的、在经济上能够持续发展的定居地。一个典型的例子是，他们从国内派许多白人去殖民地维持军事占领，却根本没有考虑这些白人自身的生存和繁衍问题。这样做的结果是，这些殖民者不得不大量地与当地土著人结婚生子，造成南美洲白人与印第安人大量混血的现象。

英国对其在北美的殖民活动从最初阶段就对人的定居和生存问题给予了关注，殖民地的经营权和管理权也基本掌握在有关个人和组织的手中，各种政策相当灵活，其主要目标就是建立稳定而永久的殖民地。尽管最初的努力遭受挫折，但英国人还是在1607年建立了在北美的第一个永久定居地——詹姆斯敦。

早期英国人越过大西洋移民美洲的旅程异常艰难。他们搭乘狭小、拥挤的船只，在6至12个星期的旅程里，只能吃到很少的食物，许多旅客在半路上就病死了。船只因经常遭受暴风雨的袭击而破烂不堪，甚至沉没在茫茫的大海里。

那些疲乏的旅客看到美洲海岸时，人人都有如释重负之感。一位历史学家写道："百里之外传来的气息，有如满园花木那样馥郁芳香。"最先进入移民眼帘的新大陆是一片苍翠的密林。在密林中，居住着对外来闯入者充满敌意的印第安人。因此，移民们一方面要应付艰苦的日常生活，另一方面又要提防印第安人的袭击。但是，那从北向南延伸2 100公里的一望无际的原始大森林是一座巨大的宝库，不仅给移民提供充裕的粮食和燃料，还是他们盖房子、制家具、造船以及出口货物的原料来源。

需要特别指出的是，最早去新大陆的两批英国移民有着截然不同的动机。1607年在詹姆斯敦定居的移民主要是为了寻求更大的经济机会而离开英国故土；而1620年乘"五月花号"在马萨诸塞普利茅斯登陆的移民则是为逃避政治压迫、追求宗教自由来到美洲。在"五月花号"船上，这些追求宗教自由的人们通过了一个叫做《五月花公约》的政治文件，要求移民们同心协力为良好的秩序和生存建立一个文明政治社会，并制定颁布符合殖民地全体人民利益的公平的法律、法令、条例、规章，设立治理机构。为此，这批移民备受人们尊敬，不仅赢得了"朝圣者"（Pilgrims）的美名，而且成为现代美国人精神上的祖先。

England was the first country to compete with Spain for claims in the New World, although it was too weak to do this openly at first. But **Queen Elizabeth** of England supported such explorations as early as the 1570s.

Sir Humphrey Gilbert led the first English settlement efforts. He did not establish any lasting settlement. He died as he was returning to England. Gilbert's **half brother Sir Walter Raleigh** continued his work. Raleigh sent a number of ships to explore the east coast of North America. He called the land **Virginia** to honor England's unmarried Queen Elizabeth. In 1585, about 100 men settled on Roanoke

Island, off the coast of the present-day state of **North Carolina**. These settlers returned to England a year later. Another group went to Roanoke the next year. This group included a number of women and children. But the supply ships Raleigh sent to the colony failed to arrive. When help got there in 1590, none of the settlers could be found. History experts still are not sure what happened. Some research suggests that at least some of the settlers became part of the Indian tribe that lived in the area.

One reason for the delay in getting supplies to Roanoke was the attack of the Spanish Navy against England in 1588. King Phillip of Spain had decided to invade England. But the small English ships combined with a fierce storm defeated the huge Spanish fleet. As a result, Spain was no longer able to block English exploration. England discovered that supporting colonies so far away was extremely costly. So Queen Elizabeth took no more action to do this. It was not until after her death in 1603 that England began serious efforts to start colonies in America.

In 1606, the new English King, **James I**, gave two business groups permission to establish colonies in Virginia, the area claimed by England. Companies were organized to carry out the move. The **London Company** sent 100 settlers to Virginia in 1606. The group landed there in May, 1607 and founded **Jamestown**. It was the first permanent English colony in the New World.

The colony seemed about to fail from the start. The settlers did not plant their crops in time so they soon had no food. Their leaders lacked the farming and building skills needed to survive on the land. More than half the settlers died during the first winter.

The businessmen controlling the colony from London knew nothing about living in such a wild place. They wanted the settlers to search for gold, and explore local rivers in hopes of finding a way to the East. One settler knew this was wrong. His name was Captain **John Smith**. He helped the colonists build houses and grow food by learning from the local Indians. Still, the Jamestown settlers continued to die each year from disease, lack of food and Indian attacks. The London Company sent 6,000 settlers to Virginia between 1606 and 1622. More than 4,000 died during that time.

History experts say that all the settlers surely would have died without the help of the local **Powhatan Indians**. The Indians gave the settlers food. They taught them how to live in the forest. And the Powhatan Indians showed the settlers how to plant new crops and how to clear the land for building. The settlers accepted the Indians' help. Then, however, the settlers took whatever else they wanted by force. In 1622, the local Indians attacked the settlers for interfering with Indian land. Three hundred forty settlers died. The colonists answered the attack by destroying the Indian tribes living along Virginia's coast. Slowly, the settlers recognized that they would have to grow their own food and survive on their own without help from England or anyone else. The Jamestown colony was clearly established by 1624. It was even beginning to earn money by growing and selling a new crop: tobacco.

The other early English settlements in North America were much to the north of Virginia, in the present state of Massachusetts. The people who settled there left England for different reasons than those who settled in Jamestown. The Virginia settlers were looking for ways to earn money for English businesses. The settlers in Massachusetts were seeking religious freedom.

King Henry VIII of England had separated from the **Roman Catholic Church**. His daughter, Queen Elizabeth, established the **Protestant religion** in England. It was called the **Church of England**, or the Anglican Church. The Anglican Church, however, was similar to that of the Roman Catholic Church. Not all Protestants liked this. Some wanted to leave the Anglican Church and form religious groups of their own. In 1606, members of one such group in the town of Scrooby did separate from the Anglican Church. About 125 people left England for Holland. They found problems there too, so they decided to move again. . . to the New World. These people were called **Pilgrims**, because that is the name given to people who travel for religious purposes.

About 35 Pilgrims were among the passengers on a ship called the *Mayflower* in 1620. It left England to go to Virginia. But the *Mayflower* never reached Virginia. Instead, it landed to the North, on **Cape Cod Bay**. The group decided to stay there instead of trying to find Jamestown.

The Pilgrims and the others on the *Mayflower* saw a need for rules that would help them live together peacefully. They believed they were not under English control since they did not land in Virginia. So they wrote a plan of government, called the **Mayflower Compact**. It was the first such plan ever developed in the New World. They elected a man called **William Bradford** as the first governor of their **Plymouth colony**. We know about the first 30 years of the Plymouth colony because William Bradford described it in his book, *Of Plymouth Plantation*.

As happened in Jamestown, about half the settlers in Plymouth died the first winter. The survivors were surprised to find an Indian who spoke English. His name was **Squanto**. He had been

Mayflower **on her way to the New World**

kidnapped by an English sea captain and had lived in England before returning to his people. The Pilgrims believed Squanto was sent to them from God. He made it possible for them to communicate with the native people. He showed them the best places to fish, what kind of crops to plant and how to grow them. He provided them with all kinds of information they needed to survive. The settlers invited the Indians to a feast in the month of November to celebrate their successes and to thank Squanto for his help. Americans remember that celebration every year when they **observe** the **Thanksgiving holiday**.

Other English settlers began arriving in the area now called **New England**. One large group was called the **Puritans**. Like the Pilgrims, the Puritans did not agree with the Anglican Church. But they did not want to separate from it. The Puritans wanted to change it to make it more holy. Their desire for this change made them unwelcome in England. The first ship carrying Puritans left England for America in 1630. By the end of that summer, 1,000 Puritans had landed in the northeastern part of the new country. The new English King, Charles, had given permission for them to settle the Massachusetts Bay area.

The Puritans began leaving England in large groups. Between 1630 and 1640, 20,000 sailed for New England. They risked their lives on the dangerous trip. They wanted to live among people who believed as they did, people who honored the rules of the Bible. Puritans believed that the Bible was the word of God. The Puritans and other Europeans, however, found a very different people in the New World. They were America's native Indians.

Words, Expressions and Notes

Queen Elizabeth 伊丽莎白女王（1533—1603），即伊丽莎白一世，第一个登上英国王位的女王，在任期间（1558—1603）恢复英国国教，击败西班牙无敌舰队，发展工商业和海外贸易，促进文化艺术的繁荣，终生未婚。

Sir Humphrey Gilbert 汉弗莱·吉尔伯特爵士（1539—1583），英国军人、航海家

half brother 同父异母或同母异父的兄弟

Sir Walter Raleigh 沃尔特·罗利（1552—1618），英国探险家，早期美洲殖民者

Virginia 弗吉尼亚殖民地

North Carolina 北卡罗来纳殖民地

James I 詹姆斯一世（1566—1625），英国国王（1603—1625）

London Company 伦敦公司，又称为弗吉尼亚公司（Virginia Company），早期英国负责开拓美洲殖民地的两个股份制公司之一。另一个是普利茅斯公司（Plymouth Company）。

Jamestown 詹姆斯敦，弗吉尼亚东部一村庄，1607年英国在此建立其在北美的第一个殖民地。

John Smith 约翰·史密斯（1580—1631），英国探险家，詹姆斯敦殖民地主要创建者，后任殖民地总督（1608）。

Powhatan Indians 波瓦坦印第安人。波瓦坦原为弗吉尼亚一带一个印第安部落首领的名字。据约翰·史密斯写的《弗吉尼亚史》记载，有一次他被波瓦坦印第安人俘虏后正要被处决时，波瓦坦的女儿波卡洪塔斯（Pocahontas）将他救下。波卡洪塔斯后来与英国人结婚，并于1616年去英国，受到上流社会的礼遇。这也成为早期英国人与印第安人交往的一段佳话。

Roman Catholic Church 罗马天主教

Protestant religion 新教，指不受天主教或东正教控制的其他基督教

Church of England（= Anglican Church）英国国教

Pilgrims *n.* 朝圣者；早期移居美洲的英国新教徒

Mayflower "五月花号" 轮船

Cape Cod Bay 科德角海湾

Mayflower Compact 《五月花号公约》，世界上第一份征得被统治者同意而组建政府的法律文件

William Bradford 威廉·布雷德福（1590—1657），北美英国清教徒殖民者，后被选为普利茅斯殖民地总督。

Plymouth colony 普利茅斯殖民地

Of Plymouth Plantation 《普利茅斯殖民史》

Squanto 斯匡托（1585?—1622），一个印第安土著人，曾给予新英格兰地区第一批移民的生存极大的帮助。

observe *v.* 庆祝

Thanksgiving holiday 感恩节

New England 新英格兰地区，位于美国大陆东北角，濒临大西洋，毗邻加拿大。新英格兰地区包括现在美国的6个州，由北至南分别为缅因州、新罕布什尔州、佛蒙特州、马萨诸塞州、罗德岛州、康涅狄格州。马萨诸塞州首府波士顿是该地区的最大城市以及经济与文化中心。

Puritans *n.* 清教徒。基督教新教中的一派，16世纪起源于英国，主张简化宗教礼仪，提倡勤俭、清洁的生活。

Questions for Comprehension and Discussion

1. How did Virginia get its name?
2. What did the businessmen in London want the first settlers to do in America? Why were they wrong?
3. How did the Indians help the settlers living in Jamestown?
4. Why has the Mayflower Compact been considered a very important document in American history?
5. Who was Squanto? What role did he play in early American history?
6. Thanksgiving is considered the first authentic American holiday. How did it come into being?

4 Clashes Between the Settlers and the Natives

定居者与土著人之间的冲突

大约 2.5 万年以前，一队亚洲人跨越白令海来到北美洲，成为新大陆第一批原始居民。在随后的数千年间，他们在生息繁衍的同时由北向南逐步推进，最后占据了南北美洲的各个角落，在新大陆上创造出许许多多各有特点的印第安文化。

然而，无论这些居住在平原、高山、沙漠或丛林的印第安部落的文化有多么大的区别，他们都有一个重要的共同点，那就是，几乎所有的印第安人都认为，人是大自然的一部分。无论他们周围的动物是河狸还是海鸥，是鳄鱼还是美洲虎，他们都把这些动物当成大自然的一分子，理所当然地认为它们都有权利分享这个地球。诚然，印第安人也猎杀动物，就如同动物之间相互捕杀一样，但这仅仅是为维持最基本的生活。他们用动物的皮毛做衣服，用树木搭建居所，在地上挖洞种庄稼，把地球当做人类的母亲。一个历史故事曾经这样描述：当一个白种人手把手教一个印第安人犁地时，印第安人拒绝这样做，原因是犁地如同"把一把刀子插进母亲的身体"。

在印第安文化中，人、神灵和动物都是相互联系的。印第安人拒绝土地私有制。他们认为，太阳、水、空气、植物和动物都是神灵所创造，而它们本身也是神灵。因此，与这些神灵息息相关的土地不可能成为某人的私有物。当一个白人抱怨印第安人的马匹跑到他家的牧场吃草时，印第安人的答复是："难道是你让草生长的吗？"

当以大自然为中心的印第安文化与以土地私有制为中心的欧洲文化在新大陆不期而遇时，一场冲突便在所难免。然而，这场激烈程度超出大多数人预想的冲突是如此血腥和残酷，以至于几乎导致了一个民族的消亡。

Many different native American groups lived on the east coast of what would become United States. They spoke many different languages. Some were farmers, some were hunters. Some fought many wars, others were peaceful. These groups are called tribes. Their names are known to most Americans—the **Senecas**, the **Mohawks**, the **Seminole**, the **Cherokee**, to name only a few.

These tribes had developed their own cultures many years before the first European settlers arrived. Each had a kind of religion, a strong **spiritual belief**. Many tribes shared a similar one. The Indians on the east coast shared a highly developed system of trade. Researchers say different tribes of native Americans traded goods all across the country.

The first recorded meetings between Europeans and the natives of the east coast took place in the 1500s. Fishermen from France and the **Basque area of Spain** crossed the Atlantic Ocean. They searched for whales along the east coast of North America. They made temporary camps along the coast. They often traded with the local Indians. The Europeans often paid Indians to work for them. Both groups found this to be a successful relationship. Several times different groups of fishermen tried to establish a permanent settlement on the coast, but the severe winters made it impossible. These fishing camps were only temporary.

The first permanent settlers in New England began arriving in 1620. They wanted to live in peace with the Indians. They needed to trade with them for food. The settlers also knew that a battle would result in their own quick defeat because they were so few in number. Yet, problems began almost immediately. Perhaps the most serious was the different way the American Indians and the Europeans thought about land. This difference created problems that would not be solved during the next several hundred years.

Land was extremely important to the European settlers. In England, and most other countries, land meant wealth. Owning large amounts of land meant a person had great wealth and political power. Many of the settlers in this new country could never have owned land in Europe. They were too poor. And they belonged to minority religious groups. When they arrived in the new country, they discovered no one seemed to own the huge amounts of land. Companies in England needed to find people willing to settle in the new country. So they offered land to anyone who would **take the chance** of crossing the Atlantic Ocean. For many, it was a dream come true. It was a way to improve their lives. The land gave them a chance to become wealthy and powerful.

American Indians believed no person could own land. They believed, however, that anyone could use it. Anyone who wanted to live on and grow crops on a piece of land was able to do so. The American Indians lived within nature. They lived very well without working very hard. They were able to do this because they understood the land and their environment. They did not try to change the land. They might farm in an area for a few years. Then they would move on. They permitted the land on which they had farmed to become wild again. They might hunt on one area of land for some time, but again they would move on. They hunted only what they could eat, so the numbers of animals continued to increase. The Indians understood nature and made it work for them.

The first Europeans to settle in New England in the Northeastern part of America were few in number. They wanted land. The Indians did not fear them. There was enough land for everyone to use and plant crops. It was easy to live together. The Indians helped the settlers by teaching them how to plant crops and survive on the land. But the Indians did not understand that the settlers were going to keep the land. This idea was **foreign to the Indians**. It was like to trying to own the air, or the clouds. As the years passed, more and more settlers arrived, and took more and more land. They cut down trees. They built fences to keep people and animals out. They demanded that the Indians stay off their land.

Religion was another problem between the settlers and the Indians. The settlers in New England were very serious about their Christian religion. They thought it was the one true faith and all people should believe in it. They soon learned that the Indians were not interested in learning about it or changing their beliefs. Many settlers came to believe that Native Americans could not be trusted because they were not Christians. The settler groups began to fear the Indians. They thought of the Indians as a people who were evil because they had no religion. The settlers told the Indians they must change and become Christians. The Indians did not understand why they should change anything.

The European settlers failed to understand that the Native American Indians were extremely religious people with a strong belief in unseen powers. The Indians lived very close to nature. They believed that all things in the universe depend on each other. All native tribes had ceremonies that honored a creator of nature. American Indians recognized the work of the creator of the world in their everyday life.

Other events also led to serious problems between the Native Americans and the settlers. One serious problem was disease. The settlers brought sickness with them from Europe. For example, the disease smallpox was well known in Europe. Some people carried the bacteria that caused smallpox, although they did not suffer the sickness itself. Smallpox was unknown to Native Americans. Their bodies' **defense systems** could not fight against smallpox. It killed whole tribes. And, smallpox was only one such disease. There were many others.

The first meetings between settlers and Native Americans were the same in almost every European settlement on the east coast of America. The two groups met as friends. They would begin by trading for food and other goods. In time, however, something would happen to cause a crisis. Perhaps a settler would demand that an Indian stay off the settler's land. Perhaps a settler, or Indian, was killed. Fear would replace friendship. One side or the other would answer what they believed was an attack. A good example of this is the violent clash called **King Philip's War**.

A Plains Indian tribe holds a council meeting on horseback.

Matacom was a leader of the Wampanoag tribe that lived in the northernmost colonies. He was known to the English as King Philip. Without the help of his tribe, the first European settlers in that area might not have survived their first winter. The Wampanoag Indians provided them with food. They taught the settlers how to plant corn and other food crops. The two groups were very friendly for several years. As the years passed, however, fear and a lack of understanding increased. Matacom's brother died of a European disease. Matacom blamed the settlers. He also saw how the increasing numbers of settlers were changing the land. He believed they were destroying it.

One small crisis after another led to the killing of a Christian Indian who lived with the settlers. The settlers answered this by killing three Indians. A war quickly followed. It began in 1675 and continued for almost two years. It was an extremely cruel war. Men, women and children on both sides were killed. Researchers believe more than 600 settlers were killed. They also say as many as 3,000 Native Americans died in the violence.

History experts say the tribe of Indians called the **Narraganset** were the true victims of King Philip's War. The Narraganset were not involved in the war. They did not support one group or the other. However, the settlers killed almost all the Narraganset Indians because they had learned to fear all Indians. This fear, lack of understanding and the failure to compromise were not unusual. They strongly influenced the European settlers' relations with Native Americans in all areas of the new country.

Words, Expressions and Notes

Senecas 塞纳卡印第安人，易洛魁联盟中最大的部落，居住在美国东北部地区。

Mohawks 莫霍克印第安人，居住在美国东北部和加拿大。

Seminole 西米诺尔印第安人，居住在佛罗里达和俄克拉何马地区。

Cherokee 切落基印第安人，居住在美国东北部地区。

spiritual belief 精神信仰

Basque area of Spain 西班牙巴斯克地区，位于西班牙北部。

take the chance（of doing sth） 冒险做某事

foreign to the Indians 对印第安人来说是从未想到过的

defense systems （身体的）防御系统

King Philip's War 菲力普王的战争。菲力普原名 Metacom，是万帕诺亚格（Wampanoag）印第安部落的酋长，曾组织部落联盟在新英格兰地区抗击英国移民。

Narraganset 纳拉干西特印第安人，居住在罗得岛殖民地，现已灭绝。

Questions for Comprehension and Discussion

1. What was the immediate cause of problems between the newly-arrived settlers and the Indians?
2. Why did the first European settlers want very much to own land in the New World?
3. Why did the Indians feel so close to nature?
4. What were the major differences between European settlers and the Indians in religion?
5. Do you think it is possible to find a way to solve the problems between European settlers and the native Indians?
6. Can history teach us any way to lessen the conflict between cultures? Is cultural conflict inevitable?

Unit 2   The Colonial Times

5   Colonial Expansion: The Northeastern America

殖民地在东北部地区的扩张

弗吉尼亚殖民地创建人约翰·史密斯在 1607 年说："美利坚的天时地利为人的居住造就了一个最好的地方。"

17 世纪初期，出现了一股从欧洲到北美的移民潮流。在三个多世纪里，这股潮流从最初的几百名英格兰移民漂洋过海，逐渐演变为千百万人势如潮水的大迁移。他们在各种强大动机的推动下，终于在美洲这片荒凉的大陆上建立起新的文明。

昌然新大陆得天独厚，资源丰富，但是，为了取得当时移民还不能制造的物品，与欧洲的贸易至关重要。在这方面，北美大陆东部沿大西洋的海岸线对于移民来说极为有用。在西边，茂密的森林和高大的阿巴拉契亚山脉阻挡着移民向西发展，只有猎人和商人才敢冒险进入那荒芜的地方。因此，在 100 年的时间里，移民们都只在沿海一带建立密集的居住地。

1630 年以后，马萨诸塞海湾区域（波士顿）的定居点在开发新英格兰中起了重要的作用。位于北美东北部的新英格兰地区是美国文明最重要的发源地之一。这里原为冰河地带，土壤贫瘠多石，平地稀少，夏季短，冬季长，是一个不适宜耕作的地方。为适应这样的环境，新英格兰人克服重重困难，为生存进行了顽强的斗争。他们利用水力，建立水车磨坊以及锯木厂。大批木材可以用来制造船只，优良的港口可以促进贸易，而大海又是财富的极大来源。在马萨诸塞，仅捕鳕鱼这一行业就能成为该地区迅速繁荣的基础。

在新英格兰地区，教会严格控制着社会。但全体居民，由于拓荒生活的艰苦，共同负担着社会责任。新英格兰人居住在港口附近的乡镇里，过的是市镇生活，不少人还经营工商业。公共牧地和公共林地可以满足在附近小块农田中工作的城市居民。由于住地集中，学校、教堂、乡镇议会也成立了，市民利用这些地方来商讨各项与公众利益有关的事情。在乡镇会议上，移民们通过讨论公共问题，获得宝贵的自治经验。在教育方面，哈佛大学于 1636 年在马萨诸塞成立，马萨诸塞海湾地区 1647 年开始实行义务小学教育。即使人们以今天的眼光来观察，新英格兰人重视教育的程度也实在令人惊叹。

艰难的生活和至高无上的宗教并没能束缚每一个公民的思想。罗杰·威廉斯是一个反叛的牧师，对没收印第安人土地的权利、政教合一的好处，他都表示怀疑。他因为"散布反对地方长官权威的危险的新思想"，终于被立法机构放逐。他跑到附近的罗得岛向友好的印第安人购买土地，不久便在罗得岛上建立了一个殖民地，其原则是人们可以有信仰的自由，政教必须永远分离。

透过早期新英格兰人艰苦奋斗的顽强精神和独立思考的优良品质，我们似乎在朦胧中看到了美利坚的未来。

The Puritans were one of the largest groups from England to settle in the Northeastern area called Massachusetts. They began arriving in 1630. The Puritans had formed the **Massachusetts Bay Company** in England. The King had given the company an area of land between the Charles and Merrimack Rivers.

17

The Puritans were Protestants who did not agree with the Anglican Church. The Puritans wanted to change the church to make it more holy. They were able to live as they wanted in Massachusetts. Soon they became the largest religious group. By 1690, fifty thousand people were living in Massachusetts. Puritans thought their religion was the only true religion and everyone should believe in it. They also believed that church leaders should lead the local government, and all people in the colony should pay to support the Puritan church. The Puritans thought it was the job of government leaders to tell people what to believe. Some people did not agree with the Puritans who had become leaders of the colony. One of those who disagreed was a Puritan **minister** named **Roger Williams**.

Roger Williams believed as all Puritans did that other European religions were wrong. He thought the native Indian religions were wrong too. But he did not believe in trying to force others to agree with him. He thought that it was a sin to

The Puritans walk to church, carrying their guns and Bibles.

punish or kill anyone in the name of Christianity. And he thought that only church members should pay to support their church. Roger Williams began speaking and writing about his ideas. He wrote a book saying it was wrong to punish people for having different beliefs. Then he said that the European settlers were stealing the Indians' land. He said the King of England had no right to permit people to settle on land that was not his, but belonged to the Indians. The Puritan leaders of the **Massachusetts Bay Colony** forced Roger Williams to leave the colony in 1636. He traveled south. He bought land from local Indians and started a city, **Providence**. The Parliament in England gave him permission to establish a new colony, **Rhode Island**, with Providence as its capital. As a colony, Rhode Island accepted people of all religious beliefs, including Catholics, **Quakers**, Jews and even people who denied the existence of God. Roger Williams also believed that governments should have no connection to a church. This idea of **separating church and state** was very new. Later it became one of the most important of all America's governing ideas.

Other colonies were started by people who left Massachusetts to seek land. One was **Connecticut**. A group led by Puritan minister **Thomas Hooker** left Boston in 1636 and went west. They settled near the Connecticut River. Others soon joined them. Other groups from Massachusetts traveled north to find new homes. The King of England had given two friends a large piece of land in the North. The friends divided it. **John Mason** took what later became the colony of **New Hampshire**. **Ferdinando Gorges** took the area that later became the state of **Maine**. It never became a colony, however. It remained a part of Massachusetts until after the United States was created.

The area known today as New York State was settled by the **Dutch**. They called it New Netherland. Their country was the **Netherlands**. It was a great world power, with colonies all over the world. A business called the Dutch West India Company owned most of the colonies. The Dutch claimed American land because of explorations by **Henry Hudson**, an Englishman working for the Netherlands. The land the Dutch claimed was between the Puritans in the North and the **Anglican** tobacco farmers in the South. The

Dutch were not interested in settling the territory. They wanted to earn money. The Dutch West India Company built trading posts on the rivers claimed by the Netherlands. People in Europe wanted to buy goods made from the skins of animals trapped there. In 1626, the Dutch West India Company bought two islands from the local Indians. The islands are **Manhattan Island** and **Long Island**. Traditional stories say the Dutch paid for the islands with some trade goods worth about 24 dollars. The Dutch West India Company tried to find people to settle in America. But few Dutch wanted to leave Europe. So the colony welcomed people from other colonies, and other countries. These people built a town on Manhattan Island. They called it **New Amsterdam**. It was soon full of people who had arrived on ships from faraway places. It was said you could hear as many as 18 different languages spoken in New Amsterdam. In 1655, the governor of New Netherland took control of a nearby Swedish colony on **Delaware Bay**. In 1664, the English did the same to the Dutch. The English seized control of New Amsterdam and called it New York. That ended Dutch control of the territory that now is the states of New York, New Jersey and Delaware.

Most of the Dutch in New Amsterdam did not leave. The English permitted everyone to stay. They let the Dutch have religious freedom. The Dutch were just not in control any more. The **Duke of York** owned the area now. He was the brother of **King Charles II of England**. The King gave some of the land near New York to two friends, Sir George Carteret and Lord John Berkeley. They called it **New Jersey**, after the English island where Carteret was born. The two men wrote a plan of government for their colony. It created an **assembly** that represented the settlers. It provided for freedom of religion. Men could vote in New Jersey whatever their religion. Soon, people from all parts of Europe were living in New Jersey. Then King Charles took control of the area. He sent a royal governor to rule. But the colonists were permitted to make their own laws through the elected assembly. The King of England did the same in each colony he controlled. He collected taxes from the people who lived there, but permitted them to govern themselves.

One religious group that was not welcome in England was the Quakers. Quakers call themselves Friends. They believe that each person has an inner light that leads them to God. Quakers believe they do not need a religious leader to tell them what is right. So, they had no **clergy**. Quakers believe that all people are equal. The Quakers in England refused to recognize the King as more important than anyone else. They also refused to pay taxes to support the Anglican Church. Quakers believe that it is always wrong to kill. So they would not fight even when they were forced to join the army. They also refuse to promise loyalty to a king or government or flag or anyone but God. The English did not like the Quakers for all these reasons. Many Quakers wanted to leave England, but they were not welcome in most American colonies. One Quaker changed this. His name was **William Penn**.

William Penn was not born a Quaker. He became one as a young man. His father was an Anglican, and a good friend of the King. King Charles borrowed money from William's father. When his father died, William Penn asked that the debt be paid with land in America. In 1681, the King gave William Penn land which the King's Council named Pennsylvania, meaning Penn's woods. The Quakers now had their own colony. It was between the Puritans in the North and the Anglicans in the South. William Penn said the colony should be a place where everyone could live by Quaker ideas. That meant treating all people as equals and honoring all religions. It also meant that anyone could be elected. In most other colonies, people could believe any religion, but they could not vote or hold office unless they were a member of the majority church. In Pennsylvania, all religions were equal.

Words, Expressions and Notes

Massachusetts Bay Company 马萨诸塞海湾公司，经英王特许成立于 1629 年的海外贸易公司，1630 年在北美建立马萨诸塞海湾殖民地以及城市波士顿。

minister *n.* 教士

Roger Williams 罗杰·威廉斯（1603—1683），北美英国激进派清教徒教士，罗得岛殖民地创建人，后任该殖民地首任总督。

Massachusetts Bay Colony 马萨诸塞海湾殖民地

Providence *n.* 普罗维登斯，罗得岛首府

Rhode Island 罗得岛殖民地

Quakers *n.* （基督教）贵格会教徒

separating church and state 政教分离

Connecticut *n.* 康涅迪格殖民地

Thomas Hooker 托马斯·胡克（1586—1647），康涅迪格的清教徒牧师，宣称人民选举行政官员是上帝所授的权利，因而被誉为"美国民主之父"。

John Mason 约翰·梅森（1586—1635），早期北美大陆英国殖民者，新罕布什尔殖民地的创建人

New Hampshire 新罕布什尔殖民地

Ferdinando Gorges 费迪南多·戈吉斯（1566—

1647），早期北美大陆英国殖民者，缅因殖民地的创建人

Maine *n.* 缅因州，是新英格兰地区的主要部分。

Dutch *n.* 荷兰人

Netherlands *n.* 荷兰

Henry Hudson 亨利·哈得逊（？—约1611），英国航海家、探险家，美国的哈得逊河（Hudson River）、加拿大的哈得逊湾（Hudson Bay）都以其姓氏命名。

Anglican *a.* 英国的

Manhattan Island 曼哈顿岛

Long Island 长岛

New Amsterdam 新阿姆斯特丹

Delaware Bay 特拉华湾

Duke of York 约克公爵

King Charles II of England 英国国王查尔斯二世

New Jersey 新泽西殖民地

assembly *n.* 议会

clergy *n.* 神职人员

William Penn 威廉·佩恩（1644—1718），英国基督教新教贵格会领袖，宾夕法尼亚殖民地创建人

Questions for Comprehension and Discussion

1. Why did large groups of Puritans leave England for America since 1630?

2. Who was Roger Williams? What did he think and do in the early years of Massachusetts colony?

3. Why were Roger Williams's ideas very important in early American history?

4. What is the history of New York?

5. What is the belief of the Quakers?

6. How did Pennsylvania get its name?

6 Colonial Expansion: The South

殖民地在南部地区的扩张

与注重工商业发展的新英格兰及中部诸殖民地不同的是，弗吉尼亚、马里兰、南北卡罗来纳和佐治亚等南方殖民地以农业为主。弗吉尼亚的詹姆斯敦是新大陆最早的英国殖民地。1606年12月下旬，在伦敦殖民公司资助之下，大约100人乘船到新大陆来探险。他们的目标并不是在荒野上成家立业，而是梦想找到黄金和钻石。面对严酷的现实，移民们在约翰·史密斯船长的坚强领导下，在印第安人的帮助下，逐步掌握了玉米等农作物的种植，才使这一小块殖民地在最初几年得以维持下去。

1612年，有一件事使弗吉尼亚的经济起了巨大的变化，这就是人们发现了弗吉尼亚烟叶加工的方法，使它适合欧洲人的口味。第一批烟叶于1614年运抵伦敦，10年之内，烟叶成为弗吉尼亚主要的财源。

随着新移民的不断到来，在南方，像在其他殖民地一样，人们由于在海岸附近的殖民地里找不到肥沃的土地，便开始向内地推进。不久，人们发现西部的山区颇可立足。因此，南方内地很快就有了欣欣向荣的田庄。一个典型的例子是，有一位精明能干的测量师名叫波得·杰斐逊，仅用一碗混合甜饮料就换了160公顷土地，并在上面建立了自己的农庄。他就是美国《独立宣言》作者、美国第三任总统托马斯·杰斐逊的父亲。

大西洋海岸地区和内陆殖民地之间，早已存有明显的裂痕。内地地区的人在政治辩论上常常侃侃而谈，抨击旧习惯和旧传统的惰性。由于来自旧殖民地的人可以轻而易举地在边疆地区建立一个新家庭，这有效地防止了旧殖民地当局阻挠进步和改革。海岸地区的当权人物不得不常常放宽政策，放宽取得土地的条件以及宗教习惯的限制等，否则，人们都要离开旧殖民地，相继到边区去谋生了。在一个正处于发展中的朝气蓬勃的社会里，故步自封是行不通的。向山地和内陆推进，对后来整个美国的前途有着重大的意义。

The most northern of the Southern colonies was **Maryland**. The King of England, Charles I, gave the land between Virginia and Pennsylvania to **George Calvert** in 1632. George Calvert was also called Lord Baltimore. He was a Roman Catholic. George Calvert wanted to start a colony because of religious problems in England. Catholics could not openly observe their religion. They also had to pay money to the government because they did not belong to the Anglican Church which was the Church of England. George Calvert never saw the colony that was called Maryland. He died soon after he received the documents. His son Cecil Calvert became the next Lord Baltimore, and received all the land. He had the power to collect taxes, fight wars, make laws and create courts in Maryland. Cecil Calvert named his brother Leonard as the colony's first governor. Cecil Calvert believed that English Catholics could live in peace in Maryland with people who believed in Protestant religions. So he urged Catholics to leave England. To get more settlers, he permitted them to own their farms and gave them some power in local politics. Some Catholics did go to Maryland, but not as many as expected. Protestants were in the majority. In 1649, Lord Baltimore accepted a **Toleration Act** passed by the local government. It guaranteed freedom of religion... but only for Christians.

King Charles II of England gave away more land in America in 1663. This time, he gave to eight English lords the land known as **Carolina**. It extended south from Virginia into an area known as Florida. Spain controlled Florida. Spain also claimed the Southern part of Carolina. Spanish, French and English settlers had tried to live in that area earlier. But they were not successful. But the eight new owners promised 40 hectares of land to anyone who would go to Carolina to live. They also promised religious freedom. The first successful Carolina settlers left England in 1670. They built a town in an area where two rivers met. They called it Charles Town, for King Charles. Spanish ships attacked the port city many times, but the settlers kept them away. The settlers planted all kinds of crops to see what would grow best. They found rice was just right for the hot wet land. Their pigs and cattle did so well that settlers in Carolina started selling meat to the **West Indies**. Many of Charles Town's settlers came from **Barbados**, a port used in the West Indies slave trade. The settlers began buying black slaves to help grow the rice. By 1708, more blacks than whites lived in southern Carolina. The work of slaves made possible a successful economy.

Northern Carolina grew much more slowly than the Southern part of the colony. Many settlers to this area were from nearby Virginia. People who did not agree with the Anglican Church were not welcome in Virginia. Some of them moved south to the Northern part of Carolina. History experts say that the area that became North Carolina may have been the most democratic of all the colonies. The people generally did not get involved in each other's lives. They permitted each other to live in peace. They faced danger together from pirates who made the North Carolina coast their headquarters. Experts say the people in northern Carolina were independent thinkers. In 1677, some of them rebelled against England. They did not like England's **Navigation Acts**. These laws forced people in Carolina to pay taxes to England on goods sold to other colonies. Some northern Carolina settlers refused to pay this tax. They even set up their own government and tried to break free of England. But the English soldiers in the colonies stopped the rebellion by arresting its leader. The differences between the people of northern Carolina and southern Carolina became too great. The owners of the colony divided Carolina into two parts in 1712.

The last English colony founded in the New World was **Georgia**. It was established in 1732, under King George II. Georgia was the idea of a man named **James Oglethorpe**. He wanted to solve the debtor problem in England. Debtors are people who cannot re-pay money they owe. At that time, debtors were placed in prison. This made it impossible for them to earn the money needed to pay their debts. Oglethorpe wanted to create a colony where debtors could go instead of going to prison. He wanted it to be a place where people could have good lives. But not many debtors wanted to go to Georgia. The people who settled there were much like the people in the other colonies. They did not agree with all of Oglethorpe's ideas. They wanted to do things he did not believe were right—like drinking alcohol and owning slaves. The settlers won in the end. They did not accept Oglethorpe's ideas about how they should live. Life was not easy in Georgia. Spaniards and pirates captured ships of all nations along the coast. Spain controlled Florida and also claimed Georgia and the Carolinas. Border fights were common. Oglethorpe lost all his money trying to establish Georgia. King George took control of the colony in 1752.

As all these new colonies were being established nearby, the colony of Virginia was growing. A way of life was developing there that was very different from that found in the North. Most people in Virginia at this time were members of the Church of England. Religion was not as important a part of their lives as it was to the people in the North. In the New England colonies, the clergy were considered the most important people in town. In the Southern colonies, rich land owners were more important. People in Virginia did not live in towns, as people did in Massachusetts. They lived along rivers on small farms or on large farms called plantations. Living on a river made it easy to send goods to other nations by ship. Virginians were sending large amounts of tobacco to England on those ships. It was the crop that earned them the most money.

Growing tobacco destroys the elements in the soil that support plant life. After a few years, nothing grows well on land that has been planted with tobacco. A farmer has to stop planting anything on the land every few years. That means he needs a lot of land. He also needs many workers. So tobacco farmers in Virginia began to buy land and workers. At first, they bought the services of poor people who had no money or jobs. These people were called **indentured servants**. They made an agreement to work for a farmer for a period of four to seven years. Then they were freed to work for themselves. In 1619, a Dutch ship brought some Africans to Jamestown. They had been kidnapped from their homes by African traders and sold to the ship's captain. He sold them to the Virginia settlers. Those first blacks may have been treated like

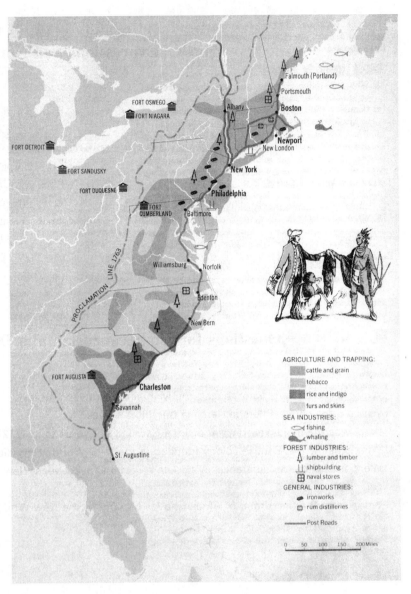

Colonial America in 1750

indentured servants. Later, however, colonists decided to keep them as slaves so they would not have to continue paying for workers. Indians did not make good slaves because they could run away. Blacks could not. They had no place to go. Slowly, laws were approved in Virginia that made it legal to keep black people as slaves. By 1750, there were more Africans in Virginia than any other group.

History experts continue to debate if slavery caused prejudice in America or prejudice caused slavery. No one knows the answer. Most Europeans of the 17th century felt they were better than African people. The reasons for this included the Africans' different customs, religion and the black color of their skin. Europeans believed the color black represented danger and death. Slavery in the American south affected the history of the United States for many years. It divided the people and led to a great **civil war**.

Words, Expressions and Notes

Maryland 马里兰殖民地

George Calvert 乔治·卡尔弗特（1580—1632），英国下议员、国务大臣，北美马里兰殖民地的创建者

Toleration Act 《容忍法案》

Carolina 卡罗来纳殖民地，1729 年被分为北卡罗来纳和南卡罗来纳。

West Indies （拉丁美洲）西印度洋群岛

Barbados （拉丁美洲）巴巴多斯岛

Navigation Acts 《航海条例》，英国于 17 世纪中期

至 18 世纪颁布的由英国轮船从事航运的一系列法律，后成为英国保护贸易的手段。

Georgia 佐治亚殖民地

James Oglethorpe 詹姆斯·奥格尔索普（1696—1785），英国将军、下议员，佐治亚殖民地创建者，并担任首任总督。

indentured servants 契约仆役，指 1700 至 1900 期间来到北美与人订约充当仆役若干年以偿付赴北美的旅费和维持生活的异乡客。

civil war 内战

Questions for Comprehension and Discussion

1. Why did the Calverts want to start the Maryland colony?

2. Why did the early settlers in Carolina buy black slaves?

3. What was the major reason that divided Carolina in two parts in 1712?

4. What was the last English colony founded in the New World? How did it get its name?

5. What is the major difference in people's social life between New England colonies and southern colonies?

6. When were the first group of African slaves brought to the New World? And how?

7 Slavery Coming to America

奴隶制来到美洲

在美国，一些白人以他们是第一批建立詹姆斯敦的英国人的后裔而倍感自豪。然而，如果历史有知，把1619年——比搭乘"五月花号"在马萨诸塞普利茅斯登陆的移民还早一年——抵达詹姆斯敦的20个黑人的后代都一一记录在案的话，许多黑人也应该享有同样的荣耀。作为非洲移民的先行者（尽管是被迫的），这20个黑人在詹姆斯敦建立后仅仅12年便来到新大陆。如今，他们的总人数已经超过3 000万。

黑人对美国的建国和发展的贡献通常被人们所忘记，这其中的主要原因是，在到达新大陆的最初3个世纪里，他们几乎都是作为奴隶在默默无闻地劳作。其实，在北方新崛起的矿山、工厂和港口，哪个地方没有浸透着他们在辛勤劳动中洒落的汗水？从南方种植园出产的糖、烟草和棉花，哪样产品上没有映射着他们遭受非人折磨后从黝黑皮肤上渗出的鲜血？

奴隶制是一种罪恶，从英国殖民时期开始的奴隶制是美国历史上最黑暗的一页。但事实是，在殖民地时期，奴隶问题却很少受到人们的关注。大多数白人（尤其是在南方）甚至认为，因为经济发展需要，奴隶制度是再自然不过的一件事。然而，随着时间的推移和非洲裔奴隶人数的增多，奴隶制与大多数新大陆移民所信奉的"人人生而平等"的基本价值观之间的冲突愈发显现，由奴隶制所引发的社会矛盾日益突出。《独立宣言》作者、美国第三任总统托马斯·杰斐逊（他自己也拥有黑奴）曾经就美国的奴隶问题忧心忡忡地写道："每当我想到上帝是公正的，我就为祖国的前途感到不寒而栗……"杰斐逊的预感不无道理：他去世后仅35年，一场由奴隶制引发的血腥战争差一点使这个国家一分为二。

尽管北美地区的奴隶制长期以来一直受到广泛的关注和批评，但奴隶制的源头却并不在美国。下面，我们首先从世界的范围了解奴隶制的概况，然后看一看奴隶制在北美大陆的发展过程，最后再倾听一位曾经贩卖过非洲黑奴的船长约翰·纽顿面对上帝发出的深切忏悔。

Slavery is one person controlling or owning another. Some history experts say it began following the development of farming about 10,000 years ago. People forced prisoners of war to work for them. Other slaves were criminals or people who could not re-pay money they owed. Experts say the first known slaves existed in the **Sumerian society** of what is now **Iraq** more than 5,000 years ago. Slavery also existed among people in China, India, Africa, the Middle East and the Americas. It expanded as trade and industry increased. This increase created a demand for a labor force to produce goods for export. Slaves did most of the work. Most ancient people thought of slavery as a natural condition that could happen to anyone at any time. Few saw it as evil or unfair. In most cities, slaves could be freed by their owners and become citizens. In later times, slaves provided the labor needed to produce products that were in demand. Sugar was one of these products. Italians established large sugar farms beginning around the 12th century. They used slaves from Russia and other parts of Europe to do the work. By the year 1300, African blacks had begun to replace the Russian slaves. They were bought or captured from **North African Arabs**, who used them as slaves for years. By the 1500s, Spain and Portugal had American colonies. The Europeans made native Indians work in large farms and mines in the colonies. Most of the

Indians died from European diseases and poor treatment. So the Spanish and Portuguese began to bring in people from West Africa as slaves. France, Britain and the Netherlands did the same in their American colonies.

England's southern colonies in North America developed a farm economy that could not survive without slave labor. Many slaves lived on large farms called plantations. These large farms produced important crops traded by the colony, crops such as cotton and tobacco. Each plantation was like a small village owned by one family. That family lived in a large house, usually facing a river. Many separate buildings were needed on a plantation. For example, a building was needed for cooking. And buildings were needed for workers to produce goods such as furniture that were used on the plantation. The plantation business was farming. So there also were barns for animals and buildings for holding and drying crops. There was a house to smoke meat so it could be kept safely. And there was a place on the river from which goods were sent to England on ships.

An African is branded after being selected as a slave for the New World.

The plantation owner controlled the farm and saw that it earned money. He **supervised**, fed and clothed the people living on it, including the slaves. Big plantations might have 200 slaves. They worked in the fields on crops that would be sold or eaten by the people who lived on the plantation. They also raised animals for meat and milk. **Field slaves** worked very long and hard. They worked each day from the time the sun rose until it set. Many of these slaves lived in extremely poor conditions in small houses with no heat or furniture. Sometimes, five or ten people lived together in one room. **House slaves** usually lived in the owner's house. They did the cooking and cleaning in the house. House slaves worked fewer hours than field slaves, but were more closely supervised by the owner and his family.

Laws approved in the Southern colonies made it illegal for slaves to marry, own property, or earn their freedom. These laws also did not permit slaves to be educated, or even to learn to read. But some owners permitted their slaves to earn their freedom, or gave them money for good work. Other owners punished slaves to get them to work. These punishments included beatings, **withholding food** and threatening to sell members of a slave's family. Some plantation owners **executed** slaves suspected of serious crimes by hanging them or burning them alive. History experts say that people who were rich enough to own many slaves became leaders in their local areas. They were members of the local governments. They attended meetings of the **legislatures** in the capitals of their colonies usually two times a year. Slave-owners had the time and the education to greatly influence political life in the Southern colonies because the hard work on their farms was done by slaves.

Today, most people in the world **condemn** slavery. That was not true in the early years of the American nation. Many Americans thought slavery was evil, but necessary. Yet owning slaves was common among the richer people in the early 1700s. Many of the leaders in the colonies who fought for

American independence owned slaves. This was true in the Northern colonies as well as the Southern ones. One example is the famous American diplomat, inventor and businessman Benjamin Franklin. He owned slaves for 30 years and sold them at his general store. But his ideas about slavery changed during his long life. Benjamin Franklin started the first schools to teach blacks and later argued for their freedom.

Slavery did not become a force in the Northern colonies mainly because of economic reasons. Cold weather and poor soil could not support such a farm economy as was found in the South. As a result, the North came to depend on manufacturing and trade. Trade was the way colonists got the English goods they needed. It was also the way to earn money by selling products found in the New World. New England became a center for such trade across the seas. The people who lived there became shipbuilders so they could send the products to England. They used local wood to build the ships. They also sold wood and wood products. They became businessmen carrying goods around the world. The New England shipbuilding towns near the Atlantic Ocean grew quickly as a result. The largest of these towns was Boston, Massachusetts. By 1720, it had more than 10,000 people. Only two towns in England were larger: London and Bristol. More than 25 percent of the men in Boston had invested in shipping or worked in it. Ship captains and businessmen held most of the public offices.

The American colonies traded goods such as whale oil, ginger, iron, wood, and rum—an alcoholic drink made from sugarcane. Ships carried these goods from the New England colonies to Africa. There, they were traded for African people. The Africans had been captured by enemy tribesmen and sold to African slave traders. The New England boat captains would buy as many as they could put on their ships. The conditions on these ships were very cruel. The Africans were put in so tightly they could hardly move. Some were chained. Many killed themselves rather than live under such conditions. Others died of sicknesses they developed on the ship. Yet many did survive the trip, and became slaves in the Southern colonies, or in the Caribbean islands. Black slaves were needed to work on Caribbean sugar plantations. The Southern American colonies needed them to work on the tobacco and rice plantations. By 1750, almost 25 percent of the total number of people in the American colonies were black slaves. From the 1500s to the 1800s, Europeans sent about 12 million black slaves from Africa to America. Almost two million of them died on the way.

History experts say English ships carried the greatest number of Africans into slavery. One slave ship captain came to hate what he was doing, and turned to religion. His name was John Newton. He stopped taking part in slave trade and became a leader in the Anglican Church. He is famous for having written this famous song, "Amazing Grace."

Amazing Grace,
How sweet the sound,
That saved a **wretch** like me.
I once was lost but now am found,
Was blind, but now can see...

John Newton

For Your Appreciation

Amazing Grace
奇异恩典

1748 年的一天，一艘专门从事贩卖非洲黑奴的船只在大海上突遭狂风暴雨，在船只即将倾覆之际，船长竭尽全力向苍天呼救，"Lord, have mercy upon us!" 祈求得到上帝的保佑。平安度过灾难之后，他开始在信仰上有所追求，最终放弃了贩卖奴隶的罪恶行当，成为一个远近闻名的基督教牧师。他就是《奇异恩典》的作者约翰·纽顿（John Newton, 1725—1807）。

由于奴隶制是自美国有史以来一直困扰社会的话题，所以尽管作者是一位英国人，这首歌曲却成为美国人的最爱。歌曲中呈现出的圣洁、祥和、空灵、庄重的气氛，令人静气凝神。如今在美国的许多庄严隆重的场合（例如美国前总统里根的葬礼），人们都能听到这优美而动人的旋律。

Amazing Grace, how sweet the sound,	奇异恩典，如此甘甜，
That saved a wretch like me.	我等罪人，竟蒙赦免。
I once was lost but now am found,	昔我迷失，今被寻回，
Was blind, but now I see.	曾经盲目，今又重见。
' Twas Grace that taught my heart to fear.	如斯恩典，令心敬畏，
And Grace, my fears relieved.	如斯恩典，免我忧惧。
How precious did that Grace appear,	归信伊始，恩典即临，
The hour I first believed.	何等奇异，何其珍贵。
Through many dangers, toils and **snares**	冲决罗网，历经磨难，
I have already come;	风尘之中，我已归来。
'Tis Grace that brought me safe thus far	恩典眷顾，一路搀扶，
And Grace will lead me home.	靠它指引，终返家园。
The Lord has promised good to me.	主曾许诺，降福于我，
His word my hope secures.	主之言语，希望所系；
He will my shield and portion be,	此生此世，托庇于主，
As long as life **endures**.	赞美上帝，直至永生。
As long as life endures.	

Words, Expressions and Notes

Sumerian society　苏美尔社会。苏美尔（Sumer）是古代幼发拉底河下游的一个地区。

Iraq *n.* 伊拉克

North African Arabs　北非阿拉伯人

supervised *v.* 监督，指导

field slaves　在田间劳作的奴隶

house slaves　在住宅以及周围劳作的奴隶

withholding food　拒给食物

executed *v.* 处死

legislatures *n.* 立法机构

condemn *v.* 谴责

wretch *n.* 可怜的人；坏蛋

'**Twas** = It was

snares *n.* 圈套，骗局

His word my hope secures. = His word secures my hope.

He will my shield and portion be = He will be my shield and portion

endures *v.* 持续

Questions for Comprehension and Discussion

1. What is slavery? Why is it considered evil?
2. Why was slavery important for the economy of England's southern colonies in North America?
3. How did slaves live on the plantations?
4. What was the difference between a field slave and and a house slave?
5. Why did slavery not become an important force in the Northern colonies of North America?
6. Why may blacks as well as whites claim to be founders of American civilization?

8 The French and Indian War

法英七年战争

当英国人在大西洋海岸地区建立农场、种植园和市镇的时候，法国人已经在加拿大东部的圣劳伦斯河流域建立了另外一种殖民地。他们派遣的移民为数不多，但是，却有大批探险家、传教士和皮货商人。他们占领密西西比河，利用一系列的堡垒和商业口岸，成立了一个新月形状的帝国——北起东北部的魁北克，南至南方的新奥尔良。这样一来，他们势必要把英国人限制在阿巴拉契亚山脉以东的狭长地带里了。

英国人对于这种他们认为的"法国人的入侵"，早就进行了抵抗。英法移民之间的地方性冲突早在 1613 年就发生过。最后，有组织的战争终于发生，这些战争是英法世界范围冲突中在美洲的抗衡。从 1689 到 1697 年，欧洲有巴勒提拿特战争，美洲有威廉国王之战；从 1702 到 1713 年，欧洲有西班牙王位继承战争，美洲有安妮女王之战；从 1744 年到 1748 年，欧洲有奥地利王位继承战争，美洲有乔治国王之战。在这些战争里，英国虽然略占上风，但仍然胜负未定，法国在新大陆的地位还很牢固。

到了 18 世纪 50 年代，英法两国为争夺土地而厉兵秣马。1754 年，双方开始发生武装冲突，史称"法国和印第安战争"。交战一方是英国人和他们的印第安盟友，另一方是法国人和他们的印第安盟友。英法两国在北美洲的霸权，注定要由这场战争来解决。尽管未得到殖民地的全力支持，尽管在战争初期屡受挫败，英国由于占有优越的战略地位，加上指挥得法，经过 7 年奋战，英国终于赢得了最后胜利，占领了加拿大和密西西比河上游两岸之地，法国在北美建立帝国的美梦也就基本破灭了。

战争胜利的直接结果是英国在北美洲殖民地面积增加了一倍多。原来大西洋海岸一个狭长地带加上如今广阔无际的加拿大与密西西比河及阿利根尼山之间的领土，本身就可以构成一个帝国。在人口方面，以前大多数都是英国新教徒或英国化的欧洲大陆移民，现在则包括了法国的天主教徒以及为数众多的部分基督徒化了的印第安人。要保卫和治理这块巨大的领土，同时还要偿还战争消耗的巨额经费，英国必须筹集大笔经费。但问题是，钱从哪里来？英国决定向殖民地征税。

另外，在战争初期，7 个殖民地的代表召开了一次会议，旨在组成一个殖民地之间的联盟，以对付法国及其印第安盟友造成的威胁。尽管由本杰明·富兰克林提出的会议决议未被各殖民地议会所接受，但这是各殖民地走向联合的第一次尝试，是后来召开的争取民族独立的大陆会议的先驱。

最后，以乔治·华盛顿为代表的一批出生于殖民地的年轻军人在战争中积累了抗击欧洲职业军队的宝贵经验。在未来的独立战争中，正是华盛顿组建了一支殖民地的人民军队，打败了当年他曾效力的英国军队。

从这以上 3 个方面看，英国在军事上的暂时胜利为它随后在政治上的永久失败埋下了种子。

During the 18th century, Spain, France and Britain controlled land in North America. Spain controlled Florida. France was powerful in the Northern and central areas. Britain controlled the east. All three nations knew they could not exist together peacefully in North America. The situation could only be settled by war. The powerful European nations already were fighting each other for land and money all over the world. These small wars continued for more than 100 years. They were called **King William's War**, **Queen Anne's War**, **King George's War** and **the French and Indian War**.

The French and Indian War was fought to decide if Britain or France would be the strong power in North America. France and its colonists and Indian allies fought against Britain, its colonists and Indian allies. The war began with conflicts about land. French explorers had been the first Europeans in the areas around the **Great Lakes** and the **Ohio and Mississippi rivers**. France had sent traders and **trappers** to these territories and had established trading centers there. Britain claimed the same land. When the King gave land in North America to someone, the land was considered to extend from east coast to west coast, even though no one knew where the west coast was. The land along the east coast had become crowded, and settlers were moving west. White people were destroying the Indians' hunting areas. And Indians became worried that they would lose the use of their land.

The Indian tribes may have been able to resist the people moving west if they had been united. But their own conflicts kept the Indian groups apart. When Britain and France started fighting each other, some Indians helped the British. Others helped the French. The French settlers lived mainly in what was called New France. Today it is part of Canada. Life there was different from life in the British colonies to the South. There was no religious freedom, for example. All settlers in French territories had to be French and belong to the Roman Catholic Church. So, many French people who belonged to Protestant churches settled in the British colonies. France also did not like the fact that the British paid the Indians high prices for animal furs. France was more interested in the fur trade than in settling the land. The British hurt the French traders' business when they bought fur from the Indians.

One of the French trading forts was built in the area where the city of **Pittsburgh**, Pennsylvania is today. The French called it **Fort Duquesne**. The British claimed it was in Virginia and that the land belonged to them. In 1754, the governor of Virginia sent a 21-year-old colonist named George Washington to tell

Hidden by rocks and trees, the French and the Indians ambush the British.

the French to get out. This was the same George Washington who would later become the first President of the United States. The French refused to leave Fort Duquesne. So Washington and 150 men tried to force them out. They attacked a group of Frenchmen and killed ten of them. The French and Indian War had begun.

British troops under the command of **General Edward Braddock** joined George Washington at Fort Duquesne. The British general expected to fight the way battles were fought in Europe. There, troops lined up on open fields and fired their weapons as they marched toward each other. The French and Indians did not fight this way. They hid in the woods. They wore clothes that made them difficult to see. They shot at the British from behind trees. The British had more troops than the other side. But the French and Indians won the battle of Fort Duquesne. General Braddock was killed.

Most of the French and Indian War was fought along two lakes in an area of New York state near the border with Canada. One was Lake George. The other, Lake Champlain. Lake Champlain is north of Lake George. It reaches almost all the way to the city of **Montreal** in Canada. These lakes provided the best way to move troops and supplies during the French and Indian War. Few roads existed in North America at that time. The military force which controlled the lakes and rivers controlled much of North America.

The French had military bases in the cities of **Quebec** and Montreal. The British had military bases along New York's Hudson River. The area between them became the great battle ground. Fighting increased after the British defeated the French near Lake George in the last months of 1755. The French then built a new military base to control Lake Champlain and the surrounding area. The French military base was at the Southern end of Lake Champlain. They built a strong camp, the kind called a fort. They called it Fort Carillon. The fort would control Lake Champlain and the area needed to reach the Northern part of Lake George. The fort was designed to provide a strong defense against attack. The French built two big walls of logs, several meters apart. The area between the walls was filled with dirt. Later, a strong stone front was added. Troops inside the walls were well protected. The British built a similar fort at the Southern end of Lake George. They called it **Fort William Henry**.

France sent one of its best military commanders to take command of its troops in America. His name was the **Marquis de Montcalm**. General Montcalm attacked several British forts in 1757. One of these was Fort William Henry on Lake George. The British commander was forced to surrender. General Montcalm promised that the British troops would be treated fairly if they surrendered. But the Indian allies of the French did not honor the surrender agreement. They began to kill British soldiers and settlers. No one is sure how many people died. It could have been more than 1,000.

In 1758, a strong British force attacked Fort Carillon on Lake Champlain. General Montcalm was the French commander. Fort Carillon was strong enough that the smaller French force was able to defeat the bigger British force. The British withdrew, but attacked again the next year. This time the British commander was **General Jeffery Amhurst**. Amhurst was successful. The British defeated the French. They changed the name of Fort Carillon to **Fort Ticonderoga**. It became an important military center in the French and Indian War. Fort Ticonderoga would also become important later, during America's War for Independence.

The French and Indian War ended after the British defeated the French in Quebec. Britain and France signed a treaty ending the war in Paris in 1763. The British had won the French and Indian War. They took control of the lands that had been claimed by France. Britain now claimed all the land from the east coast of North America to the Mississippi River. Everything west of that river belonged to Spain. France gave all its western lands to Spain to keep the British out. Indians still controlled most of the western lands, except for some Spanish colonies in Texas and New Mexico.

The French and Indian War was one part of a world conflict between Britain and France. It was fought to decide which of the two powerful nations would rule North America. The British defeated the French in North America in 1763. As a result, it took control of lands that had been claimed by France. Britain now was responsible for almost two million people in the 13 American colonies and 60,000 French-speaking people in Canada. In addition to political and economic responsibilities, Britain had to protect all these colonists from different groups of Indians. This would cost a lot of money. Britain already had spent a lot of money sending troops and material to the colonies to fight the French and Indian War. It believed the American colonists should now help pay for that war.

Words, Expressions and Notes

King William's War　威廉国王之战（1689—1697）

Queen Anne's War　安妮女王之战（1702—1713）

King George's War　乔治国王之战（1744—1748）

the French and Indian War　法英七年战争。1756 年至 1763 年，英法双方各自在印第安部落支援下在北美争夺殖民地的战争。

Great Lakes　五大湖，美国与加拿大之间 5 个大湖的总称。除密歇根湖属美国之外，苏必利尔、休伦、伊利、安大略四湖均为两国共有。

Ohio and Mississippi rivers　俄亥俄河与密西西比河

trappers　*n.*　为获取野兽皮毛而设陷阱或捕兽机的猎人

Pittsburgh　*n.* 匹兹堡（美国城市）

Fort Duquesne　迪凯纳要塞，以法国海军名将

Abraham Duquesne 名字命名

General Edward Braddock　爱德华·布雷多克（1695—1755），英国驻北美洲英军总司令，率军远征法国迪凯纳要塞，遭伏击身亡。

Montreal　*n.* 蒙特利尔（加拿大城市）

Quebec　*n.* 魁北克省（加拿大地名）

Fort William Henry　威廉·亨利要塞

Marquis de Montcalm　德蒙卡侯爵，法军在北美地区的总指挥

General Jeffery Amhurst　杰弗利·阿默斯特（1717—1797），英国陆军元帅，1760 年率部击败加拿大的法国军队，后出任加拿大总督。

Fort Ticonderoga　泰康德罗卡要塞，英法冲突中的一处战略要地

Questions for Comprehension and Discussion

1. What countries controlled the land of North America during the 18th century?

2. In what way did the French differ from the British in settling in the New World?

3. Why did the British army lose in the early battles in the French and Indian War?

4. Why were the Indian tribes not able to resist the people moving west?

5. What was the major problem England had after it had become the master of North America?

Unit 3　The American Revolution

9　The Road to Revolution

通往革命之路

美国开国元勋之一、第二任总统约翰·亚当斯说，美国革命早在 1620 年就开始了。他说："革命在战争前就开始了。革命隐藏在人民的心里和思想里。"

但是，作为一个实际问题来看，英国和美洲的公开分裂，是从 1763 年开始的，这时距第一个定居点在詹姆斯敦建立之日已有 150 年的光阴。此时，各殖民地在经济和文化方面发展得很快，所有殖民地都已经有了多年自治的历史，总人口已达 150 多万。

在殖民地的所有发展阶段里，一个显著的特点就是英国政府对远隔重洋的美洲殖民地缺乏控制能力，各殖民地享受着高度的政治上的独立，与伦敦当局只保持着松散的联系。事实上，直到 1763 年，英国还没有一个前后一贯的殖民地政策。伦敦的基本指导原则源于根深蒂固的重商主义，即殖民地应该把原料供给母国，在工业上不应和母国竞争。但是，这个原则贯彻得很不得力，各殖民地也从来没有认为自己是卑屈的。与此相反，它们觉得自己与英国的关系就是由一些国家组成的自由联邦。在初创的阶段，殖民地大都可以根据各自的环境自由发展。除了佐治亚之外，英国政府没有直接参加过殖民地的建立。

虽然英国国会或者王室有时也会情绪激动地要求殖民地服从英国的旨意和利益，但大多数移民都采取抵制态度。由于与英国距离遥远，移民并不十分害怕英国的报复行动。除开地理因素使英国在殖民地管理上鞭长莫及之外，美国早期的生活特色也是殖民地倾向于自治的原因之一。移民从地狭人稠的欧洲国家来到这个广阔无垠的地方，因环境所致，生活方式就不得不变得以个人为重了。

另外，移民们承袭英国人为争取政治自由而进行长时期斗争的传统，把自由观念写进了弗吉尼亚的第一个特许状里。这个特许状规定，英国移民享有的自由、特权和豁免权就如"他们诞生和生长在英国本土一样"。这就是说，他们可以享受大宪章和习惯法带来的好处。

这就是为什么约翰·亚当斯说"革命隐藏在人民的心里和思想里"的真正原因。

1763 年，英国政府害怕移民迁入新领地会挑起新的印第安战争，宣布阿利根尼山、佛罗里达地区、密西西比河与魁北克之间的土地，全部留给印第安人使用，这就触犯了移民向西发展的根本利益。1764 年，英国实行新财政政策，通过食糖法增加税收。从这时起，殖民地与伦敦当局之间的关系便骤然紧张起来。

The road to revolution lasted several years. The most serious events began in 1770. War began five years later. Relations between Britain and its American colonists were most tense in the colony of Massachusetts. There were protests against the British policy of taxing the colonies without giving them **representation in Parliament**. To prevent trouble, thousands of British soldiers were sent to Boston, the biggest city in Massachusetts. On March 5, 1770, tension led to violence. This is what happened.

It was the end of winter, and the weather was very cold. A small group of colonists began throwing

rocks and pieces of ice at soldiers guarding a public building. They were joined by others, and the soldiers became frightened. They fired their guns. Five colonists were killed. The incident became known as the **Boston Massacre**.

The people of Massachusetts were extremely angry. The soldiers were tried in court for murder. Most were found innocent. The others received minor punishments. Fearing more violence, the British Parliament cancelled most of its taxes. Only the tax on tea remained. This eased some of the tensions, for a while. Imports of British goods increased. The colonists seemed satisfied with the situation, until a few years later. That is when the Massachusetts colony once again became involved in a dispute with Britain.

A Paul Revere's engraving showing the Massacre

The trouble started because the British government wanted to help improve the business of the **British East India Company**. That company organized all the trade between India and other countries ruled by Britain. By 1773, the company had become weak. The British government decided to permit it to sell tea directly to the American colonies. The colonies would still have to pay a tea tax to Britain. The Americans did not like the new plan. They felt they were being forced to buy their tea from only one company.

Officials in the colonies of Pennsylvania and New York sent the East India Company's ships back to Britain. In Massachusetts, things were different. The British governor there wanted to collect the tea tax and **enforce the law**. When the ships arrived in Boston, some colonists tried to block their way. The ships remained just outside the harbor without unloading their goods. On the night of December 16th, 1773, a group of colonists went out in a small boat. They got on a British ship and threw all the tea into the water. The colonists were dressed as American Indians so the British would not recognize them, but the people of Boston knew who they were. A crowd gathered to cheer them. That incident—the night when British tea was thrown into Boston harbor—became known as the **Boston Tea Party**.

Destroying the tea was a serious crime. The British government was angry. Parliament reacted to the Boston Tea Party by punishing the whole colony of Massachusetts for the actions of a few men. It approved a series of laws that once again changed relations between the colony and Britain. One of these laws closed the port of Boston until the tea was paid for. Other laws strengthened the power of the British governor and weakened the power of local colonial officials. In June, 1774, the colony of Massachusetts called for a meeting of delegates from all the other colonies to consider joint action against Britain.

This meeting of colonial delegates was called the **First Continental Congress**. It was held in the city of Philadelphia, Pennsylvania, in September, 1774. All the colonies except one was represented. The Southern colony of Georgia did not send a delegate. The delegates agreed that the British Parliament had no right to control trade with the American colonies or to make any laws that affected them. They said the people of the colonies must have the right to take part in any legislative group that made laws for them.

The First Continental Congress approved a series of documents that condemned all British actions in the American colonies after 1763. It approved a Massachusetts proposal saying that the people could use weapons to defend their rights. It also organized a **Continental Association** to boycott British goods and to stop all exports to any British colony or to Britain itself. Local committees were created to enforce the boycott. One of the delegates to this First Continental Congress was **John Adams** of Massachusetts. Many years later, he said that by the time the meeting was held, the American Revolution had already begun.

Britain's King George II announced that the New England colonies were in rebellion. Parliament made the decision to use troops against Massachusetts in January, 1775.

The people of Massachusetts formed a **provincial assembly** and began training men to fight. Soon, groups of armed men were doing military exercises in towns all around Massachusetts and in other colonies, too.

British officers received their orders in April, 1775. By that time, the colonists had been gathering weapons in the town of Concord, about thirty kilometers west of Boston. The British forces were ordered to seize the weapons. But the colonists knew they were coming and were prepared. Years later, **Henry Wadsworth Longfellow** wrote a poem about what happened. The poem tells about the actions of Paul Revere, one of three men who helped warn the colonial troops that the British were coming:

(Excerpt from "Paul Revere's Ride")
Listen my children and you shall hear
of the midnight ride of Paul Revere.
On the eighteenth of April in Seventy-Five
hardly a man is now alive
who remembers that famous day and year.
He said to his friend,
"If the British march by land or sea from the town tonight,
Hang a lantern aloft in the belfry arch
of the North Church tower as a signal light.
One if by land,
And two if by sea.
And I on the opposite shore will be
Ready to ride and spread the alarm
Through every **Middlesex** village and farm
For the country folk to be up and to arm."

**Paul Revere rides toward Lexington
to warn of the British advance.**

When the British reached the town of **Lexington**, they found it protected by about seventy colonial troops. These troops were called "**Minute Men**" because they had been trained to fight with only a minute's warning. Guns were fired. Eight colonists were killed. No one knows who fired the first shot in that first battle of the American Revolution. Each side accused the other. But the meaning was very clear. It was called: "the shot heard round the world."

From Lexington, the British marched to Concord, where they destroyed whatever supplies the colonists had not been able to save. Other colonial troops rushed to the area. A battle at Concord's north bridge forced the British to march back to Boston. It was the first day of America's War for Independence. When it was over, almost 300 British troops had been killed. Fewer than 100 Americans had died.

The British troops had marched in time with their **drummers and pipers**. The musicians had played a song called "Yankee Doodle." The British invented the song to insult the Americans. They said a Yankee Doodle was a man who did not know how to fight. After the early battles of the revolution, the Americans said they were glad to be Yankee Doodles.

(Excerpt from "Yankee Doodle")
Father and I went down to camp,
Along with Captain Gooding.
And there we saw the men and boys
As thick as hasty pudding.
Yankee Doodle keep it up,
Yankee Doodle **dandy,**
Mind the music and the step,
And with girls be-handy. . . .

Following the battles at Lexington and Concord, the Massachusetts government organized a group that captured Fort Ticonderoga on Lake Champlain in New York State. The other colonies began sending troops to help. And another joint colonial meeting was called: the **Second Continental Congress.**

Words, Expressions and Notes

representation in Parliament 在（英国）议会中的代表权。早期美洲殖民地的人民十分看重他们的意志能够在英国议会中得到表达，而英国统治当局却对殖民地人民采取居高临下的傲慢姿态，对他们的正当要求不闻不问。因此，殖民地人民高喊出"无代表权就无税收！"（No representation, no taxes!）的战斗口号。

Boston Massacre 波士顿惨案。1770 年 3 月 5 日，波士顿居民反对英国殖民政策遭到英国军队开枪射杀，5 人死亡。这是英国统治者与殖民地人民之间的第一次流血冲突。

British East India Company 英国东印度公司。英国政府于 1600 年特许成立对东南亚从事殖民事业的组织，1874 年解散。

enforce the law （强制）实施法律

Boston Tea Party 波士顿倾茶事件。1773 年 12 月 16 日，波士顿居民为反对英国垄断茶叶贸易，化装登上英国商船，把船上的数百箱茶叶倒入海中。此事件成为美国独立战争的直接导火索。

First Continental Congress 第一届大陆会议。在弗吉尼亚议会的倡议下，各殖民地代表于 1774 年 9 月 5 日在费城开会，"就殖民地目前的悲惨处境进行磋商"。出席该会议的代表由各殖民地人民代表会议选举出来，除佐治亚之外，各殖民地都派有代表出席，代表总数是 55 人。由于各殖民地意见分歧，会议陷于进退两难的境地：首先它必须传达出各殖民地代表坚定一致的态度，以迫使英国政府让步；但同时它又不能表现出任何偏激或"独立的精神"，以免使温和派人士惊惶（此时的殖民地仍有很多对英国抱有幻想的人士）。大会通过了一系列谴责英国的文件，其中一项对未来的美国将产生重大而深远的影响，那就是——人民有权拿起武器捍卫他们的权利。大会代表之一、美国第二任总统约翰·亚当斯后来指出："当第一届大陆会议举行之时，美国革命就已经开始。"

Continental Association 大陆联合会。第一届大陆会议期间组建的负责协调各殖民地对英国采取统一政策和行动的委员会。

John Adams 约翰·亚当斯（1735—1826），主张殖民地独立的激进政治家，《独立宣言》起草人之一，美国第二任总统

provincial assembly 地方议会

Henry Wadsworth Longfellow 亨利·华兹沃斯·朗费罗（1807—1882），美国历史上最著名的诗人之一

Hang a lantern aloft in the belfry arch 在高高的钟楼上挂上一盏灯

One if by land 如果（英军）从陆上来，就挂一盏（灯）

And two if by sea 如果从海上来，就挂两盏

Ready to ride and spread the alarm （我）随时准备骑马去报警

Middlesex 马萨诸塞殖民地的一个县名

Lexington 列克星敦，波士顿附近一小镇，因在此打响美国独立第一枪而闻名。

Minute Men （美国独立战争时期）招之即来的民兵

drummers and pipers 鼓手和风笛手

As thick as hasty pudding （意指）很多人踊跃报名参军（抗击英国军队）

dandy *a.* 服饰浮华的；极好的，第一流的

Second Continental Congress 第二届大陆会议，1775 年 5 月 10 日在费城召开。由于在脱离英国的关键

议题上存在分歧，会期异常漫长。经过长达一年的讨论至 1776 年 5 月 10 日，一项快刀斩乱麻的决议案终于通过。随后，会议要求杰斐逊等 5 人

草拟正式宣言。1776 年 7 月 4 日，会议通过《独立宣言》，宣告一个新国家的诞生。

Questions for Comprehension and Discussion

1. "No taxation without representation" became a catch phrase in the early years of American Revolution. What does it mean? Why is it important for the people in the colonies?

2. What happened in the Boston Massacre?

3. What did the British government do after the Boston Tea Party?

4. Do you know the meaning of American "gun culture"? When and where did it start?

5. Who was Paul Revere? What did he do in the American Revolution?

6. What is the meaning of "Minute Men"?

7. How did "Yankee Doodle" become a popular song in America?

10 The Birth of the Declaration of Independence

《独立宣言》的诞生

当列克星敦与康科德的枪声还在人们耳畔回响之际，第二次大陆会议于 1775 年 5 月 10 日在费城召开。刚从英国回来的本杰明·富兰克林也出席了会议——他以几个殖民地"代理人"的身份去伦敦谋求和解却毫无结果。战争是大会面临的首要问题。来自弗吉尼亚的代表帕特里·亨利指出："战争实际上已经开始，我们的同胞已经走上战场。"由杰斐逊和来自宾夕法尼亚的代表约翰·迪金森共同起草的宣言《为何必须拿起武器》发出了令人激动的号召："我们的事业是正义的。我们的联合是完美的，我们内部的资源是丰富的，并且，必要的话，我们无疑可以取得外援。我们将使用敌人迫使我们拿起的武器来保卫我们的自由，因为，我们宁愿做自由人而牺牲，也不愿做奴隶而苟存。"

当宣言还处于辩论阶段时，大陆会议就把民兵改编成大陆军，任命乔治·华盛顿为总司令。但即使这样，面对完全脱离英国走向独立的抉择，殖民地大多数人的态度却是半心半意、模棱两可的。一些人对殖民地和英国之间的关系认识不清，在效忠和反抗英王之间犹豫不决；另一些人对殖民地的力量估计不足，存在一个敢不敢独立的问题。

1776 年 1 月，托马斯·潘恩发表了他的小册子《常识》。他以活泼的文体说明了独立的必要性。他甚至攻击神圣不可侵犯的国王，嘲弄王权世袭的观念。他说，一个老实人在社会上的价值，超过有史以来所有戴上王冠的坏蛋。他以令人信服的方式提出了两个不同的选择：继续向暴君和抱残守缺的政府屈服，或者是选择自由与幸福而成立一个自给自足的独立共和国。这本小册子风行整个殖民地，不仅让信仰坚定的人们目标更加明确，而且唤起和团结了那些犹豫不决的人们，使他们也投身到脱离英国而独立的伟大事业之中。

1776 年 6 月 7 日，来自弗吉尼亚的理查德·亨利·李提出建议，主张 13 个殖民地宣布独立，建立美国联邦。一个以托马斯·杰斐逊为首的五人委员会立即奉命起草正式宣言，"列举迫使我们作出这一重大决定的原因"。

1776 年 7 月 4 日通过的《独立宣言》不仅宣告了一个新国家的诞生，而且阐明了人类自由的基本哲理。《独立宣言》的作用远不止是公开宣布独立。它揭示的观念激发了群众对美国建国大业的热忱，它使普通人民逐渐认识到个人的重要，激发他们为个人自由、自治和有尊严的生活而奋斗。《独立宣言》是人类历史上一份划时代的文献，它以其强大无比的精神力量撼动了整个西方世界，而它的主要作者托马斯·杰斐逊也因此永垂史册。

Battles had been fought between Massachusetts soldiers and British military forces in the towns of Lexington and Concord. Yet war had not been declared. Even so, citizen soldiers in each of the thirteen American colonies were ready to fight. This was the first question faced by the Second Continental Congress meeting in Philadelphia, Pennsylvania. Who was going to organize these men into an army? Delegates to the Congress decided that the man for the job was George Washington. He had experience fighting in the French and Indian War. He was thought to know more than any other colonist about being a military commander. Washington accepted the position. But he said he would not take any money for leading the new **Continental Army**. Washington left Philadelphia for Boston to take command of the soldiers there.

Delegates to the Second Continental Congress made one more attempt to prevent war with Britain. They sent another message to King George. They asked him to consider their problems and try to find a solution. The king would not even read the message. You may wonder: Why would the delegates try to prevent war if the people were ready to fight? The answer is that most members of the Congress—and most of the colonists—were not yet ready to break away from Britain. They continued to believe that they could have greater **self-government** and still be part of the British empire. But this was not to be.

Two days after the Congress appointed George Washington as army commander, colonists and British troops fought the first major battle of the American Revolution. It was called the **Battle of Bunker Hill**, although it really involved two hills: Bunker and Breed's. Both are just across the Charles River from the city of Boston. Massachusetts soldiers dug positions on Breed's Hill one night in June, 1775. By morning, the hill was filled with troops. The British started to attack from across the river. The Americans had very little gunpowder. They were forced to wait until the British had crossed the river and were almost on top of them before they fired their guns. Their commander reportedly told them: Do not fire until you see the whites of the British soldiers' eyes.

The British climbed the hill. The Americans fired. A second group climbed the hill. The Americans fired again. The third time, the British reached the top, but the Americans were gone. They had left because they had no more gunpowder. The British captured Breed's Hill. More than 1,000 had been killed or wounded in the attempt. The Americans lost about 400. That battle greatly reduced whatever hope was left for a negotiated settlement. King George declared the colonies to be in **open rebellion**. And the Continental Congress approved a declaration condemning everything the British had done since 1763.

The American colonists fought several battles against British troops during 1775. Yet the colonies were still not ready to declare war. Then, the following year, the British decided to use **Hessian soldiers** to fight against the colonists. Hessians were mostly German **mercenaries** who fought for anyone who paid them. The colonists feared these soldiers and hated Britain for using them. At about the same time, **Thomas Paine** published a little document that had a great effect on the citizens of America. He named it *Common Sense*. It attacked King George, as well as the idea of government by kings. It called for independence. About 150,000 copies of *Common Sense* were sold in America. Everyone talked about it. As a result, the Continental Congress began to act. It opened American ports to foreign shipping. It urged colonists to establish state governments and to write constitutions. On June 7, delegate **Richard Henry Lee** of Virginia proposed a resolution for independence.

"Give me liberty or give me death!" Henry Lee
urges Virginians to fight against British rule.

The resolution was not approved immediately. Declaring independence was an extremely serious step. Signing such a document would make delegates to the Continental Congress traitors to Britain. They would be killed if captured by the British. The delegates wanted the world to understand what they were doing and why. So they appointed a committee to write a document giving the reasons for their actions. One member of the committee was the Virginian, **Thomas Jefferson**. He had already written a report criticizing the British form of government. So the other committee members asked him to prepare the new document. They said he was the best writer in the group. They were right. It took him 17 days to complete the document that the delegates approved on July 4th, 1776. It was America's Declaration of Independence.

Jefferson's document was divided into two parts. The first part explained the right of any people to revolt. It also described the ideas the Americans used to create a new, republican form of government. The Declaration of Independence begins this way:

> When in the course of human events, it becomes necessary for one people to dissolve the political bands which have connected them to another, and to assume among the powers of the earth, the separate and equal station to which the laws of nature and of Nature's God entitle them, a decent respect to the opinions of mankind requires that they should declare the causes which impel them to the separation. [1]

Jefferson continued by saying that all people are equal in the eyes of God. Therefore, governments can exist only by permission of the people they govern. He wrote:

> We hold these truths to be self-evident, that all men are created equal and that they are endowed by their creator with certain unalienable rights, that among these are Life, Liberty and the pursuit of Happiness. That to secure these rights, governments are instituted among Men, deriving their just powers from the consent of the governed. [2]

The next part states why the American colonies decided to separate from Britain:

> That whenever any form of government becomes destructive of these ends, it is the right of the people to alter or abolish it. [3]

This is why the Americans were rebelling against England. The British believed the Americans were violating their law. Jefferson rejected this idea. He claimed that the British treatment of the American colonies violated the natural laws of God. He and others believed a natural law exists that is more powerful than a king. The idea of a natural law had been developed by British and French philosophers more than 100 years earlier. Jefferson had studied these philosophers in school. In later years, however, he said he did not re-read these ideas while he was writing the declaration. He said the words came straight from his heart.

The second part of the Declaration lists 27 complaints by the American colonies against the British government. The major ones concerned British taxes on Americans and the presence of British troops in the colonies. After the list of complaints, Jefferson wrote this strong statement of independence:

> That these united colonies are and of right ought to be free and independent states; that they are absolved from all allegiance to the British crown and that all political connection between them and the

---

1 在人类历史事件的进程中，当一个民族有必要解除其与另一民族相联结的政治桎梏，并按照自然法则和上帝的意旨在世界列强中取得独立与平等的地位时，对于人类舆论的真诚与尊重，要求他们必须将不得已而独立的原因予以宣布。

2 我们认为以下的真理不言而喻：人人生而平等，造物主赋予他们某些不可转让的权利，其中包括生命权、自由权和追求幸福的权利。为了保障这些权利，人们建立起经由被管辖者同意的政府。

3 任何形式的政府，一旦破坏这些目标，人民就有权利去改变它或废除它，并建立一个新的政府。

state of Great Britain is and ought to be totally dissolved; and that as free and independent states they have the full power to levy war, conduct peace, contract alliances, establish commerce and do all other acts and things which independent states may of right do. [1]

The last statement of the Declaration of Independence was meant to influence the delegates into giving strong support for that most serious step—revolution:

And for the support of this declaration with a firm reliance on the protection of divine providence we mutually pledge to each other our lives, our fortunes and our sacred honor. [2]

The signing of the Declaration of Independence

For Your Memory

Free America
自由亚美利加

（约瑟夫·沃伦博士为《美国近卫军之歌》曲调填词）

马萨诸塞殖民地议会主席约瑟夫·沃伦博士 Dr. Joseph Warren 是波士顿著名的争取殖民地独立的"自由之子社"（Sons of Liberty）的最早成员之一，也是为美国革命献身的殖民地第一位高级官员。极有可能成为美国开国元勋（founding fathers）之一的他在 1775 年 6 月的邦克山战役中

1　这些联合一致的殖民地从此成为，而且按其权利必须成为自由独立的国家；它们已经解除一切效忠于英王室的义务，从此完全断绝，并必须断绝与大不列颠王国之间的一切政治联系。作为自由独立的国家，它们享有全权去宣战、缔和、同盟、通商或采取其他一切独立国家有权采取的行动。
2　为了拥护此项宣言，我们怀着神明保佑的坚定信心，以我们的生命、我们的财产和我们神圣的荣誉，互相宣誓。

牺牲，年仅 35 岁。人们在他倒下的地方树立了纪念碑，马萨诸塞州沃伦县也因他而得名。沃伦在参战前根据《英国近卫军之歌》的曲调填写的歌曲《自由亚美利加》是美国最早广泛传唱的爱国歌曲之一，曾有力地鼓舞了殖民地人民不畏强暴、争取独立自由的斗志。

Lift up your hands **ye heroes**!
And swear with proud disdain;
The wretch that would enslave you,
Shall **lay his snares in vain**.
Should Europe empty all her force,
We'll **meet her in array**,
And fight, and shout, and shout, and fight,
For North America!

Torn from a world of tyrants,
Beneath this western sky,
We **formed a new dominion**,
A land of liberty.
The world shall own their masters here,
Then **hasten on the day**,
Huzza, huzza, huzza, huzza,
For free America.

Words, Expressions and Notes

Continental Army　独立战争时期殖民地人民组成的大陆军

self-government　*n.* 自治政府

Battle of Bunker Hill　邦克山战役（1775 年 6 月），美国独立战争时期的重要战役之一

open rebellion　公开反叛

Hessian soldiers　黑森雇佣兵。黑森（Hessen）是德国的一个州。独立战争期间，英国为应付兵力不足的问题，去德国黑森招募士兵到美国镇压争取独立的殖民地人民。

mercenaries　*n.* （以挣钱为目的的）外国雇佣兵

Thomas Paine　托马斯·潘恩（1737—1809），美国独立战争时期著名政论家，其名作《常识》在美国历史上影响巨大。

Richard Henry Lee　理查德·亨利·李（1732—1794），美国独立战争时期政治家

Thomas Jefferson　托马斯·杰斐逊（1743—1826），《独立宣言》起草人，美国第三任总统

ye heroes = you heroes

lay his snares in vain　他们的诡计不会得逞

meet her in array　群起迎击英国军队

Torn from a world of tyrants　从暴君统治的世界中脱离出来

formed a new dominion　组建了一个新国家

hasten on the day　让那一天早些到来

huzza　*int.* （表示喜悦，喝彩）好哇！

Questions for Comprehension and Discussion

1. Why did the delegates to the Second Continental Congress want to prevent war with Britain?
2. What was the meaning of the Battle of Bunker Hill?
3. What did Thomas Paine say in his small book *Common Sense*?
4. Why was Thomas Jefferson chosen for the job of writing the Declaration of Independence?
5. Why is the Declaration of Independence considered the most important document in American history?
6. What is the idea of a natural law? Why did Jefferson think that a natural law is more powerful than a king?

11 The American Revolution: Whose Side Are You On?

美国革命：你究竟站在哪一边?

在任何革命的开始阶段，人们都满怀热情期待革命一举成功。然而，严酷的事实是，在经历了最初的激情之后，人们将要面对的注注是痛苦、寒冷、饥饿、伤病和死亡。美国革命也不例外。

《独立宣言》发表后，美国人很快就在军事上陷入困境。当英国的威廉·豪将军越过纽约和新泽西追击华盛顿的部队时，托马斯·潘恩无不担忧地写道："这是考验人们灵魂的时刻。"当华盛顿战败撤离纽约时，一位观察者写下这样一段文字："很多被枪杀的反叛者都没有穿鞋或长袜，其中几个人仅穿着内裤……也没有合身的衬衣和背心。"

革命战争持续了六年多，战火蔓延到各殖民地。当英美两军在烽火连天的战场上奋力厮杀时，殖民地的人们发现大家都面临着一个同样的问题：你究竟站在哪一边?

对生活在殖民地的绝大多数英国后裔来说，对故国的感情是发自内心的，是根深蒂固的。第二次大陆会议召开于1775年5月，而《独立宣言》却到1776年7月才得以发表，为什么其间有这么长时间的耽搁? 其实，在很多人的心里，宣告独立就意味着对祖国的背叛。对于大多数人来说，这实在不是一个能够轻易作出的决定。抛弃心中的故国而创建一个新国家是每个人都未曾经历，甚至从未想到过的事。人们普遍对未来感到心中无数。

在这样的背景下，殖民地的人们在独立问题上分成了三派：一派坚定支持独立，另一派坚定效忠英国，最后就是人数众多的看风使舵派。美国历史对那些在独立战争中态度暧昧的人有一个特定的称呼，叫"阳光爱国者"（sunshine patriot），这些人密切关注战事，哪方获胜他们就倾向支持哪方。

此外，战争还让黑人和印第安人处于两难境地。尤其是印第安人，他们大多数在战争中选择支持英国的事实，使他们在未来的岁月里与白人的关系更加紧张，并为此付出了惨重代价。

Delegates to the American Continental Congress approved and signed a declaration of independence on July 4th, 1776. The new country called the United States of America was at war with Britain. Yet not everyone in the former colonies agreed on the decision. No one knows for sure how many Americans remained loyal to Great Britain. The Massachusetts political leader, John Adams, thought about 33 percent of the colonists supported independence, 33 percent supported Britain, and 33 percent supported neither side. Most history experts today think that about 20 percent of the colonists supported Britain. They say the others were neutral or supported whichever side seemed to be winning.

As many as 30,000 Americans fought for the British during the war. Others helped Britain by reporting the movements of American rebel troops. Who supported Britain? They included people appointed to their jobs by the King, religious leaders of the Anglican Church, and people with close business connections in Britain. Many members of minority groups remained loyal to the King because they needed his protection against local majority groups. Other people were loyal because they did not want change or because they believed that independence would not improve their lives. Some thought the actions of the British government were not bad enough to make a rebellion necessary. Others did not believe that the rebels could win a war against such a powerful nation as Britain.

Native American Indians did not agree among themselves about the revolution. Congress knew it had

45

to make peace with the Indians as soon as the war started, or American troops might have to fight them and the British at the same time. To prevent trouble, American officials tried to stop settlers from moving onto Indian lands. In some places, the Indians joined the Americans, but generally they supported the British. They expected the British to win. They saw the war as a chance to force the Americans to leave their lands. At times, the Indians fought on the side of the British, but left when the British seemed to be losing the battle. Choosing to fight for the British proved to be a mistake. When the war was over, **the Americans felt they owed the Indians nothing**.

John Adams, one of the great figures in American history

Black slaves in the colonies also were divided about what side to join during the American Revolution. Thousands fought for the British, because that side offered them freedom if they served in the army or navy. Some American states also offered to free slaves who served, and hundreds of free blacks fought on the American side. Many slaves, however, felt their chances for freedom were better with the British. Details are not exact, but history experts say more blacks probably joined the British in the North than in the South.

At least 5,000 African-Americans served with the colonial American forces. Most had no choice. They were slaves, and their owners took them to war or sent them to replace their sons. Others felt that a nation built on freedom might share some of that freedom with them. In the South, many slave owners kept their slaves at home. Later in the war, every man was needed, although most slaves did not fight. Instead, they **drove wagons** and **carried supplies**. Many African-Americans also served in the American navy. Blacks who served in the colonial army and navy were not separated from whites. Black and white men fought side by side during the American Revolution. History experts say, however, that most black slaves spent the war as they had always lived: working on their owners' farms.

The American rebels called themselves Patriots. They called British supporters **Tories**. Patriots often seized Tories' property to help pay for the war. They also kidnapped Tories' slaves to be used as laborers for the army. Many Tories were forced from towns in which they had lived all their lives. Some were tortured or hanged. In New Jersey, Tories and Patriots fought one another with guns, and sometimes burned each other's houses and farms.

Some history experts say the American Revolution was really the nation's first civil war. The revolution divided many families. Perhaps the most famous example was the family of **Benjamin Franklin**. Ben Franklin signed the Declaration of Independence. His son William was governor of the colony of New Jersey. He supported the King. Political disagreement about the war **tore apart** this father and son for the rest of their lives.

Different ideas about the war existed among the Patriots, too. That is because the colonies did not really think of themselves as one nation. They saw themselves as independent states trying to work together toward a goal. People from Massachusetts, for example, thought Pennsylvania was a strange place filled with strange people. Southerners did not like people from the North. And people who lived in farm areas did not communicate easily with people who lived in coastal towns and cities. This meant that the Continental Congress could not order the states to do anything they did not want to do. Congress could not demand that the states provide money for the war. It could only ask for their help. George Washington, the top general, could not take men into the army. He could only wait for the states to send them. History experts say George Washington showed that he was a good politician by the way he kept Congress and the 13 states supporting him throughout the war.

As the people of America did not agree about the war, the people of Britain did not agree about it, either. Many supported the government's decision to fight. They believed that the war was necessary to rescue loyalists from the Patriots. Others did not think Britain should fight the Americans, because the Americans had not invaded or threatened their country. They believed that Britain should leave the colonies alone to do as they wished. King George was not able to do this, however. He supported the war as a way to continue his power in the world, and to **rescue British honor** in the eyes of other national leaders. Whichever side British citizens were on, there was no question that the war was causing severe problems in Britain. British businessmen could no longer trade with the American colonies. Prices increased. Taxes did, too. And young men were forced to serve in the **royal navy**.

Benjamin Franklin, one of the most prominent figures in American Revolution

At the start of the war, the British believed that the rebellion was led by a few **extremists** in New England. They thought the other colonies would surrender if that area could be surrounded and controlled. So, they planned to separate New England from the other colonies by **taking command** of the **Hudson River Valley**. They changed this plan after they were defeated in the **Battle of Saratoga** in New York State. Later, they planned to capture major cities and control the coast from Maine in the north to Georgia in the south. They failed to do this, although they did occupy New York City for the whole war, and at times had control over Philadelphia and Charleston.

The British experienced many problems fighting the war. Their troops were far from home, across a wide ocean. It was difficult to bring in more forces and supplies, and it took a long time. As the war continued, American ships became more skilled at attacking British ships at sea. The colonial army had problems, too. Congress never had enough money. Sometimes, it could not send General Washington the things he needed. Often, the states did not send what they were supposed to. Americans were not always willing to take part in the war. They were poorly trained as soldiers and would promise to serve for only a year or so.

For Your Memory

Soldier, Soldier, Will You Marry Me?
士兵, 士兵, 你愿意娶我吗?

歌曲是反映生活的最直观和最好的方式之一。在艰难的岁月里，歌曲往往能够给社会注入激情，鼓舞同时代的人们去改变他们的社会困境。在美国独立战争时期，人们在实际斗争中，开始创作大量反映革命斗争的歌曲，几乎所有的重大历史事件都被人们用歌曲的形式加以传唱。歌曲《士兵，士兵，你愿意娶我吗?》是美国最古老的民歌之一，生动展现了美国历史画卷中独立战争时期老百姓积极支持大陆军的一个有趣侧面，歌曲中传达出的幽默也是乐观主义在早期美国人身上的具体体现。

Soldier, soldier, will you marry me,
With your **musket**, **fife** and drum?
How can I marry such a pretty girl as you,

When I got no hat to put on?
Off to the **haberdasher** she did go,
As fast as she could run,

She bought him a hat, the best that was there,
And the soldier put it on.

Soldier, soldier, will you marry me,
With your musket, fife and drum?
How can I marry such a pretty girl as you,
When I got no coat to put on?
Off to the tailor she did go,
As fast as she could run,
She bought him a coat, the best that was there,
And the soldier put it on.

Soldier, soldier, will you marry me,
With your musket, fife and drum?
How can I marry such a pretty girl as you,
When I got no boots to put on?
Off to the **cobbler** she did go,
As fast as she could run,

She bought him a pair of the best that was there,
And the soldier put them on.

Soldier, soldier, will you marry me,
With your musket, fife and drum?
How can I marry such a pretty girl as you,
When I got no pants to put on?
Off to the tailor she did go,
As fast as she could run,
She bought him a pair of the best that was there,
And the soldier put them on.

Now, soldier, soldier, will you marry me,
With your musket, fife and drum?
Well, how can I marry such a pretty girl
as you,
With a wife and three kids back home?

Words, Expressions and Notes

the Americans felt they owed the Indians nothing 这里指的是由于早期移民大量侵占印第安人的土地，一些白人内心或多或少对印第安人怀有内疚感。当印第安人在独立战争中站在英国人一边后，美国人认为他们欠印第安人的债已经抵消了。
drove wagons 赶着马（或牛）车
carried supplies 搬运补给品
Tories （美国独立战争时期的）亲英分子
Benjamin Franklin 本杰明·富兰克林（1706—1790），美国早期政治家和科学家，参加起草《独立宣言》，发明避雷针。
tore apart 分开；分裂

rescue British honor 挽救英国的尊严
royal navy （英国）皇家海军
extremists *n.* 极端分子
taking command 控制
Hudson River Valley 哈得逊河谷地区
Battle of Saratoga 萨拉托加战役（1777 年），北美独立战争的转折点
musket *n.* 滑膛枪
fife *n.* （用于军乐中的）横笛
haberdasher *n.* 男子服饰用品商
cobbler *n.* 鞋匠

Questions for Comprehension and Discussion

1. Why did some people remain loyal to the King of England during the war for independence?
2. Why did native American Indians generally support the British in the war? What was the consequence of their choice when the war was over?
3. What did black slaves do during the American Revolution?
4. Some history experts say that the American Revolution was really the nation's first civil war. Do you agree with the idea? Why or why not?
5. What were the major problems George Washington had during the war?
6. What were the major problems the British experienced during the war?

12 Winning the War for Independence

赢得独立战争

北美殖民地与大英帝国之间的冲突似乎都是由一些不起眼的小事引起的，如对一磅茶叶或一份报纸增加一丁点税收等等。但更深刻的冲突根源就隐藏在这些看似普通的问题之中：谁来统治新大陆？谁来挑选统治者？不同的社会群体怎样公平合理地分担国家的费用和分享国家的进步？当社会变革成为必需时，人民可以采用什么方法来实现必要的变革？当殖民地人民从英国国王那里寻求不到问题的答案时，他们余下的选择就只有武装斗争。可是，应该由谁来领导这场军事斗争？各殖民地的领导人十分明智地选择了华盛顿。

来自弗吉尼亚的军官乔治·华盛顿从来就不是一个思想激进者。但是，当得知列克星敦那"震撼世界的枪声"后，他在给一个朋友的信中写道："这令人很不愉快，这块幸福安宁的土地要么血流成河，要么成为奴隶的住所。多么悲哀的选择！可是一个品德高尚的人岂能面对这样的抉择畏缩不前？"

美国革命的历史重任不可避免地落在品德高尚的华盛顿的肩头，但他并不是一个超人。和平时期，华盛顿像其他弗吉尼亚绅士一样爱好打猎和跳舞；在战争时期，他在战场上犯下很多错误，有的错误甚至差一点使他全军覆没；他并没有赢得手下将军们的彻底尊敬，尽管他们服从他的命令；当他的要求被拒绝时，他也会同国会争吵不休。

但是，华盛顿身上具有的两种品质如同希望的灯塔划破了美国革命战争时期最黑暗的夜空，那就是——无私与坚毅。任何人都知道，华盛顿绝不会利用自己的地位去谋求权力、赞扬和财富，而世上其他伟人也许很难不受到这些东西的诱惑。当强大的英国军队似乎不可战胜之时，华盛顿也从未动过投降或者退缩的念头。华盛顿的同胞们深知他为国家不求回报的奉献精神，因而他们都全心全意跟随在他身后。

尽管通注胜利的道路无比坎坷，华盛顿还是以他天才的领导才能把一支组织松散、训练不足、装备落后、给养匮乏、主要由地方民兵组成的队伍整编和训练成为一支能与英军正面抗衡的正规军，最终赢得了北美独立战争的胜利。

It is December, 1776. British **General William Howe** has decided to stop fighting during the cold winter months. The General is in New York. He has already established control of a few areas near the city, including Trenton and Princeton in New Jersey. General George Washington and the Continental Army are on the other side of the **Delaware River**. The Americans are cold and hungry. They have few weapons. Washington knows that if Howe attacks, the British will be able to go all the way to Philadelphia. They will then control two of America's most important cities. He decides to attack. His plan is for three groups of troops to cross the Delaware River separately. All three will join together at Trenton. Then they will attack Princeton and New Brunswick. Washington wants to **surprise the enemy** early in the morning the day after the Christmas holiday, December 26th.

On Christmas night, 2,400 soldiers of the Continental Army get into small boats. They cross the partly frozen Delaware River. The crossing takes longer than Washington thought it would. The troops are four hours late. They will not be able to surprise the enemy at sunrise. Yet, after marching to Trenton,

49

Washington's troops do surprise the Hessian mercenaries who are in position there. The enemy soldiers run into buildings to get away. The Americans use cannons to blow up the buildings. Soon, the enemy surrenders. Washington's army has captured Trenton. A few days later, he marches his captured prisoners through the streets of the city of Philadelphia.

Washington and his men cross the Delaware River.

Washington's victory at Trenton changed the way Americans felt about the war. Before the battle, the rebels had been defeated in New York. They were beginning to **lose faith** in their commander. Now that faith returned. Congress increased Washington's powers, making it possible for the fight for independence to continue. Another result of the victory at Trenton was that more men decided to join the army. It now had 10,000 soldiers. This new Continental Army, however, lost battles during the summer to General Howe's forces near the **Chesapeake Bay**. And in August, 1777, General Howe captured Philadelphia.

Following these losses, Washington led the army to the nearby area called **Valley Forge**. They would stay there for the winter. His army was suffering. Half the men had no shoes, clothes, or blankets. They were almost starving. They built houses out of logs, but the winter was very cold and they almost froze. Many suffered from diseases such as smallpox and **typhus**. Some died. General Washington and other officers were able to get food from the surrounding area to help most of the men survive the winter. By the spring of 1778, they were ready to fight again.

General Howe was still in Philadelphia. History experts say it is difficult to understand this British military leader. At times, he was a good commander and a brave man. At other times, he stayed in the safety of the cities, instead of leading his men to fight. General Howe was not involved in the next series of important battles of the American Revolution, however. The **lead part** now went to General **John Burgoyne**. His plan was to capture the Hudson River Valley in New York State and separate New England from the other colonies. This, the British believed, would make it easy to capture the other colonies. The plan did not succeed. American General **Benedict Arnold** defeated the British troops in New York. General Burgoyne had expected help from General Howe, but did not get it. Burgoyne was forced to surrender at the town of Saratoga.

The American victory at Saratoga was an extremely important one. It ended the British plan to separate New England from the other colonies. It also showed European nations that the new country might really be able to win its revolutionary war. This was something that France, especially, had wanted ever since being defeated by the British earlier in the French and Indian War. The French government had been supplying the Americans secretly through the work of America's minister to France, Benjamin Franklin. Franklin was popular with the French people and with French government officials. He helped gain French sympathy for the American cause.

After the American victory at Saratoga, the French decided to enter the war on the American side. The government recognized American independence. The two nations signed military and political treaties. France and Britain were at war once again. The British immediately sent a message to America's Continental Congress. They offered to change everything so relations would be as they had been in 1763.

The Americans rejected the offer. The war would be fought to the end. In 1779, Spain entered the war against the British. And the next year, the British were also fighting the Dutch to stop their trade with America.

The French now sent gunpowder, soldiers, officers, and ships to the Americans. However, neither side made much progress in the war for the next two years. By 1780, the British had moved their military forces to the American South. They quickly gained control of

Ben Franklin is warmly received at Versailles Palace.

South Carolina and Georgia, but the Americans prevented them from taking control of North Carolina. After that, the British commander moved his troops to **Yorktown**, Virginia. The commander's name was **Lord Charles Cornwallis**. Both he and George Washington had about 8,000 troops when they met near Yorktown. Cornwallis was expecting more troops to arrive on British ships. What he did not know was that French ships were on their way to Yorktown, too. Their commander was **Admiral Francois Comte de Grasse**. De Grasse met some of the British ships that Cornwallis was expecting, and he defeated them. The French ships then moved into the Chesapeake Bay, near Yorktown.

The Americans and the French began attacking with cannons. Then they fought the British soldiers hand-to-hand. Cornwallis knew he had no chance to win without more troops. He surrendered to George Washington on October 17th, 1781. The war was over. American and French forces had captured or killed one half of the British troops in America. The surviving British troops left Yorktown playing a popular British song called, **"The World Turned Upside Down."**

How were the Americans able to defeat the most powerful nation in the world? Historians give several reasons. The Americans were fighting at home, while the British had to bring troops and supplies from across a wide ocean. British officers made mistakes, especially General William Howe. His slowness to take action at the start of the war made it possible for the Americans to survive during two difficult winters. Another reason was the help the Americans received from the French. Also, the British public had stopped supporting the long and costly war. Finally, history experts say America might not have won without the leadership of George Washington. He was honest, brave, and sure that the Americans could win. He never gave up hope that he would reach that goal.

The peace treaty ending the American Revolution was signed in Paris in 1783. The independence of the United States was recognized. Western and northern borders were set. Thirteen colonies were free. Now, they had to become one nation.

Words, Expressions and Notes

General William Howe 威廉·豪将军（1729—1814），驻北美英军总司令
Delaware River 特拉华河
surprise the enemy 给敌人以突然袭击
lose faith 失去信心

Chesapeake Bay 切萨皮克湾（位于弗吉尼亚与马里兰附近）
Valley Forge 福吉谷，美国革命圣地，位于宾夕法尼亚东部。1777 年冬，费城陷落，华盛顿率残兵败将来到福吉谷休整，度过了独立战争期间最艰难

的一段时光。华盛顿利用这段时间重新训练军队，把一支衣衫褴褛、未受过任何军事训练的农民军队改编成一支纪律严明、具有高度战斗力的正规军。严冬过后，华盛顿率部队杀出福吉谷，重新和英军较量，最终赢得了一个新的国家。如今，福吉谷已成为美国国家历史公园。

typhus *n.* 斑疹伤寒

lead part 领导的角色

John Burgoyne 约翰·伯戈因（1722—1792），英国将军，在萨拉托加战役中被美军包围后投降，返回英国后从事戏剧创作。

Benedict Arnold 贝尼迪克特·阿诺德（1741—1801），独立战争时期美军将领，后因私通英军逃亡英国。

Yorktown *n.* 约克敦（地名）

Lord Charles Cornwallis 查尔斯·康华里勋爵

（1738—1805），英国将军，独立战争中的英军司令，在约克敦围城战役中战败投降。

admiral *n.* 海军上将，海军将军

Francois Comte de Grasse 格拉斯（1722—1788），法国海军军官，率舰参加美国独立战争，在约克敦围城战役中对击败英军起重要作用，后在加勒比海遭英海军全歼，被俘。

The World Turned Upside Down （歌曲名）《这世界已经颠倒过来》。这原是出现于1643年的一首英国民谣歌曲，人们在歌曲中抗议当时的克伦威尔（Oliver Cromwell）政府禁止英国传统圣诞节庆祝活动的政策。英国军队在约克敦战役中失败后演奏这首曲子，恰当而幽默地表达了英国人对他们的国家从世界顶端跌落下来后感到的沮丧感。

Questions for Comprehension and Discussion

1. How did George Washington and the Continental Army get their first important victory in Trenton?

2. Why was the American victory at Saratoga an extremely important one?

3. In the war against Britain, why would the United States and France be natural allies?

4. Why did the British troops play a song called "The World Turned Upside Down" when they were beaten by the Continental Army?

5. What are the major reasons why the Americans were able to defeat the most powerful nation in the world?

6. What were the qualities that made George Washington a great commanding general of the Continental Army?

Unit 4　Creating a Nation

13　The Birth of the Constitution (Part 1)

宪法的诞生（一）

1782 年，一位名叫 J·赫克托·圣约翰·克雷夫科尔（J. Hector St. John de Crevecoeur）的法裔美国人发表了 12 篇文章，他把这些文章汇集成书，题为《美国农民来信》（*Letters from an American Farmer*）。这本书在欧洲出版后，作者一举成名，并为这个新生的国家赢得许多朋友。克雷夫科尔于 1754 年移民到新大陆，在纽约殖民地的一个农场定居。在美国革命期间，他在两个大陆都有朋友和亲戚，他自己也曾遭到英国人短期监禁。1780 年他乘船前往欧洲，住在伦敦期间，他发表了有关美国生活的文章。他曾担任法国驻纽约领事几年，1790 年回到法国安度余生。在许多年里，克雷夫科尔对新大陆敏锐而富于同情的描述，使他成为拥有最广大读者的美洲评论员。他在《来信》中这样讲道：

"当一个旅行者来到一个新大陆，来到一个现代社会，一个与他迄今所见过的社会不同的社会，这个社会本身就可供他思考。这不是像欧洲那样是由拥有一切的贵族老爷和一无所有的群氓组成的社会。这里没有贵族家庭，没有宫殿，没有国王，没有主教，没有教会控制，没有给少数人显赫权力的那种无形的权力，没有雇佣几千人的制造商，没有穷极奢侈。富人和穷人不像在欧洲那样相差甚远……这里的人们散居在一片巨大的领土上，通过良好的道路和可通航的河流相互交流，由温和政府的丝带把我们连在一起，大家都尊重法律而不畏惧其权力，因为法律是公平的。我们生气勃勃，充满实业精神，这种精神已破除镣铐，不受任何约束，因为我们每个人都为自己工作……

"这位旅行者的下一个愿望便是要知道这些人是从何处来的？他们是英格兰人，苏格兰人、爱尔兰人、法国人、荷兰人、德国人和瑞典人的混杂。由这种混杂而繁衍产生了一个现叫做美国人的种族……'哪里有面包，哪里就是祖国'，这是所有移民的座右铭。那么美国人——这个新的人到底是什么人？他们或是欧洲人，或是欧洲人的后裔，因此，他们是你在任何其他国家都找不到的混血人。我可以向你指出一个家庭，其祖父是英国人，其妻是荷兰人，其子娶一个法国女人，而他们现在的四个儿子娶了四个不同民族的妻子。他是一个美国人，他把一切古老的偏见和习俗都抛到身后，从他所接受的新的生活方式中，从他所服从的新政府里，从他所处的新的地位上，获得新的习俗。在伟大养母宽大的怀抱里，他成了一个美国人。在这里，来自世界各国的人融合成一个新的民族，总有一天，他们所付出的劳动以及他们的后代将使世界发生巨大的变化。"

在《美国农民来信》中，克雷夫科尔首次表达了一个全新的概念：美国是一个大熔炉，来自世界各国的人在这里融合成为一个新的民族。

然而，年轻而欣欣向荣的美国要成为一个世界强国，还有很长的路要走。它首先面临的紧迫问题是——这个地域如此辽阔的国家居然没有一个中央政府！

One cannot truly understand the United States without understanding its Constitution. That political document describes America's system of government. It guarantees the rights of America's citizens. Its power is greater than any president, court, or legislature. It is the law of the land and the heart of the country.

The first American states had no strong central government when they fought their war of independence from Britain in 1776. They cooperated under an agreement called the **Articles of Confederation**. The agreement provided for a Congress. But the Congress had few powers. Each state governed itself.

When the war ended, the states owed millions of dollars to their soldiers. They also owed money to European nations that had supported the Americans against Britain. The new United States had no national money to pay the debts. There was an American dollar. But not everyone used it. And it did not have the same value everywhere. The situation led to economic ruin for many people. They could not pay the money they owed. They lost their property. They were put in prison. Militant groups took action to help them. They interfered with tax collectors. They terrorized judges and burned court buildings.

The situation was especially bad in the Northeast part of the country. In Massachusetts, a group led by a former soldier tried to seize guns and ammunition from the state military force. **Shays' Rebellion**, as it was called, was stopped. But from north to south, Americans were increasingly worried and frightened. Would the violence continue? Would the situation get worse?

Many Americans distrusted the idea of a strong central government. After all, they had just fought a war to end British rule. Yet Americans of different ages, education, and social groups felt that something had to be done. If not, the new nation would fail before it had a chance to succeed. These were the opinions and feelings that led, in time, to the writing of the United States Constitution.

Even before the war ended, three men called for a change in the **loose confederation of states**. They urged formation of a strong central government. Those three men were George Washington, **Alexander Hamilton**, and **James Madison**. George Washington commanded America's troops during the revolution. He opposed the Articles of Confederation because they provided little support for his army. His soldiers often had no clothes or shoes or food. They had no medicines or blankets or bullets. During the war, Washington wrote many angry letters about the military situation. In one letter, he said: "Our sick soldiers are naked. Our healthy soldiers are naked. Our soldiers who have been captured by the British are naked!"

General Washington's letters produced little action. The 13 separate states refused to listen when he told them the war was a war of all the states. He learned they were more interested in themselves than in what his soldiers needed. After the war, there was much social, political, and economic disorder. General Washington saw once again that there was no hope for the United States under the Articles of Confederation. He wrote to a friend: "I do not believe we can exist as a nation unless there is a central government which will rule all the nation, just as a state government rules each state."

Alexander Hamilton agreed. He was a young lawyer and an assistant to General Washington during the revolution. Even before the war ended, Hamilton called for a convention of the 13 states to create a central government. He expressed his opinion in letters, speeches, and newspaper stories. Finally, there was James Madison. He saw the picture clearly. It was an unhappy picture. There were 13 governments. And each tried to help itself **at the cost of the others**. Nine states had their own navy. Each had its own army. The states used these forces to protect themselves from each other. For example, the state of Virginia passed a law which said it could seize ships that did not pay taxes to the state. Virginia did not mean ships from England and Spain. It meant ships from Maryland, Massachusetts, and Pennsylvania. James Madison often said most of the new nation's political problems grew out of such commercial problems.

In 1786, representatives from Maryland and Virginia met to discuss opening land for new settlements along the **Potomac River**. The Potomac formed the border between those two states. The representatives agreed that the issue of settling new land was too big for just two states to decide. "Why not invite Delaware and Pennsylvania to help?" someone asked. Someone else said all the states should be invited. Then they could discuss all the problems that were giving the new nation so much trouble. The idea was accepted. And a convention was set for **Annapolis**, Maryland.

The convention opened as planned. It was not much of a meeting. Representatives came from only five states. Four other states had chosen representatives, but they did not come. The remaining four states did not even choose representatives. The men who did meet at Annapolis, however, agreed it was a beginning. They agreed, too, that a larger convention should be called. They appointed the representative from New York, Alexander Hamilton, to put the agreement in writing. So Hamilton sent a message to the legislature of each state. He called for a convention in Philadelphia in May of the next year, 1787. The purpose of the convention, he said, would be to write a constitution for the United States.

Alexander Hamilton, the first Secretary of the Treasury of the U. S. A.

Many people believed the convention would not succeed without George Washington. But General Washington did not want to go. He suffered from **rheumatism**. His mother and sister were sick. He needed to take care of business at his farm, **Mount Vernon**. And he already said he was not interested in public office. How would it look if, as expected, he was elected president of the convention? George Washington was the most famous man in America. Suppose only a few states sent representatives to the convention? Suppose it failed? Would he look foolish? Two close friends, James Madison and **Edmund Randolph**, urged General Washington to go to Philadelphia. He trusted them. So he said he would go as one of the representatives of Virginia. From that moment, it was clear the convention would be an important event. If George Washington would be there, it had to be important.

James Madison of Virginia was the first delegate to arrive for the convention in Philadelphia. Madison asked the other delegates from Virginia also to arrive early. He wanted to enter the convention with a plan for a strong central government. He was sure no other state would do this. Two Virginia delegates, George Wythe and John Blair, came early as requested. Together, the three men worked on Madison's plan.

The convention was to start on May 14th. George Washington arrived the day before. He was welcomed outside Philadelphia by a military guard and the firing of cannons. Washington was the most famous man in America. He led the forces that won the war for independence from Britain. The first thing Washington did in Philadelphia was to visit Benjamin Franklin. Franklin was an important political leader in America. He also was chief of Pennsylvania's delegation to the convention. Franklin was then 81 years old. Age had weakened him. But his mind remained strong. Every important person who came to Philadelphia, even the great General Washington, visited Benjamin Franklin.

Day by day, more delegates arrived in Philadelphia for the convention. Fifty-five men in all from 12 states. Pennsylvania sent the most delegates—eight. Rhode Island sent none. A few of the delegates were very old. But many were in their twenties or thirties. The average age of the delegates was just 43 years.

This respected group was missing two important persons—John Adams and Thomas Jefferson. At the time, Adams was serving as America's representative to Britain. Jefferson was serving as the representative to France. Both men expected to continue their service to the new nation. So both were extremely interested in the convention in Philadelphia. They exchanged letters with friends to learn what was happening.

The first important decision by the delegates was choosing a president for the convention. Several urged the others to name George Washington. The delegates agreed. Washington was their choice. George Washington then officially opened the convention with a short speech. He thanked the delegates for naming him president. But he said the honor was too great. He asked the delegates to forgive him if he made mistakes. After all, he said, he had never been chairman of a meeting before. With those words, George Washington sat down. And for the next four months, he spoke only when necessary.

The first day of the convention ended well. The delegates agreed to name a small committee to write rules for the meetings. They quickly appointed three men. George Wythe of Virginia, Alexander Hamilton of New York, and Charles Pinckney of South Carolina. So far, the business of the convention was easy. The work was done in a friendly way. It was not long, however, before a serious dispute developed. The dispute was between the large states and the small states. How would they share power in a government of united states? Should states with bigger populations have more power than states with smaller populations? The dispute would sharply divide the delegates for the next four months.

Words, Expressions and Notes

Articles of Confederation 《邦联条例》，制定于 1781 年，目的是将 13 个殖民地松散地联系在一起。于 1789 年被正式宪法代替。

Shays' Rebellion 谢司起义。丹尼尔·谢司（Daniel Shays）原是美军军官，因不满政府政策于 1786 年率领马萨诸塞的农民起义。当局采用强硬手段将手里只有棍棒或草叉的农民镇压下去。暴动完全平定之后，立法当局才考虑到暴动的发生的确是由于许多不公平的事情所导致，于是采取了一些补救措施。起义首领中一些人被判处死刑，另一些人被判处监禁或罚款；谢司本人于 1787 年被判处死刑，但次年获赦免。

loose confederation of states 由各州组成的松散联邦

Alexander Hamilton 亚历山大·汉密尔顿（1757—

1804），美国开国元勋之一，大陆会议代表，建国后任首任财政部长，对国家银行和财政系统建设的贡献巨大。

James Madison 詹姆斯·麦迪逊（1751—1836），美国第四任总统，美国宪法主要起草人

at the cost of the others 以他人受损为代价

Potomac River 波托马克河，位于美国东部，流经首都华盛顿。

Annapolis 安纳波利斯，马里兰州首府

rheumatism *n.* 风湿病

Mount Vernon 弗农山，华盛顿的庄园所在地

Edmund Randolph 爱德蒙·伦道夫（1753—1813），美国第一任司法部长

Questions for Comprehension and Discussion

1. It is said that one cannot truly understand the United States without understanding its Constitution. Do you agree with this idea? Why or why not?

2. Why was the situation very bad in the new United States?

3. What might be the major reason that many Americans distrusted the idea of a strong central government?

4. Why did Washington, with Hamilton and Madison, urge the 13 states to form a strong central government?

5. What kind of a picture did James Madison see clearly in the new nation?

6. Why did George Washington not want to go to the convention in Philadelphia? Why did he later change his mind and agree to be the president of the convention?

7. Do you consider the work of writing a constitution easy or difficult? Why?

14 The Birth of the Constitution (Part 2)

宪法的诞生（二）

　　革命的成功，使美国人民有机会把他们在《独立宣言》中表达的政治理想变成法定的观念，并通过各州的宪法来纠正过去的一些不平现象。第二次大陆会议早在 1775 年 5 月 10 日开会的第一天就通过一个决议，建议各殖民地成立新的政府，"为选民们谋求幸福与安全"。于是，各殖民地先后制定了自己的"宪法"，殖民地也由"colony"变成"state"，其地位发生了质的转变。

　　然而，仅靠《邦联条例》联合在一起的各州，正如华盛顿所说，是由一根"沙土制成的绳索"维系的。该《条例》最明显的缺点是没有建立一个真正的全国性政府。这时候的美国，没有总统，没有联邦法院，没有执法机构，没有参议院，各州都可以行使自己的"主权"，州与州之间的关系如同今日的联合国各成员国之间的关系。根据《条例》组建的行使中央政府职权的"国会"也虚弱不堪。1781 年，当一个送信人把英军在弗吉尼亚约克镇投降的捷报送到国会时，国会却发觉自己囊空如洗。最后，各位议员只得自掏腰包给送信人酬劳。

　　在 1786 年的一次会议上，推动制定新宪法的三个重要人物之一———华盛顿的前助手亚历山大·汉密尔顿向出席会议的几个州的代表呼吁，请他们敦促各州委派代表，参与制定联邦政府的新宪法。一些州的代表听到这个大胆的建议后非常愤怒。可是，当他们又听说弗吉尼亚已经推选乔治·华盛顿作代表时，便默不作声了。

　　的确，与独立战争时期一样，在美国建国的最关键时刻，往往都是由华盛顿站出来力挽狂澜，拨正这艘刚刚扬起风帆的大船的航向。

　　1787 年 5 月在费城召开的会议很快就进入无休止的争论中。华盛顿为此非常恼火。他在一封信中写道："我几乎绝望…… 那些反对建立一个强有力的中央政府的人，依我看来，都是一些心胸狭隘的政客，或是一些严重受地方观念影响的人。"

　　然而，在华盛顿、汉密尔顿和麦迪逊的强力推动下，美国历史上最重要的会议终于逐步切入正题。

In May of 1787, a group of America's early leaders met in Philadelphia. They planned to change the Articles of Confederation which provided a loose union of the 13 American states. Instead of changes, however, they wrote a completely new Constitution. That political document established America's system of government and guaranteed the rights of its citizens. It is still the law of the land.

On May 29th, the delegates heard the **Virginia Plan**. This was the plan of government prepared by James Madison and other delegates from the state of Virginia. The 33-year-old governor of Virginia, Edmund Randolph, presented the plan. First, he spoke about America's existing plan of government, the Articles of Confederation. Governor Randolph praised the Articles and the men who wrote them. He called those men "wise" and "great." But, he said, the Articles were written for 13 states in a time of war. Something more was needed now for the new nation. Something permanent.

The announced purpose of the convention was to change the Articles of Confederation to make them more effective. The Virginia Plan was not a plan of proposed changes. It was much more extreme. It was, in fact, a plan for a completely new central government. Debate on the Virginia Plan began May 30th.

57

Immediately, Edmund Randolph proposed an **amendment**. The plan, he noted, spoke of a **federal union of states**. But such a federation would not work. Instead, he said, America's central government should be a national government. It should contain a **supreme legislature, executive and judiciary**.

For a few moments, there was complete silence. Many of the delegates seemed frozen in their chairs. Did they hear correctly? Most of them did not question the idea of a government with three separate parts. Several states already had such a system. But to create a central government that was "national" and "supreme"... what did these words mean exactly? What was the difference? The delegates debated the meaning of these words—federal, national, supreme—for many days. Both James Madison and Gouverneur Morris of Pennsylvania tried to explain. Madison said a federal government acts on states. A national government acts directly on the people. Morris gave this explanation. A federal government is simply an agreement based on the good faith of those involved. A national government has a complete system of operation and its own powers.

Some delegates feared that such a central government would take away power from the states. But in the end, they approved the proposal. On June 1, they began debate on the issue of a **national executive**.

The Virginia Plan offered several points for discussion. It said the national executive should be chosen by the national legislature. The executive's job would be to carry out the laws made by the legislature. He would serve a number of years. He would be paid a small amount of money. These points served as a basis for debate. Over a period of several weeks, the delegates worked out details of the executive's position and powers.

The debate over the size of the national executive lasted a long time. Finally, the delegates voted. Seven state delegations voted for a one-man executive. Three voted against the idea.

During the debate on size, other questions arose about the national executive. One question was the executive's **term**. Should he serve just once or could he be re-elected? Alexander Hamilton argued for a long term of office. He said if a president served only a

James Madison, Father of the American Constitution

year or two, America soon would have many former presidents. These men, he said, would fight for power. And that would be bad for the peace of the nation. Benjamin Franklin argued for re-election. The people, he said, were the rulers of a republic. And presidents were the servants of the people. If the people wanted to elect the same president again and again, they had the right to do this.

Delegates debated two main proposals on the question. One was for a three-year term with re-election permitted. The other was for one seven-year term. The vote on the question was close. Five state delegations approved a term of seven years. Four voted no. The question came up again during the convention and was debated again. In the final document, the president's term was set at four years with re-election permitted. Next came the question of how to choose the national executive.

It was a most difficult problem. The delegates debated, voted, re-debated, and re-voted a number of proposals. **James Wilson** proposed that the executive be elected by special representatives of the people called **electors**. The electors would be chosen from districts set up for this purpose. Several delegates disagreed. They said the people did not know enough to choose good electors. They said the plan would be too difficult to carry out and would cost too much money. One delegate proposed that the national executive be elected by the state governors. He said the governors of large states would have more votes than the governors of small states. Nobody liked this proposal, especially delegates from the small states. It was defeated.

Another proposal was to have the national executive elected directly by the people. Elbridge Gerry of Massachusetts was shocked by this idea. "The people do not understand these things," he said. "A few dishonest men can easily fool the people. The worst way to choose a president would be to have him elected by the people." So the delegates voted to have the national legislature appoint the national executive. Then they voted against this method. Instead, they said, let state legislatures name electors who would choose the executive. But the delegates changed their mind on this vote, too. They re-debated the idea of direct popular elections. The convention voted on the issue sixty times. In the end, it agreed that the **national executive should be chosen by electors named by state legislatures**.

Now, someone said, we have decided how to choose the executive. But what are we to do if the executive does bad things after being appointed? We should have some way of dismissing him. Yes, the delegates agreed. It should be possible to **impeach** the executive, to **try** him, and if guilty, remove him from office. Gouverneur Morris of Pennsylvania spoke in support of impeachment. A national executive, he said, may be influenced by a greater power to **betray his trust**. The delegates approved a proposal for removing a chief executive found guilty of **bribery, treason, or other high crimes**.

The last major question about the national executive was the question of **veto power over the national legislature**. Not one delegate was willing to give the executive complete power to reject new laws. And yet they felt the executive should have some voice in the law-making process. If this were not done, they said, the position of executive would have little meaning. And the national legislature would have the power of a dictator. James Madison offered a solution. The executive should have the power to veto a law, Madison said. But his veto could be over-turned if most members of the legislature voted to pass the law again.

The final convention document listed more details about the national executive, or president. For example, it said the president had to be born in the United States or a citizen at the time the Constitution was accepted. He must have lived in the United States for at least 14 years. He must be at least 35 years old. The executive would be paid. But his pay could not be increased or reduced during his term in office. He would be **commander-in-chief of the armed forces**. And, from time to time, he would have to report to the national legislature on the **state of the Union**.

The final document also gave the words by which a president would be sworn-in. Every four years, for more than 200 years now, each president has repeated this **oath of office**: "I do **solemnly swear** that I will faithfully execute the Office of President of the United States, and will to the best of my ability, preserve, protect, and defend the Constitution of the United States."

Words, Expressions and Notes

Virginia Plan （关于制定宪法的）弗吉尼亚方案
amendment *n.* 修正案
federal union of states 由各州组成的联盟
supreme legislature, executive and judiciary 最高立法、行政和司法机构
national executive 国家最高领导机构（或人）
term *n.* 任职期限
James Wilson 詹姆斯·威尔逊（1742—1798），美国

早期杰出的政治家，《独立宣言》签署人，美国宪法制定工作的重要推动者，华盛顿总统任命的六位首席大法官之一
electors *n.* 合格选举人；选举团成员
national executive should be chosen by electors named by state legislatures 国家领导人由各州提名的选举团成员选出
impeach *v.* 弹劾

try *v.* 审判

betray his trust 背叛人民对他的信任

bribery, treason, or other high crimes 贿赂、叛国、或其他严重罪行

veto power over the national legislature （总统）对国家立法机构拥有的否决权

commander-in-chief of the armed forces 武装部队总司令

state of the Union 国情咨文

oath of office （总统的）就职誓言

solemnly swear 庄严宣誓

Questions for Comprehension and Discussion

1. What was the first plan of the convention in Philadelphia? Was there any change in the original plan?

2. Who prepared a plan for the meeting to discuss? What was the plan called?

3. Why did many of the delegates seem frozen in their chairs when they heard someone say that America should have a national government?

4. According to the Virginia Plan, what would be the job of the executive of the national government?

5. Why did Benjamin Franklin argue for re-election of the national executive?

6. Why did the members of the convention want to limit the power of the national executive? How could they do so?

7. Do you think the words each new president speaks before he is sworn in important or not? Why?

15 The Birth of the Constitution (Part 3)

宪法的诞生（三）

跨入现代社会，几乎每一个国家都有一部成文宪法，人们对此也早已习以为常，认为这是一件理所当然之事。然而，从历史的角度看，宪法是一个相当年轻的新事物，而成文宪法的发源地则是世界最年轻的国家之一——美国。事实上，美国宪法不仅最早，而且最稳定。对于宪法，美国人一直有着特殊的感情。美国第二任总统亚当斯曾经写道："在一切自由的州中，宪法决定一切。"

1787 年 5 月在费城州议会大厦举行的会议，仅被授权对《邦联条例》加以修正。但是，正如日后麦迪逊所说的，代表们"抱着对国家的坚强信念，把《邦联条例》搁在一边，直接考虑如何建立一个全新形式的政府"。

1787 年费城有一个炎热的夏天，但比气候更热的，是美利坚合众国开国先辈们讨论新宪法的热情（甚至可以说是"火气"）。今天，当我们用当代人的眼光来观察他们制订一部关系国家命运和前途的根本大法的过程时，既为他们严肃认真的态度感到惊讶，也对他们聪明睿智的做法感到钦佩。

为保证制宪会议取得成功，大会采取了几项非同寻常的措施。首先，大会以秘密方式进行，不对任何外人开放；其次，大会作出的任何决议都可以更改；第三，会议不是讨论一个问题就了结一个问题，而是不对代表们的表决作永久记录，任何代表都可以把已经讨论过或表决过的问题重新提出来再讨论或再表决。

大会进行期间，当时身在法国的托马斯·杰斐逊得知制宪会议以秘密方式召开时大为光火。麦迪逊曾在多年以后向杰斐逊解释说："如果当时会议公开进行，每个代表都不会对已经说过的话改口，即使他知道他说错了；也不会有代表向公众承认他犯了错误。假如讨论向公众开放，大会肯定会以失败告终。"

这就是我们看到会议过程中经常对同一个问题不断进行周而复始的演讲、讨论和表决的缘由。

最后，我们再来回答一个有趣的问题：既然制宪会议不对任何人开放，为什么我们今天能够知道当年会议代表们闭门讨论的详细过程？

其实，大会开始时任命了一位记录员，可他的工作糟糕透顶，第一天会议下来，所记录的会议细节少得可怜。幸亏，有另一个人在未经大会安排的情况下也对会议作了详细的笔记。要不是他，美国建国后第一次历史性会议的许多历史细节可能永远不为人所知。他就是来自弗吉尼亚的代表麦迪逊。从会议的第一天起，他就坐在会议前排的有利位置，拼命记录下每一个代表在会上的发言。每天夜晚，他把白天的记录一一加以整理。会议结束时，麦迪逊说道："这份自我安排的工作差一点杀死我。"30 年以后，麦迪逊的全部会议记录得以公开发布。

由于大会最后通过的宪法源自詹姆斯·麦迪逊起草的《弗吉尼亚方案》，而他又在宪法制订过程中很好地协助华盛顿主持了会议，后来他被美国人民尊称为"美国宪法之父"。

Delegates spent several weeks debating details of the position and powers of the national executive. The delegates decided the executive would be chosen by electors named by state legislatures. They decided he could veto laws. And they decided he could be removed from office if found guilty of serious crimes. Then the convention reached agreement on a national judiciary. Delegates approved a **Supreme Court**. And they agreed that the national legislature should establish **a system of lower national courts**. The national executive, or president, would appoint the judges. These courts would hear cases involving national laws, the rights of American citizens, and wrong-doing by foreign citizens in the United States. The existing system of state courts would continue to hear cases involving state laws.

The delegates began to discuss creation of a national legislature. This would be the most hotly debated issue of the convention. It forced out into the open the question of equal representation. Would small states and large states have an equal voice in the central government? One delegate described the situation this way. "Let us see the truth," he said. "This is a fight for power. . . not for liberty. Small states may lose power to big states in a national legislature. But men living in small states will have just as much freedom as men living in big states." The issue **brought the deepest emotions to the surface**. One day, Gunning Bedford of Delaware looked straight at the delegates from the largest states. "Gentlemen!" he shouted, "I do not trust you. If you try to crush the small states, you will destroy the Confederation. And if you do, the small states will find some foreign ally of more honor and good faith who will take them by the hand and give them justice."

The debate on legislative representation—big states against small states—lasted for weeks that summer in Philadelphia. Delegates voted on proposals, then discussed other proposals, then voted again. By the beginning of July, they were no closer to agreement than they had been in May. As one delegate said: "It seems we are at the point where we **cannot move one way or another**." So the delegates did what large groups often do when they cannot reach agreement. They voted to create a committee. The purpose of the committee was to develop a compromise on representation in the national legislature. The so-called "Grand Committee" would work by itself for the next several days. The rest of the delegates would rest and enjoy themselves during the July 4th holiday.

July 4th, Independence Day. It was a national holiday in the United States. It marked the 11th anniversary of America's Declaration of Independence from British rule. It was a day for parades, fireworks, and patriotic speeches. The celebration was especially important in Philadelphia. It was the city where the Declaration of Independence was signed. Now it was the city where a new nation was being created. Convention president George Washington led a group of delegates to a ceremony at a Philadelphia church. They heard a speech written especially for them. "Your country looks to you with both worry and hope," the speaker said. "Your country depends on your decisions. Your country believes that men such as you, who led us in our war for independence, will know how to plan a government that will be good for all Americans."

"Surely," the speaker continued, "we have among us men who understand the **science of government** and who can find the answers to all our

Independence Hall, Philadelphia, birthplace of the Declaration of Independence and the United States Constitution

problems. Surely we have the ability to design a government that will protect the liberties we have won."

The delegates needed to hear such words. Just a few days before, Benjamin Franklin had expressed his thoughts about the convention. He was not hopeful. Franklin said: "We seem to feel our own lack of political wisdom, since we have been running around in search of it. We went back to ancient history for examples of government. We examined different forms of republics which no longer exist. We also examined modern states all around Europe. But none of these constitutions, we found, work in our situation." Franklin urged the convention to ask for God's help. He said each meeting should begin with a prayer. Hugh Williamson of North Carolina quickly ended any discussion of Franklin's idea. His words were simple. The convention, he said, had no money to pay a minister to lead the delegates in prayer.

The convention returned to its work on July 5th. Delegates heard the report of the Grand Committee about representation in the national legislature. The report had two proposals. The Grand Committee said both must be accepted or both rejected. The report described a national legislature with two houses. The first proposal said representation in one house would be based on population. Each state would have one representative for every 40,000 people in that state. The second proposal said representation in the second house would be equal. Each state would have the same number of votes as the other states.

The convention already had voted for a national legislature of two houses. It had not agreed, however, on the number of representatives each state would have in each house. Nor had it agreed on how those representatives would be elected. The proposals made by the Grand Committee on July 5th were the same as those made by Roger Sherman of Connecticut a month earlier. In the future, they would be known as the "**Great Compromise**." Delegates debated the compromise for many days. They knew if they did not reach agreement, the convention would fail. Those were dark days in Philadelphia.

Later, Luther Martin of Maryland noted that the newspapers reported how much the delegates agreed. But that was not the truth. "We were **on the edge of breaking up**," Martin said. "We were held together only by the strength of a hair." Delegates Robert Yates and John Lansing of New York had left the convention in protest. But George Mason of Virginia declared he would bury his bones in Philadelphia before he would leave without an agreement. Even George Washington was depressed. He wrote to Alexander Hamilton, who had returned to New York temporarily. "I am sorry you went away," Washington said. "Our discussions are now, if possible, worse than ever. There is little agreement on which a good government can be formed. I have lost almost all hope of seeing a successful end to the convention. And so I regret that I agreed to take part."

Next came the questions: Who could be elected to the **House and Senate**? Who would elect them? Delegates did not take long to decide the first question. Members of the House, they agreed, must be at least 25 years old. They must be a citizen of the United States for seven years. And, at the time of election, they must live in the state in which they are chosen. Members of the Senate must be at least 30 years old. They must be a citizen of the United States for nine years. And, at the time of election, they must live in the state in which they are chosen.

How long would lawmakers serve? Roger Sherman of Connecticut thought representatives to the House should be elected every year. Elbridge Gerry of Massachusetts agreed. He thought a longer term would lead to a dictatorship. James Madison of Virginia protested. "It will take almost one year," he said, "just for lawmakers to travel to and from the seat of government!" Madison proposed a three-year term. But the delegates finally agreed on two years. There were many ideas about the term for **Senators**. A few delegates thought they should be elected for life. In the end, the convention agreed on a Senate term of six years.

Then, the convention discussed the difficult issue of slavery. Slavery affected the decision on how to count the population for purposes of representation in Congress. It also affected the powers proposed for the Congress. The convention accepted several political compromises on the issue. One compromise was the "**three-fifths rule**." The population would be counted every ten years to decide how many representatives each state would have. The delegates agreed that every five **Negro slaves** would be counted as three persons. Another compromise permitted states to import slaves until the year 1808. After that, no new slaves could be brought into the country. Many of the delegates in Philadelphia did not like these compromises. But they knew the compromises kept the Southern states from leaving the convention. Without them, as one delegate said, no union could be formed.

After all the debates, **bitter arguments**, and compromises, the delegates were nearing the end of their work. Four months had passed since the convention began. The weather had been hot. Emotions had been hot, too. But that was expected. For the men in Philadelphia were deciding the future of their country. Early in September, the convention appointed five men to a **Committee of Style**. It was their job to write the document containing all the convention's decisions. William Samuel Johnson of Connecticut was chairman of the committee. The other members were Alexander Hamilton of New York, Gouverneur Morris of Pennsylvania, Rufus King of Massachusetts, and James Madison of Virginia. Of these five men, Gouverneur Morris was known for the beauty of his language. So Judge Johnson asked him to write the Constitution.

Words, Expressions and Notes

Supreme Court （美国）最高法院

a system of lower national courts 一套等级更低的国家法院体系

brought the deepest emotions to the surface 使（代表们）内心最深处的情感得以显露出来

cannot move one way or another 进退两难

science of government 政府管理科学

Great Compromise "伟大的妥协"。从美国建国开始，"妥协"就是美国政治中的一个重要概念和一项具体实践。尽管美国的建国者们各自为自己所代表的利益吵得一塌糊涂，但最后却总是归于妥协。在妥协的背后，往往显示出理性和宽容，蕴涵着对共同达成的社会契约的尊重精神。而这正是美国政治和社会稳定的关键。

on the edge of breaking up 处于分崩离析的边缘

House and Senate 众议院和参议院

senators 参议员

"three-fifths rule" "五分之三规则"，指在安排众议院席位时，一个黑人奴隶只作为一个正常人的五分之三计算。这是由于北方州担心南方州因拥有大量黑奴而取得人口上的优势，于是要求把黑奴剔除开，但南方州则威胁要退出联邦。"五分之三规则"就是双方妥协的结果。

Negro slaves 黑人奴隶

bitter arguments 激烈的争论

Committee of Style （宪法）文本润饰小组

Questions for Comprehension and Discussion

1. What issue was the most difficult one for the delegates of the convention?

2. Why did the small states feel that they were harmed in the meeting?

3. A speaker at a Philadelphia church spoke to the delegates: "Surely we have among us men who understand the science of government and who can find the answers to all our problems. Surely we have the ability to design a government that will protect the liberties we have won." Why did the delegates need to hear such words?

4. How did the convention solve the problem between big states and small states?

5. Why did Washington say that "I regret that I agreed to take part"?

6. What decision had made about slavery in the convention?

16 The Birth of the Constitution (Part 4)

宪法的诞生（四）

1787年夏天在费城州议会大厦举行的制宪会议，是一个显赫人物的聚会。各州议会所推选的代表都是一些在殖民地政府、州政府、大陆会议、法庭，或者在战场上有经验的领袖人物。新制定的宪法最终得以在大会上通过，首先得益于两个重要人物：乔治·华盛顿和本杰明·富兰克林。因为在革命时期表现出的正直与勇敢，华盛顿成为举国知名的公民，并被推选为会议主席。他原本不情愿出席会议，但在得知没有他会议很难取得成功时，便同意出席。在长达4个月的炎热气候里，他极少发言，但仅是他每天准时端坐在大会主席的椅子上这一点，就给会议代表们带来足够的信心。足智多谋的富兰克林这时已经81岁了，他总是让比他年轻的人多发言。每当代表之间有什么问题争执不休时，他便以好意的幽默和多年从事外交工作的丰富经验帮他们调解。

比较活跃的代表中，一位是宾夕法尼亚的代表古维诺尔·莫里斯。他干练果断，深切了解建立全国性政府的必要性，而他优美严谨的写作风格也使得宪法文本最后的修饰工作交由他完成。另一位是弗吉尼亚派来的詹姆斯·麦迪逊，他是一个实在的青年政治家，对政治和历史都很有研究。一位代表说："他具有勤勉和实事求是的精神……无论在什么问题上，他都是一个知识渊博的人。"

经过了16个星期的争论和深思熟虑，草拟的宪法终于在1787年9月17日，在出席各州的一致同意之下签署了。华盛顿及其他代表们都深为这庄严的气氛所感动，大家坐在席上，思潮起伏。富兰克林以其特有的诙谐打破了当时紧张的气氛。他指着华盛顿坐椅背后用辉煌的金色绘成的半轮太阳说："在会议进程中，许多争论使我时而充满希望，时而感到忧虑。我经常望着主席后面的画，不知道那到底是日出还是日落。但是，现在我终于有幸知道那是日出，是新的一天的开始。"

会议结束了，代表们"到费城大饭店去，一齐欢宴，然后愉快地互相告别"。但是，为争取建立一个更完善的联邦而进行的重要斗争还在后头。宪法必须经过各州民选代表大会通过后方能生效，而宪法本身还需要在国家发展的过程中不断完善。

The convention approved 23 parts, or articles, for the Constitution. Gouverneur Morris re-wrote them in a more simple form, so there were just seven. Article One describes the powers of the Congress. It explains how to count the population for purposes of representation. And it says who can become senators or representatives, and how long they can serve. Article Two describes the powers of the president. It explains who can be president. And it tells how he is to be elected. Article Three describes the powers of the federal judiciary. The first three articles provide a system of **"checks and balances."** The purpose is to prevent any of the three branches of government—legislative, executive, and judicial—from becoming too powerful.

Article Four explains the rights and duties of the states under the new central government. Article Five provides a system for amending the Constitution. Article Six declares the Constitution to be the highest law of the land. And Article Seven simply says the Constitution will be established when nine states approve it. In addition to the seven articles, the Constitution contains an opening statement, or preamble.

The convention prepared its own preamble. It began, "We the undersigned delegates of the states of New Hampshire, Massachusetts..." and so on. And it listed all thirteen states by name.

The Committee of Style did not think it was a good idea to list each state. After all, Rhode Island never sent a delegate to Philadelphia. And no one knew for sure if every state would approve the Constitution. So, Gouverneur Morris wrote down instead, "We the People of the United States of America..." Those simple words solved the committee's problem. Who suspected they would cause angry debate during the fight to approve the Constitution? For they made clear that the power of the central government came not from the nation's states, but directly from its citizens.

The rest of the preamble says why the Constitution was written. "...in order to form a more perfect union, establish justice, guarantee peace at home, provide for the common defense, work for the well-being of all, and hold on to the blessings of liberty for ourselves and our children...."[1] The next step was to sign the document.

On September 17th, the delegates gathered for the last time. One might think all their business finally was done. But Nathaniel Gorham of Massachusetts rose to speak. "If it is not too late," he said, "I would like to make a change. We have agreed that one Congressman will represent every 40,000 persons. I think that number should be 30,000." Gorham's proposal could have caused a bitter argument. Then, suddenly, George Washington stood up. The delegates were surprised, because he had said little all summer. "Now," Washington said, "I must speak out in support of the proposed change. It will guarantee a greater voice in the government for the people of the nation." General Washington's influence was strong. Every delegate agreed to accept the change.

Finally, it was time to sign the Constitution. Few of the delegates in Philadelphia could be sure that enough states would approve the Constitution to make it the law of the land. And few could

George Washington presides over the Constitutional Convention of 1787.

know then that Americans of the future would honor them as "fathers" of the nation. But, as several said later, they wrote the best Constitution they could. Without it, the young nation would break apart. The United States of America would disappear before it had a chance to succeed.

As the last delegates moved to the table to sign the Constitution, Benjamin Franklin looked at a painting behind the president's chair. He spoke softly to the men around him. Franklin noted that it is difficult to paint a morning sun that appears different from an evening sun. "During the past four months of this convention," he said, "I have often looked at that painting. And I was never able to know if the picture showed a morning sun or an evening sun. But now, at last, I know. I am happy to say it is a morning sun, the beginning of a new day."

---

[1] 为了建立一个更完善的联邦，树立正义，确保内部安宁，提供共同防御，增进公共福利，并保证我们自身和子孙后代永享自由的幸福……

Change has always been part of the history of the United States. Yet there has been very little national conflict. In more than 200 years, only one civil war was fought. In that war, during the 1860s, Northern states and Southern states fought against each other. Their bitter argument involved the right of the South to leave the Union and to deal with issues, especially the issue of slavery, in its own way.

America's civil war lasted four years. Six hundred thousand men were killed or wounded. In the end, the slaves were freed, and the Union was saved. **Abraham Lincoln** was president during the Civil War. He said the Southern states did not have the right to leave the Union. Lincoln firmly believed that the Union of states was permanent under the Constitution. In fact, he noted, one of the reasons for establishing the Constitution was to form a more perfect Union. His main goal was to save what the Constitution had created.

If you ask Americans about their Constitution, they probably will talk about the **Bill of Rights**. These are the first ten changes, or amendments, to the Constitution. They contain the rights of all people in the United States. They have the most direct effect on people's lives. Among other things, the Bill of Rights guarantees freedom of speech, religion, and the press. It also establishes rules to guarantee that a person suspected of a crime is treated fairly.

The Bill of Rights was not part of the document signed at the convention in Philadelphia in 1787. The delegates believed that political freedoms were basic human rights. So, some said it was not necessary to express such rights in a Constitution. Most Americans, however, wanted their rights guaranteed in writing. That is why most states approved the new Constitution only on condition that a Bill of Rights would be added. This was done, and the amendments became law in 1791.

One early amendment involved the method of choosing a president and vice president. In America's first presidential elections, the man who received the most votes became president. The man who received the second highest number of votes became vice president. It became necessary to change the Constitution, however, after separate political parties developed. Then **ballots** had to show the names of each candidate for president and vice president.

There were no other amendments for 60 years. The next one was born in the blood of Civil War. During the war, President Abraham Lincoln announced the **Emancipation Proclamation**. That document freed the slaves in the states that were rebelling against the Union. It was not until after Lincoln was murdered, however, that the states approved the Thirteenth Amendment to ban slavery everywhere in the country. The Fourteenth Amendment, approved in 1868, said no state could limit the rights of any citizen. And the Fifteenth, approved two years later, said a person's right to vote could not be denied because of his race, color, or former condition of slavery.

By the 1890s, the federal government needed more money than it was receiving from taxes on imports. It wanted to establish a tax on earnings. It took 20 years to win approval for the Sixteenth Amendment. The amendment permits the government to collect **income taxes**. Another amendment proposed in the early 1900s was designed to change the method of electing United States Senators. For more than 100 years, Senators were elected by the legislatures of their states. The Seventeenth Amendment, approved in 1913, gave the people the right to elect Senators directly.

In 1919, the states approved an amendment to **ban the production, transportation, and sale of alcohol**. Alcohol was prohibited. It could not be produced or sold legally anywhere in the United States. The amendment, however, did not stop the flow of alcohol. Criminal organizations found many ways to produce and sell it illegally. Finally, after 13 years, Americans decided that **Prohibition** had failed. It had caused more problems than it had solved. So, in 1933, the states approved another Constitutional amendment to end the ban on alcohol.

Other amendments in the 20th century include one that gives women the right to vote. It became part of the Constitution in 1920. Another amendment limits a president to two four-year terms in office. And the Twenty-Sixth Amendment gives the right to vote to all persons who are at least 18 years old. The Twenty-Seventh Amendment has one of the strangest stories of any amendment to the United States Constitution. This amendment establishes a rule for increasing the pay of Senators and Representatives. It says there must be an election between the time Congress votes to increase its pay and the time the pay raise **goes into effect**. The amendment was first proposed in 1789. Like all amendments, it needed to be approved by three-fourths of the states. This did not happen until 1992. So, one of the first amendments to be proposed was the last amendment to become law.

The 27 amendments added to the Constitution have not changed the basic system of government in the United States. The government still has three separate and equal parts: the executive branch, the legislative branch, and the judicial branch. The three parts balance each other. No part is greater than another.

Words, Expressions and Notes

checks and balances　制约与平衡。这是美国宪法规定的政府构建的基本指导原则，目的是防止权力过分集中于个别机构或领导人。

Abraham Lincoln　亚伯拉罕·林肯（1809—1865年），美国政治家，第十六任总统（1861—1865）。在其总统任期内，美国爆发内战。林肯废除了奴隶制度，击败了南方分裂势力，维护了国家的统一。内战结束后不久，林肯遇刺身亡，成为第一个遭到刺杀的美国总统。

Bill of Rights　《人权法案》，美国宪法的第一次修正，包括10条修正案，于1791年通过。

ballots　*n.* 投票，选票

Emancipation Proclamation　《解放宣言》，由林肯总统1862年9月颁布，规定从1863年1月1日起，美国南方参与叛乱各州的全部奴隶获得永久自由。

income taxes　收入所得税

ban the production, transportation, and sale of alcohol　禁止酿造、运送和出售酒类，即宪法第十八修正案。这是美国宪法中最为失败的条款，最后国会不得不在1933年颁布宪法第二十一修正案对第十八修正案予以废止。

Prohibition　美国历史上从1920年至1933年期间的禁酒时期

goes into effect　生效

Questions for Comprehension and Discussion

1. How many articles does the Constitution have?
2. What are the first three articles of the Constitution? What is the purpose of them?
3. Why did Gouverneur Morris re-write the preamble to the seven articles?
4. Benjamin Franklin said: "During the past four months of this convention, I have often looked at that painting. And I was never able to know if the picture showed a morning sun or an evening sun. But now, at last, I know. I am happy to say it is a morning sun, the beginning of a new day." Why did he say so?
5. What are the first changes to the Constitution? When did they become law?
6. Which Amendment bans slavery in the United States?
7. When were American women given the right to vote by the Constitution?
8. Why is it said that the 27 amendments to the Constitution have not changed the basic system of government in the United States?

Unit 5　The Growth of a New Nation (1)

17　George Washington

乔治·华盛顿

费城制宪会议决定，一旦13州中有9个州的议会通过，宪法便生效。但到了1787年底，只有3个州批准了这个宪法。其他州的情况怎么样呢？事实是，当时许多头脑简单的美国人认为，这个文件给他们带来了危险。他们怀疑宪法中规定的强大的中央政府可能会对他们施行暴政，用重税压迫他们，还有可能把他们拖入战争的泥沼中。

由于对这些问题的看法不同，初生的美国产生了两大派别——一派是联邦主义者，一派是反联邦主义者。前者主张建立一个强大的政府，后者主张各州保持松散的联系。争论的结果产生了《权利法案》，并把它作为联邦宪法中最初10项修正案归入全国最高法律之中。《权利法案》一经采纳，立场动摇的各州立即支持宪法。最后，在1788年6月25日，宪法正式通过。随即，联邦会议安排了第一次选举总统的事宜。当时的美国，人人都拥护乔治·华盛顿担任国家元首。果然，1789年2月4日，他当选美利坚合众国第一任总统。

华盛顿不得不又一次响应国家的召唤离开他热爱的弗吉尼亚庄园。然而，已经57岁的他对总统职位并不感兴趣。在写给一位朋友的信中，华盛顿说他感觉自己像"一个前往死刑地点的囚犯"。然而，责任毕竟是责任。可是，当他决定前往纽约宣誓成为美国总统时，却发现自己连足够的旅途费用都没有。万般无奈，他只好向朋友借钱走马上任。人人都知道华盛顿是国家最富有的人之一，他的钱到哪里去了呢？原来，美国人一向重视土地投资，华盛顿也不例外，他的财富都在土地上。1789年4月30日，华盛顿正式宣誓就职，他保证要忠实履行总统职责，并且尽他最大的能力来"维持、保护和捍卫美国的宪法"。

华盛顿是美国历史上的一个神话。他受教育不多，没有去过欧洲，没有接受过科学、法律方面的专业训练，也没有钻研过古典作品。他基本上是美国边远地区林区生活的一个产物，仅仅通过从军的经历学习和了解人类的天性而已。人们从他的口中听不到一句原创的名言警句。相反，在他的书信里，人们看到的是他对土地经纪人的不信任，对新购进却不能工作的农场机器的抱怨，对裁剪不合身的衣服的不满，对无法支付的账单的无奈等等。

然而，华盛顿身上却散发出谜一般的人格魅力和难以描述的领袖气质。战争时期，他下达命令，让那些出口成"脏"的士兵停止讲粗话。他告诫他们："在同英国人的战斗中，上帝不会帮助那些每天都咒骂他的人。"独立战争胜利后，有人建议他废除共和制自立为国王，华盛顿对此的反应竟然是为自己给世人留下这样的印象而感到羞愧！他回信告诫写信人永远不要向任何人再提出这个话题。在担任美国总统之前，戎马生涯几乎是华盛顿一生的全部写照，然而他却坚定地指出："由于剑是维护我们自由的最后手段，一旦这些自由得到确立，就应该首先将它放在一旁。"担任总统后，他又明确表示："政府的缰绳必须由一只坚定的手执掌，而对宪法的每一次违背都必须遭到谴责。如果宪法存在什么缺陷，那就加以修正，但绝不能加以践踏！"

华盛顿所具备的高尚品质使他成为新共和国的第一个德才兼备的伟大政治家。一个欣欣向荣的共和国在他英明而富有远见的领导下正式拉开了建国大业。

The United States Constitution went into effect March 4th, 1789. The Constitution was the new nation's plan of government. There was much to be done to make it work. The machinery of government was new, untested. Strong leadership was needed. It was provided by the man chosen to be the new nation's first president: George Washington.

Many historians believe there would never have been a United States without George Washington. He led the American people to victory in their war for independence from Britain. He kept the new nation united in the dangerous first years of its life. Washington had a strange power over the American people. His name still does. During his lifetime, he was honored for his courage and wisdom. After his death in 1799, he became almost god-like. People forgot that he was human, that he had faults and made mistakes. For well over 100 years, Americans found it difficult to criticize George Washington. He represented the spirit of America—what was best about the country.

Recent historians have painted a more realistic picture of Washington. They write about his weaknesses, as well as his strengths. But this has not reduced his greatness and importance in the making of the nation. The force of Washington's personality, and his influence, was extremely important at the Philadelphia convention that wrote the new Constitution. Had he not agreed to attend, some say, the convention would not have been held. Later, as the first president, he gave the new nation a good start in life.

Washington was able to control political disputes among officials of the new government. He would not let such disputes damage the nation's unity. Washington often thought of the future. He wanted the first government to take the right steps. He said some things may not seem important in the beginning, but later, they may have bad permanent results. It would be better, he felt, to start his **administration** right than to try to correct mistakes later when it might be too late to do so. He hoped to act in such a way that future presidents could continue to build on what he began.

Washington had clear, firm ideas about what was right and what was wrong. He loved justice. He also loved the **republican form of government**. Some people had difficulty seeing this part of the man. For Washington looked like an **aristocrat**. And, at times, he seemed to act like one. He attended many ceremonies. He often rode through the streets in a carriage pulled by six horses. His critics called him "king." Washington opposed rule by kings and dictators. He was shocked that some good people talked of having a **monarchy** in America. He was even more shocked that they did not understand the harm they were doing.

Washington warned that this **loose talk** could lead to an attempt to establish a monarchy in the United States. A monarchy, he said, would be a great victory for the enemies of the United States. It would prove that Americans could not govern themselves. As president, Washington decided to do everything in his power to prevent the country from ever being ruled by a king or dictator. He wanted the people to have as much self-government as possible. Such government, Washington felt, meant a life of personal freedom and equal justice for the people.

The 18th century has been described as **the age of reason and understanding for the rights of people**. Washington was a man of his times. He said no one could feel a greater interest in the happiness of mankind than he did. He said it was his greatest hope that the policies of that time would bring to everyone those blessings which should be theirs. Washington was especially happy and proud that the United States would protect people against oppression for their religious beliefs. He did not care which god people worshipped. He felt that religious freedom was a right of every person. Good men, he said, are found all over the world. They can be followers of any religion, or no religion at all. Washington's feelings about **racial oppression** were as strong as his feelings about religious oppression. True, he owned Negro slaves. But he hated slavery. "There is not a man alive," he once said, "who wishes more truly than I to see **a plan approved to end slavery**." By his order, all his slaves were freed when he died.

From the beginning, George Washington was careful to establish a good working relationship with the Congress. He did not attempt to take away any powers given to the Congress by the Constitution. By his actions, he confirmed the separation of powers of the three branches of the government, as proposed in the Constitution. The Congress, too, was ready to cooperate. It did not attempt to take away any powers given to the president by the Constitution. The Congress, for example, agreed that President Washington had the right to appoint his assistants. But Congress kept the right to approve them.

Washington as President in 1789

Washington asked some of the nation's wisest and most able men to serve in the new government. For **Secretary of State**, he chose Thomas Jefferson. At the time, Jefferson was America's representative to France. While Congress was considering Jefferson's nomination, Washington heard of threatening events in France. He learned that a mob had captured the old prison called the **Bastille**. Washington was worried. The United States had depended on France for help during its war for independence. And it still needed French help. A crisis in France could be bad for America. The information Jefferson brought home would prove valuable if the situation in France got worse. Washington also thought Jefferson's advice would be useful in general, not just on French developments.

For **Secretary of the Treasury**, Washington chose Alexander Hamilton. Hamilton had served as one of Washington's assistants during the Revolutionary War. For **Chief Justice** of the United States, he chose **John Jay**. Jay helped write the *Federalist Papers*, which are considered the best explanation of the Constitution ever written. Two delegates to the Constitutional convention were named **Associate Justices of the Supreme Court**: James Wilson and John Rutledge. For **Attorney General**, Washington wanted a good lawyer and someone who supported the Constitution. He chose Edmund Randolph of Virginia. It was Randolph who proposed the Virginia Plan to the Philadelphia convention. The plan became the basis for the national Constitution. Randolph refused to sign the document, because he did not believe it could be approved. But he worked later to help win Virginia's approval of the Constitution.

President Washington named his assistants, and the Congress approved them. The President was ready to begin work on the nation's urgent problems. And there were many. One problem was Spain's control of the **lower part** of the Mississippi River. American farmers needed to use the river to transport their crops to market. But the Spanish governor in Louisiana closed the Mississippi to American boats. There also were problems with Britain. The United States had no commercial treaty with Britain. And Britain had sent no representative to the new American government. Equally urgent were the new nation's economic problems. Two major issues had to be settled. One was repayment of loans made to support the American army in the war for independence. The other was **creation of a national money system**.

Words, Expressions and Notes

administration *n.* 政府任期

republican form of government 共和制政府，其核心是主权在民。

aristocrat *n.* 贵族

monarchy *n.* 君主制

loose talk 轻率的言谈

the age of reason and understanding for the rights of people 理性与认识到人民权利的时代

racial oppression 种族压迫

a plan approved to end slavery 通过一项计划来结束奴隶制度

Secretary of State （美国）国务卿

Bastille 巴士底监狱。它原是法国巴黎一古堡，用作国家监狱，1789 年法国大革命时被群众攻占。

Secretary of the Treasury 财政部长

Chief Justice 首席法官

John Jay 约翰·杰伊（1745—1829），美国最高法院第一任首席法官

Federalist Papers 《联邦党人文集》，是数位美国政治家在制定宪法过程中所写作的有关美国宪法和联邦制度的评论文章的合集，共收有 85 篇文章。这些文章最早连载于纽约地区的报纸，之后在 1788 年首次出版了合集。此书主要对美国宪法和美国政府的运作原理进行了剖析和阐述，是研究美国宪法的最重要的历史文献之一。

Associate Justices of the Supreme Court 最高法院（除首席法官之外的）大法官。特别需要注意的是，Associate Justices 不能按字面意思理解为"副法官"或"助理法官"。

Attorney General 司法部长

lower part 下游地区

creation of a national money system 创建一套国家金融体系

Questions for Comprehension and Discussion

1. Why was strong leadership needed when the new nation started to run?

2. In what ways can we say that George Washington represented the spirit of America?

3. Was Washington a good politician? Why or why not?

4. Why did Washington do everything in his power to prevent the country from ever being ruled by a king or dictator?

5. Why is it said that Washington was a man of his times?

6. What did George Washington think about slavery in America?

18 The Formation of a Two-Party System and the First Inaugural Speech of Thomas Jefferson

两党制的形成和杰斐逊的第一届就职演说

华盛顿被公认为是一位伟大的军事家，但他很快就证明他也是一位杰出的政治家。他知人善用，委任托马斯·杰斐逊任国务卿，又委任他在革命期间的助手亚历山大·汉密尔顿任财政部长。而这两个人的政治理念却完全相左，因而分别成为美国两党制形成的源头。

汉密尔顿和杰斐逊代表了美国早期政治生活中两股强大的力量。汉密尔顿要求加强统一，加强中央政府的权力；杰斐逊则主张更广泛、更自由的民主政治。汉密尔顿的最高目的是建立一个更有效率的机构，而杰斐逊的最高目的则是给个人以更多的自由。汉密尔顿害怕无政府状态，处处讲求秩序、效率和组织；杰斐逊害怕暴政，处处为自由着想。建国初期的美国正需要这两种力量。美国当时有这两个杰出人士，并由华盛顿及时把他们的哲学思想互相融洽和互相协调，实在是一件幸运之事。

汉密尔顿筹划建立了国家银行，并采取多项措施扶植工商业的发展。针对许多人有拒付之前的国债或者只想偿付部分国债的想法，汉密尔顿指出，美国必须有信用，坚持要全部偿还，并且主张联邦政府要负担各州因支持革命所筹借而尚未还清的债款。他的主张使联邦政府信用稳固，健康的政府财政制度也逐步建立起来。

杰斐逊和汉密尔顿的意见注注是格格不入的。在外交上，杰斐逊体会到一个强大的中央政府的确有很大的作用，但他又害怕强大的中央政府会束缚人民。因此，在其他许多方面，他又不希望中央政府过于强大。

1797年，华盛顿当了8年国家元首后，坚决拒绝再连任下去。1796年9月17日，他发表告别词，表示不再出任总统，从而开创美国历史上摒弃终身总统、和平转移权力的范例。次年，他回到自己的维农山庄园。作为对美国独立和国家的建立作出重大贡献的军事家和政治家，华盛顿被尊为美国国父；作为全世界第一个主动引退的国家元首，华盛顿为美国和世界留下了极其宝贵的政治遗产。

华盛顿退位后，他的副总统、马萨诸塞州的约翰·亚当斯当选为新总统。对于他曾经担任过的副总统职位，亚当斯评论道："这是人类所有发明中最无足轻重的职位。"亚当斯任总统期间，美国首都由费城迁注华盛顿哥伦比亚特区，而他也成为第一个住进白宫的总统。出任总统之前，汉密尔顿和杰斐逊就形成了两大派别，但亚当斯对党派政治毫无兴趣。当上总统后，他夹在二人政治斗争的漩涡中，很难在政府管理上有所作为。作为总统，他的主要建树是避免了与法国的战争。

1800年，美国人民不满意亚当斯的对内政策，希望有一个改变。在华盛顿和亚当斯任期中，联邦主义者建立了一个强大的中央政府，但有时他们却忽略了政府必须反映人民意志的原则，他们的政策疏远了广大平民百姓。

以"天赋人权"为基本政治观点的杰斐逊，获得了广大农民、店主和工人的支持。在1800年杰斐逊获胜的选举中，这些人发挥了巨大的作用。杰斐逊在写给他朋友的信中曾经这样说过："这艘大船经历了种种考验。今后，我们将使她航行在共和的航线上。她那美丽的举止，可以充分表现出造船者的英明才干。"

1801年3月4日杰斐逊在首都华盛顿发表就职演说。这是美国建国初期的一篇重要演讲，从中我们可以深切体会到杰斐逊坚定的民主思想。他在演讲中传达出的真知灼见在两百年后的当代听众心中仍可引起经久不息的共鸣。

George Washington became America's first president in 1789. He was the most famous man in the land. He commanded the forces of the American colonies in their successful rebellion against Britain. He was elected president without opposition. George Washington did not belong to a political party. There were no political parties in America at that time. This does not mean all Americans held the same political beliefs. They did not. But there were no established organizations that offered candidates for elections. Two such organizations **began to take shape** during President Washington's first administration. One was called the **Federalists**. Its leader was Treasury Secretary Alexander Hamilton. The other was called the **Republicans**. Its leader was Secretary of State Thomas Jefferson. Each group represented the political beliefs of its leader.

The **Federalist Party**, led by Treasury Secretary Alexander Hamilton, supported a strong national government with a powerful president and courts. Federalists thought **men of money and position** should rule the country. And they did in the early 1790s. Federalists controlled the Congress. They also had great influence over the nation's first president, George Washington. The Republicans, led by Secretary of State Thomas Jefferson, did not want a strong national government with unlimited powers. And they believed political power should be spread throughout the population.

The two sides carried on a war of words in their party newspapers. Historians believe Hamilton himself wrote much of what appeared in the Federalist paper. Jefferson, they believe, acted mostly as an adviser to the Republican paper. Both papers carried unsigned articles attacking the opposition. Both printed stories that were false. At times, the attacks were personal. Many people felt **two cabinet secretaries** should be above that kind of public fighting.

John Adams took office in 1797. He had served eight years as vice president under President George Washington. Now, state electors had chosen him to govern the new nation. Adams was an intelligent man. He was a true patriot and an able diplomat. But he did not like party politics. This weakness caused trouble during his presidency. For, during the late 1700s, two political parties struggled for power. He was caught in the middle.

Thomas Jefferson, on March 4th, 1801, walked to the **Capitol** to be inaugurated as the third president of the United States. As Jefferson entered the Capitol, there was the **thunder of cannon**. All the senators and representatives stood until Jefferson sat down. A few moments later, the newly-elected president rose and began to read his inaugural speech. This is what Jefferson said:

Friends and fellow citizens,
I have been called to the position of chief executive of our country. I must tell you how honored and thankful I am. But I must tell you, too, of my fears. Yes, I must tell you that the duties of your president are too much for any one man. However, I tell myself that I am not alone. When I see all your faces, I understand the wisdom of those who wrote our Constitution. For in you, the members of Congress, and in the judicial branch of our government, I know that I shall find the strength, the honesty, the courage that I shall need.

We have passed through a hard year of bitter struggle between two political parties. We have shown the world that in America all can speak, write, and think freely. The debate is over. The people have decided. Now is the time for all of us to unite for the good of all. The majority of the people have won the contest. But we must always remember that there is a minority. True, the majority must rule. But the rule of the majority must be just. The rights of the minority are equal to the rights of the majority, and must be protected with equal laws. Let us unite with hearts and minds. Let us have peace and love in our relations with each other. For without peace and love, liberty and life are sad things indeed. Let us remember that the religious freedom which we have in the United States is nothing if we do not have political freedom, if we permit men to be punished because they do not agree with the majority.

For hundreds of years in Europe, men have killed and have been killed in the name of liberty. It is not surprising, then, that even here—in our peaceful land—all cannot agree. But it is possible to have different ideas without forgetting our common wish. We are all Republicans. We are all Federalists. Most of us love our country. Most of us want it to grow. There may be among us those who want to end the union of the states, or to end our republican government. Well then, let those men speak freely, without fear. They are wrong. But America is strong enough to let them say what they wish. When men can think and speak freely, there is no danger to the nation. For those who do not agree with them also have the right to think and speak freely.

Thomas Jefferson, one of the most brilliant individuals in human history

There are some honest Americans who are afraid that a republican government cannot be strong. But I ask these good men one question. Do they want us to destroy a government which has kept us strong and free for ten years? I hope not. We have here in the United States the best and strongest government in the world. This is the only nation on the Earth whose citizens know that the government belongs to them.

Then there are some who say that men cannot govern themselves. What do they offer us instead? Government by kings? Are kings men, or are they angels? I will let history answer this question. Let us keep our union and our government by the people through their elected representatives. We are very fortunate here in the New World. Three-thousand miles of ocean separate us from the wars and the dictatorships of Europe. Here we do not suffer as the people of Europe do. Here we have a great and rich land, with room for a hundred, perhaps a thousand generations of Americans yet to be born. We— and the American children who will come after us—all have equal rights. We honor a man not because of his father, but for what the man is. We do not care what religion a man follows. In this country, men practice religion in many ways. Yet all our religions teach honesty, truth, and the love of man. All worship one God who rules the universe, who wants men to be happy in life.

Yes, we are a fortunate people. What more do we need to make us happy? We need one more thing, my fellow citizens: a wise government. A government that keeps men from injuring each other. A government that gives men freedom to live and work in peace as they wish, and does not take from them the fruit of their labor. That is good government. In my short speech, I cannot tell you all the things that I believe our government should do, and should not do. But I will tell you what I believe to be the most important principles of our government. This is what I believe in:

The same and equal justice to all men no matter what their religion, their political beliefs, or their class. Peace, trade, and friendship with all nations, but **alliances for war with no nations**. Support of the rights of the state governments which are the best defenders of our republic. A strong central government under the Constitution to protect our peace at home and our safety in other parts of the world.

We must keep the right of the people to elect their representatives. This is the safe way to change governments that make mistakes. Without the right of election, we will have bloody revolution. In our election, the majority must rule. This is the **life-blood of a republic**. If the majority is not allowed to rule, then we will have dictatorship. America should have a good **volunteer army** to protect us in peace and in the first days of war, until we use professional soldiers. But at all times, the **civil officers of the government must be first over the military officers**.

The rights of man will be of the highest importance in this government. Information, knowledge, and opinions must move easily and swiftly. We will support freedom of religion... freedom of the press... freedom of the person protected by the **habeas corpus**... and the right to trial by juries that are chosen fairly.

These are the freedoms that brought us through a revolution and that made this nation. Our wise men wrote these freedoms. Our heroes gave their lives for these freedoms. They are the stones on which our political philosophy must be built. If we make the mistake of forgetting them, let us return to them quickly. For only these rights of man can bring us peace, liberty, and safety.

Well then, my fellow citizens, I go to the position which you have given me. I am no George Washington. I cannot ask you to believe in me as you did in the man who led us through our revolution—the man who will always be **first in the love of our country**. I ask only that you give me your support and your strength.

I know that I shall make mistakes. And, even when I am right, there will be men who will say that I am wrong. I ask you to forgive my mistakes which, I promise, will at least be honest mistakes. And I ask you to support me when I am right against the attacks of those who are wrong. Always, my purpose will be to strengthen the happiness and freedom of all Americans—those who do not agree with me, as well as those who do. I need you. I go to my work as president of the United States, ready to leave that position when you and the American people decide that there is a better man for it. May the power that leads the universe tell us what is best, and bring to you peace and happiness.

Words, Expressions and Notes

began to take shape　开始形成

Federalists　*n.* 联邦主义者

Republicans　*n.* 共和主义者

Federalist Party　联邦党

men of money and position　有权势的人；社会精英

two cabinet secretaries　两位内阁部长，指汉密尔顿和杰斐逊

Capitol　*n.*（美国）国会大厦

thunder of cannon　雷鸣般的礼炮声

alliances for war with no nations　不与任何国家因战争而结成同盟

life-blood of a republic　一个共和国的生命线

volunteer army　自愿军

civil officers of the government must be first over the military officers　政府文官的权力必须高于武官的权力

habeas corpus　人身保护权

first in the love of our country　第一号爱国者（指华盛顿）

Questions for Comprehension and Discussion

1. In what ways did Jefferson's political ideas differ from those of Hamilton?

2. Why was John Adams not successful during his presidency?

3. Why did Jefferson say in his inaugural speech that "The majority of the people have won the contest. But we must always remember that there is a minority"?

4. In his inaugural speech Jefferson announced that "we are a fortunate people." Do you think so? Why or why not?

5. What are the most important principles of American government Thomas Jefferson believed in?

6. When Jefferson said "I am no George Washington," what did he really mean?

19 Lewis and Clark Expedition (Part 1)

刘易斯与克拉克远征探险（一）

杰斐逊是一个深思熟虑、富有哲学素养的人。他出现在白宫，为美国社会带来了一股尊重民意、尊重普通老百姓的清风。杰斐逊认为，一个普通的老百姓和最高级别的官员一样，都应该受到尊重。他告诫部属，要把自己当做受人民之托的工作人员。他提倡农业，鼓励向西部开拓。他深信美国是受压迫人们的避难所。受杰斐逊民主作风的影响，全国各州先后废弃了选举资格须受财产限制的规定，并通过了许多合乎人道的债务法和刑事法。

1803年，杰斐逊的一个关键举措使美国的国土面积立刻增加了一倍。西班牙一直占有密西西比河以西的地区，以及离河口不远的新奥尔良港——这是俄亥俄河和密西西比河流域美国产品船运的必经港口。杰斐逊出任总统不久，拿破仑强迫懦弱的西班牙政府把一大块叫做路易斯安那的土地还给法国。此举使美国人又怕又怒。假如拿破仑在美国西部实施开拓计划，将对美国内陆居民的贸易和安全构成极大的威胁。

为此，杰斐逊发表声明，如果法国取得路易斯安那，"从那时起，我们就必须和英国舰队及政府联合起来，欧洲战争一旦爆发，英美联军马上就进入新奥尔良"。

拿破仑知道，在短暂的和平之后，英法之间另一次战争将会爆发；他也知道在这场战争中，法国肯定会丧失路易斯安那。因此，他决定将路易斯安那出售给美国，这样既可增加国库收入，也可以使英国得不到路易斯安那。于是，美国以1 500万美元的代价，获得了两百多万平方公里的土地和新奥尔良港口。

杰斐逊鼓励人们到新扩展的西部土地上拓荒安居，但这首先需要对这块土地有所了解。于是，他决定派一支远征队前往密苏里河上游探险，了解密西西比河以西的地区，争取找到一条通往太平洋的水道。他委派他的私人秘书梅里韦瑟·刘易斯负责此任务，而刘易斯深知此行的危险，又请自己的朋友威廉·克拉克加入远征队。这就是美国历史上著名的"刘易斯与克拉克远征探险"。

The story of the Lewis and Clark exploration begins back in time on June 20th, 1803. A young man, **Meriwether Lewis**, has just received a letter from the president of the United States, Thomas Jefferson. Meriwether Lewis is a captain in the United States army. He also serves as President Jefferson's private secretary. He is 28 years old. The letter from President Jefferson says Captain Lewis will lead a group of men to explore the area from the **Missouri River** to the Pacific Ocean.

President Jefferson's letter is long. It tells Captain Lewis to draw maps of the areas in which he travels. It tells him to record a day-by-day history of his trip. And it tells him to collect plants and animals he finds. President Jefferson says Mr. Lewis is to write about the different tribes of Indians he meets. Lewis is to report about their languages, their clothing and their culture. The letter asks Lewis to return with as much information as possible about this unknown land.

In the early 1800s, much of the land that would later become the United States was unexplored. Many people believed that ancient animals like huge dinosaurs could still live in the **Far West**. Other stories told of strange and terrible people in these unexplored areas. President Jefferson wanted Lewis to confirm or prove false as many of these stories as possible. The President also wanted him to find the best and fastest way to travel across the Far Western lands. President Jefferson wanted many other questions answered. Lewis was to learn if it was possible to send trade goods by land to the Pacific coast. He was to learn if it were possible to take a boat west across the country to the Pacific Ocean. Many people believed this was possible. This idea was called the **Northwest Passage**. People thought the Northwest Passage would be a river or several rivers that linked the Atlantic and Pacific oceans. Explorers just had to find it.

President Jefferson knew that any trip to the Far West would be extremely dangerous. Those taking part could expect years of hard work. They would lack food and water. They would face dangerous Indians and have little medical help. There would be severe weather. It was possible that such a group of explorers would never return. President Jefferson chose Lewis to lead the trip because he was sure Lewis would

Meriwether Lewis and William Clark

succeed. Meriwether Lewis and President Jefferson had spent a lot of time together. President Jefferson had great respect for Lewis. He knew Captain Lewis was a strong man who had a good education. Lewis was also a successful army officer and a good leader. And, probably most important, he was a skilled hunter who was used to living outdoors for long periods of time.

Lewis knew that such a trip would be extremely difficult and dangerous. He knew that he needed another person who could lead the group if he became injured or died. He requested President Jefferson's permission to ask a friend to help him. Lewis's friend was **William Clark**. Clark was an excellent leader, and was good at making maps. Lewis wrote a letter to Clark and offered him the job. Clark accepted. The two men decided to **share the responsibility of command**. They decided to be equal in all things. Lewis and Clark had known each other for several years. They had served in the army together. Each trusted the other's abilities.

President Jefferson then sent Lewis to the city of Philadelphia. There, scientists began to teach him about modern scientific methods. He learned about plants. He learned how to tell where he was on the planet by using the stars and the sun. He learned about different kinds of animals. He also studied with a doctor, Benjamin Rush, who taught him about emergency care of the sick or wounded and about different kinds of medicine. Doctor Rush helped Lewis gather the medical supplies that would be needed for the trip.

William Clark began to choose the men they would lead across the country to the Pacific Ocean. He made sure the men understood the dangers they would face. Clark and Lewis agreed that they needed men who could add some skill to the group. They agreed they wanted men who had lived much of their lives outdoors. They wanted some good hunters. They needed others who knew how to use small boats. They also needed some men who could work with wood, and others who could work with metals. They needed a few who could repair weapons and some who could cook. Most importantly, they looked for men who could best survive the hard days ahead. Most of the men Clark chose were soldiers. Each man prepared for the trip with five months of training. In the winter of 1803, the group came together at a place they called Camp Wood. Camp Wood was north of a small village named Saint Louis in what would later become the state of Missouri. They began buying the last of the supplies they would need. And they began preparing the three boats they would use on the first part of their trip.

Lewis and Clark called their group of 32 men the **Corps of Discovery**. Their exploration began May 14th, 1804. Another group of soldiers would join the Corps of Discovery for the first part of their trip. The soldiers would return after the first winter with reports for President Jefferson about what the explorers had discovered. They left Fort Wood and traveled north on the Missouri River. It was extremely hard work from the very beginning. Their three boats were not traveling with the flow of the river, but against it. At times, they passed ropes to the shore and the men pulled the boats. Several times the ropes broke. It was difficult and dangerous work. The largest of their three boats was almost 17 meters long. This boat was called the Discovery. It carried most of their supplies, including medicine, food, scientific instruments, weapons and gifts of friendship for the Indian tribes the explorers hoped to meet.

Lewis and Clark and the men with them immediately saw the great beauty of the land. This great natural beauty was something they would write about time and again each day during their travels. Slowly, the explorers made their way north up the Missouri River. They passed the area that in the future would be Kansas City. They continued north and passed the area that would become the city of Omaha, in the future state of **Nebraska**. As each day passed, both Lewis and Clark wrote about what they saw. Clark made maps of the land and the river.

Near the present city of Sioux City, in the state of Iowa, Sergeant Charles Floyd became sick and died within a few days. The members of the Corps of Discovery buried him not far from the river. Today, a monument stands where he was buried. The Corps of Discovery again continued north in their boats on the Missouri River. They passed through what would become the state of South Dakota. Here, for the first time they met members of the Lakota called the **Teton Sioux**. The Teton Sioux were very fierce and warlike. They demanded Lewis and Clark give them one of the boats. The two leaders refused. The Sioux threatened to kill all of the group. The Corps of Discovery prepared for a fight. But it never came. The Sioux changed their minds. Clark wrote of the Teton Sioux that they were tall and nice-looking people. He said their clothing was beautifully made with many colors and designs. He said the men were proud and fierce.

Soon, the Corps of Discovery passed into what would become the state of **North Dakota**. It was now growing late in the year. The weather was becoming colder. At a place they named Fort Mandan they quickly cut trees and made temporary homes for the winter. The Missouri River began to turn to ice. Some days it was too cold to hunt animals for food. On the 17th of December, 1804, William Clark wrote in his book, "At night the temperature fell to **74 degrees below freezing**." The Corps of Discovery would stay in Fort Mandan for five months. During the winter the explorers planned for their trip to the Pacific.

It was 164 days into the trip. Lewis and Clark had traveled about 2,420 kilometers when they were stopped by the cold winter weather. They named their winter home Fort Mandan. Mandan was the name of an Indian tribe that lived nearby.

At Fort Mandan, Lewis and Clark met French Canadian hunter Toussaint Charbonneau. He was living with the Indians. He asked to join the Corps of Discovery. He also asked if his Indian wife could come too. Her name was **Sacagawea**. She was pregnant. Lewis and Clark agreed to let them join their group for two reasons. The first was that Charbonneau spoke several Indian languages. The second concerned Sacagawea. She came from the **Shoshoni** tribe that lived near the **Rocky Mountains** in the Far West. She had been captured as a young girl by another Indian tribe. Lewis and Clark knew that no Indian war group ever traveled with women. They knew that Sacagawea's presence with them would show Indians that the Corps of Discovery did not want to fight. Sacagawea gave birth to her son, Jean Baptiste Charbonneau, on February 11th, 1805. The baby, too, would make the long trip to the Pacific Ocean. He was the youngest member of the Corps of Discovery.

In early April, the Corps of Discovery prepared to travel west. The smaller group of soldiers that had aided them during their trip to Fort Mandan prepared to return south to Saint Louis. The soldiers took the larger of the three boats the group had used to follow the Missouri River. They also took Lewis and Clark's first maps, animals, plants and reports to President Jefferson. These reports provided much detail about the land and what was on it. For example, Lewis used more than one thousand words to tell about one bird.

Words, Expressions and Notes

Meriwether Lewis 梅里韦瑟·刘易斯（1774—1809），美国探险家，与克拉克率领探险队横贯大陆，进行首次到达太平洋西北岸的考察，1808年任路易斯安那州州长；由于工作不顺心，呈现忧郁症症状，1809年10月10日在去首都华盛顿述职的路途中自杀。

Missouri River 密苏里河，美国中西部重要河流，密西西比河的最长支流

Far West （美国）远西地区，指密西西比河以西地区

Northwest Passage 西北航道。早期美国人认为在大西洋与太平洋之间可能有一条航道，并进行了多次不成功的探索。直到1969年，美国破冰油轮"曼哈顿号"才第一次成功通过北美大陆与北极群岛之间的一条航道。但这与早期美国人认为有一条通过美国西北部进入太平洋的航道的想法已相去甚远。

William Clark 威廉·克拉克（1770—1838），美国军人、探险家，与刘易斯一道率领探险队横贯大陆，进行首次到达太平洋西北岸的考察。

share the responsibility of command 共同承担领导责任

Corps of Discovery （一支从事）发现的队伍

Nebraska 内布拉斯加

Teton Sioux 蒂顿苏部族，美国西部达科他印第安人的一个分支

North Dakota 北达科他

74 degrees below freezing 华氏零下74度，约等于摄氏零下23度

Sacagawea 萨卡加维亚（1788—1812），具有传奇色彩的印第安妇女，随刘易斯与克拉克探险队西征，担任向导和翻译，使探险队绝路逢生，为美国历史上第一次成功探索西部做出重大贡献。

Shoshoni （印第安人）肖肖尼部落

Rocky Mountains 落基山

Questions for Comprehension and Discussion

1. What did President Jefferson ask Captain Lewis to do in his letter to Lewis?
2. Why did the President ask Lewis to do so many things?
3. Why did the Americans want to find the Northwest Passage?
4. Why did President Jefferson choose Lewis to lead the trip?
5. What dangers would Lewis and Clark have on their way across the country to the Pacific Ocean?
6. How did Lewis get himself prepared for the dangerous trip?
7. Why did Lewis and Clark allow an Indian woman to join in their expedition team?

20 Lewis and Clark Expedition (Part 2)

刘易斯与克拉克远征探险（二）

西进运动几乎可以说是美国建国史上的头等大事。其实早在殖民地时期，第一批朝西部迁徙的人大约在 1760 年就越过了阿利根尼山（阿巴拉契亚山脉的西部）。随后，一个叫丹尼尔·布恩（Daniel Boone）的人成为美国早期西部移民的传奇人物。他不断朝西部蛮荒之地深入，率领移民定居在肯塔基、西弗吉尼亚、密苏里这些当时还是相当边远的地区，直到 1820 年他在密苏里去世为止。

这段时期的向西迁徙活动，多以沿着河流为主，这是因为河道能为人们的交通和物资的运输带来便利。但是，当西进的人们越过宽广亦汹涌的密西西比河，来到中西部大平原边缘时，他们停下脚步，踌躇不前了。移民们面对着一个前所未有的挑战：一望无际的大平原。这里不再有提供旅行便利的河流，而骑在马背上驰骋于大草原的印第安部落也成为一个新的威胁。

刘易斯与克拉克远征探险正是在这样的背景下开始的。对于北美大陆的远西地区，人们几乎一无所知。前面的平原有多大，山有多高，究竟有没有水道通注太平洋，这些都是需要实地考察才能得出结果。

刘易斯与克拉克在 1804 至 1806 年间对密西西比河以西的远征探险取得的成就，即使在 200 年后的今天看起来，仍然不可思议。在两年又 4 个月的时间里，探险队在没有任何后勤补给、考察装备极度原始的情况下横跨广袤无垠的美国西部荒野，总行程 12 400 公里。全部考察队员除一人死于阑尾炎外，全部都存活下来。仅这一点，就是一个奇迹。当这支衣衫褴褛、蓬头垢面的"发现军团"出现在圣路易斯城时，所有的人都被眼前的景象惊呆了！因为几乎所有的美国人都认为这批人早已葬身荒野。

更令人惊诧的是，刘易斯和克拉克两人在极度艰苦的条件下所开展的科学研究工作是如此出色，以至于科学家们普遍认为，即使让当代最优秀的科学考察工作者来做同样的事，也很难达到他们的高度。

刘易斯与克拉克远征探险是美国历史上报道最多、最具有科学价值的探险活动。他们没有找到传说中的西北通海水道；然而，他们的发现极大地扩展了美国人的视野，他们的艰难跋涉为随后通注太平洋沿岸的大迁徙开拓了前进的道路。

The Corps of Discovery again moved up the Missouri River as soon as the warm weather of spring began to return. Lewis wrote of seeing thousands of animals: American **bison**, deer, huge **elk** and very fast **antelope**. Lewis saw thousands of animals all feeding together.

Lewis and Clark soon decided to leave behind important information, plants and things collected from Indians. They were having problems carrying everything they were gathering. They also decided to leave extra food behind. They did this by digging a deep hole and burying everything to protect it from animals. They would do this again and again on their way west. They would collect everything on their return trip.

The explorers soon reached an area where a series of waterfalls **blocked passage** on the river. This area is near the modern city of Great Falls, Montana. Here, the Corps of Discovery pulled the boats from the water and took them over land to the river. They carried the boats almost 30 kilometers. To make the trip easier, they made wooden wheels for their boats. Later they buried the wheels with more food and things they had collected.

On July 25th, 1805, Meriwether Lewis and two other men saw a small river that was flowing to the west. All rivers before had flowed east or southeast. Lewis correctly guessed he had reached **the line that divides the North American continent**. Rain falling to the west of the imaginary line becomes rivers that flow to the Pacific Ocean. Rain that falls to the east of the line forms rivers that flow to the Atlantic Ocean or the Gulf of Mexico. Meriwether Lewis became the first American to cross this continental line. At that point, Lewis could tell from the huge mountains he saw ahead that they would find no waterway across the continent. A lot of the trip would have to be overland.

Meriwether Lewis met two Shoshoni Indian women in this same area. About 60 men from the tribe quickly arrived riding horses. They were dressed and painted for war. It was something that few white men ever saw—a Shoshoni war party prepared to fight. Lewis made peace signs. There was no trouble.

Two days later, Clark arrived with the main group. The Corps of Discovery met with the Indians. At the meeting, Sacagawea began to cry as she looked at the Shoshoni chief, Cameahwait. Cameahwait was her brother. She had not seen him since she was kidnapped many years before. Lewis and Clark

Shortly after his returning from his expedition, Meriwether Lewis posed for this portrait.

could communicate with the Shoshoni Indians. But it was not easy. Sacagawea would listen to the Shoshoni. She would then speak to her husband, Charbonneau, in the **Hidatsa language**. He would speak in French to a soldier in the group, Francis Labiche, who then spoke in English to Lewis. It took a long time, but it worked. The Corps of Discovery decided to leave the boats and continue west on horses. Sacagawea helped Lewis and Clark trade for horses. She also helped them find an Indian guide to lead them. His name was Toby. It was already the month of September when they reached the high mountains. It was also extremely cold. The explorers began to suffer from a severe lack of food. They were forced to kill and eat several of their horses.

In October they found the huge **Columbia River**. High winds and rain slowed the group's progress. On November 7th, they reached the Pacific Ocean. Clark recorded that 554 days had passed since they left their camp at Wood River near Saint Louis. They had traveled 6,648 kilometers.

For several days the Corps of Discovery camped in an area that is now the extreme southern part of **the state of Washington**. But the hunting was poor. Indians told them the hunting would be better across the Columbia River. Lewis and Clark decided to hold a vote and let the Corps of Discovery decide. The Corps of Discovery voted to move south across the river into what is now **the state of Oregon**. William Clark's black slave York and the Indian guide Sacagawea were included in the vote. History experts say this was the first free, democratic election west of the Rocky Mountains. And they say it was the first time in American history that a black slave and a woman voted in a free election.

The explorers quickly built a camp of wooden buildings on the Columbia River. They would stay there during the winter months between 1805 and 1806. They named the buildings Fort Clatsop. "Clatsop" was the name of a nearby group of friendly Indians. The area of Fort Clatsop is very near the present city of Astoria, Oregon.

The group stayed at Fort Clatsop for four months. **It rained all but twelve days**. During the long winter months, the explorers hunted and preserved food. They used animal skins to make new clothes and shoes. They also studied the Indians, fish, animals and lands near the area of the fort. Clark made extremely good maps of the area. Meriwether Lewis, William Clark and the other members of the Corps of Discovery were prepared for their return trip to Saint Louis.

Meriwether Lewis stayed inside Fort Clatsop and wrote, day after day, of the things they found. He wrote information about one hundred different animals they had seen. Of these, eleven birds, two fish, and eleven mammals had not been recorded before. He also wrote about plants and trees. He had never seen many of these before. Neither had modern science known about them. He tried to make his reports scientific. Modern scientists say his information is still good. They say he was extremely careful and provided valuable information for the time. Experts say Lewis wrote more like a scientist of today than one of his own century.

On March 23rd, 1806, the explorers left Fort Clatsop and started back up the Columbia River. Progress was slow as the Corps of Discovery climbed higher toward the mountains. They traded with Indians for horses. In the month of May they stayed with a tribe called the **Nez Perce**. The Nez Perce said it would not be possible for the explorers to cross the mountains then. The snow was still too deep. Lewis did not agree. The group went forward. They found the Nez Perce were right. The snow was several meters deep. They were forced to stop and return down the mountain. The Nez Perce agreed to provide guides to take them through the mountains. The Corps of Discovery finally crossed the mountains in the last days of June.

Lewis divided the Corps of Discovery when they left the mountains. He wanted three different groups to go three different ways to learn more about the land. Lewis and his group soon found Indians. They were members of the **Piegan tribe**, part of the **Blackfeet**, a warlike group. At first the Indians were friendly. Then, one tried to take a gun from one of the men. A fight began. Two Indians were killed. It was the only time during the trip that any fighting took place between native Americans and the Corps of Discovery. The fight forced Lewis's group to leave the area very quickly.

The three groups met again in August of 1806. Traveling on the rivers was easier that in the beginning of their trip. The explorers now were going in the same direction as the **current**. They were in a hurry to get home. They had been away for two years and five months. Each minute they traveled brought them closer to their homes, their families and friends. On September 3rd, they saw several men traveling on the river. They learned that President Jefferson had been re-elected and was still president of the United States.

A few days later, one member of the group asked Lewis and Clark if he could remain behind. He wanted to go with a group of fur traders that was returning to the area of the **Yellowstone River**. His name was John Colter. Colter returned up the river and into the wild land. Later Colter became the first American to see the Yellowstone Valley, which became the first national park, Yellowstone. He also became famous as one of the first mountain men in American history to open the way to the Rocky Mountains.

The Corps of Discovery reached Saint Louis on September 23rd, 1806. They had very little food or supplies left, but they were back. Large celebrations were held in the small town. Lewis and Clark learned that most people believed they were dead. Lewis immediately wrote a long report to President Jefferson and placed it in the mail. A few days later President Jefferson knew they had arrived home safely and their trip had been a great success.

Experts today say the Lewis and Clark trip was one of the most important events in American history. They also agree that no two men could have done a better job or been more successful. Meriwether Lewis and William Clark added greatly to the knowledge of the American Northwest. Clark's maps provided information about huge areas that had been unknown. Lewis discovered and told about 178 new plants, most of them from the Far West. He also found 122 different kinds of animals that had been recorded. There was also one great failure, however. Lewis and Clark were not able to find a way to reach the Pacific Ocean using rivers. There was no Northwest Passage that could be used by boats.

The Lewis and Clark expedition was also a political success. It helped the United States make a **legal claim to a huge amount of land** that had been bought by President Jefferson from France. The United States bought the land just as the Corps of Discovery began its trip. This land is now the middle part of the United States. It was called the **Louisiana Territory**. President Jefferson wanted the future United States to include this land, and all other land between the Atlantic and the Pacific Oceans.

Meriwether Lewis and William Clark were the first educated white Americans to travel across the land that would become the United States. They wrote about things the American public had never seen before. They saw Native Americans before the Indians were influenced by other cultures. Their success had a lasting influence. They showed Americans it was possible to travel across the country and settle in the Far West. Lewis and Clark's exploration was the beginning of the American **campaign** to settle that far away, wild land.

Words, Expressions and Notes

bison *n.* 美洲野牛

elk *n.* 美洲赤鹿

antelope *n.* 羚羊

blocked passage 阻碍通行

the line that divides the North American continent 把北美大陆分为两半的分界线。这里指落基山脉，山脉以东的水系流入大西洋，山脉以西的水系则流入太平洋。

Hidatsa language 希多特萨语

Columbia River 哥伦比亚河

the state of Washington 华盛顿州

the state of Oregon 俄勒冈州

It rained all but twelve days. 除十二天之外一直在下雨。

Nez Perce （北美印第安）内兹佩尔塞人

Piegan tribe 皮根部落，属印第安黑脚族人

Blackfeet （北美印第安）黑脚族人

current *n.* 水流

Yellowstone River 黄石河

legal claim to a huge amount of land 合法拥有大片土地的主权

Louisiana Territory 路易斯安那领地

campaign *n.* 战役；运动

Questions for Comprehension and Discussion

1. Why was it an important discovery when Lewis and other men saw a small river that was flowing to the west?

2. What is the continental line? Is there really such a line?

3. How about the Indian tribes Lewis and Clark met on their way to the Pacific Ocean? Did they have any problems with the Indians?

4. During the trip, the expedition team held an election. History experts say this election established two records in history. What are they?

5. Why did most people think that Lewis and Clark and their men were dead?

6. Why was the Lewis and Clark expedition so important to the future of the nation?

Unit 6 The Growth of a New Nation (2)

21 The Last Days of Thomas Jefferson

托马斯·杰斐逊最后的日子

在世界历史的长河中，像列奥纳多·达·芬奇这样的天才人物十分罕见。他是古老的意大利文明的最高产物，是欧洲文艺复兴时期最杰出的代表。文艺复兴时期的格言是："一个人能够做他愿意做的任何事。"而达·芬奇就充分实践了这条格言。他不仅作为画家给我们留下著名的《蒙娜·丽莎》，他还是杰出的建筑设计师和工程师。他设计了第一艘潜艇、飞机和直升机。在天文学、地质学、植物学、解剖学和数学方面他都有很深的造诣。他对改善城市的环境卫生也表现出浓厚的兴趣。此外，他还是一位音乐家。文艺复兴时期以后，英语中出现了一个新的短语：Renaissance Man，意指同时在多个领域里颇有造诣之人。

美国也出现了一个达·芬奇似的人物。与达·芬奇不同的是，他不是出生在欧洲的文明古国，而是出生在美洲一片荒原的边缘地区。他对人民、国家和政府的见解十分深刻，他的思想已经普及全世界。他就是托马斯·杰斐逊——美国的列奥纳多·达·芬奇。

只要地球上还存在自由的人，只要世界上还有希望获得自由的人，托马斯·杰斐逊的思想就会继续存在。是他亲笔写下《独立宣言》，首次阐明了人类有史以来最伟大的思想——"人人生而平等"；是他在修订自己家乡弗吉尼亚州的法律时，在悠久的文明史上首次宣布：宗教自由和政教分离不仅仅是理想，而且是绝对必要——这项了不起的创新后来写进了美国宪法；是他一手创办了美国弗吉尼亚大学，直到今天这所大学仍然是美国最受珍视的高等学府之一。

这些还远远不能代表杰斐逊的一生。他是一个充满好奇心的人，一生都在搜集印第安人的语汇，他能阅读拉丁文和希腊文，他学会了法语、意大利语和西班牙语。他热爱乡村，热爱自然，还热衷于演奏小提琴。他设计的弗吉尼亚州议会宏伟的大厦、弗吉尼亚大学美丽的校园以及他自己的家"蒙蒂切洛"（Monticello）等，证明了他是美国第一位伟大的建筑师。他先后担任国家的各种公职，从州长、驻外大使、众议员、副总统、国务卿，直至最后出任总统。

他退休后回到他热爱的家乡蒙蒂切洛，83 岁时在那里逝世。而他的"定时去世"（Timed death）在人类历史上也极其罕见，富有戏剧性：6 月末他就病入膏肓，但他周围的人都能看出来，他在极力挣扎活到《独立宣言》50 周年纪念日——1826 年 7 月 4 日那一天；7 月 3 日他整天处于半昏迷状态，可是到 7 月 4 日上午他却清醒过来；他用微弱的声音问道："今天是 7 月 4 日吗？"守护的人回答说："是的，今天是 7 月 4 日。"即刻，一代伟人溘然长逝。

Thomas Jefferson left the White House in March, 1809. His Secretary of State, James Madison, had been elected president. And Jefferson believed the nation was in good hands. He returned to his country home in Virginia and never went back to Washington again. Jefferson and the new president exchanged letters often. Jefferson offered his advice on a number of problems faced by Madison. There were many visitors to Jefferson's home. All of them were welcome. But Jefferson was happiest with the young men who came to see him. They discussed books, government, and developments in science. Jefferson answered their questions and proposed studies to improve their education.

Jefferson **believed firmly in the value of education**. His whole idea of government depended on the ability of citizens to make intelligent decisions. He spent the final years of his life building a better educational system for Virginia. Jefferson had been interested in education for most of his life. He had developed many ideas about the best way to educate the people. He believed that every citizen had the right to an education. But he understood that all people do not have the same ability to learn. Jefferson divided the people into two groups: **those who labor and those who use their minds**. He thought both should start with the same simple education—learning to read and write and count. After these things were learned, he believed the two groups should be taught separately. Those in the labor group, he thought, should learn how to be better farmers or how to make things with their hands. The other group should study science, or medicine, or law.

Jefferson did not wait long to begin working to improve education in Virginia. A group of men decided to build a college at **Charlottesville**, near Jefferson's home. Jefferson immediately offered to take a leading part in starting the school. He said he would plan the buildings and also plan what the students would study. He wrote to many of his friends—experts in education. He asked for their advice. One of the experts told Jefferson he should not include religion among the studies. Jefferson agreed. But he understood that leaving out religious studies would cause problems. He explained it this way: "We cannot always do what is absolutely best. Those with whom we act have different ideas. They have the right and power to act on their ideas. We make progress only one step at a time. **To do our fellow men the most good**, we must lead where we can, follow where we cannot. But we must still go with them, watching always for the moment we can help them move forward another step."

Jefferson began by planning a program of studies for the Charlottesville College. But he did not stop there. Before he finished, he had completed plans for a complete education system for Virginia. He proposed a school system of three steps. The first step would be elementary schools, where all children could learn reading, writing, arithmetic, and geography. These schools would be built in all areas of the state and would be paid for by the people living in each area. The second step would be colleges. . . equal to the high schools of today. He proposed that nine of these schools be built in the

The University of Virginia, planned and designed by Thomas Jefferson

state. Students would begin the study of science, or would study agriculture, or how to use their hands to make things. These schools would be paid for by the state. The third step would be a state university, where students of great ability could go to get the best of educations. The university would produce the lawyers, doctors, professors, scientists, and government leaders. Young men whose families had money would pay for their own educations. The state would pay the costs of a small number of bright students from poor families. Jefferson also proposed that the University of Virginia be built at Charlottesville. He already had begun work on the college there and offered to give it to the university.

His education program was offered to the Virginia legislature. Many law-makers thought it was excellent. But many others opposed it. They did not want to raise taxes for the large amount of money such a system would cost. The legislature, however, agreed to part of the plan. It approved a bill to help pay the cost of educating poor children. And it agreed to spend 15,000 dollars each year for a university. There was much debate about where the university should be built. Several other towns wanted the school. Finally, Charlottesville was chosen.

By this time, Jefferson had completed plans for the university buildings. He borrowed many of his ideas from the beautiful buildings of ancient Greece and Rome. The buildings were so well planned that 100 years later, when the university was to put up a new building, the builder could find no reason to change the plans drawn by Jefferson. Work began on the university immediately. But it was six years before the school was open to students. Jefferson was there almost every day, watching the workmen. He was quick to criticize any mistake or work that was not done well. When he was sick and not able to go down to the university, he would watch the work through a telescope from a window of his home. The cost of the university kept growing. And Jefferson had to struggle to get the legislature to pay for it. He also worked hard to get the best possible professors to teach at the university. He sent men throughout the United States to find good teachers. He even sent a man to Europe for this purpose. Finally, in March, 1825, the University of Virginia opened.

Jefferson's health had suffered during his years of work for the university. He was 82 years old and **feeling his age**. He suffered from rheumatism and **diabetes**, and was so weak he could walk only short distances. Jefferson also found his memory was failing. He knew he did not have much longer to live. He told a friend one day: "When I look back over the **ranks of those with whom I have lived and loved**, it is like looking over a field of battle. All fallen." As his health grew worse, Jefferson turned his thoughts to death. He wrote how he wished to be buried. He wanted a simple grave on the mountainside below his house. He drew a picture of the kind of memorial he wanted put at his grave. On this stone he wanted the statement: **"Here was buried Thomas Jefferson —author of the Declaration of American Independence, of the Virginia Law for Religious Freedom, and Father of the University of Virginia."**

He did not choose his work as governor of Virginia, Secretary of State, or president. There was not a word about his purchase of the Louisiana Territory from France, which added so greatly to the United States. Jefferson did not explain why he chose the Declaration of Independence, the law for religious freedom, and the university as his greatest works.

Writer Nathan Schachner, in his book on Jefferson, offers this explanation: "He chose those points in his life when he performed some service in the unending struggle to free the human mind. Freedom from political tyranny, freedom from religious tyranny, and finally, freedom through education—from all the tyrannies that have ever clouded and held back the human spirit." On the 4th of July, 1826, the nation began its celebration of the 50th anniversary of the Declaration of Independence. Then, from Boston, came news that former president John Adams had died. His last words were: "Thomas Jefferson still lives."

But Adams was wrong. At ten minutes before ten in the morning, on that same 4th of July, his friend, Thomas Jefferson, had died. As the news of the deaths of the two great men spread across the country, the celebrations turned to mourning and sorrow. Jefferson was buried the next day, as he had ordered, in a simple grave on the quiet mountainside. But his spirit still lives in the Declaration of Independence, the American tradition of religious freedom, and at his beloved University of Virginia.

Words, Expressions and Notes

believed firmly in the value of education 坚信教育的价值

those who labor and those who use their minds 从事体力劳动的人和从事脑力劳动的人

Charlottesville 夏洛茨维尔，位于弗吉尼亚州，杰斐逊的故乡，弗吉尼亚大学所在地。

To do our fellow men the most good 为使我们的同胞受益最大

feeling his age 受到年龄的影响（指已经行动不便等）

diabetes *n.* 糖尿病

ranks of those with whom I have lived and loved 我与之生活和我所热爱的人们

"Here was buried Thomas Jefferson—author of the Declaration of American Independence, of the Virginia Law for Religious Freedom, and Father of the University of Virginia." （杰斐逊为自己题写的墓志铭）"这里埋葬着托马斯·杰斐逊，《独立宣言》的起草人，弗吉尼亚宗教自由法令的作者，弗吉尼亚大学之父。"

Questions for Comprehension and Discussion

1. Why was Jefferson very happy with the young men who came to see him?
2. Why did Jefferson believe firmly in the value of education?
3. What did he do for the education of his home state Virginia?
4. Jefferson wrote his own epitaph: "Here was buried Thomas Jefferson—author of the Declaration of American Independence, of the Virginia Law for Religious Freedom, and Father of the University of Virginia." In a life full of achievements, why did Jefferson choose these three works for which he most wanted to be remembered?
5. Why are Jefferson's ideas important to the world?

The War of 1812 and the Birth of the National Anthem

1812 年战争与国歌的诞生

美国第一任总统华盛顿对欧洲国家之间的连年战乱十分厌恶。在他离任时，他告诫美国人民和未来的政府要特别警惕来自外国的威胁，绝不要卷入欧洲国家的政治和军事纠纷当中。华盛顿的警告被称为是"华盛顿的伟大法规"。一直到第一次世界大战为止，这条"伟大法规"一直是美国外交政策的核心。

1805 年，杰斐逊宣布美国在英法战争中保持中立。由于英法两国都采取封锁措施，美国的商业受到很大的打击。美国船只因为怕被扣留，不敢和法国或英国通商。

当时的英国海军，拥有战舰 700 余艘，海军人员近 15 万人，英国就依靠这支力量来维持英国本土的安全，保护商业，并保持和殖民地之间的关系。但是。海军人员待遇极差，很多不愿服役的水手逃到美国船只上去避难。在这种情形下，英国海军认为他们有权搜查美国船只并索回英国人。这对美国来说是很大的耻辱。此外，许多英国军官还常常拉走许多美国海员，怂恿他们加入英国海军。

1809 年，麦迪逊继杰斐逊出任美国第四任总统。美英关系日益恶化，两国迅速备战。1812 年，美国终于对英国宣战。面对战争，美国国内发生了严重分歧：西部和南部主张战争，但纽约和新英格兰都极力反对。美国政府宣战时，军事准备还远远没有完成，分布在靠近加拿大边界的沿海各据点和内地荒僻地带的正规军队，总共不到 7 000 人。增援他们的将是一些缺乏训练、纪律散漫的民兵。

战争开始时，美国对加拿大发动三路进攻，这一行动如果指挥得当，原本可以联合起来进攻蒙特利尔。但由于调度完全失误，结果英军反过来占领了底特律。

1814 年 9 月，英国军队在华盛顿附近登陆，长驱直入进入美国首都，放火烧毁国会大厦、总统宅第白宫、财政部大厦和其他政府大楼。当英军从华盛顿撤退时，俘虏了一位年长的内科医生威廉·比尼斯。由于马里兰州律师弗朗西斯·斯科特·克伊与比尼斯医生是要好的私人朋友，为此，他毅然登上了准备进攻巴尔的摩的英国舰队，为的是想办法营救比尼斯医生。在英国军舰上，他无可奈何地观看英军攻打美军守卫着的麦克亨利堡。透过硝烟和薄雾，他依稀看到堡垒上头飘扬着一面美国国旗。当炮击结束黎明到来时，他焦虑地探望前方，看看麦克亨利堡是否还在美国人手里。令他欣慰的是，那面经历了枪林弹雨的星条旗仍然在堡垒上迎风飘扬。9 月 16 日晚，克伊怀着巨大的热情创作了一首诗歌，并配上一首古老的英国饮酒歌的曲调。历史学家认为，克伊在写这首诗时，可能就想到了这支曲子。1814 年 10 月 19 日，《星条旗》首次在巴尔的摩剧院演唱。

从那以后的好多年里，这支歌一直是美国最流行的爱国歌曲之一。1931 年，美国国会作出决定，《星条旗》正式成为美国国歌。

James Madison of Virginia was elected president of the United States in 1808. He followed Thomas Jefferson in the office and served two terms. Madison's first four years were not easy. He had to deal with a foreign policy problem that Jefferson was unable to solve: increasingly tense relations with Britain. His second four years were worse. There was war.

The United States declared war on Britain in 1812. It did so because Britain refused to stop seizing American ships that traded with France—Britain's enemy in Europe. At last, **after a change in government, Britain suspended the orders against such neutral trade**. But it acted too late. The United States had declared war.

The United States navy was not ready for war. It had only a few real warships and a small number of gunboats. It could not hope to defeat the British navy, the most powerful in the world. What the United States planned to do was seize Canada, the British territory to the North. Twenty-five hundred British soldiers guarded the border. And American generals believed they could win an easy victory. They were wrong.

An American general named **William Hull** led 2,000 men across the Canadian border. British soldiers were prepared, and they forced the Americans back. The British fought so well that General Hull surrendered all his men and the city of Detroit. The next American attack was made from **Fort Niagara**, a military center in New York on the shore of **Lake Ontario**. A small group of American soldiers crossed the **Niagara River** and attacked the British. Other Americans—state soldiers of New York—refused to cross the border to help against the British. They calmly watched as British soldiers shot down the attacking Americans. The third campaign was made by General Henry Dearborn. He led an army of state soldiers from Plattsburgh, New York, to the Canadian border. He was to cross the border and attack Montreal. But the state soldiers again refused to cross the border. Dearborn could do nothing but march them back to Plattsburgh.

British forces at this time were winning victories. They captured an American fort in northern **Michigan**. And Indians—fighting for the British—captured a fort at the place now known as Chicago. Instead of marching through Canada without difficulty, the Americans found themselves trying hard to keep the British out of the state of Ohio.

By the middle of 1813, a year after the war started, British ships controlled the United States coast. Not an American ship could enter or leave any port south of New England.

The military situation was improving in the West. **William Henry Harrison**, governor of the Indiana territory, formed a large force to try to capture Detroit from the British. At the same time, Captain **Oliver Perry** built five warships on Lake Erie. With these and four he already had, Perry met and completely defeated an English naval force.

By April, 1814, **Napoleon was forced from power** in Europe. And the war between France and Britain was over. This permitted Britain to send many of its soldiers in Europe to fight against the United States.

About 4,000 British soldiers landed on the Chesapeake coast, southeast of Washington. They marched quickly toward the capital. An American general, William Winder, commanded a force two times the size of the British group. Winder was not a good general, and his troops did not defend well.

The two sides met at Bladensburg, a town ten kilometers from Washington. The British attacked and at first the American defenders held their ground. But then, British soldiers broke through the American lines, and the Americans began to run away. General Winder ordered his men back to Washington. A group of sailors refused to retreat with their artillery. Commanded by Joshua Barney, the 400 sailors chose to stand and fight. The struggle did not last long against the 4,000 British soldiers. Barney held his position for a half hour before enemy soldiers got behind his men and silenced the guns. Barney was wounded seriously. The British thought so much of his courage that they carried him to a hospital for their own soldiers at Bladensburg. Barney himself said the British officers treated him as a brother. Once the British force had smashed through Barney's navy men, nothing stood between it and Washington.

The enemy spent the night about half a kilometer from the Capitol building. The commanders of the

British force, General Robert Ross and Admiral Sir George Cockburn, took a group of men to the Capitol and set fire to it. Then the two commanders went to the White House to burn it. Before setting fire to the president's home, Cockburn took one of President Madison's hats and the seat from one of **Dolley Madison**'s chairs. The admiral found the president's table ready for dinner. As a joke, he took a glass of wine and toasted the health of "President **Jemmy**." President Madison had fled the White House earlier. He crossed the Potomac River and started toward his home in Virginia. He joined his wife on the road the second day. And they decided to wait with others about 25 kilometers from Washington. The President returned to the capital three days after he left it. The British, after burning most public buildings, had withdrawn.

The British coastal force next attacked the city of **Baltimore**. But this time, the defenses were strong, and the attack failed. Baltimore port was guarded by **Fort McHenry**. British warships sailed close to the fort and tried to destroy it with their guns.

Shells and bombs from British mortars fell like rain over Fort McHenry. But few Americans in the fort were hurt or killed. Most of the rockets and shells exploded in the air or missed. Many of them failed to explode.

On a tall staff from the center of the fort flew a large American flag. The flag could be seen by the soldiers defending the city and by the British warships. The flag also was seen by a young American. His name was **Francis Scott Key**. Key was a lawyer who once had thought of giving his life to religious work. He was a poet and writer. Key opposed war. But he loved his country and joined the army in Washington to help defend it. When the British withdrew from Washington, they took with them an American doctor, William Beanes. Key knew Beanes. And he asked President Madison to request the British commander to release the doctor. President Madison wrote such a request, and

The American flag still flew over Fort McHenry after the heavy bombarding of the British fleet.

Key agreed to carry it to Admiral Cockburn. Key also carried letters from wounded British soldiers in American hospitals. In one of the letters, a British soldier told of the excellent medical care he was being given. Cockburn agreed to free the doctor after he read the reports of good medical care given his wounded men. But Cockburn would not permit Key, the doctor, or a man who came with Key to return to land until after the attack.

Francis Scott Key watched as the shells and rockets began to fall on Fort McHenry. "I saw the flag of my country," Key said later, "waving over a city—the strength and pride of my native state. I watched the enemy prepare for his assault. I heard the sound of battle. The noise of the conflict fell upon my listening ear. It told me that 'the brave and the free' had met the invaders." All through the rainy day, the attack continued. Doctor Beanes, watching with Key, had difficulty seeing the flag. He kept asking Key if the "stars and stripes" still flew above the fort. Until dark, Key could still see it. After then, he could only hope.

Britain tried to land another force of men near the fort. But the Americans heard the boats and fired at them. The landing failed. Shells and rockets continued to rain down on Fort McHenry. At times, the fort's cannon answered. And Key knew the Americans had not surrendered. The British land force east of Baltimore spent most of the night trying to keep dry. Commanders could not decide if they should attack or retreat. Finally, orders came from the admiral: "Withdraw to your ships." A land attack against Baltimore's defenses would not be attempted. At first light of morning, British shells were still bursting in the air over the fort. The flag had holes in it from the British shells. But it still flew. The British shelling stopped at seven o'clock. Key took an old letter from his pocket and wrote a poem about what he had seen.

The flying flag inspired Francis Scott Key to write "The Star-Spangled Banner," which became the official national anthem in 1931.

> Oh, say, can you see by the dawn's early light
> What so proudly we hailed at the twilight's last gleaming?
> Whose broad stripes and bright stars, through the perilous fight
> O'er the ramparts we watched were so gallantly streaming?
> And the rocket's red glare, the bombs bursting in the air,
> Gave proof through the night that our flag was still there.
> Oh, say, does that star-spangled banner yet wave
> O'er the land of the free and the home of the brave?

For more than 100 years, Americans sang this song and remembered the attack at Fort McHenry. In 1931, Congress made "The Star-Spangled Banner" the national anthem of the United States.

For Your Appreciation

The Star-Spangled Banner

Oh, say, can you see by the dawn's early light	啊，你可看见，透过那一线曙光，
What so proudly we hailed at the twilight's last gleaming,	在暮色将尽时我们自豪地为之欢呼的旗帜，
Whose broad stripes and bright stars, through the perilous fight	经过艰险的战斗，它那阔条明星，
O'er the ramparts we watched were so gallantly streaming?	是否依然迎风飘扬在我军堡垒上？
And the rocket's red glare, the bombs bursting in the air,	火箭弹划过的红光，在空中燃烧的炸弹，
Gave proof through the night that our flag was still there.	一整夜都见证着我们的旗帜安然无恙。
Oh, say, does that star-spangled banner yet wave	啊，那星条旗是否还高高飘扬在，
O'er the land of the free and the home of the brave?	自由的国土，勇士的家乡？

Oh! thus be it ever, when freemen shall stand 　　啊，当自由的人们站在可爱的家乡，
Between their loved home and the war's desolation! 　　和战争的废墟上，愿那星条旗永久飘扬！
Blest with victory and peace, may the heav'n rescued land 　　愿上帝拯救这片土地，赐予她和平与胜利，
Praise the Power that hath made and preserved us a nation. 　　赞美那创建和保全我们国家的力量！
Then conquer we must, when our cause it is just, 　　我们正义的事业一定能够得胜，
And this be our motto: "In God is our trust!" 　　"信奉上帝！"是我们的座右铭。
And the star-spangled banner in triumph shall wave 　　胜利的星条旗将永远飘扬在，
O'er the land of the free and the home of the brave. 　　那自由的国土，勇士的家乡！

Words, Expressions and Notes

after a change in government, Britain suspended the orders against such neutral trade 英国在政府更迭之后，终止了对这种中立贸易实行敌对政策的命令。

William Hull 威廉·赫尔（1753—1825），美国陆军将军，在1812年美英战争中不战而降，以叛国罪被判处死刑，后因其在独立战争中有功获赦免。

Fort Niagara 尼亚加拉要塞

Lake Ontario 安大略湖，五大湖之一

Niagara River 尼亚加拉河，位于美国与加拿大的国境线上，河上有著名的尼亚加拉大瀑布。

Michigan 密歇根州

William Henry Harrison 威廉·亨利·哈里森（1773—1841），曾任印第安纳准州州长、众议员、参议员，1841年任美国总统仅一个月即病逝。

Oliver Perry 奥利弗·佩里（1785—1819），美国海军军官，在1812年战争期间因在伊利湖战役中击败英国舰队而闻名。其弟Matthew Calbraith Perry曾率领舰队远征（1853—1854），迫使日本改变孤立政策而与西方建立外交和贸易关系。

Napoleon 拿破仑一世（1769—1821），法兰西第一帝国皇帝

was forced from power 被迫退位

Dolley Madison 多莉·麦迪逊，麦迪逊总统的妻子

Jemmy 杰米，麦迪逊总统的昵称

Baltimore 巴尔的摩，马里兰州中部港口城市

Fort McHenry 麦克亨利要塞

Francis Scott Key 弗朗西斯·斯科特·克伊（1779—1843），美国国歌歌词作者

Questions for Comprehension and Discussion

1. "Little Jemmie" Madison was frustrated as the president for eight years. What was the main cause?
2. What made the United States declare war on Britain in 1812?
3. Why did the American army want to seize Canada first in the war? Did they succeed in doing so?
4. Why was London able to send more soldiers to America in 1814?
5. Where was the military situation better for the Americans?
6. Did the British succeed in attacking the city of Baltimore? How did the Americans defend Fort McHenry?

23 "Remember the Alamo!"

"牢记阿拉莫!"

1812 年美英之战，也可以说是第二次独立战争，因为在这之前，美国与欧洲列强——尤其是与英国——并没有真正取得平等地位。英国尽管在外交上承认了美国的独立，但并不甘心从北美全线撤退，而是企图以加拿大为基地卷土重来。第二次反英战争胜利之后，美国才受到一个独立国家应有的诗遇，国家的团结和爱国的情绪也因战争而得到加强。革命以来，美国所经历的种种严重困难，已经克服了大部分。国家统一大业完成后，自由和秩序已逐渐平衡；国家需要偿还的债务越来越少，而西部广大的处女地正待开发。和平、繁荣和社会进步交织成一幅美好的国家前景。

随着岁月的流淌，向西开拓的人们，不断越过流注大西洋的那些河流的发源处，翻过阿巴拉契亚山脉，把密西西比河和俄亥俄河一带逐渐变成新的边疆地区。移民们陆续来到荒地之后，很多人既务农又狩猎，舒适的有多间房屋的大木屋代替了独间小木屋，井水代替了河水，生活环境大为改善。随着农民而来的还有医生、律师、店主、编辑、牧师、机械工和政治家，这些人在西部组成了一个生气蓬勃的社会。新的州也不断加入联邦：1816 年的印第安纳州，1817 的密西西比州，1818 年的伊利诺伊州，1819 年的阿拉巴马州，1820 年的缅因州和 1821 年的密苏里州。与大西洋沿岸的情况完全不同的是，在西部这样一个崭新的社会里，人们的地位与他们的家庭背景、祖传产业或者教育程度都毫无关系；他们的地位完全根据他们的品行和能力而定。

美国最初的六位总统都出生于当时的豪门贵族，其中有四位来自弗吉尼亚：华盛顿、杰斐逊、麦迪逊和 1817 年任总统的詹姆斯·门罗；还有两位来自新英格兰地区：约翰·亚当斯和他的儿子、1925 年任第六任总统的昆西·亚当斯。然而，这个传统终于在 1928 年的选举中被打破：安德鲁·杰克逊，一个出生于西部平民家庭，14 岁时成为孤儿，1812 年率领军队在新奥尔良打败英军的英雄当选美国第七任总统。他的当选显示出美国西部逐渐走向成熟，美国的人口重心和政治重心开始从沿海地区向西部转移。

在安德鲁·杰克逊总统的任期内，美国移民大量涌入原本属于墨西哥的得克萨斯地区，并在那里引发了一系列的事件。事件的高峰发生于 1836 年 3 月，正当得克萨斯的定居者们准备开会讨论独立问题时，墨西哥统治者圣安纳率领大批军队包围了圣安东尼奥城的一座叫阿拉莫的教堂。3 月 6 日，墨西哥军队攻占阿拉莫，残忍地杀死全部 188 名守卫者。"牢记阿拉莫!"从此成为美国历史上最能激发人们爱国热情的一句战斗口号。

In the early 1830s, the territory of Texas belonged to Mexico. Many Americans had moved to Texas, because they could buy a lot of land with little money. The government of Mexico expected the settlers to speak Spanish, to become **Roman Catholics**, and to accept Mexican traditions. The settlers did not. And the situation became tense. **Andrew Jackson** was president of the United States at that time. For the most part, he could do little to influence the situation in Texas. The United States had a treaty of friendship with Mexico. It was to **remain neutral** during the conflict.

Americans in Texas held a convention in April, 1833. They prepared a list of appeals to the leader of Mexico, General **Santa Anna**. The Texas settlers asked Santa Anna to end a tax on goods imported into

the territory. They asked him to **lift a ban** on new settlers from the United States. And they asked that Texas be organized as a separate state of Mexico. One of the Americans, **Stephen Austin**, carried the appeals to Mexico City. He spent six months negotiating with the Mexican government. General Santa Anna promised to honor all the requests except one. He would not make Texas a separate state, although he said that might be possible someday. Stephen Austin was satisfied. He left the Mexican capital to return to Texas. On his way home, to his surprise, Austin was arrested. He was arrested because of a letter he wrote earlier, when his negotiations with Mexican officials seemed to be failing. He had said it might be best if the people declared Texas a separate state. Austin was put in prison in Mexico City for a year and a half.

Austin urged the people of Texas to remain loyal to Mexico. But talk of rebellion already had begun. The settlers already were calling themselves "Texans." Minor **hostilities** broke out between Texans and local Mexican officials. The Mexican army **threatened action**. When Austin returned from prison, he was chosen to negotiate with the commander of Mexican forces. The commander refused to negotiate. It appeared that war would come. The Texans began to organize their own army.

In November, 1835, representatives from all parts of Texas held a convention to discuss the situation. They had no plans to take Texas out of the Mexican Republic. In fact, a proposal to do that was defeated by a large vote. However, the Texans took action to protect themselves against Santa Anna, who had declared himself dictator. They organized a temporary state government. They organized a state army. And they made plans for another convention to begin on March 1st.

Before the Texans could meet again, Santa Anna led an army of 7,000 men across the **Rio Grande River** into Texas. The first soldiers reached **San Antonio** on February 23rd. The Texas forces withdrew to an old Spanish **mission church** called the **Alamo**. On March first, the second Texas convention opened. This time, the representatives voted to declare Texas a free, independent and sovereign republic. They wrote a constitution based on the constitution of the United States. They created a government. David Burnet was named president. And **Sam Houston** was to continue as commander of Texas forces.

On the second day of the convention, a letter came from the Alamo in San Antonio. The letter was addressed to the people of Texas and all Americans. The commander of Texas forces at the Alamo wrote:

"I have been under an artillery attack for 24 hours and have not lost a man. The enemy has demanded our surrender. Otherwise, he said, he will kill every one of us. I have answered his demand with a cannon shot. Our flag still waves proudly from the walls. I shall never surrender or retreat."

"I call on you—in the name of liberty, of patriotism, and everything dear to the American character—to come to our aid with all speed. If my appeal is not answered, I will fight as long as possible, and die like a soldier who never forgets what he owes his own honor and that of his country." The letter from the Alamo closed with the words: "Victory or Death."

Representatives at the convention wanted to leave immediately to go to the aid of the Texans in San Antonio. But Sam Houston told them it was their duty to remain and create a government for Texas. Houston would go there himself with a small force. The help came too late for the 188 men at the Alamo. Santa Anna's forces captured the Spanish mission on March 6th. When the battle ended, not a Texan was left alive. Sam Houston ordered all Texas forces to withdraw northeast—away from the Mexican army.

One group of Texans did not move fast enough. Santa Anna trapped them. He said the Texans would not be harmed if they surrendered. They did. One week later, **they were marched to a field and shot**. Only a few escaped to tell the story. Santa Anna then moved against Sam Houston. He was sure his large army could defeat the remaining Texas force. President Andrew Jackson and Sam Houston were close friends. When told of Houston's retreat, the President pointed to a map of Texas. He said: "If Sam Houston is worth anything, he will make his stand here." Jackson pointed to the mouth of the San Jacinto

River.

The battle of San Jacinto began at four o'clock in the afternoon. There were about 800 Texans. There were two times that many Mexicans. The Mexicans did not expect the retreating Texans to turn and fight. But they did. Shouting "Remember the Alamo!" the Texans ran at the Mexican soldiers. Eighteen minutes later, the battle was over. Santa Anna's army was destroyed. About half of the Mexicans were killed or wounded. The other half were captured. Only two Texans were killed. Twenty-three, including Sam Houston, were wounded.

The Texans found Santa Anna the next day, wearing the clothes of a simple Mexican soldier. Santa Anna begged for mercy. Houston told him: "You might have shown some at the Alamo." Many of the Texans wanted to shoot the Mexican general. But Houston said he was worth more alive than

The battle of defending the Alamo—a defender (Davy Crockett) is clubbing Mexicans with his rifle.

dead. On May 14th, 1836, Texas President Burnet and General Santa Anna signed a treaty. The treaty made Texas independent.

1836 was a presidential election year in the United States. Andrew Jackson had served for eight years. He did not want another term. He supported his Vice President, **Martin Van Buren**. Jackson's opposition to the demands for more states' rights, and his attack on the Bank of the United States, had created problems for his Democratic Party. Texas also was a problem. Slavery was legal in the new Republic of Texas. Most northerners in the United States opposed slavery anywhere. Jackson felt that if he recognized Texas, the Democrats would lose votes in the presidential election. So Jackson decided not to act on Texas until after the election.

Opposition to the Democrats came from a **coalition political party**. Members of the party called themselves **Whigs**. Three Whigs ran for president in 1836 against Martin Van Buren. The Whigs did not expect any of their candidates to win. But they hoped to get enough votes to prevent Van Buren from gaining a majority. Then the House of Representatives would have to decide the election. And a Whig might have a better chance. The plan failed. Van Buren won.

Andrew Jackson had only a few months left as president. It seemed that much of his time was occupied with one question. That was the request by the **Republic of Texas** to become a state of the Union. Jackson wanted to make Texas a state. But more important was the Union itself. The issue of slavery in Texas was critical. Jackson said: "To give statehood to Texas now, or to recognize its independence, would increase the bitterness between the North and South. Nothing is worth this price."

Remember the Alamo
牢记阿拉莫

当特拉维斯上校同他率领的志愿者们在阿拉莫保卫战中流尽最后一滴血时，这座位于得克萨斯的教堂就注定要进入美利坚合众国的史册。如今，阿拉莫已被尊称为"得克萨斯自由的摇篮"（Cradle of Texas Liberty），而 188 名为得克萨斯的自由献出生命的烈士的英勇事迹也成为一个国家的记忆。

美国流行歌曲作家、以《黑衣人》（"The Man in Black"）闻名的约翰尼·卡什（Johnny Cash, 1932—2003）在他的美国建国 200 周年专辑中，用歌声回顾了阿拉莫保卫战这一重大历史事件。

And a hundred and eighty were challenged by **Travis** to die
By the line that he drew with his sword when the battle was nigh
Any man that would fight to the death crossed over
But him that would live, better fly
And over the line went a hundred and seventy nine

Hey Santa Anna, we're killing your soldiers below!
That men, wherever they go will remember the Alamo

Bowie lay dying, but his powder was ready and dry
Flat on his back, Bowie killed him a few in reply
And young **David Crockett** was singing and laughing
With gallantry fears in his eyes
For God and for freedom, a man more than willing to die

Hey Santa Anna, we're killing your soldiers below!
That men, wherever they go will remember the Alamo

And then they sent a young scout from the **battlements, bloody and loud**
With the words of farewell from **a garrison valiant and proud**
"Grieve not little darling, my dying, if Texas is sovereign and free
We'll never surrender and ever with liberty be"

Hey Santa Anna, we're killing your soldiers below!
That men, wherever they go will remember the Alamo

Words, Expressions and Notes

Roman Catholics 罗马天主教徒

Andrew Jackson 安德鲁·杰克逊（1767—1845），美国将军，1812 年率军在新奥尔良打败英军的英雄，后任美国第七任总统（1829—1837）。

remain neutral 保持中立

Santa Anna 圣安纳（1794—1876），墨西哥将军、总统，镇压得克萨斯反叛失败被俘（1836）；在随后的墨西哥战争中（1846—1848）以失败告终；后实行独裁统治（1853—1855），被推翻后流亡国外。

lift a ban 解除禁令

Stephen Austin 史蒂芬·奥斯丁（1793—1836），美国得克萨斯殖民地开拓者

hostilities *n.* 敌视；对抗

threatened action 威胁要采取行动

Rio Grande River 格兰德河，北起落基山脉，朝南流入墨西哥湾，全长三千多公里，其中作为美国与墨西哥界河部分有约两千公里。

San Antonio 圣安东尼奥，得克萨斯南部城市

mission church 教区教堂

Alamo 阿拉莫，原是一座教堂，得克萨斯革命期间被起义者占领作为军事要塞。

Sam Houston 萨姆·休斯敦（1793—1863），得克萨斯共和国总统（1836—1838），得克萨斯并入美国后任美国参议员、得克萨斯州州长，美国内战前夕因拒绝效忠南方而辞职。

they were marched to a field and shot 他们被押送到一片田野并被枪决

Martin Van Buren 马丁·范·布伦（1782—1862），美国第八任总统

coalition political party 联合政党

Whigs 辉格党，美国共和党的前身

Republic of Texas 得克萨斯共和国，成立于得克萨斯革命后，1845 年被并入美国成为得克萨斯州。

Travis（Colonel William Barrett Travis） 特拉维斯上校（1809—1836），美国律师和军人，得克萨斯革命领袖，率领志愿军在保卫阿拉莫教堂的战斗中被墨西哥军队杀害。

By the line that he drew with his sword when the battle was nigh 在战斗即将打响之际，在他用剑划的一道线旁

But him that would live, better fly 要想活命的，赶快走开

Bowie（James Bowie） 鲍伊（1796—1836），得克萨斯美国移民领袖，在阿拉莫战斗中被墨西哥军队杀害。

Flat on his back, Bowie killed him a few in reply 鲍伊（受伤）躺在地上，杀死几个敌人作为回敬

David Crockett 大卫·克罗克特（1786—1836），美国边疆开发者、众议员，其征服边疆的经历在美国广泛流传，在阿拉莫战斗中被墨西哥军队杀害。

With gallantry fears in his eyes 眼里只有英雄豪杰的担忧（担心不能充分展示自己的英勇）

battlements *n.* 城垛

bloody and loud 浑身血迹斑斑

a garrison valiant and proud 一座英勇而自豪的堡垒

Grieve not little darling 亲爱的，不要悲伤

Questions for Comprehension and Discussion

1. Why did many Americans want to move to Texas in the early 1830s?
2. Who was the ruler of Mexico then?
3. Why did the people in Texas take action to protect themselves against Santa Anna?
4. What is Alamo? What happened there?
5. Why has "Remember the Alamo!" become a battle cry in the history of the United States?

$\mathscr{24}$ The Mexican War

墨西哥战争

美国作家亨利·大卫·梭罗（Henry David Thoreau）常常散步锻炼。他注意到，每当他毫无目的、自由自在地漫游时，他总是朝着西方走去。他在 1845 年写道："我一定会走向俄勒冈，而不是走向欧洲。"梭罗的话正好表达了许多美国人同样的感受。这时的美国，领土不断朝西扩展，跨越森林、原野和山岭。在这广阔的土地上，居住着近 2 000 万人民，组成一个拥有 31 个州的联邦。这是一片希望无穷的大地，工业欣欣向荣，农业兴旺发达。

1846 年 5 月的一天，很多人拥到国会听一位来自密苏里州的参议员托马斯·哈特·本顿（Thomas Hart Benton）讲演。他在演说中认为，当时还不属于美国的俄勒冈必须成为美国的一部分。他说："白种人的大篷车已经登上落基山，已经散布在太平洋的海岸，不出几年，那里将生活着庞大的人群。"他甚至还说，美国西进的浪潮迟早会改变整个世界。

本顿的话在美国人心中引发巨大的共鸣。一位杂志记者写道："我们的天命就是要占据整个大陆。"美国从此时起便进入一个所谓"天定命运论时代"（The Age of Manifest Destiny）。这是一个扩张主义盛行的时代，许多年轻人涌向西部，其他人则想着朝阿拉斯加、墨西哥、加勒比海地区，甚至更远的地区扩展。美国与墨西哥的战争就是在这样的背景下爆发的。

美国的"西进运动"既有群众性移民、领土扩张和大规模开发的特点，也起到打压和排斥老牌殖民主义国家英国、法国和西班牙在新大陆势力的作用。这场运动的最大受害者有两个：一个是祖祖辈辈居住在西部的印第安人，而另一个就是主权国家墨西哥。

In the middle 1840s, the United States offered to buy California from Mexico. The government of Mexico refused to negotiate. American President **James Polk** felt that the use of force was the only way to make Mexico negotiate. So, in the spring of 1846, he ordered American soldiers to the Rio Grande River. The Rio Grande formed part of the border between the United States and Mexico.

General **Zachary Taylor** commanded the American force. He sent one of his officers across the river to meet with Mexican officials. The Mexicans protested the movement of the American troops to the Rio Grande. They said the area was Mexican territory. The movement of American troops there, they said, was an act of war. For almost a month, the Americans and the Mexicans kept their positions. Then, on April 25th, General Taylor received word that a large Mexican force had crossed the border a few kilometers up the river. A small force of American soldiers went to investigate. They were attacked. All were killed, wounded, or captured. General Taylor quickly sent a message to President Polk in Washington. It said war had begun.

The message arrived at the White House on May 9th. A few days later, President Polk asked Congress to recognize that war had started. He asked Congress to give him everything he needed to win the war and bring peace to the area. A few members of Congress did not want to declare war against Mexico. They believed the United States was responsible for the situation along the Rio Grande. They were out-voted. President Polk signed the war bill. Later, Polk wrote: "We had not gone to war for conquest. But it was clear that in making peace we would, if possible, get California and other parts of Mexico."

Many Americans opposed what they called "Mr. Polk's war." Whig Party members and **Abolitionists** in the North believed that slave-owners and southerners in Polk's administration had planned the war. They believed the South wanted to win Mexican territory for the purpose of spreading and strengthening slavery. President Polk was troubled by this opposition. But he did not think the war would last long. He thought the United States could quickly force Mexico to sell him the territory he wanted. Polk secretly sent a representative to former Mexican dictator Santa Anna. Santa Anna was **living in exile in Cuba**. Polk's representative said the United States wanted to buy California and some other Mexican territory. Santa Anna said he would agree to the sale, if the United States would help him return to power.

General Zachary Taylor

President Polk ordered the United States navy to let Santa Anna return to Mexico. American ships that blocked the port of **Vera Cruz** permitted the Mexican dictator to land there. Once Santa Anna returned, he failed to honor his promises to Polk. He refused to end the war and sell California. Instead, Santa Anna organized an army to fight the United States. American General Zachary Taylor moved against the Mexicans. He crossed the Rio Grande River. He marched toward Monterrey, the major trading and transportation center of northeast Mexico. The battle for Monterrey lasted three days. The Mexicans surrendered.

Then General Taylor got orders to send most of his forces back to the coast. They were to join other American forces for the invasion of Vera Cruz. While this was happening, Santa Anna was moving his army north. In four months, he had built an army of 20,000 men. When General Taylor learned that Santa Anna was preparing to attack, he left Vera Cruz. He moved his forces into a position to fight Santa Anna.

Santa Anna sent a representative to meet with General Taylor. The representative said the American force had one hour to surrender. Taylor's answer was short: "Tell Santa Anna to go to hell." The battle between the United States and Mexican forces lasted two days. Losses were heavy on both sides. On the second night, Santa Anna's army withdrew from the battlefield. Taylor had won another victory.

Other American forces were victorious, too. General **Winfield Scott** had captured the port of Vera Cruz and was ready to attack Mexico City. **Commodore Robert Stockton** had invaded California and had raised the American flag over the territory. **Stephen Kearny** had seized Santa Fe, the capital of New Mexico, without firing a shot. Still, the war was not over. President Polk's "short" war already had lasted for more than a year. Polk decided to send a special diplomatic representative to Mexico. He gave the diplomat the power to negotiate a peace treaty whenever Mexico wanted to stop fighting.

A **ceasefire** was declared. But attempts to negotiate a peace treaty failed. Santa Anna tried to use the ceasefire to prepare for more fighting. So General Scott ended the ceasefire. His men began their attack on Mexico City. The fighting lasted one week. The government of Mexico surrendered. Santa Anna stepped down as president. Manuel de la Peña y Peña—president of the supreme court—became **acting president**.

On February 2nd, 1848, the United States and Mexico signed a peace treaty. Mexico agreed to give up California and New Mexico. It would recognize the Rio Grande River as the southern border of Texas. The United States would pay Mexico 15 million dollars. It also would pay more than three million dollars in damage claims that Mexico owed American citizens. The terms of the treaty were those set by President Polk. Yet he was not satisfied with just California and New Mexico. He wanted even more territory. But he realized he probably would have to fight for it. And he did not think Congress would agree to extend the war. So Polk sent the peace treaty to the Senate. It was approved. The Mexican Congress also approved it. The war was officially over.

The United States now faced the problem of what to do with the new lands. President Polk wanted to form territorial governments in California and New Mexico. He asked Congress for immediate permission to do that. But the question of slavery delayed quick congressional action. Should the new territories be opened or closed to slavery? Southerners argued that they had the right to take slaves into the new territories. Northerners disagreed. They opposed any further spread of slavery. The real question was this: Did Congress have the power to control or bar slavery in the territories?

Until Texas became a state, almost all national leaders seemed to accept the idea that Congress did have this power. For 50 years, Congress had passed resolutions and laws controlling slavery in United States territories. Northerners believed Congress received the power from the constitution. Southern slave owners disagreed. They believed the power to control slavery remained with the states.

There were some who thought the earlier **Missouri Compromise** could be used to settle the issue of slavery in California, Oregon, and New Mexico. They proposed that the line of the Missouri Compromise be pushed west, all the way to the Pacific Coast. Territory north of the line would be free of slavery. South of the line, slavery would be permitted. Everyone agreed that governments had to be organized in the territories. But there seemed to be no way to settle the issue of slavery.

Words, Expressions and Notes

James Polk　詹姆斯·波尔克（1795—1849），美国第十一任总统（1845—1849），在任期间发动墨西哥战争，兼并得克萨斯，向西部进行领土扩张。

Zachary Taylor　扎卡里·泰勒（1784—1850），美国军队将军，在墨西哥战争中成为英雄后成为美国第十二任总统，就职16个月后病逝。

Abolitionists　*n.* 废除黑奴主义者

living in exile in Cuba　流亡在古巴

Vera Cruz　韦拉克鲁斯，墨西哥港口城市

Winfield Scott　温菲尔德·斯科特（1786—1866），美国军队将领，在墨西哥战争中率部队攻入墨西哥城，从而结束战争。

Commodore Robert Stockton　海军准将罗伯特·斯托克顿

Stephen Kearny　斯蒂芬·卡尼，美国军队将领，在墨西哥战争中两次负伤，曾短时任加利福尼亚州长。其侄儿菲利普·卡尼（Philip Kearny）在墨西哥战争中失去一臂，后成为美国内战时期著名的独臂将军。

ceasefire　*n.* 停火

acting president　代理总统

Missouri Compromise　密苏里妥协案。1820年在密苏里作为自由州或是蓄奴州加入联邦问题上南北双方达成的一项妥协方案。方案主要内容是：密苏里作为蓄奴州加入联邦；从马萨诸塞州分出缅因州作为自由州；美国南北双方的分界线从北纬38°43′改为36°30′。此方案使南北双方在奴隶制上的冲突暂时得到缓解。

Questions for Comprehension and Discussion

1. Why did the United States want to buy California from Mexico?
2. Why did President James Polk have to use force to make the Mexicans negotiate?
3. President James Polk said, "We had not gone to war for conquest. But it was clear that in making peace we would, if possible, get California and other parts of Mexico." What do you think of his idea?
4. Why did the movement of Americans to the West so often lead to conflict with other people?
5. What part did the army play in the nation's expansion westward?

Unit 7   A Nation Divided (1)

25   The Coming of the Civil War

内战的来临

19 世纪中叶，世界上任何国家都没有像美国那样令其他国家感兴趣，也没有任何国家能像美国一样吸引那么多游客。不过，来访者很快便会发现，事实上存在着两个美国：北方的美国和南方的美国。

在北方，新英格兰和中部大西洋沿岸各州是制造业、商业和金融业的中心。这一地区的主要产品有纺织品、木材、服装、机械、皮革和毛织品。同时，航运业也已相当发达，挂着美国国旗的船只，载着各国的货物，航行在世界各国之间。在南方，虽然沿海一带产稻米，路易斯安那州产糖，边区各州种植烟草和其他农作物，还有一些零星制造业，然而，主要的财源却是棉花。由于海湾平原的肥沃黑土得到了充分开发，棉花产量在 19 世纪 50 年代几乎增长了一倍；货车、驳船和火车把大捆大捆的棉花运到北方和南方的市场。棉花为北方的纺织厂提供了原料，而且在全国出口商品中，棉花占了一半以上。

由于发展速度不平衡，北方和南方的利害冲突逐渐明显，双方之间的和睦受到潜在的威胁。南方人对北方商人经营棉花获得的巨大利润愤愤不平，并把南方的落后归咎于北方的扩张。另一方面，北方人则宣称，南方之所以比较落后，应完全归咎于奴隶制度——这是南方经济体制中非常重要的"特有制度"。

在共和国成立初期，当北方各州考虑是否应该立即或逐步解放奴隶时，许多领袖认为奴隶制不久便会完全消失。开国领袖华盛顿曾说，他深切希望能采取一些计划，"使奴隶制度可以在不知不觉之间，逐渐而有效地被废除"。当 1808 年奴隶买卖被禁止时，很多南方人士都认为奴隶制度不需多久就会寿终正寝。

事实却与人们美好的期望背道而驰。在那以后的岁月中，南方开始大规模种植棉花，与此同时，制糖业和烟草业也在发展，这就使得黑人奴隶成为南方农业必不可少的劳动力。新的经济因素，使贩卖奴隶比从前更加有利可图。奴隶制度已成为南方地区的经济基础。

到 19 世纪 50 年代，过去不受关注的奴隶问题突然变得非常急迫，正如杰斐逊曾经预言的那样，"如同午夜的火警钟声"。1852 年，哈丽雅特·比彻·斯托夫人出版了小说《汤姆叔叔的小屋》(Uncle Tom's Cabin)。这本书指出，残暴与奴隶制度是分不开的，自由与奴隶制社会是水火不容的。北方的年轻选民们被小说深深感动。这本书激起了广大人民反对奴隶制度的热情，因为它打动了人的基本情感——对不平等现象的愤慨，以及对遭受无情剥削的弱者的同情。

这时，有一个人不打算把反对奴隶制度仅仅停留在口头上。他要采取大胆行动，用武装斗争的方式推翻奴隶制。他就是约翰·布朗。

During the first half of the 1800s, the question of slavery in the United States remained a problem. The nation's leaders found no way to settle the issue. After the war with Mexico in 1849, when the United States got California and New Mexico, the dispute over slavery became more threatening.

In 1850, President Zachary Taylor died after serving about a year and a half in office. Taylor's Vice President, **Millard Fillmore**, took his place. Early in his administration, President Fillmore signed the **Compromise of 1850**. That Compromise helped settle a national dispute over slavery and the western territories. It ended a crisis between northern and southern states. It prevented a civil war. The 1850 Compromise did not, however, end slavery in the United States. So the issue did not really die. It continued to affect the nation.

An old slave with his grandchildren

In 1852, an American woman published a book about slavery. She called it *Uncle Tom's Cabin*. The woman, **Harriet Beecher Stowe**, wrote the book for one reason. She wanted to show how cruel slavery was. Stowe's words painted a picture of slavery that most people in the North had never seen. They were shocked. Public pressure to end slavery grew strong. Abolitionists wanted to free all slaves immediately.

In the autumn of 1859, the American crisis seemed to cool. There had been elections in most states of the North and South. The people had rejected candidates of extreme ideas and elected moderate men. Only in a few states of the North did anti-slavery extremists rule. And pro-slavery extremists held power in only a few states of the deep south. People saw the elections as a sign of hope that reasonable men might find a way to settle the bitter dispute over slavery. But these hopes fell on October 17th, 1859, with the news that a group of Abolitionists had attacked the Virginia town of **Harpers Ferry**.

The attack was led by **John Brown**, an old anti-slavery extremist. Many believed him insane. He had gone to Kansas and fought bitterly against pro-slavery forces. Once, to answer an attack on the town of Lawrence, Brown and his men pulled five men and boys from their homes and murdered them. The wife of one of the men said Brown told her: "If a man stands between me and what I believe to be right, I will take his life as coolly as I would eat my breakfast."

Brown lost a son in a pro-slavery attack on his home at Osawatomie, Kansas. Brown and his friends were forced to flee. They watched as the pro-slavery men burned the town. Brown shook with grief and anger. "I have only a short time to live," he said, "only one death to die. And I will die fighting for this cause. There will be no more peace in this land until slavery is done for. I will give them something else to do than to extend slave territory. I will carry this war into the South."

To fight a war against slavery, Brown needed money and guns. He went to Massachusetts and New York. He spoke at town meetings and met privately with Abolitionist leaders. In these private talks, Brown said it was too late to settle the slave question through politics or any other peaceful way. He said the only answer was a slave rebellion. It would be bloody, Brown said, and this was terrible. But slavery itself was a terrible wrong—the same as murder. Only blood, he said, would wash away the wrongs of slavery. Brown said God meant for him to begin this rebellion by invading Virginia with a military force he already was organizing. Brown said even if the rebellion failed, it would probably lead to a civil war between North and South. In such a war, he said, the North would break the chains of the black man on the battlefield.

Brown won the support of a group of Abolitionist leaders. They formed a secret committee and called themselves the "Secret Six." They agreed to advise Brown and, more importantly, to raise 1,000 dollars for him. From New England, Brown went to Chatham, Canada. He went there for a secret convention he had called to form a revolutionary government. This government would rule all the slave territory that Brown and his men could capture. Forty-six representatives went to the convention—34 Negroes and 12 whites. Brown told them of his plan. He said he was sure that southern slaves were ready for rebellion. He said they would rise up at the first sign of a leader who wished to break their chains.

"But what if troops are brought against you?" one man asked. Brown answered that his men would fight in the mountains, where a small force could stop a much larger one. He said his men would be well-trained in mountain fighting. Brown said he expected his small force to grow much larger. He would invite the slaves he freed to join his army. And he said he thought that all the free Negroes of the North would come to fight slavery with him. The representatives approved Brown's **constitution**. And they named him commander-in-chief.

Brown had decided to strike at Harpers Ferry, a town of about 2,500 people. It was in northern Virginia about 100 kilometers north of Washington. Harpers Ferry was built on a narrow finger of land where the Shenandoah River flowed into the Potomac River. There were two bridges. One crossed the Shenandoah. The other, a railroad bridge, crossed the Potomac to Maryland. John Brown chose Harpers Ferry because there was a factory there that made guns for the army. There also was an arsenal where several million dollars' worth of military equipment was kept. Brown needed the guns and equipment for the slave army he hoped to form.

Old Brown arrived at Harpers Ferry early in July, 1859. Two of his sons, Owen and Oliver, and another man came with him. They rented an old house on a farm in Maryland not far from Harpers Ferry. Brown told people that he was a cattle buyer from New York. Brown's men joined him, one or two at a time, over the next several months. They traveled at night so no one would see them. Once they reached the farm house, they had to stay in hiding. Week by week, the little force grew. But it grew too slowly. By the end of summer, there were still less than 20 men hiding in the old house. Brown wrote letters to his supporters in the North. He asked for more money and more men. He got little of either. His supporters were afraid. Too many people knew of Brown's plans. The "Secret Six" feared they would face criminal charges if Brown attacked Harpers Ferry. Brown's men grew tired of the small, crowded rooms of the farm house. Brown knew he must act soon or his young men would begin leaving.

On Saturday, October 15th, three men arrived to join the group. One of them brought 600 dollars in gold for Brown's use. Brown saw the gold as a sign that God wanted him to act. He told his men they would strike the next night. Brown held **religious services** Sunday morning and prayed for God to help him free the slaves. Then he called his men around him to explain to them his battle plan. They would seize the two bridges at Harpers Ferry and close them. Next, they would capture the **armory** and the rifle factory. They would capture as many people as possible. They would use the people as hostages for protection against any soldiers that might be sent against them.

The army had no men near Harpers Ferry. Brown believed he would have all the time he needed. He believed his only opposition might be local groups of **militia**. He did not fear these civilian soldiers. The old man thought he and his men could hold Harpers Ferry until slaves in the area rebelled and joined them. Brown knew that Maryland and western Virginia were full of people opposed to slavery. He expected many of them to come to his aid. The 22 men rested until dark, listening to rain hit the roof of the farm house.

About eight o'clock, Brown called his group. "Men," he said, "get your weapons. We are going to the Ferry." A wagon was brought out and a horse tied to it. In the wagon were a few tools and some extra guns. Brown climbed into the wagon and started it toward town. Two of his men stepped out in front of the wagon, leading the way. The others walked behind. It was a dark and cold night. A light rain was falling. There was no one else on the road. After a time, they reached the high ground above the Potomac. Below them, across the river, lay the town of Harpers Ferry. Most of the town was sleeping. Only a few lights shone through the rain. John Brown was ready for his final struggle against slavery.

Words, Expressions and Notes

Millard Fillmore　米勒德·菲尔莫尔（1800—1874），美国第十三任总统（1850—1853），对奴隶制妥协，签署奴隶逃亡法。

Compromise of 1850　《1850年妥协案》，南北双方在奴隶制问题上的又一次妥协，主要内容是：加利福尼亚以自由州加入联邦，但允许南方奴隶主到北方自由州搜寻逃走的奴隶。这一妥协案为南北双方今后更大的冲突埋下了隐患。

Uncle Tom's Cabin　《汤姆叔叔的小屋》

Harriet Beecher Stowe　哈丽雅特·比彻·斯托（1811—1896），美国女作家，其长篇小说《汤姆叔叔的小屋》对反对奴隶制的斗争起过推动作用。

Harpers Ferry　哈珀斯渡口

John Brown　约翰·布朗（1800—1859），美国激进的废奴主义者，在袭击弗吉尼亚哈珀斯渡口军火库的战斗中受伤被捕，后被判处绞刑。

constitution　*n.* 章程

religious services　宗教仪式

armory　*n.* 军械库

militia　*n.* 民兵

Questions for Comprehension and Discussion

1. Why did the dispute over slavery become more threatening after the war with Mexico in 1849 and after the United States got California and New Mexico?
2. Why did people in the North get shocked when they read *Uncle Tom's Cabin*?
3. What made John Brown say "I have only a short time to live"?
4. John said that he was sure that Southern slaves were ready for rebellion. Do you think so? Why?
5. Why did Brown decide to strike at Harpers Ferry, a town of about 2,500 people?
6. What do you think of John Brown's plan? Were he and his men well-prepared for the attack?

26 John Brown's Raid at Harpers Ferry

约翰·布朗袭击哈珀斯渡口

在很长一段时间里，反对奴隶制度运动的主要方式，是帮助奴隶们逃到北方的安全地带，或是越境潜到加拿大去。经过周密组织，被称为"地下铁道"的秘密逃亡路线，在 19 世纪 30 年代已遍布北方各地，其中以西北地区最为成功。仅在俄亥俄一州，1830 年至 1860 年间，获得帮助而逃亡成功的奴隶，估计不下 4 万人。各地反奴隶制度组织也急剧增加，到 1849 年总数已达约 2 000 个，拥有会员约 20 万人。

19 世纪 50 年代，北方各州的废奴主义情绪越来越强烈，并受到自由土地运动的鼓动，该运动强烈反对把奴隶制度发展到未设州的地区。而这时南方的政治领袖、专业人士以及大多数教会牧师在北方废奴主义的压力下，不仅不再为奴隶制度感到歉意，反而成为这个制度的狂热支持者，认为奴隶制度是必要而永久的制度。他们甚至宣称："奴隶制度是一个国家从野蛮走向文明的阶梯。"

随着南北双方在奴隶制度这个老问题上的争论变得越来越激烈，一位高而瘦的伊利诺伊州的律师从全国风起云涌的政治辩论中脱颖而出，他就是亚伯拉罕·林肯。

林肯一向认为奴隶制度是一种罪恶。他在 1854 年的一次演说中强调，国家一切立法都必须建立在限制奴隶制度和最后予以废除的原则之上。1858 年，林肯在伊利诺伊州参议员竞选中成为伊利诺伊州老资格参议员斯蒂芬·道格拉斯的对手。6 月 17 日，林肯在接受共和党提名时发表了一篇重要演说，为从此以后的美国历史定下了基调："分裂之家不能持久。我相信我们的政府不能永远忍受一半奴役一半自由的状况。我不认为联邦会瓦解，我也不认为这个国家会没落——不过，我认为，分裂的局面将会终止。"尽管道格拉斯最后以微弱多数连任参议员，但林肯也因此成了全国大名鼎鼎的政治家。

当关于奴隶制的辩论方兴未艾之际，反奴隶制的狂热人士约翰·布朗率人袭击弗吉尼亚哈珀斯渡口的联邦军械库，使南北之间的冲突更加尖锐。1859 年 10 月的这次袭击从战术上讲是彻头彻尾的失败，但就布朗的更大目标而言，他取得了辉煌的胜利：它引起了全国的关注，加剧了地区之间的紧张状况，并且导致了全国性内战的最后爆发。

With his force of less than twenty men, John Brown moved through the darkness down to the bridge that crossed the Potomac River. Two men left the group to cut the telegraph lines east and west of Harpers Ferry. At the bridge, Brown's men surprised a railroad guard. They told him he was their prisoner. The guard thought they were joking until he saw their guns. Once across the bridge, Brown and his men moved quickly. They captured a few people in the street and another guard at the front gate of the government armory. They seized the armory, then crossed the street and seized the **supply center**. Millions of dollars' worth of military equipment was kept there.

After leaving a few men to guard the prisoners, Brown and the others went to the gun factory across town. They seized the few people who were there and captured the factory. **Without firing a shot**, Brown now controlled the three places he wanted in Harpers Ferry. Brown planned to use the people he had captured as hostages. The militia would not attack if there was danger of harming the prisoners.

Brown had decided to capture, as his best hostage, Colonel Lewis Washington. The Colonel was a **descendant** of president George Washington. He lived on a big farm near Harpers Ferry. Brown sent some of his men to capture the old colonel and free his slaves. They returned from the Washington farm after midnight. They brought Colonel Washington and ten slaves. They also captured another farmer and his son. The slaves were given spears and told to guard the prisoners. Then, at the far end of the Potomac River bridge, the first shots were fired. Brown's son, Watson, and another man fired at a railroad guard who refused to halt. A bullet struck his head, but did not hurt him seriously. The guard raced back across the bridge to the railroad station. He cried out that a group of armed men had seized the bridge.

A photograph of John Brown about three years before the Harpers Ferry Raid

A few minutes later, a train from the west arrived at Harpers Ferry. The wounded guard warned the trainmen of the danger at the bridge. Two of the trainmen decided to investigate. They walked toward the bridge. Before they could reach it, bullets began **whizzing past them**. They ran back to the train and moved it farther from the bridge.

Brown finally agreed to let the train pass over the bridge and continue on to Baltimore. The train left at sunrise. By this time, word of Brown's attack had spread to Charles Town, more than 12 kilometers away. Officials called out the militia, ordering the men of Charles Town to get ready to go to the aid of Harpers Ferry. Soon after sunrise, men began arriving at Harpers Ferry from other towns in the area. They took positions above the armory and started shooting at it.

Brown saw that he was surrounded. His only hope was to try to negotiate a ceasefire and offer to release his 30 hostages, if the militia would let him and his men go free. Brown sent out one of his men and one of the prisoners with a white flag. The excited crowd refused to recognize the white flag. They seized Brown's man and carried him away. Brown moved his men and the most important of his hostages into a small brick building at the armory. Then he sent out two more of his men with a prisoner to try to negotiate a ceasefire. One of them was his son, Watson.

This time, the crowd opened fire. Watson and the other raider were wounded. Their prisoner escaped to safety. Watson was able to crawl back to the armory. One of the youngest of Brown's men, William Leeman, tried to escape. He ran from the armory and jumped into the Potomac, planning to swim across the river. He did not get far. A group of militia saw him and began shooting. Leeman was forced to hide behind a rock in the middle of the river. Two men went out to the rock with guns and shot him. His body lay in the river for two days. Later, more people were killed. One was the mayor of Harpers Ferry, Fontaine Beckham.

After the mayor's death, a mob went to the hotel where one of Brown's men had been held since he was seized earlier in the day. They pulled him from the hotel and took him to the bridge over the river. Several members of the mob put guns to his head and fired. They pushed his body off the bridge and into the water. Across town, three of Brown's men were in trouble at the gun factory. The factory was built on an island in the Shenandoah River. The island was now surrounded by militia. Forty of the soldiers attacked the factory from three sides. They pushed the three raiders back to a small building next to the river. The three men fought as long as possible. Then they jumped through a window into the river. They tried to swim to safety. Men with guns were waiting for them. Bullets fell around the three like rain. One man was hit. He died instantly. Another was wounded. He was pulled to land and left to die. The third man escaped death. He was captured and held for trial.

All through the afternoon and evening, Brown's men at the armory continued to exchange shots with the militia. Several more on both sides were killed or wounded. One of those was another of Brown's sons, Oliver. He was shot and seriously wounded. Night fell. Then, a militia officer, Captain Sinn, walked up to the small building held by Brown. He shouted to the men inside that he wished to talk. Brown opened the door and let him in. For almost an hour, the two men talked. They talked about slavery and the right to rebel against the government.

Brown was **furious** that the crowd outside had refused to honor his **white flag of truce** earlier in the day. He told Sinn that his men could have killed unarmed men and women, but did not do so. "That is not quite correct," Captain Sinn said. "Mayor Beckham had no gun when he was shot."

"Then I can only say I am most sad to hear it," said Brown.

"Men who take up guns against the government," said Sinn, "must expect to be shot down like dogs."

The President of the United States in 1859 was **James Buchanan**. When Buchanan learned of the attack, he wanted immediate action. He sent a force of **Marines** to Harpers Ferry, under the command of **army Colonel Robert E. Lee**.

Brown and his men were trapped inside the brick building. They held a few hostages whom they hoped to exchange for their freedom. Colonel Lee wrote a message to John Brown demanding his surrender. He did not think Brown would surrender peaceably. So, he planned to attack as soon as Brown rejected the message. As expected, Brown refused to surrender. He said he and his men had the right to go free. As soon as Brown spoke, the signal was given. The Marines attacked. They broke open a small hole in the door of the brick building. One by one, the Marines moved through the hole. They fought hand-to-hand against the men inside. After a brief fight, they won. John Brown's rebellion was crushed.

A few hours after Brown was captured, the Governor of Virginia and three Congressmen arrived in Harpers Ferry. They wanted to question Brown. Brown had been wounded in the final attack. He was weak from the loss of blood. But he welcomed the chance to explain his actions. The officials first asked where Brown got the money to organize his raid. Brown said he raised most of it himself. He refused to give the names of any of his supporters. Then the officials asked why Brown had come to Harpers Ferry. "We came to free the slaves," Brown said, "and only that."

He continued: "I think that **you are guilty of a great wrong against God and humanity**. I believe anyone would be perfectly right to interfere with you, so far as to **free those you wickedly hold in slavery**. I think I did right. You had better—all you people of the South—prepare yourselves for a settlement sooner than you are prepared for it.

"You may get rid of me very easily. I am nearly gone now. But this question is still to be settled... this Negro question, I mean. That is not yet ended."

The raid on Harpers Ferry increased the bitterness of the national dispute over slavery. Members of the Democratic Party called the raid a plot by the Republican Party. Republican leaders denied the charge. They said the raid was the work of one man—one madman—John Brown. Still, they said, he had acted for good reason: to end slavery in America. Southern newspapers condemned Brown. Some said his raid was an act of war. Some demanded that he be executed as a thief and murderer. Many southerners said all of the North was responsible for the raid. They believed all northerners wanted a slave rebellion in the South. And it was such a rebellion that southerners feared more than anything else. New measures were approved throughout the South to prevent this. Military law was declared in some areas. Slave owners threatened to beat or hang any Negro who even looked rebellious.

The Governor of Virginia decided to try Brown in a state court. He believed a federal court trial would take too long. If Brown were not brought to trial quickly, he said, people might attack the jail and kill him.

John Brown's lawyers tried to show that his family had a history of madness. They tried to prove that Brown, too, was mad. They asked the court to declare him innocent because of **insanity**. Brown protested. He said the lawyers were just trying to save his life. He did not want such a defense. The matter of insanity was dropped.

Brown's lawyers then argued that he was not guilty of the three crimes with which he was charged. First, they said, he could not be guilty of treason against Virginia, because he was not a citizen of Virginia. Second, he could not be guilty of plotting a slave rebellion, because he had never **incited** slaves against their owners. And third, he could not be guilty of murder, because he had killed only in self-defense. The trial lasted five days. The jury found John Brown guilty of all three charges.

John Brown was executed on December 2nd, 1859. His death created a wave of public emotion throughout the country. In the North, people mourned. One man wrote: "The events of the last month or two have done more to build northern opposition to slavery than anything which has ever happened before. . . than all the anti-slavery pamphlets and books that have ever been written."

In the South, people cheered. But their happiness at Brown's punishment was mixed with anger at those who honored him. As the nation prepared for a presidential election year, **the South renewed its promise to defend slavery. . . or leave the Union.**

Words, Expressions and Notes

supply center （军事）物资储存中心
without firing a shot 未放一枪一弹
descendant n. 后代
whizzing past them （子弹）从身旁嗖嗖地飞过
furious a. 愤怒的
white flag of truce 休战的白旗
James Buchanan 詹姆斯·布坎南（1791—1868），第十五任美国总统（1857—1861）
Marines n. （美国）海军陆战队
army Colonel Robert E. Lee 陆军上校罗伯特·李（1807—1870），美国军人，内战爆发后任南方军

总司令，以出色的战略战术多次击败北方军队，最终失败投降。
you are guilty of a great wrong against God and humanity 你们因违背上帝和人性而罪恶深重
free those you wickedly hold in slavery 解救那些处于你们邪恶奴役之下的人们
insanity n. 精神错乱
incited v. 煽动
the South renewed its promise to defend slavery. . . or leave the Union 南方重申了它的诺言：要么保卫奴隶制，要么离开联邦

Questions for Comprehension and Discussion

1. Why did John Brown and his men want to attack the gun factory?
2. Why did Brown want to capture Colonel Lewis Washington?
3. What happened when Brown wanted to negotiate a ceasefire?
4. John Brown said when he was captured, "You may get rid of me very easily. I am nearly gone now. But this question is still to be settled. . . this Negro question, I mean. That is not yet ended." What do you think of his words?
5. Why were there different reactions toward John Brown's death between the North and the South?
6. How did John Brown's raid help to move the nation toward the Civil War?

27 The First Shots of the Civil War

内战第一枪

布朗组织的武装起义虽然失败了，但其意义和影响都是非常深远的。这次起义实际上给未来的废奴运动指明了唯一的正确方向——武装斗争。1860 年，远在欧洲的马克思就指出：“现在世界上发生的最大事件，一是由于布朗的死而展开的奴隶运动，二是俄国的奴隶运动。”

1860 年的总统选举是美国历史上斗争最为激烈的选举之一。尽管南方各州都拒绝林肯，但在北方工人和西部农民的积极支持下，林肯成功当选。选举结果刚一出来，南卡罗来纳州立即召开特别大会，宣布“南卡罗来纳及其他各州，在美利坚合众国的名义下所组成的联邦，从此解散”。南方其他各州立即仿效南卡罗来纳的做法，并于 1861 年 2 月 8 日成立了“南部邦联”。

1861 年 3 月 4 日，亚伯拉罕·林肯宣誓就任美国第十六任总统。在就职演说中，他拒绝承认这一分裂，认为这在“法律上是无效的”，同时呼吁大家努力恢复团结。但是南方人对此不仅置若罔闻，反而在 4 月 12 日，炮轰南卡罗来纳州查尔斯顿港口联邦军队驻守的萨姆特要塞。美国内战的第一枪终于打响。刹那间，北美大陆战争阴云密布，南北双方剑拔弩张。

北方人迟疑不决的观望态度被萨姆特要塞的炮火一扫而光。林肯总统最初准备征召 75 000 名志愿军，其中分配给俄亥俄州的名额仅为 13 000 人，但该州竟有 30 万人涌入征兵站。北方人民的参战热情由此可见一斑。

在南方，人们的情绪更是高昂，因为他们相信他们的事业，就如同他们的先辈与英国殖民者的战斗一样是正义的，并且会得到全世界的支持。在最初退出联邦的 7 个州里，人们迅速响应他们的“总统”杰斐逊·戴维斯的号召积极备战。这时，南北双方都焦急地等待着迄今仍忠于联邦的各奴隶制州表态。4 月 17 日，弗吉尼亚州迈出决定性的一步，宣布脱离联邦。阿肯色、田纳西和北卡罗来纳亦很快效仿。弗吉尼亚州的退出是对联邦最沉重的打击，因为出生于该州的元老政治家们不仅是美国独立革命和制定宪法的中坚，而且其中有 5 人当过总统。另外，弗吉尼亚的退出还使联邦军队遭受巨大损失：著名军事指挥官罗伯特·李上校为忠于他的州，辞去了指挥联邦部队的职务。

战争的火药味在整个北美大陆弥漫。即将交战的南北双方，都以为自己胜券在握，严重低估了对方的斗志和实力。尤其是在北方，人们甚至乐观地认为，“三十天内就可以有效地平息这场地方性骚乱”。他们未曾料到的是，这场他们原以为能够轻而易举结束的战斗，将会演变成一场纵横数千公里的惨烈厮杀，而参加搏斗的双方，都将要付出几十万血肉之躯的沉重代价。

By February 1st, 1861, seven Southern states had withdrawn from the United States of America. They created their own independent nation, the **Confederate States of America**. The South **seceded** because a Republican, Abraham Lincoln, had been elected president. Southerners believed Lincoln would support a constitutional ban on slavery. They were afraid their way of life **was about to end**.

On a cold and cloudy day in March, 1861, Abraham Lincoln became the 16th president of the United States. In his inaugural speech, the new president announced the policy he would follow toward the Southern states that had left the Union. Lincoln said no state had a legal right to secede. He said the Union could not be broken. He said he would enforce federal laws in every state. And he promised not to surrender any federal property in the states that seceded. Lincoln said if force was necessary to protect the Union, then force would be used. His policy was soon tested.

Just before sunrise on the morning of April 12th, 1861, the first shot was fired in the American Civil War. A heavy mortar roared, sending a shell high over the harbor at Charleston, South Carolina. The shell dropped and exploded above **Fort Sumter**, a United States fort on an island in the harbor. The explosion was a signal for all southern guns surrounding the fort to open fire. Shell after shell smashed into the island fort. The booming of the cannons woke the people of Charleston. They rushed to the harbor and cheered as the bursting shells lighted the dark sky.

At Fort Sumter, Major Robert Anderson and his men waited three hours before firing back at the Confederate guns. Anderson could not use his most powerful cannons. They were in the open at the top of the fort, where there was no protection for the gunners. Too many of his small force would be lost if he tried to fire these guns. So Anderson had his men fire the smaller cannon from better-protected positions. These, however, did not do much damage to the Confederate guns.

The shelling continued all day. A big cloud of smoke rose high in the air over Fort Sumter. The smoke was seen by United States navy ships a few miles outside Charleston Harbor. They had come with the ship bringing food for the men at Sumter. There were soldiers on these ships. But they could not reach the fort to help Major Anderson. Confederate boats blocked the entrance to the harbor. And confederate guns could destroy any ship that tried to enter. The commander of the naval force, Captain Fox, had hoped to move the soldiers to Sumter in small boats. But the sea was so rough that the small boats could not be used. Fox could only watch and **hope for calmer seas**.

Confederate shells continued to smash into Sumter throughout the night and into the morning of the second day. The fires at Fort Sumter burned higher. And smoke filled the rooms where soldiers still tried to fire their cannons. About noon, three men arrived at the fort in a small boat. One of them was Louis Wigfall, a former United States senator from Texas, now a Confederate officer. He asked to see Major Anderson. "I come from **General Beauregard**," he said. "It is time to put a stop to this, sir. The flames are raging all around you. And you have defended your flag bravely. Will you leave, sir?" Wigfall asked.

Major Anderson was ready to stop fighting. His men had done all that could be expected of them. They had fought well against a much stronger enemy. Anderson said he would surrender, if he and his men could leave with honor. Wigfall agreed. He told Anderson to lower his flag and the firing would stop.

Down came the United States flag. And up went the white flag of surrender. The battle of Fort Sumter was over. More than 4,000 shells had been fired during the 33 hours of fighting. But no one on either side was killed. One United States soldier, however, was killed the next day when a cannon exploded as Anderson's men prepared to leave the fort.

President Abraham Lincoln asked the states of the Union for 75,000 soldiers to help end the Southern rebellion. Northern states quickly formed military groups and sent them to Washington. But border states—those between the North and South—refused to send any. Some prepared to leave the Union and join the Confederacy.

The first state to secede after the start of the Civil War was Virginia. It was an important state because of its location. It was just across the Potomac River from Washington. Virginia's decision to secede cost the Union a military commander of great ability. He was Robert E. Lee. Lee was a Virginian and had served in the United States army for more than thirty years. Lincoln asked him to be head of the army when General Winfield Scott retired. Lee said he could not accept the job. He said he opposed **secession** and loved the Union. But, he said, he could not make war on his home state. Lee resigned from the army. He did not really want to fight at all. But soon after his resignation, he agreed to command the forces of Virginia.

The storm of battle spread across the United States in the summer of 1861. For several months, small fights had flashed like lightning around the edge of this great storm. Soldiers fought **pro-southern rioters** in the streets of Baltimore and Saint Louis. A Confederate supporter shot and killed a famous young officer from the North. Untrained soldiers of both sides fought in the mountains of western Virginia. So far, the fighting **had not claimed many lives**. But very soon, the storm would **break in all its fury**.

For more than a month, **General Irvin McDowell** had been building a Union army in northern Virginia, just across the Potomac River from

The rebel flag flew over Fort Sumter on April 14th, 1860, as troops began cleanup after their successful bombardment.

Washington. He had more than 30,000 men at bases in Arlington and Alexandria. Late in June, McDowell received orders: "March against the Confederate army of General Pierre Beauregard."

General McDowell's huge Union army left Arlington on the afternoon of July 16. It was a hot day, and the road was dusty. The march was not well organized, and the men traveled slowly. They stopped at every stream to drink and wash the dust from their faces. Some of the soldiers left the road to pick fruits and berries from bushes along the way. To some of those who watched this army pass, the lines of soldiers in bright clothes looked like a long circus parade. Most of these men had not been soldiers long. Their bodies were soft, and they tired quickly. It took them four days to travel the 45 kilometers to Centreville, the final town before **Bull Run**. The battle would start the next morning—Sunday, July 21st.

The road from Washington was crowded early Sunday morning with horses and wagons bringing people to watch the great battle. Hundreds of men and women watched the fight from a hill near Centreville. Below them was Bull Run. But the battleground was

General "Stonewall" Jackson

covered so thickly with trees that the crowds saw little of the fighting. They could, however, see the smoke of battle. And they could hear the sounds of shots and exploding shells. From time to time, Union officers would ride up the hill to report what a great victory their troops were winning.

In the first few hours of the battle, Union forces were winning. McDowell had moved most of his men to the left side of Beauregard's army. They attacked with artillery and pushed the Confederate forces back. It seemed that the Confederate defense would break. Some of the Southern soldiers began to run. But others stood and fought. One Confederate officer, trying to prevent his troops from moving back, pointed to a group led by **General T. J. Jackson** of Virginia. "Look!" He shouted. "There is Jackson... standing like a stone wall! Fight like the Virginians!"

The Confederate troops refused to break. The fighting was fierce. The air was full of flying bullets. A newsman wrote that the whole valley was boiling with dust and smoke. A Confederate soldier told his friend, "Them Yankees are just marching up and being shot to hell." Neither side would give up. Then, a large group of **Johnston**'s troops arrived by train and joined in the fight. Suddenly, Union soldiers stopped fighting and began pulling back. General McDowell and his officers tried to stop the retreat, but failed. Their men wanted no more fighting.

The fleeing Union soldiers threw down their guns and equipment, thinking only of escape. Many did not stop until they reached Washington. It was a bitter defeat. But it made the North recognize the need for a real army—one trained and equipped for war.

Words, Expressions and Notes

Confederate States of America （美国）南部邦联

seceded *v.* 退出，脱离

was about to end 即将结束

Fort Sumter 萨姆特要塞，美国内战第一枪在此打响。

hope for calmer seas 期待着大海更加平静一些

General Beauregard 博勒加德将军，南方军将领

secession *n.* 分离

pro-southern rioters 支持南方的聚众闹事者

had not claimed many lives 还未造成很大的伤亡

break in all its fury 猛烈地爆发

General Irvin McDowell 欧文·麦克道威尔准将，北方军将领

Bull Run 公牛溪，南北双方在内战中的第一次大战之地。战役以南方联军的胜利结束，北方军死伤约2 900 人，南方联军约2 000 人。此战役既鼓舞了南方军队的士气，也使北方真正意识到内战的艰巨性。

General T. J. Jackson 托马斯·杰克逊将军（1824—1863），南方军传奇人物，在公牛溪战役中获得"石墙杰克逊"（Stonewall Jackson）的绰号，1863 年在自己人的走火事件中受伤致死。

Johnston（Joseph Eggleston） 约瑟夫·约翰斯顿将军（1807—1891），南方联军上将，从未战败，但与南方"总统"戴维斯长期不和，1865 年向北方军将领谢尔曼将军投降。

Questions for Comprehension and Discussion

1. Why did some Southern states withdraw from the United States in 1861?
2. Why did Lincoln want to use force to protect the Union?
3. What happened at Charleston, South Carolina in April 12th, 1861?
4. Why had Major Anderson surrendered to Confederate forces in Fort Sumter?
5. What did Robert E. Lee do after he resigned from the Union army?
6. The battle of Bull Run was considered the first important battle during the Civil War. Who won the battle? How did a Confederate general named Thomas Jackson get his nickname "Stonewall"?

28 The Battle of Shiloh

西洛大战

    1861 年的夏天，参战双方都非常渴望能够早日投入战斗并赢得胜利。就资源而言，北方占有决定性的优势，它拥有 23 个州，2 200 万的人口，而南方只有 11 个州和 900 万人口。北方在工业上的优势，更超过其人力上的优势，它有制造武器、弹药、生产服装及其他各种用品的设备。同样，北方的铁路网，也有助于联邦军队取胜。

    但是，从军事的角度看，南方却强于北方。首先，南方各州早就为战争在作准备，前任总统布坎南及其内阁在下台之前就把相当多的武器弹药运往南方，同时还给南方派去同情奴隶制的军官。"南部邦联"成立后，他们大量夺取属于联邦军队的武器和兵工厂。其次，南方因维持其奴隶制的需要，常年都组建民兵。战争打响后，这些人很快就转为正规军。第三，南方人认为他们是为自己的独立而战，士气异常高昂。此外，南方军队还拥有一些杰出的军事指挥官。

    然而，乐观的气氛笼罩着整个北方，甚至连林肯总统本人对战争也抱有不切合实际的看法。与当时北方的普遍舆论一样，他认为只要占据了"南部邦联"建立在弗吉尼亚的"首都"里士满，南方政权自然就会垮台。"向里士满进军！"的口号一度响彻整个北方。据一个士兵事后回忆，当时北方士兵个个摩拳擦掌，跃跃欲试，"唯恐自己会错过进攻里士满的战役"。然而，当北军在"公牛溪"战役中首次与南军正面交锋时，当 36 000 人的北方大军在"石墙"杰克逊将军的铜墙铁壁前败下阵来仓皇逃窜时，乐观的情绪才开始止步于严酷的现实。由于战场距华盛顿如此之近，北方的领袖们十分害怕南方军队会乘机攻打首都。此刻他们才意识到，训练一支装备精良的正规部队有多么紧迫。国会立即通过法案，授权总统召集 50 万志愿军。

    林肯在战争初期犯下的最大错误莫过于委任乔治·麦克莱伦为陆军总司令。事实证明，他是一个只会纸上谈兵的军事庸才，一个嘴上夸夸其谈内心胆小如鼠的人。他整天忙于制订军事计划，从事军队的组织和检阅，然后就是寻找各种借口，不让军队投入战斗。

    就在麦克莱伦无休止地军事息工的同时，北方的另一位军事指挥官却在田纳西州西洛大战中脱颖而出，他就是尤利塞斯·格兰特。当北方的人们在战役结束后得知自己的军队死伤数目高达 13 000 人后，愤怒地要求林肯总统解除格兰特的职务。林肯总统回答道："我离不开这个人，因为他敢于战斗。"事实证明，只有依靠像格兰特这样勇猛顽强、敢于战斗、不怕牺牲的军事指挥官，北方才能最终打败南方获得内战的胜利。

    In July, 1861, Union soldiers of the North and Confederate soldiers of the South fought the first major battle in America's Civil War. They clashed at Manassas, or Bull Run, Virginia, less than 50 kilometers from Washington. The Union soldiers fought furiously. But two large Confederate forces broke the Union attack.

    Northerners had expected to win the battle of Bull Run. They believed the Confederacy would fall if the Union won a big military victory early in the war. Now, however, there was great fear that southern soldiers would seize Washington. The Union needed to build and train an army quickly. President Abraham Lincoln named General **George McClellan** to do this. McClellan was 34 years old. The young general had two important tasks. He must defend Washington from attack. And he must build an army to

strike at enemy forces in Virginia. McClellan wasted no time. He put thousands of troops into position around the city. And he built 48 forts. After this rush of activity, however, little more happened for a long time. McClellan told his wife: "I shall **take my own time** to make an army that will be sure of success. As soon as I feel my army is well-organized and well-trained and strong enough, I will force the rebels to a battle."

General George McClellan

McClellan kept making excuses for why he would not move against the enemy. His excuses became a continuing source of trouble for President Lincoln. The public, the press, and politicians all demanded that McClellan do something. They wanted to win the war... and win it right away.

McClellan commanded the biggest army in the Union, the **Army of the Potomac**. But it was not the only army. Others were battling Confederate forces in the west. The Confederates had moved up through Tennessee into the border state of Kentucky. They built forts and other defensive positions across the Southern part of the state. They also blocked as many railroads and rivers as they could. Their job was to keep Union forces from invading the South through Kentucky. One of the Union Generals in the area was **Ulysses Grant**. Grant had served in the army for 20 years. He had fought in America's war against Mexico and had won honors for his bravery. When that war ended, he was sent to an army base far from his wife and children. He did not like being without them. And he did not like being an officer in peace time. Grant began to drink too much alcohol. He began to be a problem. In 1854, he was asked to leave the army. When the Civil War started, Grant organized a group of unpaid soldiers in Illinois. With the help of a member of Congress, he was named a General. All of the other Union generals knew Ulysses Grant. Few had any faith in his abilities. They were sure he would always fail.

Grant, however, had faith in himself and his men. He believed he could force Confederate soldiers to withdraw from both Kentucky and Tennessee. Then he would be free to march directly into the deep south—Mississippi. Two Confederate forts stood in Grant's way. They were in Tennessee, close to the Kentucky border. United States navy gunboats captured the first, Fort Henry, on the Tennessee River. That fort was easy to attack and not well-defended. The fighting was over by the time Grant and his men got there. The second, Fort Donelson, was nearby on the Cumberland River. It was stronger and defended by 20,000 soldiers. Grant surrounded the fort and let the navy gunboats shell it. The fighting there lasted several days.

At one point, the Confederates tried to break out of the fort and escape. They opened a hole in the Union line and began to retreat. Suddenly, however, their commanding officer decided it would be wrong to retreat. He ordered them back to the fort. After that, there was no choice. The Confederates would have to surrender. The commanding officer sent a message to General Grant. "What were the terms of surrender?" Grant's answer was simple: "No terms except unconditional and immediate surrender." The Confederates gave up Fort Donelson. Grant took 14,000 prisoners. It was the greatest Union victory since the start of the war. Ulysses Grant was a hero. Newspapers called him "Unconditional Surrender" Grant.

After the Union victory at Fort Donelson, Confederate forces withdrew from Tennessee. They moved farther south and began to re-group at Corinth, Mississippi. Confederate Generals hoped to build one big army to stop Ulysses Grant. They would have to move fast. Grant was marching toward Corinth with 40,000 men. Another 35,000, under the command of Don Buell, were to meet him on the way. Grant arrived in the area first. He waited for Buell 30 kilometers from Corinth, near a small country meeting hall called Shiloh Church. Confederate General **Albert Sydney Johnston** was waiting, too. He had more than

40,000 men, about the same as Grant. And he was expecting another 20,000. But when he learned that grant was nearby, he decided not to wait. He would attack immediately.

Johnston did not know it, but his attack came as a surprise to the Union army. Union officers had refused to believe reports that Johnston was on the move. They said his army was not strong enough to attack. Union troops did not prepare defensive positions. They had no protection when the battle began. The fighting at Shiloh was the bitterest of the war. It was not one battle, but many. Groups of men fought each other all across the wide battlefield. From a distance, they shot at each other. Close up, they cut each other with knives. The earth became red with blood. The dead and wounded soon lay everywhere. At first, the Confederates pushed Grant's army back. They had only to break through one more line and victory would be theirs. But **in the thick of the struggle**,

General Ulysses Grant

General Johnston was shot in the leg. The bullet cut through an artery. Johnston bled to death before help arrived. Any hope for a Southern victory at Shiloh died with him. By the time the fighting began again the next day, **General Buell** had arrived to help Grant. The Confederate army retreated. The Union army let it go.

Shiloh. The word itself came to mean death and destruction. The battle of Shiloh had **brought home to the American people**, both of the North and South, the horror of war. It was the first time so many men—100,000—had fought against each other in the western world. It was the American people's first real taste of the **bloodiness of modern warfare**. As one soldier who fought there said: "It was too shocking, too horrible. I hope to God that I may never see such things again." The North won the battle of Shiloh. But it paid a very high price for victory. More than 13,000 union soldiers were killed, wounded, or missing. On the Confederate side, more than 10,000 soldiers were killed or wounded.

The North celebrated the news of its victory. But joy quickly turned to anger when the public learned of the heavy losses. People blamed General Grant. They demanded that President Lincoln dismiss him. Lincoln thought of the two men who were now his top military commanders: McClellan and Grant. They were so different. McClellan organized an army and then did nothing. Grant organized an army and moved. Lincoln said of Grant: "I cannot do without this man. He fights."

For Your Memory

The Day the Sun Stood Still
那一天太阳停止了转动

如果说 1861 年 7 月的公牛溪战役打掉了北方企图速战速决的乐观情绪的话，1862 年 4 月的西洛之战则让战争双方彻底认识到这场内战的残酷和血腥：南北双方 10 万大军在田纳西河旁鏖战厮杀两天两夜，一时间炮声震天，天昏地暗，血流成河，尸横遍野，交战双方分别付出死伤一万多人的惨重代价。

歌曲《那一天太阳停止了转动》根据一个亲自参加西洛大战的南方军队军官的日记而创作。在日记中，这位军人详细记录了那极其惨烈的兄弟之间的血战。他在日记中写道："在那大炮轰鸣、子弹横飞、被上帝所抛弃的山冈上，连阳光的阴影也无处躲藏；一个人一生的时间，也比不上战场上一分钟那么漫长……"

On the 12th of April, 1861, Confederate guns opened fire on Fort Sumter in Charleston Harbor, thus beginning the bloodiest conflict in American History—620,000 **casualties**—more than all other American wars combined.

The Civil War remains this nation's single most defining experience, **ultimately giving new meaning to the word: Freedom**. **Walt Whitman**, a young newspaperman, destined to become America's greatest poet, wrote: "Future years will never know the **seething hell** and the black **infernal** background of this war—and it is best they should not—the real war will never get in the books."

We were young and **bound for glory**
Itching for a fight like you
Bring hell and **purgatory**
To the boys who wore **the blue**
And I thought I'd seen it all
Till the day night wouldn't fall
Oh how the sun did blaze
Wouldn't go down for days

I got shot and lost my rifle
When the first **wave** hit the **rise**
And the guns rolled out like thunder
And the black smoke burned my eyes
And I watched it all unfold
Just the way the Bible told
Joshua's endless day
Keeping the night at bay
And the soldiers kept a-coming
Till the ground looked like a sea of blue and gray
And I watched them from a distance
Wondering if I would've fought or run away
The day the sun stood still
How they **beat the bloody drums**
And the seconds moved like hours
But the sunset never comes
And the cannons shake the ground
And the bullets **test your will**
Even shadows found no cover
On that **godforsaken** hill

The day the sun stood still
I watched them lean their shoulders
To the fearful **hail of lead**
And I prayed for night to save us
And I cried and bowed my head
But the sun just kept a-creeping
'Cross a cold indifferent sky
Casting a deadly glow on all the men below
All the hours in a lifetime
Don't add up to one whole minute in that sun
And the heroes and the cowards
Look the same when they have fallen by the gun

The day the sun stood still
And the North and South looked west
But the evening star was sleeping
And the daylight wouldn't rest
Out on the killing floor
The red sun on the hill
Shining down on all the dead men
With a strange and **eerie chill**
The day the sun stood still

Do not judge what your brother does
Till you've walked a mile
Rank by bloody file
Who's to say if you'll run or stay and fight?

The day the sun stood still
Is just beneath the skin

In the soul of every soldier

Every battle that he's in

The day the sun stood still

Will **haunt** your dreams at night

And **stalk** your every sunrise

Though you will not know it till

The day the sun stands still

How they'll beat the bloody drums

And the seconds moved like hours

But the sunset never comes

And the cannons shake the ground

And the bullets test your will

Even shadows find no cover

On some godforsaken hill on

The day the sun stood still. . .

The day the sun stood still. . .

Words, Expressions and Notes

George McClellan 乔治·麦克莱伦 (1826—1885)，美国将军，南北战争初期曾任联邦军总司令，后被林肯总统撤职。

take my own time 慢慢来；不着急

Army of the Potomac 波托马克军团，美国南北战争时期东部战区联邦军队的主要军团

Ulysses Grant 尤利塞斯·格兰特 (1822—1885)，美国将军，内战中 (1864 年) 被林肯总统任命为联邦军总司令，后任美国第十八任总统 (1869—1877)。

Albert Sydney Johnston 阿尔伯特·约翰斯顿 (1803—1862)，南方军将领，参加过得克萨斯独立革命和墨西哥战争，内战爆发后成为南方军将领，1862 年在田纳西州西洛大战中用突袭战术重创北方军队，但自己在激战中亦受伤而亡。他的死直接导致南方联军的溃败。

in the thick of the struggle 在激战中

General Buell (Don Carlos Buell) 布尔将军 (1818—1898)，北方联邦军队将领

brought home to the American people 向美国人活生生展示了 (战争的恐怖)

bloodiness of modern warfare 现代战争的血腥

casualties n. 死伤人数

ultimately giving new meaning to the word：Freedom 最终予以自由新的含义。这里"新的含义"指北方军队和人民不仅是为国家的统一而战，同时也为他人的自由——南方黑人奴隶的自由而战，即真正的自由不仅仅是自己的自由，也包括他人的自由。

Walt Whitman 沃尔特·惠特曼 (1819—1892)，美国 19 世纪最著名的诗人，主要作品为《草叶集》。

seething hell 沸腾的地狱

infernal a. 地狱般的

bound for glory 准备为光荣而战

itching for a fight 跃跃欲试以求一战

purgatory n. 炼狱

the blue 蓝色的军装，又指北军 (这是因为北方军队身着蓝色军装；南方军队穿灰色军装，因此又称为 the gray)。

wave n. 一波攻击

rise n. 高地

Joshua's endless day 约书亚没有尽头的一天。此典故源自圣经《旧约》第六卷《约书亚记》。约书亚是古代以色列领导人摩西的继任者。约书亚在书中说道："And the sun stood still, and the moon stopped, until the nation took vengeance on their enemies."

Keeping the night at bay 钳制住夜晚 (使其不得动弹)。意指时间过得太慢。

beat the bloody drums 敲响带血的战鼓。南北战争时期，交战双方仍然沿袭欧洲战争的传统，都有鼓队在战场上助威。

test your will 考验你的意志

godforsaken a. 被上帝抛弃的

hail of lead 枪林弹雨

Casting a deadly glow 投下死亡的火光

eerie chill （在阳光下人们感到的却是）令人恐惧的寒冷

Do not judge what your brother does / Till you've walked a mile / Rank by bloody file / Who's to say if you'll run or stay and fight? 不要去评价一位士兵在战场上的表现。当你走在浑身上下血迹斑斑的士兵队伍中间时，你能知道哪位士兵是英雄，哪位是懦夫吗？

haunt v. 萦绕；挥之不去

stalk v. 笼罩

Questions for Comprehension and Discussion

1. Where did the North and the South fight their first major battle?
2. Why did General McClellan keep making excuses for delaying military moves against the enemy?
3. Why did all the Union generals who knew Ulysses Grant have no faith in his abilities?
4. Why did Newspapers call General Grant "Unconditional Surrender" Grant?
5. Why is it said that "the battle of Shiloh had brought home to the American people, both of the North and South, the horror of war"?
6. Why did President Lincoln refuse to dismiss General Grant?

Unit 8   A Nation Divided (2)

29   The Emancipation Proclamation

《解放宣言》

1862 年 4 月，格兰特将军率领的大军在田纳西州的西洛与南方叛军遭遇。这是内战以来最大规模的对抗，10 万士兵血战两天，战场上双方死尸堆积如山。美国内战的惨烈和血腥在此时彻底显现。

格兰特将军在战场上表现出来的军事才能令人刮目相看。他坚决果断，打破旧的军事传统，运用灵活机动的战术，尽管伤亡惨重，但联邦军队最终还是取得了胜利。

当西部及南部战线不断传来捷报时，作为联邦主力的麦克莱伦的 11 万大军却仍在东部战线上一动不动。林肯于 3 月免除了他总司令的职务，但仍让他指挥军队。出于无奈，麦克莱伦率领大部队试图进攻里士满。他的进攻计划完全不切合实际，而他又刚愎自用，不顾他人劝告，以致在 6 月底 7 月初，部队遭到南方军总司令罗伯特·李将军的沉重打击，麦克莱伦率领残兵败将狼狈逃窜。9 月，林肯命令麦克莱伦的部队再次阻击南方军队。17 日，麦克莱伦部队与罗伯特·李的部队遭遇，南军受到阻击。18 日晚，罗伯特·李的部队撤退，仓皇渡过波托马克河，麦克莱伦在战斗处于优势的情况下却放弃乘胜追击的大好机会，让敌人安全返回南方。

至此，联邦军队在西线和南线取得的显著胜利都被东部战线的败绩抵消，联邦军队败多胜少，战场上的主动权始终掌握在南方叛军手中。

在国内军事形势仍然不明朗的时候，国际局势却有非同寻常的发展：英国、法国等国家已经准备承认"南部邦联"为独立国家！

面对严峻的形势，林肯认识到"事情越来越糟"，他感到，"我们必须拿出最后一张牌，并且改变我们的策略，否则我们就要输了"。

这"最后的一张牌"就是：《解放宣言》。

America's Civil War of the 1860s began as a struggle over a state's right to leave the Union. President Abraham Lincoln firmly believed that a state did not have that right. And he declared war on the Southern states that did leave. Lincoln had one and only one reason to fight: to save the Union. In time, however, there was another reason to fight: to free the Negro slaves.

Lincoln had tried to keep the issue of slavery out of the war. He feared it would weaken the Northern war effort. Many men throughout the North would fight to save the Union. They would not fight to free the slaves. Lincoln also needed the support of the four slave states that had not left the Union: Delaware, Kentucky, Maryland, and Missouri. He could not be sure of their support if he declared that the purpose of the war was to free the slaves. Lincoln was able to follow this policy, at first. But the war to save the Union was going badly. The North had not won a decisive victory in Virginia, the heart of the Confederacy. To guarantee continued support for the war, Lincoln was forced to recognize that the issue of slavery was, in fact, a major issue. And on September 22nd, 1862, he announced a new policy on slavery

in the rebel Southern states. His announcement became known as the Emancipation Proclamation.

American newspapers printed the Proclamation. This is what it said:

> I, Abraham Lincoln, President of the United States and Commander-in-Chief of the army and navy, do hereby declare that on the first day of January, 1863, all persons held as slaves within any state then in rebellion against the United States, shall then become and be forever free.
>
> The government of the United States, including the military and naval forces, will recognize and protect the freedom of such persons, and will interfere in no way with any efforts they may make for their actual freedom.

President Abraham Lincoln

For political reasons, the proclamation did not free slaves in the states that supported the Union. Nor did it free slaves in the areas around Norfolk, Virginia, and New Orleans, Louisiana.

Most anti-slavery leaders praised the Emancipation Proclamation. They had waited a long time for such a document. But some did not like it. They said it did not go far enough. It did not free all of the slaves in the United States—only those held by the rebels. Lincoln answered that the Emancipation Proclamation was a **military measure**. He said he made it under his wartime powers as Commander-in-Chief. As such, it was legal only in enemy territory. Lincoln agreed that all slaves should be freed. It was his personal opinion. But he did not believe that the Constitution gave him the power to free all the slaves. He hoped that could be done slowly, during peacetime.

Lincoln's new policy on slavery was welcomed warmly by the people of Europe. It won special praise in Britain. The British people were deeply concerned about the Civil War in America. The United States navy had blocked Southern exports of cotton. The British textile industry, which depended on this cotton, was almost dead. Factories were closed. Hundreds of thousands of people were out of work. The British government watched and worried as the war continued month after month. Finally, late in the summer of 1862, British leaders said the time had come for them to **intervene**. They would try to help settle the American dispute. Britain would propose a peace agreement based on Northern recognition of Southern rights. If the North rejected the agreement, Britain would recognize the Confederacy.

Then came the news that President Lincoln was freeing the slaves of the South. Suddenly, the Civil War was a different war. No longer was it a struggle over Southern rights. Now it was a struggle for human freedom. The British people strongly opposed slavery. When they heard that the slaves would be freed, they gave their support immediately to President Lincoln and the North. Britain's peace proposals were never offered. The Emancipation Proclamation had cost the South the recognition of Britain and France.

The South was furious over the Proclamation. Southern newspapers attacked Lincoln. They accused him of trying to create a slave rebellion in states he could not occupy with troops. They also said the Proclamation was an invitation for Negroes to murder whites. The Confederate Congress debated several resolutions to fight Lincoln's Proclamation. One resolution would make slaves of all Negro soldiers captured from the Union army. Another called for the execution of white officers who led black troops. Some Southern lawmakers even proposed the death sentence for anyone who spoke against slavery.

In the North, most people cheered the new policy on slaves. Some, however, opposed it. They said the policy would cause the slave states of the Union to secede. Those states would join the Confederacy. Or, they said, it would cause freed slaves to move north and take away jobs from whites. There also was another reason. 1862 was a congressional election year. The Democratic Party was the opposition party at that time. Party leaders believed their candidates would have a better chance of winning if they opposed the policy. Democrats said the policy was proof that anti-slavery extremists were in control of the government.

Abraham Lincoln announced the Emancipation Proclamation on September 22nd, 1862. But Lincoln said he would not sign the Proclamation until the first day of 1863. That gave the Southern states 100 days to end their rebellion, or face the destruction of slavery.

Some people thought Lincoln would withdraw the Proclamation at the last minute. They did not believe he would sign a measure that was so extreme. They said the new policy would only make the South fight harder. And, as a result, the Civil War would last longer. Others charged that the Proclamation was illegal. They said the Constitution did not give the president the power to violate the property rights of citizens.

Lincoln answered the charges. He said: "I think the Constitution gives the Commander-in-Chief special powers under the laws of war. The most that can be said, if so much, is that slaves are property. Is there any question that, by the laws of war, property—both of enemies and friends—may be taken when needed."

Just before the first of the year, a congressman asked the president if he still planned to sign the Emancipation Proclamation.

"My mind is made up," Lincoln answered. "It must be done. I am driven to it. There is no other way out of our troubles. But although my duty is clear, it is in some way painful. I hope that the people will understand that I act not in anger, but in expectation of a greater good."

The morning of New Year's Day was a busy time for Lincoln. It was a tradition to open the White House on that day so the President could wish visitors a happy new year. After the last visitor had gone, Lincoln went to his office. He started to sign the Emancipation Proclamation. Then he stopped. He said:

> "I never, in all my life, felt more sure that I was doing right than I do in signing this paper. But I have been shaking hands all day, until my arm is tired. When people examine this document, they will say, '**He was not sure about that.**' But anyway, it is going to be done."

With those words, he wrote his name at the bottom of the paper. He had issued one of the greatest documents in American history.

For Your Memory

Slavery Chain Done Broke at Last
奴隶制的枷锁终于被打碎

1862 年 12 月 31 日晚，美国北方的黑人聚集在全国各地，与许多白人一起翘首等待《解放宣言》的正式发表。当林肯总统签署文件的消息传来，各地会场发出阵阵欢呼："哈利路亚！哈利路亚！我们解放了！我们解放了！"黑人们如同久旱逢甘霖那样欣喜若狂，载歌载舞，欢庆解放。

Slavery chain done broke at last,
Broke at last, broke at last;
Slavery chain done broke at last,
Gonna praise God till I die.

Slavery chain done broke at last,
Broke at last, broke at last;
Slavery chain done broke at last,

Gonna praise God till I die.

Way up in that valley
Just praying on my knees,
Telling God about my troubles,
Yes and to help me if He please.

Slavery chain done broke at last,
Broke at last, broke at last;
Slavery chain done broke at last,
Gonna praise God till I die.

Well, I told Him how I suffer,
In the **dungeon** and the chain;
And the days were with head bowed down,
And my broken flesh and pain.
Slavery chain done broke at last,
Broke at last, broke at last;
Slavery chain done broke at last,
Gonna praise God till I die.

Well, I know my Jesus heard me,
'Cause the spirit spoke to me;
Said: "Rise now my children,
Then you too shall be free."

Slavery chain done broke at last,
Broke at last, broke at last;
Slavery chain done broke at last,
Gonna praise God till I die.

There's no more weary children,
'Cause my Jesus set me free.
And there's no more **auction block**
Since He gave me liberty.

Slavery chain done broke at last,
Broke at last, broke at last;
Slavery chain done broke at last,
Gonna praise God till I die. . . .

Words, Expressions and Notes

military measure 军事措施
intervene *v.* 介入，干涉
He was not sure about that. 他在这个问题上可不是那么有信心。这里指人们看见总统的字迹时可能说出的话。其原因是林肯总统一整天都忙于会见客人并同他们握手，签字时由于疲乏而手有些抖动。
gonna = going to 这是非标准英语，但大量用于口语和歌曲中。

way up in that valley 在那遥远的山谷
dungeon *n.* 地牢
'cause = because 在歌曲或诗歌中，为了减少音节，时常会对一些常用词汇采用缩写的形式。
auction block 拍卖的站台。美国贩卖黑奴时期，常强迫黑奴们站在临时搭建的站台（甚至木箱）上拍卖，以便奴隶主挑选。这是对黑人人格的极大侮辱。

Questions for Comprehension and Discussion

1. Why did Lincoln not abolish slavery at the beginning of the war instead of on January 1st, 1863?
2. Why did Lincoln try to keep the issue of slavery out of war?
3. What forced Lincoln to recognize that the slavery was an important issue that could not be avoided?
4. Why was Lincoln's new policy on slavery welcomed warmly by the people of Europe?
5. How did the Emancipation Proclamation change the goals for which the Union was fighting?
6. How did Lincoln justify the issuance of the Emancipation Proclamation?

30　The Gettysburg Address

葛底斯堡演说

1863 年 1 月 1 日，林肯总统正式签署《解放宣言》，使叛乱各州的奴隶获得自由，并号召他们参加北方的军队。宣言为战争中的北方指明了新的政治方向：他们不只是为了拯救联邦而战，而且也是为了废除奴隶制度而战，同时还是为人类的自由而战。这就使北方立刻在南北双方的对垒中取得了道德上的制高点，让正义与文明同北方连在一起。在国内，人们欢欣鼓舞，大批黑人踊跃参军；在国外，英国、法国等欧洲大国一夜之间改变了看法，纷纷转而支持北方。

尽管林肯总统在 1862 年 11 月解除了麦克莱伦的职务，但北方部队在东部仍然没有取得进展。1863 年上半年，联邦军队在几次重要的战役中均失利。尤其是在钱塞洛斯维尔（Chancellorsville）的血战中，联邦军队更遭到惨败，损兵折将近两万人。但南方也为它的胜利付出了高昂的代价："石墙" 杰克逊将军在混战中被自己人误伤致死。

1863 年 6 月，罗伯特·李将军认定北方军队在钱塞洛斯维尔的惨败正是给南方的一个机会，于是他挥师北上，率领大部队进入宾夕法尼亚州，北方形势顿时出现危机。林肯当即下令，调集邻近州 12 万军队迎战。7 月 1 日，双方在葛底斯堡展开大会战。

葛底斯堡战役是美国历史上最血腥的战争，也是内战的转折点。双方近18 万士兵相互发射炮弹，轮番端着刺刀冲杀，不断同敌人在地上翻滚着进行生死搏斗，枪炮声、战鼓声、呐喊声、咒骂声、哀号声此起波伏，震天动地。鏖战三天后，南方军队最终承受不住巨大的伤亡，败下阵来。厮杀之后，整个战场变成巨大的停尸场，田野和树林中布满残肢断臂的扭曲尸体。四处散落的残破大炮和弹药车，肿胀的马尸，打碎的步枪和弹匣，刻印在银铜装饰物上母亲和妻儿的画像把这场战争的悲剧性气氛推向高潮。

此战役以后，南方军队元气大伤，从此再没有实力进犯北方。

几个月之后，林肯总统来到葛底斯堡，出席阵亡将士墓地落成仪式。在这里，他发表了美国历史上最简短、但却是阐释民主信念最雄辩动人的讲话——《葛底斯堡演说》。

In November 1863, President Abraham Lincoln traveled to **Gettysburg**, Pennsylvania. He was to make a speech opening a **military cemetery** there. Five months earlier, Confederate General Robert E. Lee had marched his army up from Virginia to invade the North. The Union Army of the Potomac went after him. They met at Gettysburg in the bloodiest battle of America's Civil War.

The battle of Gettysburg lasted three days. General Lee threw his men against the Union Army. The Northern soldiers refused to break. Lee, at last, had to stop fighting. Badly hurt, his army went back to Virginia. Lee left behind a battlefield covered with Confederate dead. More than 3,000 Confederate soldiers had been killed. Union losses were almost as heavy. Two thousand five hundred Union soldiers had been killed. The terrible job of clearing the battlefield fell to the Union soldiers who had won the battle. Many thousands on both sides had been wounded. The wounded were moved to medical centers for treatment. The dead were buried. Most of the bodies were buried where they fell. The Confederate dead generally were buried together in large, shallow graves. Union troops who fell were buried in separate graves all over the battlefield.

A few weeks after the battle, the governor of Pennsylvania visited Gettysburg. As he walked over the battlefield, he saw where rains had washed away the earth covering many of the fallen soldiers. He said men who died so bravely should have a better resting place than that. The governor said a new cemetery should be built for the bodies of the Union soldiers. He asked the governors of other northern states to help raise money for the cemetery. Within a month, there was money enough to buy a large area of the battlefield for a military cemetery. Work began almost immediately. The human remains were moved from other places on the battlefield and put into graves in the new cemetery.

The governor planned a ceremony in November 1863, to **dedicate** the Gettysburg cemetery. He invited governors and congressmen from each state in the Union. He asked a former senator and governor of Massachusetts, **Edward Everett**, to give the dedication speech. An invitation was sent to the White House, too. The governor asked President Lincoln to come to the ceremony. He asked Lincoln to say a few words. Lincoln agreed to do so. He felt it was his duty to go. He wanted to honor the brave men who had died at Gettysburg. Lincoln hoped his words might **ease the sorrow** over the loss of these men and **lift the spirit** of the nation.

Lincoln was advised to talk about democracy. He recently had received a letter from a man in Massachusetts. The man had just returned from a visit to Europe. The man told Lincoln that Europeans saw the war more clearly than Americans, who were in the middle of it. He said they saw it as **a war between the people and an aristocracy**. The South, he said, was ruled

Lincoln was making his address at Gettysburg on November 19th, 1863.

by a small group of aristocrats. He said once the people understood that it was a war for democracy, they would win it quickly. The man urged Lincoln to explain to the common people that the war was not the North against the South, but democracy against the enemies of democracy.

Lincoln was busy during the two weeks before the ceremony at Gettysburg. He did not have much time to work on his speech. He decided what to say. But he did not choose the exact words he would use. Lincoln left Washington November 18th for the train ride to Gettysburg. The train stopped in Baltimore. A crowd waited to see him. An old man came up and shook Lincoln's hand. He told the president that he had lost a son in the fighting at Gettysburg. Lincoln said he understood the man's sorrow. Lincoln said to the old man: "When I think of the **sacrifices of life still to be offered**, and the hearts and homes to be made lonely before this terrible war is over, **my heart is like lead**. I feel at times like hiding in a deep darkness."

Lincoln arrived at Gettysburg at sundown. He had dinner. Then he went to his room to complete the speech he would give the next day. He worked for several hours. Finally, it was done. The next morning, Lincoln, on horseback, led a slow parade to the new cemetery. A huge crowd waited before the place where Lincoln and the other important visitors would sit. Military bands played. Soldiers saluted.

The ceremonies began with a prayer. Then Edward Everett rose to speak. Everett stood silent for a moment. He looked out across the battlefield and the crowds that now covered it. He began to talk about the Civil War and what had caused it. He spoke about Lee's invasion of the North. He told how northern cities would have fallen had Lee not been stopped at Gettysburg. He praised the men who had given their lives in the great battle. Everett spoke for almost two hours. He closed his speech with the hope that the nation would come out of the war with greater unity than ever before.

Then Lincoln stood up. He looked out over the valley, then down at the papers in his hand. He began to read:

Four score and seven years ago, our fathers brought forth on this continent, a new nation, **conceived in Liberty**, and dedicated to the **proposition** that all men are created equal. [1]

Now we are engaged in a great civil war testing whether that nation or any nation so conceived and so dedicated, can long endure. We are met on a great battlefield of that war. We have come to dedicate a portion of that field, as a final resting place for those who here gave their lives that that nation might live. It is altogether fitting and proper that we should do this. [2]

But, in a larger sense, we cannot dedicate—we cannot consecrate—we cannot hallow this ground. The brave men, living and dead, who struggled here, have consecrated it, far above our poor power to **add or detract**. [3]

The world will little note, nor long remember what we say here, but it can never forget what they did here. It is for us the living, rather, to be dedicated here to the unfinished work for which they who fought here have thus far so nobly advanced. It is rather for us to be here dedicated to the great task remaining before us—that from these honored dead we take increased devotion to that cause for which they gave the **last full measure of devotion**—that we here highly resolve that these dead shall not have died in vain that this nation, under God, shall have a new birth of freedom—and that government of the people, by the people, for the people, shall not perish from the earth. [4]

The crowd applauded for several minutes. Then the people began to leave. Lincoln turned to a friend. **He said he feared his speech had been a failure.** He said he should have prepared it more carefully. Edward Everett did not agree with Lincoln. He said the president's speech was perfect. He said the president had said more in two minutes than he, Everett, had said in two hours. Newspapers and other publications praised Lincoln's Gettysburg address. Said one: "The few words of the President were from the heart, to the heart. They cannot be read without emotion."

For Your Memory

The Battle Hymn of the Republic
共和国战歌

朱莉娅·沃德·豪（Julia Ward Howe）是一位反对奴隶制诗人。1861 年 11 月的一天夜晚，

---

1 八十七年前，我们的先辈在这块大陆上建立了一个新的国家，它孕育于自由之中，信奉人人生而平等的理念。

2 当前，我们正在进行一场规模巨大的内战，以考验我们的国家，或者任何一个拥有同样理想和信念的国家，能否长久生存。我们今天聚集在这场战争的一片广阔的战场上，为的是要把战场上一小块土地奉献给那些为国家生存而英勇捐躯的人们，以作为他们最后的安息之地。我们这样做是恰当而合理的。

3 然而，从更广的意义上来说，我们无法奉献这片土地，我们没有能力使它成为圣地，也不可能把它变成人们的景仰之所。那些曾经在这里战斗的勇士，无论活着的还是死去的，早已将这块土地神圣化了，而这远非我们菲薄的能力所能左右。

4 世界将很难注意到，也不会长久记得我们今天在此地所说的话，然而对英雄们的业绩，人们将永志不忘。我们活着的人应该做的，就是要献身于英雄们曾在此为之奋斗、努力推进，但尚未完成的事业。我们应该做的，就是要投入到他们遗留给我们的伟大任务中去。先烈们已将自己的全部精诚贡献给我们的事业，我们应从他们那里获取更多奉献精神，下定决心不让先烈们白白死去，目的是让我们的国家在上帝的庇护下，重获自由的新生，让我们这个民有、民治、民享的政府永世长存。

她看到波托马克河南面一队队北方军队正开赴前线，士兵们高唱着流行歌曲《约翰·布朗的遗体》。一个朋友建议她为这支行军歌重新填歌词。第二天她在黎明前起床，找到笔和纸，写下了《共和国战歌》。这时她幼小的女儿还在身旁酣睡。歌曲像野火一样燃遍全国，成为美国的《马赛曲》。一时间，南北双方的士兵都唱着这首歌奔赴战场。

1862年2月，这首歌未署名发表在《大西洋月刊》上，立刻赢得像拉尔夫·沃尔多·埃默森和亨利·华兹沃思·朗费罗这些杰出文学家的高度赞扬。但更重要的是，联邦军立即把它作为自己的行军歌。这是唯一一首最终能超越地方偏见而成为全国性歌曲的内战歌曲。在未来的西美战争、第一次和第二次世界大战期间，大批的美国士兵都是唱着这首行军歌走向战场的。

Mine eyes have seen the glory of the coming of the Lord. He is trampling out the vintage where the **grapes of wrath** are stored. He hath loosed the fateful lightning of his terrible swift sword. His truth is marching on.	眼前忽见上帝降临，闪耀万丈光芒， 他将积满怒火的山冈化为一马平川， 手中锐利无敌神剑放出闪电金光， 让真理传遍四方。
Glory, glory! **Hallelujah**! Glory, glory! Hallelujah! Glory, glory! Hallelujah! His truth is marching on.	光荣，光荣！哈利路亚！光荣，光荣！哈利路亚！ 光荣，光荣！哈利路亚！让真理传遍四方。
I have seen Him in the watchfires of a hundred circling camps. They have builded Him an altar in the evening dews and damps. I can read His righteous sentence by the dim and flaring lamps. His day is marching on.	上帝显现的环形军营里篝火熊熊， 人们身披夜间的露水为他建一座神坛， 昏暗摇曳的灯光里他作出公正的判决： 让真理传遍四方。
Glory, glory! Hallelujah! Glory, glory! Hallelujah! Glory, glory! Hallelujah! His truth is marching on.	光荣，光荣！哈利路亚！光荣，光荣！哈利路亚！ 光荣，光荣！哈利路亚！让真理传遍四方。

Words，Expressions and Notes

Gettysburg 葛底斯堡，宾夕法尼亚南部一小镇

military cemetery 军事公墓

dedicate v. 为（建筑物等）举行落成仪式

Edward Everett 爱德华·埃弗雷特（1794—1865），美国政治家、演说家和教育家，与林肯总统同在葛底斯堡国家公墓落成典礼上发表演说。

ease the sorrow 减轻悲痛

lift the spirit 提高士气

a war between the people and an aristocracy 人民与贵族特权阶层之间的一场战争

sacrifices of life still to be offered （人民在内战中）还将付出生命的代价

my heart is like lead 我的心像铅一般沉重

conceived in Liberty 孕育于自由之中

proposition n. 主张

add or detract 增加或减少

last full measure of devotion 最后的全部奉献，指献出了生命

He said he feared his speech had been a failure. 林肯认为他的演说是一个失败。美国历史学家对此解释说，由于林肯之前的爱德华·埃弗雷特的演说长达两小时，现场的听众误以为林肯总统也可能会发表同样长的演说。当大多数人在埃弗雷特的演说结束后正在伸一伸腿，动一动手臂，为接

下来的长篇演说做一点身体上的准备时，林肯总统的演说就已经结束。由于没有集中注意力倾听，现场的人们只是礼节性地拍了拍手。这就是林肯认为演说不成功的原因。然而，人们从第二天的报纸上细细品味林肯的讲话后，才逐渐认识到这篇演说的伟大之处。

grapes of wrath 愤怒的葡萄，典出《圣经·启示录》，意指愤怒和暴力的起因。

Hallelujah *int.* 哈利路亚，表示赞美、欢乐或感谢。

Questions for Comprehension and Discussion

1. Why was the battle at Gettysburg a turning point in the war?

2. Why did the governor of Pennsylvania want to build a military cemetery for the Union soldiers who died in the battle?

3. Why did President Lincoln agree to attend the ceremony at Gettysburg?

4. Lincoln said, "When I think of the sacrifices of life still to be offered, and the hearts and homes to be made lonely before this terrible war is over, my heart is like lead. I feel at times like hiding in a deep darkness." What do you think about Lincoln's words?

5. Why did people say that "The few words of the president were from the heart, to the heart"?

31 The Assassination of Abraham Lincoln

林肯总统遭遇暗杀

就在北方人民庆祝葛底斯堡战役的胜利时，西部战线又传来捷报，格兰特将军的部队攻克了密西西比河上的重要战略据点维克斯堡，南方军队被俘士兵达 29 000 人。这是南北战争期间联邦军队俘获人数最多的一次。

经过 1863 年下半年的几次大战役，南方军队在物资方面捉襟见肘，而北方军队在战争中迅速成长起来，兵力和武器日渐增强，战略战术日益成熟。1864 年 3 月，林肯正式任命格兰特将军为北方军总司令，改变了之前联邦部队缺乏统一指挥、各战区司令各自为战的局面。格兰特就任后，立刻制定对南方军队采取"分而歼之"的战略，并撤掉那些颟顸无能的将军，启用智勇双全的将军威廉·谢尔曼（William Sherman）任密西西比河战区司令，这些措施为联邦军队的最后胜利打下了基础。

1864 年，格兰特将军开始向南方"首都"里士满发动稳步而坚决的进军；与此同时，谢尔曼将军指挥的西线大军也接二连三取得辉煌战果。谢尔曼是坚决对南方叛军实施无情打击的少数北方将军之一。他的名言"战争就是地狱"（War is hell.）至今被广泛流传。他率领大军长驱直入，占领南方重大工业城市亚特兰大后，又开始了"向海洋进军"（March to the Sea）的计划。谢尔曼率领大军直扑南方主要工业品供应州佐治亚，一路上，南方人的粮食、衣物、马匹等有用物品一律征用，其他则全部烧毁和破坏，包括庄稼、房屋、工厂、铁道和桥梁。其结果是，他的军队经过的地方，"连乌鸦也找不到落足之处"。谢尔曼表示，他就是要用这种"焦土政策"彻底摧毁南方人的斗志，让他们永远不敢再造反。这也是几十年之后，战争双方基本和解时，南方人民仍然不肯原谅谢尔曼的原因。

1865 年 2 月 17 日，南方军在锐不可当的谢尔曼大军面前望风败逃，放弃了南卡罗来纳州首府哥伦比亚。查尔斯顿城由于通往内陆的铁路线被切断，未经一战该城便落入联邦部队之手。与此同时，格兰特的部队也在东线不断取得战果。4 月 2 日，罗伯特·李将军被迫下令放弃里士满。一周后，他在弗吉尼亚被联邦军队包围，无路可逃，宣布投降。至此，持续 4 年的内战，终于以北方的胜利而告终。

正当北方各地人民欢天喜地庆祝胜利之际，一个噩耗如同晴天霹雳般从首都传来：林肯总统遇刺身亡。

On April 9th, 1865, Confederate General Robert E. Lee surrendered his army to Union General Ulysses Grant. Within weeks, America's Civil War would be over. When people in Washington learned of Lee's surrender, they hurried to the White House. They wanted to hear from President Abraham Lincoln. The crowd did not know that it would be one of his last speeches.

President Lincoln spoke several days after General Lee's surrender. The people expected a victory speech. But Lincoln gave them something else. Already, he was moving forward from victory to the difficult times ahead. The Southern rebellion was over. Now, he faced the task of re-building the Union. Lincoln did not want to punish the South. He wanted to re-join the ties that the Civil War had broken. So, when the people of the North expected a speech of victory, he gave them a speech of reconstruction, instead. On the night of April 11th, Lincoln appeared before a crowd outside the White House. He held a candle in one hand and his speech in the other.

"Fellow citizens," Lincoln said. "We meet this evening not in sorrow, but in gladness of heart. The surrender of the main army of the Confederacy gives hope of a righteous and speedy peace. The joy cannot be held back. By these recent successes, we have had pressed more closely upon us the question of reconstruction."

"We all agree," Lincoln continued, "that the so-called seceded states are **out of their correct relation with the Union**. We also agree that what the government is trying to do is get these states back into their correct relation."

Confederate General Robert E. Lee

"I believe it is not only possible, but in fact easier to do this without deciding the legal question of whether these states have ever been out of the Union. Finding themselves safely at home, it would be of no importance whether they had ever been away."

There was cheering and applause when President Lincoln finished, but less than when he began. The speech had been **too long and too detailed to please the crowd**. Lincoln, however, believed it a success. He hoped he had made the country understand one thing: the great need to forget hatred and bitterness in the difficult time of re-building that would follow the war. The president continued to discuss his ideas on reconstruction over the next few days. On Friday, April 14th, he

Lincoln with his military officers during the Civil War

agreed to put this work aside for a while. In the afternoon, he took his wife Mary for a long drive away from the city. In the evening, they would go to the theater.

One of the popular plays of the time, called *Our American Cousin*, was being performed at Ford's Theater, not far from the White House. The **Secretary of War** did not want the Lincolns to go alone. He ordered an army officer to go with them. The President and Mrs. Lincoln sat in special seats at Ford's Theater. The **presidential box** was above and to one side of the stage. A guard always stood outside the door to the box. On this night, however, the guard did not remain. He left the box unprotected.

President Lincoln settled down in his seat to enjoy the play. As he did so, a man came to the door of the box. He carried a gun in one hand and a knife in the other. The man entered the presidential box quietly. He slowly raised the gun. He aimed it at the back of Lincoln's head. He fired. Then the man jumped from the box to the stage three meters below. Many in the theater recognized him. He was an actor: **John Wilkes Booth**. Booth broke his leg when he hit the stage floor. But he pulled himself up, shouted: "**Sic semper tyrannis!**"—Thus ever to tyrants!—and ran out the door. He got on a horse and was gone.

The attack was so quick that the audience did not know what had happened. Then a woman shouted, "The President has been shot!"

Lincoln had fallen forward in his seat, unconscious. Someone asked if it was possible to move him to the White House. A young army doctor said no. The President's wound was terrible. He would die long before reaching the White House. So Lincoln was moved to a house across the street from Ford's Theater. A doctor tried to remove the bullet from the President's head. He could not. Nothing could be done, except wait. The end was only hours away.

Cabinet members began to arrive, while wild reports spread through the city: the Confederates had declared war again! There was fighting in the streets! An official of the War Department described the situation. "The extent of the plot was unknown. From so horrible a beginning, what might come next. How far would the bloody work go. The safety of Washington must be looked after. The people must be told. The assassin and his helpers must be captured."

Early the next morning, April 15th, Abraham Lincoln died. A prayer was said over his body. His eyes were closed. The news went out by telegraph to cities and towns across the country. People read the words, but could not believe them. To millions of Americans, Abraham Lincoln's death was a personal loss. They had come to think of him as more than the President of the United States. He was a trusted friend. People hung black cloth on their doors in sorrow. Even the South mourned for Lincoln, its former enemy. Southern General Joe Johnston said: "Mr. Lincoln was the best friend we had. His death is the worst thing that could happen for the South."

Messages of regret came from around the world. British labor groups said they could never forget the things Lincoln had said about working people. Things such as: "The strongest tie of human sympathy should be one **uniting all working people of all nations and tongues**."

A group representing hundreds of French students sent this message: "In President Lincoln we mourn a fellow citizen. There are no longer any countries shut up in narrow frontiers. Our country is everywhere where there are neither masters nor slaves. Wherever people live in liberty or fight for it. We look to the other side of the ocean to learn how a people which has known how to make itself free knows how to preserve its freedom."

The assassination of Abraham Lincoln touched the imagination of America's writers. Many tried to put their feelings into words. Walt Whitman wrote several poems of mourning. Here is part of one of them, "**O Captain! My Captain!**"

> Here captain! Dear father!
> This arm beneath your head!
> It is some dream that on the deck,
> You've fallen cold and dead.
> My captain does not answer, his lips are pale and still,
> My father does not feel my arm, he has no pulse nor will.
> **The ship is anchor'd safe and sound**, its voyage closed and done,
> From fearful trip the **victor ship comes in with object won**;
> **Exult o shores**, and ring o bells!
> **But I with mournful tread**,
> Walk the deck my captain lies,
> Fallen cold and dead.

Abraham Lincoln was assassinated in the spring. That is the time of year when lilac plants burst into flower throughout much of the United States. One of Walt Whitman's most beautiful poems in honor of Lincoln is called, "**When Lilacs Last in the Dooryard Bloomed.**" Here is part of that poem.

When lilacs last in the dooryard bloom'd
And **the great star early droop'd in the western sky** in the night,
I mourned, and yet **shall mourn with ever-returning spring**.
Ever-returning spring, **trinity** sure to me you bring,
Lilac **blooming perennial** and drooping star in the west,
And thought of him I love...
Coffin that passes through lanes and streets,
Through day and night with the great cloud darkening the land...
With the countless torches lit,
With the silent sea of faces and the **unbared heads**...
With the tolling, tolling bells' perpetual clang,
Here, coffin that slowly passes,
I give you my sprig of lilac.

Words, Expressions and Notes

out of their correct relation with the Union 超出了与联邦的正确关系

too long and too detailed to please the crowd 由于（讲话）太长太详细而不能取悦听众

Secretary of War = War Secretary 陆军部长，总统内阁成员之一

presidential box （福特剧院里的）总统包间

John Wilkes Booth 布思，美国演员，公开主张奴隶制，刺杀林肯总统后在被追捕时毙命。

Sic semper tyrannis! = Thus ever to tyrants. "这就是暴君的下场！"——这句话原是弗吉尼亚州的警句，种族主义分子布思用这句话来表达他对林肯总统的仇恨。

uniting all working people of all nations and tongues 联合所有国家和讲所有语言的劳动人民

"O Captain! My Captain!" 《啊，船长！我的船长！》诗人惠特曼为悼念林肯而作的著名诗歌。在诗歌中，作者把美国比作一艘大船，而林肯就是这艘船的掌舵人。

The ship is anchor'd safe and sound 这艘船安全地抛锚停泊

victor ship comes in with object won 胜利的大船完成使命归来

Exult o shores 啊，海岸，欢呼吧！

But I with mournful tread 但我却迈着悲痛的步伐

When Lilacs Last in the Dooryard Bloomed 《当丁香花最近在院子里开放的时候》，诗人惠特曼为悼念林肯而作的著名长诗

the great star early droop'd in the western sky 巨星从西方的天空早早坠落

shall mourn with ever-returning spring 每当春回大地时都要哀悼

trinity n. （基督教的）三位一体，即圣父、圣子和圣灵合为一神。诗歌在此把林肯总统神化了。

blooming perennial 终年绽放

unbared heads 戴着帽子的人们

Questions for Comprehension and Discussion

1. Why did President Lincoln not give people a victory speech?

2. Why did Lincoln want to make the country understand the need to forget hatred and bitterness brought by the war?
3. Why is it said that "to millions of Americans, Abraham Lincoln's death was a personal loss"?
4. Why did people around the world also mourn for Lincoln's death?
5. Why did poet Walt Whitman compare Abraham Lincoln to "Captain"?

32 The End of the Civil War

内战的结束

　　林肯的不幸去世使全美沉浸在悲伤之中，全国上下到处一片哭泣之声。他的死也在国外引起巨大震动，各国进步人士和人民都为失去这位伟大的"奴隶的解放者"而感到痛惜。马克思在1865年对林肯作出了深刻的评价："林肯是一个不会被困难所吓倒，不会为成功所迷惑的人；他不屈不挠地迈向自己的伟大目标，从不轻举妄动，他稳步向前，从不倒退；他既不因人民的热烈拥护而冲昏头脑，也不因人民的情绪低落而灰心丧气；他用仁慈心灵的光辉缓和严峻的行动，用幽默的微笑照亮为热情所蒙蔽的事态；他谦虚地、质朴地进行自己宏伟的工作，绝不像那些天生的统治者们那样做一点点小事就大吹大擂。总之，他是一位达到了伟大境界而仍然保持自己优良品质的罕有的人物。这位出类拔萃和道德高尚的人竟是那样谦虚，以至于在他成为殉道者倒下去之后，全世界才发现他是一位英雄。"

　　在1861年到1865年的内战炮火中，南方奴隶制度被彻底摧毁，北方取得了决定性的胜利。但欢庆胜利之后，北方发现各种难题接踵而来：战后的南方满目疮痍，经济基础崩溃，各种社会基础设施完全毁坏；人们精神委靡不振，基本生活毫无保障；黑人尽管获得自由，在经济上却不能自立；南方反动的种植园主时刻准备复仇，恢复奴隶制度……如何抚平战争的创伤，在废墟上实施南方的重建，成为内战结束后的首要问题。从1865年到1877年，美国进入艰难的南方战后重建时期。

General William Sherman

　　President Abraham Lincoln did not live to see the final surrender of the armies of the Confederacy. However, before he was murdered on April 14th, 1865, the war was really over. The surrender of Robert E. Lee, early in April, brought an end to four years of bloody fighting. Several other Confederate armies were still in the field. But they were too small and too weak to continue the fight.

　　One army was in North Carolina, commanded by General Joe Johnston. Five days after Lee's surrender, Johnston asked for a meeting with General **William Sherman**, the Commander of Union forces in North Carolina. Sherman met with Johnston a few days later. He offered him the same surrender terms that General Lee had accepted. He said the Confederates must give up their weapons and promise to fight no more. Then they would be free to return to their homes. Johnston said he could not accept these terms. Johnston said he had the power to surrender all the Confederate armies everywhere in the South. He said he would do so if Sherman agreed on a political settlement.

　　The two generals met again the next day. Sherman listened as Johnston explained his demands. Most of them, Sherman accepted. He believed that President Lincoln wanted to help the South as much as possible. He had heard Lincoln say that he wanted to make it easy for the Southern states to return to the

Union. When the agreement was completed, Sherman sent it immediately to Washington for approval by the new president, **Andrew Johnson**. The agreement seemed to give the South everything it wanted.

Instead of surrendering to Sherman, the Confederate armies would break up. The soldiers would return to their homes, taking their weapons with them. They would sign a promise not to fight again and to obey state and federal laws. In exchange for this, Sherman said the President would recognize state governments in the South which promised to support the Constitution. He said federal courts would be established in the South again. And he said the President, as well as he could, would protect the political rights promised to all people by the Constitution of the United States and the **state constitutions**. And Sherman said the United States government would not interfere with any of the Southern people, if they remained peaceful and obeyed the laws.

President Johnson held a cabinet meeting to discuss the agreement Sherman had signed. War Secretary **Stanton** and the other members of the cabinet were violently opposed to it. They said Sherman had no power to make any kind of political settlement. President Johnson rejected the agreement. He said Johnston's army must surrender within 48 hours, or be destroyed. He said the surrender terms could be no better than those given General Lee.

Johnston decided to surrender. On April 26th, his army laid down its weapons. One by one, the remaining armies surrendered. The soldiers began returning home. Many of them were bitter. They wanted to continue to fight. They spoke of **guerrilla war** against the **Yankees**. But most of the Confederate commanders opposed this. Many, like **cavalry** General **Nathan Bedford Forrest**, urged their men to accept defeat. Said Forrest in a farewell speech to his men:

> It is a clear fact that we are beaten. We would be foolish to try to fight further. The government which we tried to establish is at an end. Civil War—such as you have just passed through—naturally causes feelings of bitterness and hatred. We must put these feelings aside. Whatever your responsibilities may be, meet them like men. You have been good soldiers. You can be good citizens.

Confederate President **Jefferson Davis** fled south after the fall of his government. He hoped to get across the Mississippi River. He believed that he could form a new Confederate army. If this failed, he planned to escape to Mexico.

President Lincoln had hoped that Davis would escape. He felt that punishing Davis would only create more bitterness and make reconstruction—the rebuilding of the South—more difficult. But President Johnson did not share Lincoln's feelings. He believed Davis had a part in the plot to kill Lincoln. He said Davis must be captured. On May 10th, Union forces found the Confederate president's camp in Southern Georgia. They seized him and took him to Fort Monroe, Virginia. He remained there for many months under close guard. His trial was never held. And finally, in 1867, he was freed.

Jefferson Davis

Late in May, 150,000 Union soldiers, representing every one of the Union armies, came to Washington. They came to take part in a big parade—a victory march through the city. For two days, the soldiers marched past the White House. Many of the marching men had fought at Bull Run, at **Fredericksburg**, **Antietam**, Gettysburg, **Petersburg**, and **Appomattox**. Sherman's western army was there from battles at Shiloh, **Vicksburg**, **Murfreesboro**, **Chickamauga**, and **Atlanta**. The soldiers marched proudly past the president and other government leaders.

All along the way, from the Capitol building to the White House, were huge crowds of cheering people. Hour after hour, the soldiers passed. Never had the city seen such a celebration. Each group of soldiers had its band and carried its own battle flags. Some proudly carried flags that had been torn in fierce fighting. Finally, late on the second day, the final group of soldiers passed the White House. The grand parade was over. The battle flags were put away, and the marching bands fell silent. The war was ended. Now, men could look about them and count the cost of the war.

Four years of bloody fighting had saved the Union of states. The Northern victory had settled for all time the question of whether states could leave the Union. And it had **put to rest** the great problem of slavery, which had troubled the nation for so many years. But the costs were great. More than 600,000 men of the North and South lost their lives. Hundreds of thousands more were wounded. Many had lost their arms or legs.

The war cost the North almost three and one-half thousand million dollars. It was almost as costly to the Confederates. Most of the war was fought in the Southern states. And most of the war damage was there. Hundreds of cities and towns suffered damage. Some—like Atlanta—were completely destroyed by Union forces. The damage outside the populated areas was almost as great. Union armies had marched across the South leaving behind them widespread destruction. Farm houses and buildings had been burned; animals and crops seized or destroyed.

Transport in the South was especially hard hit. Union soldiers had destroyed most of the railroads. The few Confederate trains that escaped capture were worn out from heavy use. River boats had been destroyed, and roads and bridges were in terrible condition. The South had no money to rebuild. Businessmen and rich landowners had put their money in Confederate bonds... now completely worthless. Confederate war debts would never be paid. There was also the question of the four million former slaves. They were free now. But few could take care of themselves. They needed jobs and training.

The people of the South faced a difficult future. They had been defeated in battle. Their economy was destroyed. In many areas, there was little food and the people were hungry. Farmers could not plant crops, because they had no seed and no animals to break the ground. There was no money for rebuilding.

Words, Expressions and Notes

William Sherman 威廉·谢尔曼（1820—1891），联邦军队著名将领，是内战时期少数主张对南方实施坚决打击的北方将领之一，曾参加公牛溪、维克斯堡战役，率军横越佐治亚州，攻克亚特兰大，1869 年任美国陆军总司令。

Andrew Johnson 安德鲁·约翰逊（1808—1875），美国第十七任总统（1865—1869）

state constitutions （美国）各州的宪法

Stanton （Edwin Stanton）斯坦顿（1814—1869），美国陆军部长，主张对南方重建实施严厉措施，与安德鲁·约翰逊总统发生争吵，诱发弹劾总统事件。

guerrilla war 游击战

Yankees （南方人对北方人的蔑称）北方佬

cavalry n. 骑兵

Nathan Bedford Forrest 福雷斯特（1821—1877），南方军将领，战后成为三 K 党魁首。

Jefferson Davis 杰斐逊·戴维斯（1808—1889），内战时期南方联盟总统，战后被监禁两年。

Fredericksburg 弗雷德里克斯堡，位于弗吉尼亚，1862 年 12 月联邦军队曾在此地败给由罗伯特·李将军指挥的南方联军。

Antietam 安提塔姆，位于马里兰州。1862 年 9 月联邦军队与南方联军在此地激战，双方投入兵力 12 万，死伤惨重，最后南方联军撤退。

Petersburg 彼得斯堡，位于弗吉尼亚州东南部的城市，北方联军总司令格兰特将军在 1864 至 1865 年率军围困该城达 10 个月，最终于 1865 年 4 月 2 日攻下该城，为攻打南方"首都"里士满扫清了道路。

Appomattox 阿波马托克斯，位于弗吉尼亚州的一个村庄，1865 年 4 月 9 日罗伯特·李将军指挥的南

136

方联军在此地被包围后向北方军队投降。

Vicksburg 维克斯堡，位于密西西比州的战略要地，联邦军队在 1862 至 1863 年包围维克斯堡城，并最终于 1863 年 7 月 4 日攻克该城。该战役是北方联军的重大胜利，使北方控制了密西西比河水道，并让格兰特的西部大军能投入到弗吉尼亚的战场上去，以夺取内战的最后胜利。

Murfreesboro 默弗里斯波罗，位于田纳西州中部的城市。南北双方于 1862 年 12 月 3 日至 1863 年 1 月 2 日在此激战。

Chickamauga 乞卡摩戞，位于佐治亚州北部。南北

双方军队于 1863 年 9 月在这里交手，北方军受挫，几近崩溃，在乔治·托马斯将军（George Henry Thomas）的沉着冷静指挥下才避免了更大的失败。

Atlanta 亚特兰大，南方最重要的城市。联邦军队 10 万大军在谢尔曼将军的指挥下从 1864 年 7 月 20 日至 9 月 2 日对亚特兰大实施包围打击并最终攻克该城。这次战役的胜利对林肯总统再次当选总统发挥了积极的作用。

put to rest 平息

Questions for Comprehension and Discussion

1. Why did Sherman accept most of the terms Johnston demanded?
2. Why were President Johnson and his cabinet members violently opposed to the agreement Sherman had signed?
3. What did General Nathan Bedford Forrest tell his soldiers? Why did he say so?
4. What were the direct results of the war?
5. Why is it said that "the people of the South faced a difficult future"?

Unit 9   Settling the West

33   The Gold Rush and the Story of Cowboys

淘金热与牛仔的故事

早在建国前的殖民地时期，第一批西进的人们就越过阿巴拉契亚山朝密西西比河流域进发。但是，直到1865年，真正得到开发的地区只延伸到密西西比河沿岸各州的西部。在这个新开辟的狭窄地带以外，还有大片无人占据的荒地。这片荒地连接着广阔的大草原，大草原又与生长着稀疏树林的平原接壤，一直延伸到落基山脉。在这绵延1 600公里的巨大山脉里，蕴藏着丰富的金、银及其他金属。在山的西侧，荒无人烟的平原和沙漠一直伸展到丛林满布的海岸线和太平洋。除了加利福尼亚定居区及零星小村落外，居住在这些地方的只有印第安人。

第一次淘金热发生在加利福尼亚。1848年1月24日的早晨，有个叫詹姆斯·马歇尔的人涉水走过一条小溪，忽然，他看到河里有东西在闪光。他弯下腰去，竟捡起来好几块金子！一年后的1849年，这条几年前还处于原始状态的山谷就挤满了成千上万的淘金者，以致人们为这些疯狂的人们取了个特别的名字：Forty-Niners，专指那些在1849年到加利福尼亚淘金的人。

从加利福尼亚开始，人们先后在科罗拉多、内华达、蒙大拿、怀俄明、达科他、阿拉斯加等地方发现金矿。采矿者涌向这些地区，逐步建立村镇，打下了永久定居的基础。

在得克萨斯州，养牛早就是一项重要事业，内战后尤见繁荣。赶牛人赶着得州的长角牛，穿过开放的公共地带，向北走去。牛群边走边吃，到堪萨斯州的铁路运输站时，已长得膘肥体壮。不久，这样的"长征"就成为常事了。向北移动的牛群，在几百公里的征途上，留下了无数的足迹。由于有利可图，在科罗拉多、怀俄明、堪萨斯、内布拉斯加和达科他等地区，也出现了巨大的牧场。西部的城市因成为屠宰业和肉类加工中心而繁荣起来，而一种最纯粹的美国文化——牛仔文化也应运而生。

Soon after the Civil War ended in 1865, thousands of land-hungry Americans began to move west. The great movement of settlers continued for almost forty years. The great empty west, in time, became completely settled. The discovery of gold had already started a great movement to California.

Men had rushed to the gold fields with hopes of becoming rich. A few found gold. The others found only hard work and high prices. When their money was gone, they gave up the search for gold. But they stayed in California to become farmers or businessmen or laborers. Some never gave up the search for riches. They moved back toward the east, searching for gold and silver in the wild country between California and the Mississippi River.

Each new gold rush brought more people from the East. Mining camps quickly grew into towns with stores, hotels, even newspapers. Most of these towns, however, lived only as long as gold was easy to find. Then they began to die. In some of the gold centers, big mining companies bought up all the land from those who first claimed it. These companies brought in mining machines that could dig out the gold from deep underground and separate it from the rock that held it. These companies needed equipment and other supplies. Transportation companies were formed. They carried supplies to the mining camps in huge wagon trains pulled by slow-moving oxen. Roads were built, and in some places, railroads.

The great wealth taken from the gold and silver mines was usually invested in other businesses: shipping, railroads, factories, stores, land companies. More jobs were created in the West. And living conditions got better. More and more people decided to leave the crowded East for a new life in the West. But the big eastern cities

The gold seekers, also known as **Forty-Niners**, started a massive movement of people to California.

continued to grow. New factories and industrial centers were built. People moved from the farms to find work in the cities.

The growth of these industrial centers created a big demand for food, especially meat. Chicago quickly became the heart of the meat industry. Railroads brought animals to Chicago, where packing companies killed them and prepared the meat for eastern markets. Special railroad cars kept the meat cold, so it would remain fresh until sold. As the meat industry grew, the demand for fresh meat increased. More and more cattle were needed.

There were millions of cattle in Texas, but no way to get them to the eastern markets. The closest point on the railroad was Sedalia, Missouri, more than 1,000 kilometers away. Some cattlemen believed it might be possible to walk cattle to the railroad, letting them feed on the open grassland along the way. Early in 1866, a group of Texas cattlemen decided to try this. They put together a huge herd of more than 260,000 cattle and set out for Sedalia.

There were many problems on that first cattle drive. The country was rough; grass and water sometimes hard to find. **Bandits** and Indians followed the herd trying to steal cattle. Farmers had put up fences in some areas, blocking the way. Most of the great herd was lost along the way. But the cattlemen believed they had proved that cattle could be walked long distances to the railroad. They believed a better way to the railroad could be found, with plenty of grass and water.

The cattlemen got the Kansas Pacific Railroad to extend its line west to Abilene, Kansas. There was a good **trail** from Texas to Abilene. Cattlemen began moving their herds up this trail across the Oklahoma territory and into Kansas. At Abilene, the cattle were put on trains and carried to Chicago. In the next four years, more than 1.5 million cattle were moved north over the **Chisholm trail** to Kansas. Other trails were found as the railroad moved farther west.

Trail drives usually began with the **spring round-up**. Cattlemen would send out cowboys to search the open grasslands for their animals. As the cattle were brought in, the young animals were **branded**— marked to show who owned them. Then they were released with their mothers to spend another year in the open country. The other cattle were put together for the long drive to Kansas. Usually, they were moved in groups of 2,500 to 5,000 animals. Twelve to twenty cowboys took them up the trail.

The cowboys worked hard on a trail drive. They had to keep the herd together day and night and protect it from bad men and Indians. They had to keep the cattle from moving too fast or running away. If they moved too fast, they would lose weight, and their owner would not get as much money for them. The cowboys would walk the cattle only 20 to 30 kilometers a day. The cattle could feed all night and part of the morning before starting each day. If the grass was good, and the herd moved slowly, the cattle would get heavier and bring more money.

In the early 1880s, the price of cattle rose to fifty dollars each, and many cattlemen became rich. Business was so good that a 5,000-dollar investment in the cattle industry could make 45,000 dollars in four years. More and more people began raising cattle. And early cattlemen greatly increased the size of their herds. Within a few years, there was not enough grass for all the cattle, especially along the trails. There was so much meat that the price began to fall.

There were two severe winters that killed hundreds of thousands of cattle. An extremely dry summer killed the grass, and thousands more died of hunger. The cattle industry itself almost died. Cattlemen also had problems with farmers and sheepmen. Farmers coming west would claim grassland used by the cattle growers. They would put up fences and plow up the land to plant crops. Other settlers brought huge herds of sheep to compete with cattle for the grass, and the sheep always won. Cattle would not eat grass where sheep had eaten. Violence broke out. Cattle growers fought the farmers and sheepmen for control of the land. The cattlemen finally had to settle land of their own, putting up fences and cutting the size of their herds. They no longer could let their cattle run free on public lands.

By the late 1800s, the years of the cowboys were ending. But the story of the cowboy and his difficult life would not be forgotten. Even today, the cowboy lives in movies, on television, and in books. When one thinks of the "wild west" of America, he does not think of the miners who opened the way to the West. Nor does he think of the men who struggled to build the first railroads across the wild land. And one does not think of the farmers who pushed slowly westward to fence, plow, and plant the land.

The words "wild west" bring to mind just one character: the cowboy. His difficult fight to protect his cattle on the long trail was an exciting story. It has been told by many writers. Perhaps the best-known was a young easterner, **Owen Wister**. He worked as a cattleman for several years, then wrote about the heroic life of the cowboy in a book called *The Virginian*. Another easterner who came west to learn about the cowboy was the artist **Frederick Remington**. Remington was a cowboy for only two years. But he spent the rest of his life painting pictures of the West and writing about it. His exciting works made the West and the cowboy come to life for millions who never saw a real cowboy.

For Your Appreciation

Cowboy Code
牛仔守则

在从农牧业国家过渡到工业化国家的过程中，美国出现了一门特殊的新职业：西部牛仔。事实是，牛仔作为一门职业仅持续了大约30年时间，但它却在历史长河的这一瞬间发展成为地道的、生命力极强的美国本土文化（毋庸置疑，美国绝大多数文化传统都带有欧洲的烙印）。一个多世纪以来，从小说到电影，从歌曲到广告，从娱乐舞台到政治舞台，人们无处不能看到牛仔的身影。究其原因，西部牛仔这一形象不仅直接传达了美国人民早期在与西部残酷自然环境进行抗争中展现出来的传统个人主义精神，更重要的是，它还为生活在急遽变迁中的当代美国社会各阶层的人们提供了急需的道德标准与精神支柱。从下面的《牛仔守则》中我们可以发现，无论是从道德的层面还是从精神的层面上看，西部牛仔全然就是美国人心目中最完美的英雄形象的化身。

The Cowboy must never shoot first, hit a smaller man, or **take unfair advantage**. He must never **go back on his word**, or **a trust confided in him**. He must always tell the truth. He must be gentle with children, the elderly, and animals. He must not **advocate or possess racially or religiously intolerant ideas**. He must help people in distress. He must be a good worker. He must keep himself clean in thought, speech, action, and personal habits. He must respect women, parents, and his nation's laws. The Cowboy is a patriot.

Words, Expressions and Notes

bandits　*n.*　土匪

trail　*n.*　（荒野中的）小道

Chisholm trail　奇泽姆小道，从得克萨斯州的圣安东尼奥至堪萨斯州的阿比林之间的一条著名的道路，因印第安商人 Jessie Chisholm 而得名。

spring round-up　在春天把牛围在一起准备出发

branded　*v.*　用烧红的烙铁在牛身上打上表明牛归属的烙印

Owen Wister　欧文·韦斯特（1860—1938），美国作家，其长篇小说《弗吉尼亚人》是第一部直接描写西部牛仔的重要文学作品。

Frederick Remington　弗雷德里克·雷明顿（1861—1909），美国油画家、雕塑家，作品以描绘西部生活著称。

take unfair advantage　用不公平的手段使他人吃亏

go back on his word　言而无信

a trust confided in him　（背弃）别人对他的信任

advocate or possess racially or religiously intolerant ideas　主张或持有种族或宗教上的偏见

Questions for Comprehension and Discussion

1. What did people do after they gave up the search for gold in the West?
2. How did the gold rush help develop the West?
3. Why did some cattlemen in Texas try to walk their cattle to the railroad?
4. What did the cowboys do along the way to the railroad?
5. Why have the stories of the West remained a familiar part of American folklore?
6. Who wrote a book about cowboys first? What is the name of the book?
7. What do you think about cowboys after reading the "Cowboy Code"?

34 Early Country Music: Cowboy Songs

美国早期乡村音乐：牛仔歌曲

西部大量的牧场带来了一种多姿多彩的生活，那些性格粗犷、衣着鲜明的牧牛人也自然成为这种生活的中心人物。美国第二十五届总统西奥多·罗斯福在他的回忆录中谈到他在达科他的个人经历时说："我们过着自由而粗犷的生活，骑着马，带着枪，在仲夏的烈日下工作。广阔的平原在我们的热泪中闪动。我们也经历过晚秋的夜晚，守护牛群时难忍的寒冷。不过，我们感到我们的脉搏与这粗犷的生活在一起跳动；在我们的心里，充满了工作的荣耀和生活的欢乐。"

在1866年至1888年间，大约有600万头牛从得州放牧到科罗拉多、怀俄明、蒙大拿等地的高原上过冬。养牛业的兴旺发达，在1885年达到最高峰，当时的草原，已经不足以满足这么多长途跋涉的牛群吃草的需要了，而且这些草原，也开始被纵横交错的铁路线所割裂。在牧牛人身后不远之处，有许多草原蓬车在吱吱作响，农民把他们的妻儿，还有拉车的马、乳牛和猪群也带了来。根据《定居法案》，他们圈定所得的土地，用铁丝网围起来。原来未经合法手续取得土地的牧牛人都被赶了出去。不久，这片具有浪漫气氛的西部荒原与放牛人一道，便不复存在了。

尽管真正的西部牛仔早已随着历史烟尘的消散而远去，但牛仔们粗犷的形象、丰富的经历和他们在动荡生活中展示出的鲜明性格特征却扎下根来，成为一种繁荣兴旺的美国本土文化。从韦斯特1902年的小说《弗吉尼亚人》开始，牛仔就一直成为美国小说、电影、电视、歌曲和广告中的英雄和主角。下面就让我们在音乐和歌声中去重温美国这段独特的历史，去细细品味当年牛仔在西部草原生活中的喜怒哀乐吧！

The cattle industry started in Texas during the 1870s. With its growth came a new kind of worker—the man who watched and took care of the cattle. These men who watched the cows and rode with them as they moved across the wild lands were often young. Just boys. And so they were called "cowboys." People all over the world have seen all sorts of films about the cowboy. And he is often shown in television shows. But the real life of the cowboy is not often shown. His

Oklahoma cowboys pause during a roundup in the 1890s.

work has been hard, and his life lonely and full of danger. The cowboy has told his own story in many songs and ballads. Hundreds of these have come from cowboys whose names are not known. They just sang these songs as they rode on the saddles of their horses across the cattle lands; or, as they sat at their campfires at night.

They sang about the things that were close to them: horses and cows and danger and death. Often,

they sang about the long ride to the cattle markets where the cows were sold for beef, as in this song called, "Get Along Little **Dogie**." Dogie is another name for a young cow, especially one which wanders away from the herd. The song tells how the young cowboy keeps driving the dogies forward. He feels sorry for them, because they will soon be sold for meat. But that's their hard luck, not his. And he keeps pushing them on while he sings.

As I was a-walking one morning for pleasure
I **spied** a young cowboy a-riding along
Well his hat was shoved back and his **spurs** were a-jingling
And as he was riding, he was singing this song

Whoopie-ti-yi-yo, get along little dogies
It's your misfortune and none of my own
Whoopie-ti-yi-yo, get along little dogies
You know that **Wyoming** will be your new home

It's early in the springtime we round up the dogies
We cut them and brand them and **bob off their tails**
We round up the horses, load up the **chuck-wagon**,
And then throw the dogies out on the north trail.

Whoopie-ti-yi-yo, get along little dogies
It's your misfortune and none of my own
Whoopie-ti-yi-yo, get along little dogies
You know that Wyoming will be your new home

Well your mother was raised **way down** in Texas
Where the **jimson weed** and **old choice** grow
We'll fill you up on those **prickly pears briers**,
Until you are ready for **Idaho**

Whoopie-ti-yi-yo, get along little dogies
It's your misfortune and none of my own
Whoopie-ti-yi-yo, get along little dogies
You know that Wyoming will be your new home

One of the most famous of cowboy ballads is this one, called "**The Chisholm Trail**."

Oh come along boys and listen to my tale
I'll tell you about my troubles on the old Chis'm Trail
Come a ti yi yippy yay yippy yay come a ti yi yippy yippy yay

On a ten dollar horse and a forty dollar saddle
Ridin' and a **punchin'** them Texas cattle
Come a ti yi yippy yay yippy yay come a ti yi yippy yippy yay

We left old Texas October twenty-third
Drivin' up the trail with **a 2-U herd**

Come a ti yi yippy yay yippy yay come a ti yi yippy yippy yay

There's mud in the **gully** and dust in the **draw**
The bossman's **meaner** than my mother-in-law
Come a ti yi yippy yay yippy yay come a ti yi yippy yippy yay

Got a hole in my hat where the rain runs in
Got a hole in my boot where it runs out again
Come a ti yi yippy yay yippy yay come a ti yi yippy yippy yay

Well the water's gettin' scarce and we're runnin' out of light
Looks like we're gonna have to drive 'em all night
Come a ti yi yippy yay yippy yay come a ti yi yippy yippy yay

Spent two days lookin' for **muley-headed** calf
Ain't been to sleep in a week and a half
Come a ti yi yippy yay yippy yay come a ti yi yippy yippy yay

I woke up one morning on the old Chis'm Trail
With a rope in my hand and a cow by the tail
Come a ti yi yippy yay yippy yay come a ti yi yippy yippy yay

Well it's bacon and beans most every day
I'd as soon be eatin' that **prairie hay**
Come a ti yi yippy yay yippy yay come a ti yi yippy yippy yay

Well the days are hot and the nights are cold
This cowboy life is gettin' **mighty old**
Come a ti yi yippy yay yippy yay come a ti yi yippy yippy yay

I reckon I'm as crazy as a **Catahoula pup**
I've tried and I've tried but I can't give it up
Come a ti yi yippy yay yippy yay come a ti yi yippy yippy yay

Well I went to the boss to **draw my roll**
He **figured me out nine dollars in the hole**
Come a ti yi yippy yay yippy yay come a ti yi yippy yippy yay

Well there ain't no leavin' so I guess I'm gonna stay
I'll be punchin' them cattle for the rest of my days
Come a ti yi yippy yay yippy yay come a ti yi yippy yippy yay

Day and night, the horse was at the cowboy's side. A cowboy was as proud of his horse as he was of his skill in riding him. There is this feeling in the song "I Ride An Old Paint." A paint, or pinto, is a horse of three or more different colors.

I ride an old paint, lead **an old Dan**
Going to Montana to **throw the houlihan**
Feed them in the **coulees**, and water in the draw

Tails are all **matted**, and their backs are all raw
Ride around little dogies, ride around them slow
They're fiery and snuffy and are raring to go

Old Bill Jones had two daughters and a song
One went to college, and the other went wrong
His wife got killed in a **free-for-all fight**,
But still he keeps a-singing from morning till night
Ride around little dogies, ride around them slow
They're fiery and snuffy and are raring to go

I've worked in your town, worked on your farm,
All I got to show's the muscle in my arm,
Blisters on my feet, and callous on my hand,
I'm going to Montana to throw the houlihan.
Ride around little dogies, ride around them slow,
They're fiery and snuffy and are raring to go.

When I die, take my saddle from the wall
Put it on my pony, lead him out of his stall
Tie my bones to his back, turn our faces to the West
We'll ride the prairie that we love the best
Ride around little dogies, ride around them slow
They're fiery and snuffy and are raring to go
Ride around little dogies, ride around them slow
The fiery and snuffy are raring to go

The cattle herds were driven a very long way to the cattle markets and had to be kept and watched on the open trail for many weeks. And the trail took the cowboys over rough country in all kinds of weather. The wild prairie lands were not friendly to men or animals. It was a lonely land. And the howling of wolves and winds at night made it more so. Across this strange land, no man in the early days of the West knew just where death was waiting for him. A listener hears the mournful feeling cowboys had for the prairie in this song called, "The Dying Cowboy." He does not want to be buried out in these wild lands—in the lone prairie—as the song says. Still, the dying cowboy does not get his wish. There is no choice. He can be buried only in the lone prairie in a narrow grave six by three. Six feet deep and three feet wide.

Oh bury me not on the lone prairie
These words came low and mournfully
From the **pouted lips** of a youth who lay
On his dying bed at the close of day

Oh bury me not on the lone prairie
Where the **coyote** howls and the wind blows free
In a narrow grave just six by three
Bury me not on the lone prairie

It matters not I've oft been told
Where the body lies when the heart grows cold

Yet grant oh grant this wish to me
Bury me not on the lone prairie

Oh bury me not on the lone prairie
Where the coyote howls and the wind blows free
In a narrow grave just six by three
Oh bury me not on the lone prairie

He **wailed in pain** and o'er his brow
Death's shadows fast were gathering now
He thought of his friends and his home but **nigh**
As the cowboys gathered to see him die

Oh bury me not on the lone prairie
These words came low and mournfully
From the pouted lips of a youth who lay
On his dying bed at the close of day

For Your Enjoyment

Red River Valley

From this valley they say you are leaving
We shall miss your bright eyes and sweet smile
For you take with you all, all the sunshine
That has brightened our pathway awhile

Then come sit by my side if you love me
Do not hasten to **bid me adieu**
Just remember the Red River Valley
And the cowboy that's loved you so true

For a long time, my darling, I have waited
For the sweet words you never would say
Now at last all my fond hopes have vanished
For they say that you're going away

Then come sit by my side if you love me
Do not hasten to bid me adieu
Just remember the Red River Valley
And the cowboy that's loved you so true

146

Words, Expressions and Notes

dogie　*n.* 无母犊牛

spied　*v.* 看见

spurs　*n.* 踢马刺

Wyoming　*n.* 怀俄明州

bob off their tails　剪短牛尾巴（以利于上膘）

chuck-wagon　*n.* 为牛仔装运并提供食物的大车

way down　很远

jimson weed　［植］曼陀罗

old choice　一种可供牛吃的野草

prickly pears briers　一种多刺植物

Idaho　爱达荷州

The Chisholm Trail　（歌曲）《奇泽姆小道》，参见上篇注释

punchin' (them cattle)　赶牛放牧

a 2-U herd　蜿蜒前进的牛群形成两个 U 型

gully　*n.* 溪谷；水沟

draw　*n.* 洼地

meaner　*a.* 更小气刻薄的

muley-headed　*a.* 无角的（牛）

Ain't ＝ am not 或 is not 或 are not　非标准英语，多用于口语中。

prairie hay　草原上的草

mighty old　极其糟糕的；该死的

Catahoula pup　牧牛犬幼崽。Catahoula，一种美国牧羊犬，由路易斯安那州的一个印第安人部落得名。

draw my roll　领薪水

figured me out nine dollars in the hole　计算出我倒差（老板）9 美元

an old Dan　一头老牛

throw the houlihan　抛绳索套牛

coulees　*n.* 深冲沟

matted　*v.* 缠结在一起

They're fiery and snuffy and are raring to go　牛的脾气暴躁倔强，不肯朝前走

free-for-all fight　混战

pouted lips　撅起的嘴唇

coyote　*n.* 北美草原狼

wailed in pain　痛苦地哀号

nigh　*adv.* 在近处

bid me adieu　对我说再见

Questions for Comprehension and Discussion

1. How did a new kind of worker, "the cowboy," come into being?

2. How about the life of a cowboy?

3. Why does the life of a real cowboy differ very much from that of cowboys shown in the films and television shows?

4. What are the usual subjects of cowboy songs?

5. Why would the dying cowboy not want to be buried out in the lone prairie?

6. Do you think the American cowboy culture will or will not fade out in the future? Why?

35 The Indian Wars of the West (Part 1)

西部印第安战争 （一）

20 世纪之前的美国历史一直伴随着白种人朝西迁徙的脚步声。从早期殖民地时期人们越过阿巴拉契亚山脉，到西进先驱丹尼尔·布恩开垦肯塔基，再到 19 世纪上半叶人们开始在密西西比河沿岸定居，这时西进运动已经有近百年的历史。1862 年美国通过《定居法案》，法案规定：一个公民只要他有能力在西部定居和开垦，就可以免费获得 65 公顷土地。东部的农民蜂拥般移居到西部的平原和河谷，20 年前还是野牛出没的地方顿时冒出许多村落；养牛的牧民把从得克萨斯州到密西西比河上游广阔的草原占为己有；在山区，矿工们在内华达、蒙大拿、科罗拉多等地开掘矿道，城镇也随之建立起来。

面对白种人的迁徙狂潮，远西地区的原著居民印第安人既愤怒也无奈。一些部落拿起武器奋起反抗，但大多数印第安人在美国政府和军队的强大压力下，只有忍气吞声，听从命运的安排。1854 年 12 月，在濒临太平洋的美国西北部一个现在称为西雅图的地方，一位名叫西雅图的印第安酋长面对美国政府要求他放弃印第安人的传统领土而去政府规定的"保留地"居住的要求，发表了以下催人泪下的讲话：

"不知有多少世纪，苍天为我的人民洒下多少动情的泪水。亘古不变的事物，如今却要改变了。今天晴空万里，明天却可能阴云密布。但是我的话语如同星星，永世不变。白人头领说，华盛顿的大首领向我们表示友好和善意。这是他的好意，因为我们知道，他根本无需我们以友谊作为回报。他的子民众多，如广袤平原上无边的青草。我的族人寥寥，如风暴肆虐后平原上零星的树木。白人大首领捎信给我们，希望购买我们的土地，不过他允许我们保留足够的土地过安逸的生活。这看来的确合理，甚至是慷慨的，因为我们红种人已经没有要求受到尊重的权利了；这也是明智的，因为我们已不再需要辽阔的土地了。

"但我只有一个要求：我们将有权回来祭扫我们的祖先。在我的人民看来，这儿的每一寸土地都是神圣的。每一个山坡，每一条山谷，每一块平原和树林，都因我的族人早已远去的喜怒哀乐而变得圣洁无比……"

The American nation began to expand west during the middle 1800s. People settled in the great open areas of the **Dakotas**, **Utah**, Wyoming, and California. The movement forced the nation to deal with great tribes of native American Indians. The Indians had lived in the western territories for hundreds of years. Settlers and cattle ranchers pushed the Indians out of their homelands. The result was a series of wars between the tribes and the federal government.

At first, the United States government had just one policy to deal with the Indians. It was brutal. Whenever white men wanted Indian land, the tribes were pushed farther west. If the Indians protested, or tried to defend their land, they were destroyed with crushing force. By the middle 1800s, almost all the eastern Indians had been moved west of the Mississippi River. They were given land in **Indian Territory** in what is now the state of Oklahoma. The government described these Indians as "civilized." This meant they were too weak to cause more trouble. Many agreed to follow the ways of the white men.

The Indians of the western grasslands were different. They refused to give up their way of life. These

plains Indians were always on the move, because they hunted buffalo—the American bison. They followed great groups of the animals across the grassy plains. At that time, there were millions of these animals in the American west. The Indians of the plains depended on the buffalo for almost everything they needed. Many of them were fierce fighters. The plains Indians did not want white men crossing their hunting lands. They often tried to destroy the wagon trains carrying settlers to California and Oregon.

Going west! People pass around Independence Rock, Wyoming.

The United States army was given the job of keeping peace. Soldiers were sent to build roads and forts in the western plains. They tried to protect the wagon trains from Indian attacks. They tried to keep white settlers from invading Indian lands. There were many fights between the soldiers and the plains Indians. The soldiers had more powerful weapons. They usually won.

Some plains Indians tried to live peacefully with the white men. One such group was part of the Sioux tribe, called Santee Sioux. It was the largest and most powerful group in the west. The Santee Sioux lived along the Northeastern edge of the **Great Plains** in what is now the state of **Minnesota**. They signed treaties with the government giving up 90 percent of their land. The Santee agreed to live in a small area. In exchange, the United States agreed to make yearly payments to the tribe. This made it possible for the Indians to buy food and other things from white traders.

Trouble started, however, in the summer of 1862. The government was late giving the Indians their yearly payment. As a result, the Indians lacked the money to buy food. The white traders refused to give the Indians **credit** to buy food. One trader said: "If they are hungry, let them eat grass." The Indians were hungry. Soon, their hunger turned to anger. Finally, the local Indian chief called his men together. He gave the orders for war. Early the next morning, the tribe attacked the trading stores. Most of the traders were killed, including the man who had insulted the Indians. He was found with his mouth filled with grass. The governor of Minnesota sent a force of state soldiers to stop the Indian revolt. The soldiers had artillery. They killed several hundred Indians in battle. They hanged several others. Soon, the revolt was over.

Trouble came next to parts of Colorado and Wyoming. This is where the Sioux Indians and the **Cheyenne** Indians lived. The chief of the Lakota Sioux tribe was named **Red Cloud**. The Indians fought bitterly to keep white men out of their hunting grounds. After two years of fighting, with many deaths on both sides, the government decided the struggle was too costly. It asked for peace. The Sioux and the Cheyenne agreed. They were given a large area of land north of Wyoming in the Dakota territory. They also were given the right to use their old hunting lands farther north. The government agreed to close a road used by whites to cross the hunting grounds. And all soldiers were withdrawn from Sioux country.

The war ended and peace came to the Sioux and the Cheyenne. With peace came a new United States policy toward other Indians of the West. The government decided to put aside an area of land for each tribe. The land was called a "**reservation**." Each tribe would live on its own reservation. Most of the

149

reservations were in Indian territory in what is now the state of Oklahoma. Other reservations were in Dakota near the land of the Sioux.

The government believed it would cost less money and fewer lives to keep Indians on reservations. The Indians would be away from possible trouble with white settlers. Instead of moving freely over the plains to hunt buffalo, the Indians would live in one place. They would receive food and money from the government. Officials came from Washington to explain this new policy to the Indians. A big meeting was held. Chiefs representing many tribes attended. The chiefs spoke, one after another, to the government officials.

All of the chiefs said they, too, wished to live in peace with the white men. But many questioned the decision to move to reservations. One who did so was Chief Ten Bears of the **Comanche** tribe. He said:

> There are things which you have said to me that I do not like. You said you wanted to put us on a reservation. You said you would build houses for us. I do not want your houses. I was born on the plains where the wind blows free, and there is nothing to break the light of the sun. I was born where everything breathed a free breath. I want to die there... not within walls.

So the government and the Indians reached a compromise. The tribes were given reservations in Indian territory. But they were also given permission to hunt buffalo in a wide area south of the reservations. The Indians agreed to give up all their old lands. They agreed to live in peace on the reservations. In exchange, the United States promised to give the Indians all the food, clothing, and other things they needed. It also promised to give them schools and medical care.

The Indians were not happy with this agreement. They did not

The Indians' way of life—hunting the buffalo

want to give up their old ways of living. However, they saw they had no choice. The government was too strong. They waited weeks, then months, for help to move to the new reservations. They could not understand the delay in carrying out the agreement. The delay was in Washington, D. C. Congress could not agree on how much money to spend on the Indians. So the lawmakers refused to approve the agreement. They left the situation unsettled. Again, Indians were forced to watch angrily as white settlers began moving onto lands they had agreed to give up. As the whites moved in, the buffalo and other animals left. The Indians had difficulty finding food.

Soldiers shared their food with the Indians. It was not enough. Western officials sent urgent messages to Washington asking for supplies for the Indians. No supplies could be sent until Congress approved the money to buy them. As before, some of the Indians became angry and refused to wait any longer. Their anger led to new fighting. In the end, it was a fight that failed to win back their land.

Words, Expressions and Notes

Dakotas *n.*（南北）达科他州

Utah *n.* 犹他州

Indian Territory 印第安准州，即后来的俄克拉何马州。美国政府在 19 世纪初强迫印第安人定居的区域。

plains Indians 生活在平原上的印第安人

Great Plains （位于加拿大和美国中西部的）大平原。这是世界上最大的平原之一，约占加拿大领土面积的 18% 和美国领土面积的 15%。

Minnesota *n.* 明尼苏达州

credit *n.* 信用，赊欠

Cheyenne *n.* 沙伊安印第安人部落

Red Cloud 红云（1822—1909），印第安俄格拉拉苏（Oglala Sioux）部落首领，率领印第安人在 19 世纪 60 年代成功阻止白人对怀俄明、蒙大拿和南达科他部分地区的占领。

reservation *n.* 保留地，美国政府划给印第安人居住的地方

Comanche *n.* 科曼奇印第安人部落

Questions for Comprehension and Discussion

1. Why was there a series of wars between the Indian tribes and the federal government during the middle 1800s?
2. What was the old policy of the United States to deal with the Indians?
3. Why would the Indians kill the traders in Minnesota in the summer of 1862?
4. What was the new United States policy toward the Indians of the West?
5. Why did many Indians not want to move to reservations?

36 The Indian Wars of the West (Part 2)

西部印第安战争（二）

美国历史上的"印第安战争"（The Indian Wars）泛指从殖民地时期起白人与印第安人之间爆发的战争；而"西部印第安战争"则专指越过密西西比河后朝太平洋沿岸地区迁徙的白人与印第安人之间爆发的一系列武装冲突，冲突总数达 950 次之多。

在处理早期冲突时，美国政府对印第安人采取的是极其残忍的政策——驱赶、清剿和杀戮，全然不顾这些世世代代居住在美洲大陆土著居民的传统和感情。一直到 19 世纪 70 年代，美国人才逐渐意识到对待印第安人的不公，成立了"国家印第安人权利协会"等组织。1881 年，一个最早为印第安人鸣冤叫屈的妇女海伦·杰克逊（Helen Jackson）出版了《百年耻辱》（*A Century of Dishonor*），此书立即成为对白人迫害印第安人的起诉书。作者在书中指出："在过去的三十年中，太平洋大陆架上的印第安人所遭受的欺凌、压榨和杀戮，可怕得令人难以置信。"但具有讽刺意味的是，当这个白人良心运动兴起之时，印第安人实际上对白人再也不构成任何威胁了。

从 19 世纪 60 年代至 80 年代，印第安人对入侵他们家园的白人展开了最后的殊死搏斗，其中影响最大的莫过于 1876 年发生在蒙大拿的一次战役。美国内战中涌现的英雄乔治·卡斯特将军率领一支部队把印第安人驱赶回保留地。这位毕业于西点军校，在内战结束时仅 25 岁就晋升为少将的军事天才，此时早已名扬全国。而他自己也踌躇满志，期待着有朝一日当上美国总统。然而，骄傲自大、对印第安人不屑一顾的他却中了埋伏，他与两百多名士兵被一举歼灭。从此，卡斯特成为美国历史上最具争议的一个人物，他的名字也在军事上成为狂妄自大的代名词。

1890 年 12 月 28 日，在南达科他一个叫"伤膝溪"（Wounded Knee Creek）的地方，联邦军队袭击了一个印第安部落，三百多印第安人被杀死，史称"伤膝溪屠杀"（Wounded Knee Massacre）。至此，北美大陆印第安民族长达 300 年反抗外来入侵者的历史悲剧终于落下最后一幕。正如印第安宗教领袖黑鹿（Black Elk）指出的那样："一个民族的梦想就在那里消亡。"

During the 1800s, the federal government forced native American Indians to live in special areas. These were called reservations. The Indians no longer could move freely over the Great Plains to hunt buffalo. White men were settling there. The situation resulted in violence.

The government sent soldiers to force the Indians to move to reservations. But the soldiers could not keep them there. Groups of Indians would leave the reservations in the spring. They followed the buffalo across the plains. Some raided the homes of White settlers. They stole horses and cattle. At the end of the summer, the Indians would return to the reservations. And the government would give them food for the winter.

As years passed, fewer Indians left the reservations to live the old life on the plains. It became difficult to find buffalo. The plains were becoming empty. Only a few years before, millions of buffalo lived on the Great Plains. Then railroads were built across the country. White men came to claim the grasslands. They put up fences. Cowboys came up from Texas with huge groups of cattle. They forced the buffalo away or killed them. The Indians tried to prevent this killing. Angry groups of Indians often attacked White buffalo hunters. But the army was too strong. Soldiers killed or captured many Indians.

Finally, most Indians gave up the struggle. They surrendered their guns and horses. They went back to the reservations and became farmers.

All this was taking place in what is now the South-central part of the United States. Far to the North, another struggle was taking place involving the great Sioux Indian tribe. The Sioux had signed a treaty with the government in 1868. The treaty gave them a large reservation in what is now Nebraska, South Dakota, and Wyoming. The Black Hills in Dakota were part of the reservation. These hills were important to the Sioux. In their religion, the Black Hills were a holy place. They were the center of their world, where the gods lived. They were the place where Indian fighters went to speak with the great spirit.

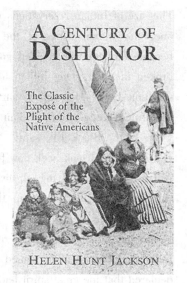

A Century of Dishonor, **an offending stain in American history**

In 1873, the Black Hills suddenly became important to white men, too. Gold was discovered there. Treaties and religion meant nothing to the White miners who rushed to the Black Hills to search for gold. At first, the Indians killed some of the miners. They chased others away. But more miners came. The Sioux tribe asked the government to enforce the treaty. Tribal leaders asked the government to keep White men away from the reservation. The army sent soldiers to remove the miners. The soldiers ordered the miners to leave. But they made no effort to enforce the order. Again the Indians protested. This time, the government sent officials to negotiate a new treaty. It asked the Sioux Indians to give up the Black Hills. Some of the Indian leaders refused to negotiate. One who rejected the invitation was **Sitting Bull**. "I do not want to sell any land to the government," Chief Sitting Bull said. He held a little dust between his fingers. "Not even this much."

This resistance did not stop government efforts to get the Black Hills for the miners. The War Department sent General **George Crook** to punish the Indians and force them back to their reservation. Crook led a large force into Sioux country. He surprised an Indian village, capturing hundreds of horses. There was another clash a few months later. This time, the result was very different. The Indians gave the army its worst defeat in almost a century.

Sitting Bull with his family members

The battle took place near the **Little Bighorn River**. General **George Custer** led 212 soldiers in search of the Indian leader, **Crazy Horse**. As General Custer moved through the river valley, he sent men ahead to explore the area. His men returned with reports that thousands of Indians were waiting to attack. Custer refused to listen. He pushed forward. Soon, his forces were surrounded by Indians. In less than an hour, the Indians killed the general and every one of his men. The white soldiers lay dead at Little Bighorn. And Custer's name would go down in history as a symbol of foolish pride in battle. The battle at Little Bighorn was a serious defeat for the United States Army. But the Indians' victory did not last long. Within a year, the army forced most of the Sioux to surrender. It took the Black Hills for the miners. It moved the Indians to a new reservation.

In the next few years, the same thing happened to other Indian tribes throughout the west. Under great pressure from White settlers, the government took land from the Indians and opened it to settlement.

The size of Indian reservations was reduced again and again. One by one, the Indian tribes of the west changed. Their fierce fighters became farmers who needed government help. They were weak and broken in spirit. One Indian leader named **Black Elk** described the situation best. He was a survivor of a battle at a place called **Wounded Knee**. Many Indian women and children had died there. Years later, Black Elk said: "I did not know then how much was ended. When I look back now from this high hill of my old age, I can still see the dead lying all over the ground. And I can see that something else died there in the bloody mud, and was buried. A people's dream died there."

Some Indians turned to religion during this difficult time. An Indian religious leader named **Wovoka** gained influence. Wovoka declared that the great spirit had chosen him to prepare the Indians for a new world. He said the New World would arrive soon. And it would

General George Custer

be a wonderful world. There would be no White men, he said. And all dead Indians would come back to life. Wovoka warned that new soil would rise up and cover the world like a flood. He said Indians could escape destruction by dancing a special dance. It was called the Ghost Dance. Wovoka said the Ghost Dance would make Indians powerful. He said it would even protect them from bullets fired by the White men's guns.

Thousands of Indians in the American west listened to Wovoka's message. They believed him. And they began to dance for long hours every day. On the Sioux reservations, all other activities stopped. Children no longer went to school. No one did anything but dance. All this frightened White officials. They tried to arrest some Indian leaders to stop the dancing. The arrests led to fighting. And the fighting led to a final battle in which the army defeated the Indians completely. The Indian wars were over. Wovoka himself told his followers: "Our trails are covered with grass and sand. We cannot find them. Today I call upon you to travel a new trail. It is the only trail now open—the White man's road."

Words, Expressions and Notes

Sitting Bull 坐牛（约 1831—1890），印第安苏人首领，领导苏人抗拒白人侵占印第安人土地的斗争，参加小比格霍恩战役，在"鬼舞"（Ghost Dance）暴动中被杀害。

George Crook 乔治·克鲁克（1829—1890），美国将军

Little Bighorn River 小比格霍恩河，著名的小比格霍恩战役就发生在此。

George Custer 乔治·卡斯特（1839—1876），美国骑兵军官，在内战中战绩卓著，率部袭击蒙大拿小比格霍恩河附近的印第安人营地时因轻敌而战败身亡。

Crazy Horse 疯马（约 1840—1877），具有传奇色彩的苏族印第安人领袖，率领族人抵抗白人入侵大草原，投降后被杀。

Black Elk 黑鹿（1863—1950），印第安人宗教领袖，致力于调和印第安传统文化和白人基督教文化，1904 年改信基督教。

Wounded Knee（Creek） 伤膝溪

Wovoka 瓦午卡（约 1856—1932），印第安巫师，声称接受上帝的旨意，引导印第安人跳"鬼舞"（Ghost Dance）以期重新获得失去的土地。"鬼舞"事件成为 1890 年 12 月 15 日印第安人首领"坐牛"被杀和 12 月底"伤膝溪屠杀"的直接导火索。

Questions for Comprehension and Discussion

1. How did the federal government deal with the Indians during the 1800s?
2. Why did the buffalo become fewer and fewer on the Great Plains?
3. Why did the white men often break the treaties they had signed with the Indians?
4. How did the Indians give the federal army its worst defeat in almost a century?
5. An Indian leader said: "Our trails are covered with grass and sand. We cannot find them. Today I call upon you to travel a new trail. It is the only trail now open—the White man's road." What is your opinion about his words?

Unit 10　Becoming an Industrial Giant

37　Cultivation of the West and the Story of the Statue of Liberty

西部的农业化和自由女神铜像的故事

　　内战在美国历史上刻下了一道清晰的印迹。从经济方面看，战争的需求大大地刺激了制造业，促进了大规模生产和铁路网的建设，同时还促进了科学和发明。这就为战后美国西部的农业化和逐步迈向工业化强国奠定了坚实的基础。

　　战争的结束和印第安人反抗的平定让美国的经济潜力如火山般爆发出来。《定居法案》的颁布、机器和新技术在农业上的广泛应用，使过去向西部的缓慢扩展变成一场如野火蔓延的运动。从 1860 年至 1890 年，尽管全国人口增加一倍多，美国农业生产的粮食、棉花和肉类，不但可以充分满足美国人的需要，并且剩余量日益增加。而此时全世界绝大多数其他国家的人民每天都还挣扎在饥饿的边缘。

　　农业机器的广泛应用是取得这一了不起成就的首要原因。在 1800 年，一个农民用镰刀在一天之内只能收割五分之一公顷土地上的小麦；当他使用新发明的收割机后，一天的收割面积竟达两公顷半。其他农业机器如自动捆扎机、脱粒机、播种机、切割机、去皮机、去壳机、奶油分离机、撒肥机、种薯机、干草机、孵卵机等也如雨后春笋一样涌现出来。取得这一成就的第二个原因就是西部的开发和利用。只有如此广阔的西部平原，才能为农业机器的大规模应用提供足够宽广的舞台。

　　在 19 世纪的各种伟大发明中，最不起眼的可能要数带刺铁丝网。然而，这个美国伊利诺伊州农民约塞夫·格里登（Joseph Glidden）1874 年的发明却给美国西部带来意想不到的变化：它大大加快了西部平原的农业化步伐，并使西部自由而浪漫的牧场时代走向终点。

　　农业革命反过来又对工业产生了巨大的推动作用。规模巨大的工厂、钢铁厂，横贯大陆的铁路线，繁华的城市，迅速布满在这块广袤的土地上。但是，工业化的各种问题也随之而来，如有些大企业力图垄断市场及生产，工人劳动条件恶劣、工资偏低、劳动时间过长等等，劳资双方的矛盾日益加深。

　　在这样的背景下，1886 年，塞缪尔·冈珀斯建立了美国劳工联合会。这一时期公众对工会怀有敌意。在冈珀斯的领导下，劳工联合会避免激进的政治纲领，摆脱雇主们试图强加给劳工的激进形象，把精力集中在诸如工资和工作条件等所谓"面包与黄油"一类问题上，提出工人所要求的也是其他人所要求的——更好的生活、合理的工资、良好的工作条件及自我提高的时间。在其后的八十年里，冈珀斯进行不懈斗争，其主要目标就是为工人争取最直接的权益，如每天 8 小时工作制等。

　　After the Indians were defeated, thousands of settlers hurried west. Some hoped to find new, rich farmland. The soil they left behind was thin and overworked. Their crops were poor. Some simply hoped to buy any kind of farmland. They did not have enough money to buy farmland in the east. Others came from other countries and hoped to build new lives in the United States. All the settlers found it easy to get

land in the west. In 1862, Congress had passed the **Homestead Act**. This law gave every citizen, and every foreigner who asked for citizenship, the right to claim government land. The law said each man could have 65 **hectares**. If he built a home on the land, and farmed it for five years, it would be his. He paid just ten dollars to record the deal.

Claiming land on the Great Plains was easy. Building a farm there and working it was not so easy. The wide flat grasslands seemed strange to men who had lived among the hills and forests of the East. Here there were few hills or trees. Without trees, settlers had no wood to build houses. Some built houses partly underground. Others built houses from blocks of earth cut out of the grassland. These houses were dark and dirty. They leaked and became muddy when it rained. There were no fences on the great plains. So it was hard to keep animals away from crops.

Settlers in the American west also had a problem faced by many people in the world today. They had little fuel for heating and cooking. With few trees to cut for fuel, they collected whatever they could find. Small woody plants. Dried grass. Cattle and buffalo wastes. Water was hard to find, too. And although the land seemed rich, it was difficult to prepare for planting. The grass roots were thick and strong. They did not break apart easily. The weather also was a problem. Sometimes months would pass without rain, and the crops would die. Winters were bitterly cold.

Most of the settlers, however, were strong people. They did not expect an easy life. And as time passed, they found solutions to most of the problems of farming on the great plains. Railroads were built across the West. They brought wood for homes. Wood and coal for fuel. Technology solved many of the problems. New equipment was invented for digging deep wells. Better pumps were built to raise the water to the surface. Some of the pumps used windmills for power.

The fence problem was solved in 1874. That was the year "**barbed wire**" was invented. The sharp metal barbs tore the skin of the men who stretched it along fence tops. But they prevented cattle from pushing over the fences and destroying crops. New farm equipment was invented. This included a plow that could break up the grassland of the plains. And farmers learned techniques for farming in dry weather.

Grover Cleveland was elected President of the United States in 1884. He was the first Democratic Party candidate to win the White House in almost 28 years.

Cleveland began his administration by announcing that he would reduce waste in the government. He would make government more like business. He said he would support reforms to let ability—not politics—decide who would get government jobs. Democratic Party leaders were quick to protest. They explained to Cleveland that the party owed jobs to those who had worked for his victory. Cleveland had to compromise. He permitted about 80,000 government jobs to be taken from Republicans and given to Democrats. This left 12,000 jobs. These would be given to people who did the best on government examinations. Cleveland's decision angered Republican reformers who had voted for him. They accused him of surrendering to the leaders of the Democratic Party.

On other issues, however, Cleveland refused to compromise. He opposed government economic aid to any industrial group. He vetoed a bill giving aid to farmers whose crops had failed. And he vetoed another bill giving more money to men who had served as soldiers during America's Civil War of the 1860s. The president also showed his independence by investigating gifts of public land that the government had made to the railroad, wood, and cattle industries. He found that many of these land grants were made illegally. He got back much of the land. He opened it to settlers.

President Cleveland also was concerned about a growing number of labor disputes that took place in the United States in the late 1800s. He proposed that Congress create a labor committee to help settle the disputes.

Congress failed to act on this proposal. But its lack of action did not stop the rise of a labor organization that had been formed a few years earlier. The group soon would become the most important labor union in the United States. It was the **American Federation of Labor**, or AFL. Led by **Samuel Gompers**, the AFL was different from earlier labor groups. It did not try to put all workers into one union. Instead, it tied together a number of different unions and gave them general leadership.

The AFL was different in other ways. It did not oppose the economic system of capitalism. It said only that labor should get more of the earnings of capitalism. The AFL also opposed extremists who used labor protests to change the social system. What the AFL called for were things workers wanted immediately. Higher wages. A shorter workday. Better working conditions. One of its first demands was an eight-hour workday. This demand led to a number of strikes and protests throughout the country.

The most serious incident took place in Chicago's **Haymarket Square**. More than one thousand union supporters went to a meeting there organized by an extremist. They stood calmly and listened to speeches. Just before the meeting ended, someone threw a bomb into a group of policemen. The bomb exploded with a **blinding flash**. Seven policemen were killed. The other policemen began shooting at the crowd. Some people in the crowd fired back. When it was all over, ten persons had been shot to death. Fifty others were hurt. The incident **set off** a wave of fear and anger across the country. The public demanded action against union extremists. The Haymarket Square violence slowed the growth of organized labor in the United States for many years. It would be some time before labor became a powerful force in national events.

In the spring of 1886, President Cleveland announced that he was to be married. The ceremony took place in the White House. A few months later, President Cleveland and the First Lady went to New York City for the official ceremony welcoming the **Statue of Liberty**. The statue was a gift to the people of the United States from the people of France. It represented the alliance between their two countries during America's war for independence from Britain. The statue was the creation of French artist **Frederic-Auguste Bartholdi**. He decided to make a statue that would represent freedom—a Statue of Liberty. He said it should stand on an island in New York Harbor. There, he said, it would welcome all who came to America through that gateway.

Bartholdi decided to make a copper statue in the image of a woman—Lady Liberty. High above her head, she would hold a torch of freedom to light the world. The statue's face was the face of Bartholdi's mother. The artist asked French

The Statue of Liberty

engineer **Gustave Eiffel** to build a steel support to hold the heavy statue. Eiffel was the man who later built the Eiffel Tower in Paris. The statue was built in France. Then the pieces were sent across the Atlantic Ocean. It was rebuilt in New York.

Grover Cleveland and his wife were not the only Americans to attend the Statue of Liberty ceremonies in 1886. Thousands of people crowded onto ships in the harbor to watch the great event. Thousands of others crowded the shorelines around the harbor. Everyone cheered wildly when a signal was given and a huge cloth fell from the statue. Lady Liberty stood holding her torch high for freedom. Under her feet were the broken chains of tyranny. **Below the statue was a poem**. It called to the poor and oppressed people of the world. It told them to come to America to find a land of hope and freedom.

Give me your tired, your poor,
Your **huddled masses yearning to breathe free**,
The **wretched refuse** of your **teeming shores**.
Send these, the homeless, **tempest-tost** to me,
I lift my lamp beside the golden door. [1]

The Statue of Liberty was a great success. It was one of the great engineering wonders of its time. And it filled Americans with pride in their tradition of freedom and openness to people from all lands.

Words, Expressions and Notes

Homestead Act   《定居法案》，又称《宅地法》，美国国会 1862 年通过的法案，规定凡连续耕种公有土地 5 年的农户即可获得 65 公顷土地的所有权。

hectares   *n.* 公顷

barbed wire   带刺的铁丝

Grover Cleveland   格罗菲·克里夫兰（1837—1908），两度任美国总统（1885—1889，1893—1897）。

American Federation of Labor（AFL）   美国劳工联合会

Samuel Gompers   塞缪尔·冈珀斯（1850—1924），美国劳工领袖，组建美国劳工联合会，以政策保守闻名，主张通过劳资协议维护工人的利益。

Haymarket Square   （芝加哥）干草广场，1886 年 5 月 4 日干草市场骚乱发生地

blinding flash   刺眼的火光

set off   引起

Statue of Liberty   自由女神铜像

Frederic-Auguste Bartholdi   巴托尔迪（1834—1904），法国雕塑家，纽约港自由女神铜像的作者

Gustave Eiffel   埃菲尔（1832—1923），法国土木工程师，巴黎埃菲尔铁塔的建造者

Below the statue was a poem.   铜像下有一首诗。这是指美国女诗人埃玛·拉扎勒斯（Emma Lazarus, 1849—1887）为自由女神像创作的十四行诗《新的巨像》（The New Colossus）。

huddled masses yearning to breathe free   渴望自由呼吸挤成一团的人们

wretched refuse   不幸的社会渣滓

teeming shores   拥挤的海岸

tempest-tost   *a.* 在暴风雨中颠簸飘摇的

Questions for Comprehension and Discussion

1. Why was the Homestead Act a great encouragement to the cultivation of American West?
2. What were the problems the farmers in the West had to face?
3. Why was the "barbed wire" an important invention for the West?
4. Why was President Cleveland concerned about the increasing labor disputes that took place in the United States in the late 1800s?
5. Why was the growth of organized labor in the United States slowed by Chicago's Haymarket Square violence?
6. Why did France give the Statue of Liberty as a gift to the United States?

---

1 把你们拥挤土地上不幸的社会垃圾，//穷困潦倒而渴望呼吸自由的芸芸众生，//连同那些无家可归、四处漂泊的人们送来，//我高举明灯守候在这金色的大门！

38 Industrial Revolution and Mass Immigration

工业革命与移民浪潮

在内战后不到 50 年的时间中，美国迅速从一个农业化的国家发展为一个工业化和城市化的国家。美国在这个过程中爆发出来的惊人能量令人瞠目结舌。1844 年电报技术的改进，使美洲大陆相距遥远的各地被电线杆和电线网连接起来。1876 年电话发明后，很快就普及全国，促进了社会和经济生活的发展。1867 年发明的打字机、1888 年发明的加法机和 1897 年发明的现金计数器，更加速了工商业的发展。1886 年铸造排字机、轮转印刷机和折报机发明后，一小时内就可以印刷 24 万份每份 8 页的报纸。爱迪生发明的电灯给千家万户带来了光明。爱迪生还发明了留声机，并和乔治·伊斯曼合作改进了电影。这些伟大的发明，加上其他许多科学技术的应用，使各行各业的生产力达到了一个崭新的高度。

在这种工业新秩序中，城市成了神经中枢，它集中了所有的经济力量，积聚了巨大的资金、众多的企业和金融机构、宽阔的铁路车场、烟囱林立的工厂，以及大批的工人。无数的乡村几乎在一夜之间便变成了市镇，市镇又扩展为城市。在 1830 年，只有 1/15 的人口居住在城镇；到 1860 年，比例已达 1/6；至 1890 年，更是提高到 3/10。在 1860 年，没有一个城市有上百万的人口，但 30 年后，纽约、芝加哥和费城人口都超过 100 万。在 30 年的时间里，费城和巴尔的摩人口增加了一倍，堪萨斯城和底特律的人口增加了 4 倍，克利夫兰增加了 6 倍，芝加哥增加了 10 倍。一些在内战开始时仅有几间房屋的小村落，人口竟增加了 50 倍甚至 50 倍以上。

其实，在这些巨大变化的后面，除了农业革命和工业革命的因素之外，还有一股巨大的推动力量，那就是内战后如潮水般涌来的世界各国的移民。

The "Lady of Liberty" holds a bright torch high over the harbor of New York City. Her torch of freedom was a welcome signal to millions of **immigrants** arriving to begin a new life in America.

American life was changing. And it was changing quickly. Before 1860, the United States had an agricultural economy. After 1860, the country began to change from an agricultural to an industrial economy. In 1860, American shops and factories produced less than two thousand million dollars' worth of goods. Thirty years later, in 1890, American factories produced ten thousand million dollars' worth. By then, more than five million persons were working in factories and mines. Another three million had jobs in the building industries and transportation.

Year after year, production continued to increase. And the size of the industrial labor force continued to grow. A great many of the new industrial workers came from American farms. Farm work was hard, and the pay was low. Young men left the family farms as soon as they could. They went to towns and cities to look for an easier and better way of life. Many of them found it in the factories. A young man who worked hard and learned new skills could rise quickly to better and better jobs. This was not only true for farmers, but also for immigrants who came to the United States from foreign countries. They came from many different lands and for many different reasons. But all came with the same hope for a better life in a new world.

In the 1850s, America's industrial revolution was just beginning. Factories needed skilled workers—

men who knew how to do all the necessary jobs. Factory owners offered high pay to workers who had these skills. British workers had them. Many had spent years in British factories. Pay was poor in Britain, and these skilled workers could get much more money in America. So, many of them came. Hundreds of thousands. Some factories—even some industries—seemed completely British.

Cloth factories in **Fall River**, Massachusetts, were filled with young men from Lancashire, England. Most of the workers in the shipyards of San Francisco were from Scotland. Many of the coal miners in America were men from the British mines in **Wales**. Many were farmers who came to America because they could get land for nothing. They could build new farms for themselves in the rich land of the American West.

One of the best-liked songs in Britain then was a song about the better life in America. Its name: "To the West." Its words helped many men decide to make the move to America.

> To the west, to the west, to the land of the free
> Where mighty Missouri rolls down to the sea;
> Where a man is a man if he's willing to toil,
> And the poorest may harvest the fruits of the soil.
> Where the young may exult and the aged may rest,
> Away, far away, to the land of the west.

To another group of immigrants, America was the last hope. Ireland in the 1840s **suffered one crop failure after another**. Hungry men had to leave. In 1850 alone, more than 117,000 people came to the United States from Ireland. Most had no money and little education. To those men and women, America was a magic name.

Throughout Europe, when times were hard, people talked of going to America. In some countries, organizations were formed to help people **emigrate** to the United States. A Polish farmer wrote to such an organization in **Warsaw**: "I want to go to America. But I have no money. I have nothing but the ten fingers of my hands, a wife, and nine children. I have no work at all, although I am strong and healthy and only 45 years old. I have been to many towns and cities in Poland, wherever I could go. Nowhere could I earn much money. I wish to work. But what can I do? I will not steal, and I have no work. So, I beg you to accept me for a journey to America."

As the years passed, fewer people were moving to America for a better job. Most were coming now for any job at all. Work was hard to find in any of the cities in Europe. A British lawmaker told parliament in 1870 that Englishmen were leaving their country, not because they wanted to, but because they had to. They could not find work at home. He said that even as he spoke, hundreds were dying of hunger in London and other British cities. They were victims of the new revolution in agriculture and industry. Small family farms were disappearing. In their places rose large modern farms that could produce much more. New machines took the place of men. And millions of farmers had to look for other work. Some found it in the factories. Industry was growing quickly, but not quickly enough to give jobs to all the farmers out of work.

In the next ten years, millions of people made the move from Britain, Germany, and the **Scandinavian countries**. But then, as industry in those countries grew larger, and more jobs opened, the flood of immigration began to slow. The immigrants now were coming from Southern and Eastern Europe. Anti-Jewish feeling swept Russia and Poland. Violence against Jews caused many of them to move to America. In the late 1880s, **cholera** spread through much of Southern Italy. Fear of the disease led many families to leave for the United States. Others left when their governments began building up strong armies. Young men who did not want to be soldiers often escaped by moving to America. Big armies were costly, and many people left because they did not want to pay the high taxes. Whatever the reason, people continued to immigrate to the United States.

These new immigrants were not like those who came earlier. These new immigrants had no skills. Most were unable to read or write. Factory owners found that these Eastern and Southern Europeans were hard workers. They did not protest because the work was hard and the pay was low. They did not demand better working conditions. They did not join unions or strike. Factory owners began to replace higher-paid American and British workers with the new immigrants. Business leaders wanted more of the new workers. They urged the immigrants to write letters to their friends and relatives in the old country. "Tell them to come to America, that there are plenty of jobs."

Within a few years, foreign-born workers held most of the unskilled jobs in many American industries. American workers began to protest. They demanded an end to the flood of immigration.

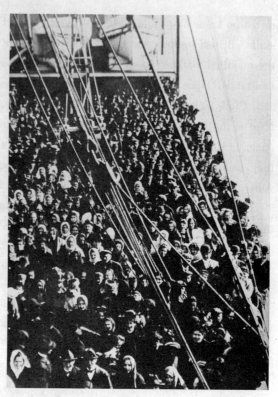

Immigrants crowded the deck of a ship arriving at Ellis Island in 1906.

Words, Expressions and Notes

immigrants *n.* （移入的）移民
Fall River 落河城，位于马萨诸塞州东南部，曾经是美国重要的纺织工业基地。
Wales *n.* （英国）威尔士
suffered one crop failure after another 粮食连年歉收。爱尔兰 19 世纪 40 年代发生土豆饥荒，史称"土豆大饥荒"（Great Potato Famine），该灾难造成 100 多万爱尔兰人死亡，并引发大规模移民浪潮。
emigrate *v.* 移居外国
Warsaw *n.* 华沙，波兰首都
Scandinavian countries 斯堪的纳维亚诸国
cholera *n.* 霍乱

Questions for Comprehension and Discussion

1. What happened to American life after 1860?
2. Why did large numbers of Europeans come to the United States from foreign countries?
3. Why did a great many of Irish people leave their country for America in the middle of the 19th century?
4. How did the first group of Chinese come to America?
5. Why did the American Congress pass a law to bar Chinese immigration in 1882? What happened after that?

The Spanish-American War

美西战争

美国内战给国家造成了巨大的创伤。身体上的伤口易于复原，而心灵上的创伤却需要更多的时间去愈合。在世界历史上，不乏由于重大突发事件而导致一个国家出现空前团结统一局面的例子。19 世纪 90 年代美国与西班牙之间的争端正好给心灵上仍有裂痕的美国提供了这样一个机会。

那时，西班牙还统治着佛罗里达半岛以南的小岛古巴，而美国与古巴的贸易当时正非常兴旺。1895 年，古巴人对西班牙暴政的愤怒终于爆发成为争取独立的战争。大多数美国人同情古巴人，但克利夫兰总统却决定保持中立。不过，3 年以后，当麦金利总统当政，美国战舰缅因号停泊于哈瓦那港口时，忽遭摧毁，260 名海员丧生。此事立刻激起全国民众的愤慨。数月后，美国决定武装干涉。

对西班牙的战争进展迅速，战事进行的 4 个月中，美国从未遭受重大挫折。战争胜利后，从波士顿到旧金山，汽笛声响彻云霄，旗帜到处飞扬，全国上下一片欢呼声。美西战争不仅让南北战争的阴霾完全散尽，还把美国推向了一个世界强国的位置。

战争中涌现出一位名叫西奥多·罗斯福的英雄。他率领美国第一义勇骑兵团到古巴作战。战后，他在古巴的英勇行为使他当上了纽约州长。就任纽约州长几个月后，罗斯福于 1899 年 4 月 10 日在芝加哥发表了《赞艰苦奋斗》(In Praise of the Strenuous Life) 的演讲，这是他最受人们欢迎的演讲之一。特别值得注意的是，他把清朝末年的中国作为讲演主题的一个反面例证。透过一个多世纪的历史烟云，我们今天来听他的讲话，仍然振聋发聩：

"我们这一代人用不着面临我们先辈所面临的那种任务，但是，我们也有自己的任务，要是我们没能完成我们的任务，我们就要遭到不幸。我们绝不能扮演中国的角色，要是我们重蹈中国的覆辙，自满自足，贪图自己疆域内的安宁享乐，渐渐地腐败堕落，对国外的事情毫无兴趣，沉溺于纸醉金迷之中，忘掉了奋发向上、苦干冒险的高尚生活，整天忙于满足我们肉体暂时的欲望，那么，毫无疑问，总有一天我们会突然发现中国今天已经发生的这一事实：畏惧战争、闭关锁国、贪图安宁享乐的民族在其他好战、爱冒险的民族的进攻面前是肯定要衰败的。"

两年以后，西奥多·罗斯福成为美国第二十六任总统。

Unlike other presidents of the late 1800s, **William McKinley** spent much of his presidency dealing with foreign policy. The most serious problem involved Spain. Spain ruled Cuba at that time. Cuban rebels had started a fight for independence. The Spanish government promised the cuban people equal rights and self-rule, but in the future. The rebels did not want to wait. President McKinley felt Spain should be left alone to honor its promises. He also felt responsible for protecting the lives and property of Americans in Cuba. When riots broke out in Havana, he ordered the **battleship _Maine_** to sail there. One night in early 1898, a powerful explosion sank the _Maine_. More than 250 American sailors died.

William McKinley

There was some evidence the explosion was caused by an accident in the ship's fuel tanks. But many Americans blamed Spain. They demanded war to free Cuba and make it independent.

President McKinley had a difficult decision to make. He did not want war. As he told a friend: "I fought in our Civil War. I saw the dead piled up. I do not want to see that again." But McKinley also knew many Americans wanted war. If he refused to fight Spain, his Republican Party could lose popular support. So, he did not ask Congress for a declaration of war right away. He sent a message to the Spanish government, instead. McKinley demanded an immediate ceasefire in Cuba. He also offered his help in ending the revolt. By the time Spain agreed to the demands, McKinley had made his decision. He asked Congress for permission to use military force to bring peace to Cuba. Congress agreed. It also demanded that Spain withdraw from Cuba and give up all claims to the island. The President signed the congressional resolution. The Spanish government immediately broke relations. On April 25th, 1898, the United States declared war on Spain.

The American Navy was ready to fight. It was three times bigger than the Spanish navy. It also was better trained. A ship-building program begun 15 years earlier had made the American Navy one of the strongest in the world. Its ships were made of steel and carried powerful guns. Part of the American Navy at that time was based in Hong Kong. The rest was based on the Atlantic coast of the United States. Admiral **George Dewey** commanded the **Pacific Fleet**. Dewey had received a message from the **Assistant Secretary of the Navy, Theodore Roosevelt**. If war broke out, it said, he was to attack the Spanish naval force in **the Philippines**. The Spanish force was commanded by Admiral Patricio Montojo.

The American fleet arrived in **Manila Bay** on May 1st. It sailed toward the line of Spanish ships. The Spanish fired first. The shells missed. When the two naval forces were 5,000 meters apart, Admiral Dewey ordered the Americans to fire. After three hours, Admiral Montojo surrendered. Most of his ships were sunk. Four hundred of his men were dead or wounded. American land forces arrived several weeks later. They captured Manila, giving the United States control of the Philippines.

Dewey was suddenly a hero. Songs and poems were written about him. Congress gave him special honors. A spirit of victory spread across the nation. People called for an immediate invasion of Cuba. Unlike the Navy, America's Army was not ready to fight. When war was declared, the Army had only about 25,000 men. Within a few months, however, it had more than 200,000. The soldiers trained at camps in the Southern United States. One of the largest camps was in Florida. Cuba is just 150 kilometers off the coast of Florida.

Two weeks after the Spanish-American War began, the Army sent a small force to Cuba. The force was ordered to inspect the North coast of Cuba and to take supplies to Cuban rebels. That invasion failed. But the second one succeeded. Four hundred American soldiers landed with guns, bullets, and supplies for the rebels. Next, the Army planned to send 25,000 men to Cuba. Their goal was the **Port of Santiago** on the South coast. American ships had trapped a Spanish naval force there earlier.

One of the commanders of the big American invasion force was Theodore Roosevelt. Roosevelt had resigned as Assistant Secretary of the Navy when the war started. He organized a group of horse soldiers. Most of the men were cowboys from America's southwest. They could ride and shoot well. Some were rich young men from New York who simply shared Roosevelt's love of excitement. The group became known as Roosevelt's "**Rough Riders**."

As the Americans landed near Santiago, Spanish forces withdrew to positions outside the city. The strongest force was at **San Juan Hill**. The Spanish soldiers used smokeless gunpowder. This made their artillery hard to find. The Americans did not have the smokeless powder. But they had **Gatling machine guns** which poured a stream of bullets at the enemy. When the machine guns opened fire, American soldiers began moving up San Juan Hill. Several American reporters watched. Later, one of them wrote this report:

"I have seen many pictures of the charge on San Juan Hill. But none seem to show it as I remember it. In the pictures, the men are running up the hill quickly in straight lines. There seem to be so many men that no enemy could stand against them."

"In fact," said the reporter, "there were not many men. And they moved up the hill slowly, in a close group, not in a straight line. It seemed as if someone had made a terrible mistake. One wanted to call to these few soldiers to come back."

The American soldiers were not called back. They reached the top of San Juan Hill. The Spanish soldiers fled. "All we have to do," an American officer said, "is hold on to the hill. And Santiago will be ours." American Commander General William Shafter sent a message to Spanish Commander General Jose Toral. Shafter demanded Toral's surrender. While he waited for an answer, the Spanish naval force tried to break out of Santiago Harbor. The attempt failed, and the Americans took control of the port. The loss destroyed any hope that Spain could win the war. There was now no way it could send more soldiers and supplies to Cuba. General Toral agreed to a short ceasefire so women and children could leave Santiago. But he rejected General Shafter's demand of unconditional surrender. American artillery then attacked Santiago. General Toral defended the city as best he could. Finally, on July 17th, he surrendered. The United States promised to send all his soldiers back to Spain.

Theodore Roosevelt

In the next few weeks, American forces occupied **Puerto Rico** and the Philippine capital of Manila. America's war with Spain was over. It had lasted just ten weeks. The next step was to negotiate terms of a peace treaty. The negotiations would be held in Paris. The victorious United States demanded independence for Cuba. It demanded control over Puerto Rico and **Guam**. And it demanded the right to occupy Manila. The two sides agreed quickly on the terms concerning Cuba, Puerto Rico, and Guam. But they could not agree on what to do about the Philippines. Spain rejected the American demand for control. It did not want to give up this important colony.

The two sides negotiated for days. Finally, they reached an agreement. Spain would give all of the Philippines to the United States. In return, the United States would pay Spain 20 million dollars. With this dispute ended, the peace treaty was quickly completed and signed.

Words, Expressions and Notes

William McKinley 威廉·麦金利（1843—1901），美国第二十五任总统（1897—1901），发动美西战争，吞并夏威夷，被刺杀。

battleship *Maine* "缅因号"战舰

George Dewey 乔治·杜威（1837—1917），美国海军上将

Pacific Fleet （美国海军）太平洋舰队

Assistant Secretary of the Navy 海军部长助理

Theodore Roosevelt 西奥多·罗斯福（1858—1919），美国第二十六任总统，曾因调停日俄战争而获

1906 年诺贝尔和平奖。

the Philippines 菲律宾（群岛），美西战争前为西班牙所控制。

Manila Bay 马尼拉湾

Port of Santiago （古巴）圣地亚哥港

Rough Riders "莽骑兵"，罗斯福招募的参加美西战争的第一志愿骑兵团

San Juan Hill 圣胡安山战役（1898 年 6 月 22 日至 24 日）所在地。西奥多·罗斯福和他的"莽骑兵"在此战役后名声大噪。

Gatling machine guns 加特林机枪，一种多管机枪，由美国人 Richard Gatling 发明。

Puerto Rico 波多黎各，原西班牙殖民地，美西战争

前后成为美国的一个实行自治的自由联邦。

Guam 关岛

Questions for Comprehension and Discussion

1. What was the direct cause of Spanish-American War?
2. How did the American navy defeat the Spanish naval force in the Philippines?
3. Why were Theodore Roosevelt and his group called "Rough Riders"?
4. How long did America's war with Spain last? Why was it so short?
5. Why has the United States been called a "world power" since it defeated Spain in the war?

$\mathcal{40}$ The Progressive Movement

进步运动

处于世纪之交的美国，工业、农业和科学技术都取得巨大的进展，全国的免费教育也基本实现。在与西班牙的战争取得胜利后，美国从一个为自身生存而奋斗的国家一跃成为一个世界强国。然而，善于思考的美国人，对于他们社会、经济以及政治的现状依旧不感到心满意足。因为大型企业——托拉斯集团的垄断地位似乎更加根深蒂固，地方政府和市政府往往为腐败政客所把持。一种物质主义的幽灵，似乎日渐影响到社会的健康发展。

其实，1884年当选的克利夫兰总统就已经注意到美国社会出现的新问题，并设法加以控制。他在任职期间签署了《州际商业条例》，纠正了铁路运输上的不少弊端。另外，他还大胆地向关税壁垒提出挑战。1890年，在本杰明·哈里森总统的任期内，美国通过了《谢尔曼反托拉斯法》，其目的就是要打破垄断，禁止妨碍州际贸易的一切合并。但由于该法律用词含糊，所以刚通过时收效不大。

无论是在国内事务还是在国际事务方面，西奥多·罗斯福当政正好与美国政治生活的新纪元相吻合。正是他领导着美国进入了一个伟大的社会进步的年代。

罗斯福出生于纽约的一个富有家庭，小时候身体虚弱，可是他以钢铁般的意志锻炼身体，成了十分活跃的野外体育活动爱好者。他从哈佛大学毕业后进入州立法机构，在政治上遭受几次失败后，有两年时间他在达科他领地经营农牧场。接着他在纽约当上了警察局总长，随后在麦金利政府时期出任海军部长助理。西班牙战争中，他在古巴的英勇行为使他步入政坛，当上纽约州长。1900年他成为威廉·麦金利竞选总统时的副总统候选人。麦金利在1901年遭暗杀后，罗斯福接任了总统职务。

罗斯福是一个生气勃勃、永不言败的人。他曾说："向强有力的事物挑战，去夺取辉煌的胜利，即使遭受挫折也比苟且偷安强得多，因为得过且过的人生活在暗淡的暮光之中，既体验不到胜利的欢乐，也尝受不到失败的痛苦。"

1902年至1908年，是一个社会批评与改革的年代。在这一时期中，几乎每一位著名人物，不论是政治家、哲学家、学者，还是文学家，他们所获得的名气总是和参与改革运动有关。这时的英雄们都是改革者，他们强烈抗议从18世纪农村式共和国继承下来的一些原则和实施办法，因为它们被证明已不适合20世纪都市化国家的需要。早在1873年时，马克·吐温就曾经以他的仔细观察，写了一本《镀金时代》(*The Gilded Age*)，讽刺和批判美国社会的政治腐败和投机风气。厄普顿·辛克莱 (Upton Sinclair) 1906年出版的小说《屠场》(*The Jungle*)，更是无情揭露了美国芝加哥大型肉类食品加工企业的恶劣生产环境和对工人的残酷剥削。书中描写的血腥肮脏的场面，竟使罗斯福总统倒了吃饭的胃口；但这也促使他下定决心，打击垄断集团，铲除腐败，采取实际措施以改善民众的生活和工作条件。由于罗斯福政府有效地执行反托拉斯的法律，他荣获"托拉斯打击者"的美名。

In September, 1901, President William McKinley was assassinated. His Vice President, Theodore Roosevelt, succeeded him.

Theodore Roosevelt became president at the beginning of the 20th century. It was a time of rapid changes in American society. The changes were a result of technology. Great progress had been made, for example, in transportation. Almost every American city had a street railroad, or trolley. These systems were powered by electricity. Thousands of Americans owned automobiles. And **Henry Ford** was planning a low-cost version which even more people could buy. Great progress had been made in communications. There were telephones in almost every business office in the cities and in many homes. And Italian inventor **Guglielmo Marconi** had sent the first wireless message across the Atlantic Ocean.

It was clear that the United States had made great progress in technology. Yet many believed it had made little progress in social issues. These people felt America's natural resources were being misused. They felt America's farmers were poorer than they should be. They felt America's industries were unfair to workers. Since the late 1800s, a spirit of reform had been growing in the United States. It started among farmers and led to the creation of a new political party—the **Populists**. Then organized labor joined the movement. Then middle class Americans. Not everyone agreed on ways to solve society's problems. But they were united in the belief that social progress had to be made. The future of American democracy, they said, depended on the success of the **Progressive Movement**. The man who came to represent the spirit of reform most of all was the new president, Theodore Roosevelt.

In the early 1900s, a group of wealthy American businessmen agreed to join their railroads. They formed a company, or **trust**, to control the joint railroad. The new company would have complete control of rail transportation in the American West. There would be no competition. President Roosevelt believed the new company violated the **Sherman Anti-trust Law**. The law said it was illegal for businesses to interfere with trade among the states. Roosevelt said he would make no compromises in enforcing the law. He asked the Supreme Court to break up the railroad trust. "We are not," Roosevelt said, "attacking these big companies. We are only trying to do away with any evil in them. We are not hostile to them. But we believe they must be controlled to serve the public good."

The Supreme Court ruled against the railroad trust. In the next few years, other trusts would be broken up in the same way. The American people called this **trust-busting**. And they called Theodore Roosevelt the **trust-buster**. Roosevelt made several speeches explaining his position on big business. Everywhere he went, he found wide public support. Later, he told a friend why people liked him so well. He said: "I put into words what is in their hearts and minds, but not in their mouths."

President Roosevelt won even more public support for his actions during a labor crisis in the coal industry. The incident was one of many in American history in which a president had to decide if he should interfere in private industry. Coal miners went on strike in the spring of 1902. They demanded more pay and safer working conditions. Mine owners refused to negotiate. One even insulted the miners. He said: "The rights and interests of the laboring man will be protected and cared for. It will not be the labor activists who take care of him. It will be the Christian men to whom God in his great wisdom has given the control of the property interests of this country." This **self-serving use of religion** made many Americans support the striking workers.

After several months, President Roosevelt invited coal mine owners and union leaders to a meeting in Washington. He asked them to keep in mind that a third group was involved in their dispute: the public. He warned that the nation faced the possibility of a winter without heating fuel. Roosevelt said: "I did not call this meeting to discuss your claims and positions. I called it to appeal to your love of country." The union leaders said they were willing to have the President appoint an independent committee to settle the strike. They said they would accept the committee's decision as final. The mine owners rejected the idea. One warned the President not even to talk about it. Such talk, he said, was illegal interference in private industry.

That made Theodore Roosevelt angry. Later, he said: "If it were not for the high office I held, **I** would have taken him by the seat of the pants and the nape of the neck and thrown him out the window." Finally, Roosevelt got both sides to agree to a compromise. Mine owners agreed to have an independent committee study the miners' demands. And the miners agreed to return to work until the study was completed. Several months later, the report was ready. The committee proposed that miners accept a smaller pay increase in exchange for improved working conditions. Both sides accepted the proposal. The coal strike ended.

Not everyone was happy. Many people still felt Roosevelt had no right to interfere. Roosevelt disagreed. "My business," he said, "is to see fair play among all men—capitalists or wage-workers. All I want to do is see that every man has a fair deal. No more, no less." Roosevelt believed the United States needed a strong leader. He planned to strengthen the presidency whenever he could.

Roosevelt was an active, noisy man. As one writer described him: "Theodore is always the center of action. When he goes to a wedding, he wants to be the bride. When he goes to a funeral, he wants to be the dead man." Many of Roosevelt's friends thought he was an **over-grown boy**. "You must always remember," one said, "that the President is about six years old."

A 1904 cartoon shows Teddy Roosevelt battling all the monster-trusts.

Another friend sent this message to Roosevelt on his 46th birthday: "You have made a very good start in life. We have great hopes for you when you grow up."

Theodore Roosevelt loved outdoor activities. He especially loved the natural beauty of the land. He worried about its future. Roosevelt wrote: "I recognize the right and duty of this generation to develop and use the natural riches of our land. But I do not recognize the right to waste them, nor to rob—by wasteful use—the generations that come after us." Roosevelt set aside large areas of forest land for national use. He created 50 special areas to protect wildlife. And he established a number of national parks.

Words, Expressions and Notes

Henry Ford 亨利·福特（1863—1947），美国汽车制造商，发明装配线生产法，使美国成为汽车大国。

Guglielmo Marconi 马可尼（1874—1937），意大利物理学家，无线电报系统的发明人，获得1909年诺贝尔物理学奖。

Populists *n.* 平民党党员。美国政治舞台在1891至1908年间活跃着一个叫平民党（People's Party or

Populist Party）的政治团体，主要受到南方和西部农民的支持。1904年后该党影响逐渐衰微，1908年后消失，但其部分理念后来融入美国的政府体系之中。

Progressive Movement 进步运动。严格说来，美国的进步运动并不是一个前后连贯、有明确政治纲领的运动，而是在普通民众的强烈要求下，以及在罗斯福总统的强力推动下，国家实施的一系列改革，触及政治、经济、法律、文化等各方面。改革的焦点是自工业化与城市化以来，大量社会财富逐步集中在极少数人手中的根本性问题。进步运动使美国朝社会文明和公正的方向迈出了一大步。

trust *n.* 托拉斯，垄断企业

Sherman Anti-trust Law 《谢尔曼反托拉斯法》

trust-busting *n.* 打击或解散托拉斯

trust-buster *n.* 打击或解散托拉斯的人

self-serving use of religion 把宗教加以自我利用。这是指罗斯福总统通过有利于自己的宗教解释来为自己的政治目标服务的言论："关心劳工不只是工会的事务，而且是信仰基督教的人的事务。"

I would have taken him by the seat of the pants and the nape of the neck and thrown him out the window. 我会毫不犹豫把他抓起来扔出窗外。

over-grown boy 长不大的小孩；老顽童

Questions for Comprehension and Discussion

1. Why were there great changes in American society at the beginning of the 20th century?

2. Why did many people not feel satisfied with the progress in social issues?

3. Why did Roosevelt want to break up the railroad trust?

4. How did Roosevelt solve the labor crisis in the coal industry?

5. A writer once described Roosevelt: "Theodore is always the center of action. When he goes to a wedding, he wants to be the bride. When he goes to a funeral, he wants to be the dead man." What do you think about his description of Roosevelt?

6. Why has Theodore Roosevelt been considered a pioneer in environment and wildlife protection?

Unit 11　An Age of Changes

41　The United States in World War I

第一次世界大战中的美国

新泽西州州长伍德罗·威尔逊以"新自由"（New Freedom）为口号，精神抖擞地投入到1912年的总统竞选，他在竞选演说中表明的"民族的新生不是来自上层阶级而是来自下层民众"的观点，获得大众的广泛好感并使他登上总统宝座。在他的领导下，美国政府在改革关税、整顿银行、控制托拉斯并调查大公司违法乱纪行为等方面都有建树。但是，威尔逊总统在历史上的地位，主要并不是因他对社会改革的无比热诚，而是由于神奇的命运把他投入第一次世界大战后，他作为战时总统所起的作用，以及在战后不稳定的世界里所担当的和平奠基人的工作。

1914 年欧洲战争的爆发震惊了美国公众。起初，战鼓声尚似遥远，但不久人们就感到战事对美国经济和政治的影响。到 1915 年，本来已略见萧条的美国工业，随着西方盟国订单的到来而再度欣欣向荣。交战双方都利用宣传工具来煽动美国公众的情绪。同时，英、德两国阻挠美国公海航运的行动也引起了威尔逊政府的强烈抗议，而美、德两国之间的争端也日趋显现。

1915 年 2 月，德国军事领导人宣布要击毁在英伦三岛周围海上行驶的一切商船。威尔逊总统警告说，美国绝不放弃在公海上贸易的传统权利，并宣布美国将要求德国对美国船只和生命的损失承担"绝对责任"。1915 年春，一艘英国客轮"卢西塔尼亚"号被击沉，死难者近 1 200 人，其中有美国人 128 名，这件事使美国人极为愤怒。威尔逊虽然是最致力于和平的美国总统，但他在目击德国的残暴，特别是其潜艇战后深信，德国的胜利将是军国主义在欧洲的胜利，势必将危及美国的安全。1917 年 4 月 2 日，5 艘美国商船被德国潜艇击沉。4 月 6 日，美国对德国宣战，并立即动用其军事资源。到 1918 年 10 月，开抵法国的美国军队超过 175 万人。

第一次世界大战是第一场惨烈的现代化战争，杀伤力巨大的潜水艇、飞机和坦克第一次投入实战。在四年多的战争中阵亡人数近 1 000 万人，其中 11.5 万多美国军人失去了生命。

萨拉热窝的枪声触发了一场世界风暴，尽管美国人试图远离这场风暴，但最终还是被这场风暴改变了他们的生活方式。从此，作为一个经济和军事大国，美国不可避免地要抛弃开国领袖华盛顿不要卷入外国冲突的历史性告诫，开始进入它在全球事务中的新角色。

In 1914, Europe exploded into flames as World War I began. It was a war no nation really wanted. But no nation seemed able to stop it. The assassination of **Austria's archduke Franz Ferdinand** in the city of **Sarajevo** was the spark that set off the explosion.

The Austrian archduke was murdered by **Serbian nationalists**. They opposed Austrian control of their homeland. After the assassination, Austria declared war on **Serbia**. One of Serbia's allies was Russia. Russia agreed to help Serbia in any war against Austria. Austria had allies, too. The most important was Germany. Germany wanted Russia to stay out of the war. When Russia refused, Germany declared war on Russia. Then Germany declared war on Russia's close ally, France. Britain entered the war a few days later when Germany violated the neutrality of **Belgium**.

171

One nation after another entered the conflict to protect its friends or to honor its treaties. Within a week, most of Europe was at war. On one side were the **Central Powers**: Germany and **Austria-Hungary**. On the other side were the **Triple Entente Allies**: France, Britain, and Russia. Many other nations took sides. **Bulgaria** and **Turkey** joined the Central Powers. **Italy**, **Romania**, **Portugal**, and **Greece** joined the Allies.

The United States hoped to stay out of the war. **President Wilson** immediately declared American neutrality. He said: "It is a war with which we have nothing to do, whose causes cannot touch us." Most Americans agreed with President Wilson. They did not want to get involved in the fighting. However, many found it difficult to remain neutral in their hearts. Some Americans had family roots in Germany. They supported the Central Powers. A greater number of Americans had

President Wilson

family roots in Britain or France. They supported the Allies. Yet the official American policy was neutrality. The United States planned to continue to trade with both sides.

After three years of fighting, Europe's lands were filled with the sights and sounds of death. But still, the armies of the Allies and the Central Powers continued to fight. The United States had tried to keep out of the European conflict. It declared its neutrality. In the end, however, neutrality was impossible. Germany was facing starvation because of a British **naval blockade**. To break the blockade, German submarines attacked any ship that sailed to Europe. That included ships from neutral nations like the United States. The German submarines sank several American ships. Many innocent people were killed.

German submarine attacks finally forced the United States into the war. It joined the Allies: Britain, France, and Russia. Like most Americans, President Wilson did not want war. But he had no choice. Sadly, he asked Congress for a declaration of war. Congress approved the declaration on April 6th, 1917. It was not long before American soldiers reached the European continent. They marched in a parade through the streets of Paris. The people of France gave them a wild welcome. They cheered the young Americans. They threw flowers at the soldiers and kissed them.

The Americans marched to the burial place of the **marquis de Lafayette**. Lafayette was the French military leader who had come to America's aid during its war of independence from Britain. The United States wanted to re-pay France for its help more than a hundred years earlier. An American army officer made a speech at the tomb. He said: "Lafayette, we are here!"

And so the Americans were there. They were ready to fight in the bloodiest war the world had ever known. Week by week, more American troops arrived. By October, 1917, the American army in Europe totaled 100,000 men. The leader of that army was General **John J. Pershing**. Pershing's forces were not sent directly into battle. Instead, they spent time training, building bases, and preparing supplies. Then a small group was sent to the border between **Switzerland** and Germany. The Americans fought a short but bitter battle there against German forces. The Germans knew the American soldiers had not fought before. They tried to frighten the Americans by waving their knives and guns in a fierce attack. The Americans surprised the Germans. They stood and fought back successfully.

1918 was the final year of the most terrible war the world had ever

General John J. Pershing

known. But World War I did not end quickly or easily. The German army made a final effort to defeat the Allies. The United States had entered the conflict. And Germany wanted a victory before large numbers of American troops could get to Europe. Germany's effort became easier after it signed a peace treaty with the new **Bolshevik** government in Russia. The treaty made it possible for Germany to use all its forces against the Allies on its western border. In the end, however, Germany's plan failed. Allied troops pushed back the German attack in a series of bloody battles. The addition of American soldiers greatly increased allied strength.

General Pershing used a weapon new to the world of war: air power. Airplanes were used first simply as "eyes in the sky." They discovered enemy positions so ground artillery could fire at them. Then they were used as fighter planes. They carried guns to shoot down other planes. Finally, planes were built big enough to carry bombs. General Pershing also used another new weapon of war: tanks. He put these inventions together for his battle plan against Germany.

On November 11th, 1918, a **truce** was signed ending the hostilities of World War I. The Central Powers, led by Germany, had lost. The Allies, led by Britain, France, and the United States, had won. The war had lasted four years. It had taken the lives of ten million persons. It had left much of Europe in ruins. It was described as **"the war to end all wars."**

The immediate task was to seek agreement on terms of a peace treaty. The Allies were filled with bitter anger. They demanded a treaty that would punish Germany severely. They wanted to make Germany weak by destroying its military and industry. And they wanted to ruin Germany's economy by making it pay all war damages. Germany, they said, must never go to war again.

President Woodrow Wilson of the United States did not agree completely with the other allies. He wanted a peace treaty based on justice, not bitterness. He believed that would produce a lasting peace.

In early December, President Wilson sailed to France. The voyage across the Atlantic Ocean lasted nine days. He arrived at the port of **Brest** on December 13th. Wilson felt very happy. Thirteen, he said, was his lucky number.

French citizens stood along the railroad that carried him from Brest to Paris. They cheered as his train passed. In Paris, cannons were fired to announce his arrival. And a huge crowd welcomed him there. The people shouted his name over and over again: "Wilson! Wilson! Wilson!" the noise sounded like thunder. French premier **Georges Clemenceau** commented on the event. He said: "I do not think there has been anything like it in the history of the world." People cheered President Wilson partly to thank America for sending its troops to help fight against Germany. But many French citizens and other Europeans also shared Wilson's desire to establish a new world of peace. They listened with hope as he made an emotional speech about a world in which everyone would reject hatred... a world in which everyone would join together to end war, forever.

More than 25 nations that helped win the war sent representatives to the peace conference in Paris. All took part in the negotiations. Wilson hoped the other Allied leaders would accept his plan for a new international organization. The organization would be called the **League of Nations**. Wilson believed the League could prevent future wars by deciding fair settlements of disputes between nations. He believed it would be the world's only hope for a lasting peace.

Words, Expressions and Notes

Austria's archduke Franz Ferdinand 奥地利的弗兰茨·费迪南德大公（奥匈帝国皇太子）

Sarajevo 萨拉热窝，前南斯拉夫重要城市，现波斯尼亚首都。

Serbian nationalists 塞尔维亚民族主义分子

Serbia *n.* 塞尔维亚

Belgium *n.* 比利时

Central Powers （第一次世界大战时的）同盟国，由德国和奥匈帝国等中部欧洲国家组成。

Austria-Hungary *n.* 奥匈帝国（1867—1918）

Triple Entente Allies 协约国，由英、法、俄组成。

Bulgaria *n.* 保加利亚

Turkey *n.* 土耳其

Italy *n.* 意大利

Romania *n.* 罗马尼亚

Portugal *n.* 葡萄牙

Greece *n.* 希腊

President Wilson 威尔逊总统（Thomas Woodrow Wilson, 1856—1924），美国第二十八任总统

naval blockade 海上封锁

marquis de Lafayette 拉斐德侯爵（1757—1834），法国将军，曾参加美国独立战争

John J. Pershing 约翰·潘兴（1860—1948），美国著名将军，在第一次世界大战中指挥在欧洲的美国远征军。

Switzerland *n.* 瑞士

Bolshevik *n.* 布尔什维克；俄国共产党

truce *n.* 停战协定

the war to end all wars 结束一切战争的战争。这是人们对第一次世界大战的结论性说法。事实证明，这种说法过于乐观和天真，因为大约二十年后就爆发了第二次世界大战。

Brest *n.* 布勒斯特，法国西部港口

Georges Clemenceau 克列孟梭（1841—1929），法国政治家，第三共和国总理

League of Nations 国际联盟，1920 年建立的国际组织，于 1946 年解散。

Questions for Comprehension and Discussion

1. What caused the war to break out in 1914?

2. Why did the United States want to remain neutral in the war?

3. Why did the United States become involved in World War I?

4. Why did the American soldiers march to the burial place of the marquis de Lafayette when they arrived in France?

5. What new weapons were used by American general Pershing in the war? How did the new weapons work?

6. What was the new international organization President Wilson suggested? What was its purpose?

42 The Roaring Twenties and the Scopes Trial

喧嚣的二十年代与斯科普斯审判案

第一次世界大战过后，美国迎来历史上少有的一段空前繁荣时期。

这时期的美国，经济欣欣向荣，各种新发明、新产品让人应接不暇。由于以自动化、标准化和流水线为特点的大规模生产方式的普遍应用，汽车、收音机迅速普及，彻底改变了人们几百年来固有的生活方式。另一方面，去欧洲开阔了眼界的士兵带回许多新的思想和观点，社会中接受过高中和大学教育的人越来越多。这些因素都对美国文明的中心——清教主义——造成强烈冲击，知识分子阶层和年轻的一代普遍对美国传统文化的基本价值开始产生怀疑。

变化与守旧是20世纪20年代美国社会出现的两股巨大力量，它们之间的碰撞也使得这段时期不可避免地成为美国20世纪上半叶最令人激动的10年。

美国政府的政策在这段时期带有明显的保守色彩。首先是美国移民政策的重要变更。一段时间以来，国内反对无限制移民的情绪逐渐高涨，最终导致1924年的《移民配额法》和1929年关于限定每年的移民人数为15万人的法令。其次，1919年通过的禁止酿造和销售酒类的第18条宪法修正案，也成为清教主义盛行的象征。禁酒令本是为了扫除国内的酗酒现象，但其结果却是制造出数以千计生产和出售私酒的违法窝点，为各种应运而生的犯罪勾当创造了条件。此外，广泛的违法行为也使禁酒令成为道德上的一种伪善。尽管早就被公认为是一项失败的政策，美国一直到1933年才通过第21条宪法修正案取消了禁酒令。

20世纪20年代也是美国保守与变革两股力量猛烈碰撞的时代，其中最富有戏剧性的一幕于1925年在田纳西州上演。一位名叫约翰·斯科普斯的中学生物教师无意之中卷入了一场美国历史上最轰动的审判。由于争论的焦点涉及达尔文"人是从猿进化而来"的基本理论，这次审判在美国历史上也被戏称为"猴子审判"（Monkey Trial）。此案由于有美国各大新闻媒体的高度关注，有对垒双方在法庭上的戏剧性表演，最后再加上保守法官的荒唐判决，这场新旧思想的大对决的审判为变化中的美国社会增添了喜剧色彩。尽管在强大的宗教力量面前科学没能取得压倒性胜利，随之而来的一股科学普及和思想解放的清风却吹遍了美利坚大地。

The administrations of President **Warren Harding** and **Calvin Coolidge** were a time of economic progress for most Americans. Many companies grew larger during the 1920s, creating many new jobs. Wages for most Americans increased. Many people began to have enough money to buy new kinds of products. The strong economy also created the right environment for many important changes in the day-to-day social life of the American people. The 1920s are remembered now as an exciting time that historians call "**The Roaring Twenties.**"

The 1920s brought a feeling of freedom and independence to millions of Americans, especially young Americans. Young soldiers returned from the World War with new ideas. They had seen a different world in Europe. They had faced death and learned to enjoy the pleasures that each day offered. Many of these young soldiers were not willing to quietly accept the old traditions of their families and villages when they returned home. Instead, they wanted to try new ways of living.

Many young Americans, both men and women, began to challenge some of the traditions of their

x

Unit 11

y

b

e

h

k

n

parents and grandparents. For example, some young women began to experiment with new kinds of clothes. They no longer wore dresses that hid the shape of their bodies. Instead, they wore thinner dresses that uncovered part of their legs. Many young women began to smoke cigarettes, too. Cigarette production in the United States more than doubled in the ten years between 1918 and 1928. Many women also began to drink alcohol with men in public for the first time. And they listened together to a

Cars crowded New York's Fifth Avenue in 1921.

popular new kind of music: **jazz**. Young people danced the **fox trot**, the **Charleston**, and other new dances. They held one another tightly on the dance floor, instead of dancing far apart.

It was a revolution in social values, at least among some Americans. People openly discussed subjects that their parents and grandparents had kept private. There were popular books and shows about unmarried mothers and about homosexuality. The growing film industry made films about all-night parties between unmarried men and women. And people discussed the new ideas about sex formed by **Sigmund Freud** and other new thinkers. An important force behind these changes was the growing independence of American women. In 1920, the nation passed the 19th amendment to the constitution, which gave women the right to vote. Of equal importance, many women took jobs during the war and continued working after the troops returned home. Also, new machines freed many of them from spending long hours of work in the home washing clothes, preparing food, and doing other jobs.

Education was another important force behind the social changes of the 1920s. More and more Americans were getting a good education. The number of students attending high school doubled between 1920 and 1930. Many of the schools now offered new kinds of classes to prepare students for useful jobs. Attendance at colleges and universities also increased greatly. And colleges offered more classes in such useful subjects as teacher training, engineering, and business administration.

Two inventions also helped cause the social changes. They were the automobile and the radio. The automobile gave millions of Americans the freedom to travel easily to new places. And the radio brought new ideas and experiences into their own homes.

Probably the most important force behind social change was the continuing economic growth of the 1920s. Many people had extra money to spend on things other than food, housing, and other basic needs. They could experiment with new products and different ways of living.

Of course, not all Americans were wearing strange new "**flapper**" clothes or dancing until early in the morning. Millions of Americans in small towns or rural areas continued to live simple, quiet lives. Life was still hard for many people including blacks, foreigners, and other minority groups. The many newspaper stories about independent women reporters and doctors also did not represent the real life of the average American woman. Women could vote. But three of every four women still worked at home. Most of the women working outside their homes were from minority groups or foreign countries.

The films and radio stories about exciting parties and social events were just a dream for millions of Americans. But the dreams were strong. And many Americans—rich and poor—followed with great interest each new game, dance, and custom.

The wide interest in this kind of popular culture was unusually strong during the 1920s. People became extremely interested in exciting court trials, disasters, film actors, and other subjects. For example, millions of Americans followed the sad story of Floyd Collins, a young man who became trapped while exploring underground. Newsmen reported to the nation as rescue teams searched to find him. Even the *New York Times* newspaper printed a large story on its front page when rescuers finally discovered the man's dead body.

Many of the Americans were fearful of the many changes that had taken place in American society. Science became an enemy to many of these traditional, religious Americans. Science seemed to challenge the most basic ideas taught in the Bible. The conflict burst into a major public debate in 1925 in a trial over Charles Darwin's idea of evolution.

British scientist Charles Darwin published his books *The Origin of the Species* and *The Descent of Man* in the 19th century. The books explained Darwin's idea that humans developed over millions of years from apes and other animals. Most Europeans and educated people accepted Darwin's theory by the end of the 19th century. But the book had little effect in rural parts of the United States until the 1920s.

William Jennings Bryan led the attack on Darwin's ideas. Bryan was a rural Democrat who ran twice for president. He lost both times. But Bryan remained popular among many traditional Americans. Bryan told his followers that the theory of evolution was evil, because it challenged the traditional idea that God created the world in six days. He accused scientists of violating God's words in the Bible. Bryan and his supporters called on local school officials to ban the teaching of evolution. Some state legislatures in the more conservative Southeastern part of the country passed laws making it a crime to teach evolution theory.

In 1925, a young science teacher in the Southern state of Tennessee challenged the state's new teaching law. The teacher, **John Scopes**, taught Darwin's evolution ideas. Officials arrested Scopes and put him on trial. Some of the nation's greatest lawyers rushed to Tennessee to defend the young teacher. They believed the state had violated his right to free speech. And they thought Tennessee's law against teaching evolution was foolish in a modern, scientific society. America's most famous lawyer, **Clarence Darrow**, became the leader of Scopes's defense team. Bryan and other religious conservatives also rushed to the trial. They supported the right of the state of Tennessee to ban the teaching of evolution.

John Scopes in 1925

The trial was held in the small town of Dayton, Tennessee. Hundreds of people came to watch: religious conservatives, free speech supporters, newsmen, and others.

The high point of the trial came when Bryan himself sat before the court. Lawyer Clarence Darrow asked Bryan question after question about the Bible and about science. How did Bryan know the Bible is true? Did God really create the earth in a single day? Is a day in the Bible 24 hours? Or can it mean a million years?

Bryan answered the questions. But he showed a great lack of knowledge about modern science. The judge found Scopes guilty of breaking the law. But in the battle of ideas, science defeated conservatism. And a higher court later ruled that Scopes was not guilty.

The Scopes evolution trial captured the imagination of Americans. The issue was not really whether one young teacher was innocent or guilty of breaking a law. The real question was the struggle for

America's spirit between the forces of modern ideas and those of traditional rural conservatism. The trial represented this larger conflict.

The most famous popular event of the 1920s was the brave action of pilot **Charles Lindbergh** when he flew an airplane across the Atlantic Ocean without stopping. He was the first man in history to do this. Lindbergh flew his plane alone from New York to France in May 1927. His flight set off wild celebrations across the United States. Newspapers carried story after story about Lindbergh's success. President Coolidge and a large crowd greeted the young pilot when he returned to Washington. And New York congratulated Lindbergh with one of the largest parades in its history. Americans liked Lindbergh

William Jennings Bryan, the prosecutor, died five days after the trial ended.

because he was brave, quiet, and handsome. He seemed to represent everything that was best about their country.

Words, Expressions and Notes

Warren Harding 沃伦·哈定（1865—1923），美国第二十九任总统（1921—1923），因其政府腐败无能而声名狼藉。

Calvin Coolidge 卡尔文·柯立芝（1872—1933），美国第三十任总统（1923—1929）

The Roaring Twenties （美国历史上）喧嚣的 20 世纪 20 年代

jazz *n.* 爵士乐，主要源于美国黑人的一种音乐形式，起始于 19 世纪末 20 世纪初，但在 20 世纪 20 年代得到很大的发展。由于爵士乐具有自由、奔放、喧闹等特点，而这正好与这一特定时期的社会特点相吻合，因此美国的 20 世纪 20 年代又被称为"爵士时代"（Jazz Age）。

fox trot 狐步舞

Charleston *n.* 查尔斯顿舞，起源于美国南卡罗来纳州查尔斯顿的一种黑人交谊舞。

Sigmund Freud 西格蒙德·弗洛伊德（1856—1939），奥地利精神病学家

flapper *n.* （特指 20 世纪 20 年代行为和服饰不受传统束缚的）年轻女孩

The Origin of the Species 《物种起源》，达尔文最重要的科学著作

The Descent of Man 《人类的遗传》，达尔文的科学著作

William Jennings Bryan 威廉·布赖恩（1860—1925），美国国会议员、国务卿，在斯科普斯审判案中担任控方律师，因其保守的宗教立场遭到辩方的猛烈批判，审判结束 5 天后即去世。

John Scopes 约翰·斯科普斯（1900—1970），田纳西州中学生物教师，因在课堂上讲授达尔文的进化论而卷入美国历史上最著名的一场法律诉讼。

Clarence Darrow 克来伦斯·达罗（1857—1938），美国著名律师，因在许多重大案件中担任被告辩护人而闻名全国。

Charles Lindbergh 查尔斯·林德伯格（1902—1974），美国飞行员，单独完成首次横越大西洋不着陆飞行。

Questions for Comprehension and Discussion

1. Why are the 1920s called "The Roaring Twenties"?
2. Why did the young people want to have new ways of living in the 1920s?
3. What were the new ways of living the young people were trying in the 1920s?
4. When did American women have the right to vote?
5. Why is it said that education was another important force behind the social changes of the 1920s?
6. Why were there many Americans who were fearful of the many changes in American society?
7. What is the importance of the Scopes trial in Tennessee?
8. How did Charles Lindbergh become a great American hero? Why?

43 The Arts of the 1920s

20世纪20年代的艺术

对大多数美国人来说，20世纪20年代是一个乐观主义盛行的年代，是一个国家开始在汽车上兜风的年代。这一时期，一种全新的音乐形式突然在全国流行开来，它就是爵士乐。这种源于黑人文化的音乐，以其自由奔放、充满活力与情感的音乐语汇，立刻成为美国文化生活中的重要组成部分。因此，作家斯科特·菲茨杰拉德形象地把这个狂热的时代称为："爵士时代"（Jazz Age）。

无情抨击社会成为这个时期美国文学的主调。新闻记者兼批评家门肯对美国人生活中的虚伪和腐败现象进行了毫不留情地鞭挞，门肯在1924年创办《美国水星》（American Mercury）杂志，以犀利的文笔攻击守旧派的愚蠢和庸俗，一时成为争论的中心。

在当时严肃的小说家中，没有一个比美国文学界第一个诺贝尔文学奖得主辛克莱·刘易斯拥有更多的读者。他把小说当做一门高级新闻学，用优秀记者的讽刺笔调和技巧，创作了以美国中产阶级的生活作主题的《大街》和《巴比特》等讽刺小说，给庸俗的市侩文化以致命的一击。

另一位作家欧内斯特·海明威却避开描写正统的美国社会。他笔下的人物，即使是美国人，也不是出现在正统的美国社会里，而是在西班牙斗牛，在意大利开救护车，在非洲狩猎，在古巴钓鱼。海明威是一个严谨而才华横溢的作家，他的文体以简洁著称，绝不借助于华丽的辞藻。他在叙事时，或寓情于景，或情景并茂，常常在平淡中显露出惊人之笔。当他描写救护车的担架上躺着一个奄奄一息的士兵，鲜血一滴一滴落在担架下面的男主人公身上时，就写下这样的句子："血滴得很慢，像太阳下山后冰柱上滴下来的水。"

而斯科特·菲茨杰拉德与海明威正好相反，他的人生经历和他的作品都完全融入被他称为的"爵士时代"中去，他自己也成为这个时代的代言人。菲茨杰拉德的作品，哪怕是初涉文坛时的稚嫩之作，也都文笔流畅，结构谨严。在小说《了不起的盖茨比》里，菲茨杰拉德运用精巧的构思和完美的形式，从不同角度和不同层次表现财富与青春的矛盾，表现"美国梦"的破灭。在这部篇幅不长的佳作中，菲茨杰拉德对那个有钱人的世界可谓了如指掌，不管里面的人物是否富有，他把每个人的外表、神情和谈吐都写得惟妙惟肖、淋漓尽致。故事的叙述者，和菲茨杰拉德一样，若即若离地在小说中出现，这就使情节显得更加客观。而且，这本书即使在最乌烟瘴气的场面里，也有不绝如缕的动人哀怨；在故事巧妙的结尾阶段，幽怨暗恨竟如泉水喷涌，让读者难以释怀。

20世纪20年代对于美国的文学和艺术来说是一个生气勃勃的年代，是一个离经叛道的年代，也是一个收获颇丰的年代。通过这个时代的洗礼，一大批艺术家用内容丰富和风格创新的作品，为美国的文学和艺术赢得了世界性声誉。

There were many changes in the social customs and day-to-day life of millions of Americans during the administration of President Calvin Coolidge. Many young people began to challenge the traditions of their parents and grandparents. They experimented with new ideas and ways of living. People of all kinds became very interested in the new popular culture. Radio and films brought them exciting news of court trials, sports heroes, and wild parties. However, the 1920s also was one of the most active and important

periods in the more serious arts. Writers, painters, and other artists produced some of the greatest work in the nation's history.

Most Americans approved strongly of the economic growth and improved living conditions during the 1920s. They supported the conservative Republican policies of President Calvin Coolidge. And they had great faith in the country's business leaders and economic system. However, many of the nation's serious artists had a different and darker view of society. They were troubled deeply by the changes they saw. They believed that Americans had become too interested in money and wealth. These artists rejected the new business society. And they also questioned the value of politics. Many of them believed that the First World War in Europe had been a terrible mistake. These artists had little faith in the political leaders who came to power after the war. They felt a need to protest the way the world was changing around them.

The spirit of protest was especially strong in serious American writing during the 1920s. Many of the greatest writers of this period hated the new business culture. One such writer was **Sinclair Lewis**. He was the first American to win the Nobel Prize for literature. Lewis wrote about Americans living in the towns and villages in the central part of the United States. Many of the people in his books were foolish men and women with empty values. They chased after money and popularity. In his famous book, *Main Street*, Lewis joked about and criticized small-town business owners. Social criticism also was central to the writing of the newspaper writer, **H. L. Mencken**, from the eastern city of Baltimore. Mencken considered most Americans to be stupid and violent fools. He attacked their values without mercy.

Sinclair Lewis

Of course, many traditional Americans reacted strongly to such criticism. For example, some religious and business leaders attacked Mencken as a dangerous person whose words were treason against the United States. But many young people thought Mencken was a hero whose only crime was writing the truth.

The work of Lewis, Mencken, and a number of other writers of the 1920s has been forgotten by many Americans as the years have passed. But the period did produce some truly great writing. One of the greatest writers of these years was **Ernest Hemingway**. Hemingway wrote about love, war, sports, and other subjects. He used short sentences and rough words. His style was sharper and different from traditional American writing. And his strong views about life set him apart from most other Americans.

Another major writer was **F. Scott Fitzgerald**. Fitzgerald wrote especially about rich Americans searching for happiness and new values. His books were filled with people who rejected traditional beliefs. His book *The Great Gatsby* is considered today to be one of the greatest works in the history of American writing.

A third great writer of the 1920s was **William Faulkner**. Faulkner wrote about the special problems and ways of life in the American South. His books explored the emotional tension in a society still suffering from the loss of the Civil War sixty years before. Some of Faulkner's best books were *The Sound and the Fury*, *As I Lay Dying*, and *Absalom, Absalom*. Like Hemingway, he won the Nobel Prize for literature.

The 1920s also produced the greatest writer of theater plays in

F. Scott Fitzgerald

American history, **Eugene O'Neill**. O'Neill was an Irish-American with a dark and violent view of human nature. His plays used new theatrical methods and ways of presenting ideas. But they carried an emotional power never before seen in the American theater. Some of his best-known plays were ***Mourning Becomes Electra***, ***The Iceman Cometh***, and ***A Long Day's Journey into Night***.

A number of American writers also produced great poetry during the 1920s. Probably the most famous work was ***The Waste Land***, a poem of sadness by the writer **T. S. Eliot**.

There also were important changes in American painting during the 1920s. Economic growth gave many Americans the money to buy art for their homes for the first time. Sixty new museums opened. Slowly, Americans learned about serious art.

Actually, American art had been changing in important ways since the beginning of the century. In 1908, a group of New York artists arranged a historic show. These artists tried to show real life in their paintings. They painted new kinds of subjects. For example, **George Bellows** painted many emotional and realistic pictures of the sport of boxing. His work, and the painting of other realistic artists, became known as the **"Ash Can" school of art**.

Another important group of modern artists was led by the great photographer **Alfred Stieglitz**. This group held a major art show in 1913 in New York, Chicago, and Boston. The show presented modern art from Europe. Americans got their first chance to see the work of such painters as **Pablo Picasso** and **Georges Braque**. The show caused a huge public debate in the United States. Traditional art critics accused the organizers of the show of trying to **overthrow** Christianity and American values. Former president Theodore Roosevelt and others denounced the new art as a threat to the country.

However, many young American painters and art lovers did not agree. They became very interested in the new art styles from Europe. They studied them closely. Soon, **Charles Demuth**, **Joseph Stella**, and other American painters began to produce excellent art in the new cubist style. **John Marin** painted beautiful views of sea coasts in New York and Maine. And such artists as **Max Weber** and **Georgia O'Keefe** painted in styles that seemed to come more from their own imagination than from reality. As with writing, the work of many of these serious modern painters only became popular many years later.

The greatest American designer of buildings during the 1920s was **Frank Lloyd Wright**. Wright believed that architects should design a building to fit its location, not to copy some ancient style. He used local materials in new ways. Wright invented many imaginative methods to combine useful building design with natural beauty. But again, most Americans did not know of Wright's work. Instead, they turned to local architects with traditional beliefs. These architects generally designed old and safe styles for buildings— for homes, offices, colleges, and other needs.

Frank Lloyd Wright

Writers and artists now look back at the "Roaring 1920s" as an extremely important period that gave birth to many new styles and ideas. Hemingway's style of writing continues to influence American writers more than half a century later. Many painters say the period marked the real birth of modern American art. And architecture students in the United States and other countries now study the buildings of Frank Lloyd Wright. The changes in American society caused many of these artists much sadness and pain in their personal lives. But their expression of protest and rich imagination produced a body of work that has grown in influence with the passing years.

Words, Expressions and Notes

Sinclair Lewis　辛克莱·刘易斯（1885—1951），美国作家，获 1930 年诺贝尔文学奖。

Main Street　《大街》，辛克莱·刘易斯的长篇小说

H. L. Mencken　门肯（Henry Louis Mencken，1880—1956），美国新闻记者兼批评家，著有语言名著《美国语言》（*The American Language*）。

Ernest Hemingway　欧内斯特·海明威（1899—1961），美国著名作家，获 1954 年诺贝尔文学奖。

F. Scott Fitzgerald　斯科特·菲茨杰拉德（1896—1940），美国作家，以描写"爵士时代"的作品著称。

The Great Gatsby　《了不起的盖茨比》，斯科特·菲茨杰拉德的著名长篇小说

William Faulkner　威廉·福克纳（1897—1962），美国著名作家，获 1950 年诺贝尔文学奖。

The Sound and the Fury　《愤怒与喧嚣》，威廉·福克纳的长篇小说

As I Lay Dying　《当我弥留之际》，威廉·福克纳的长篇小说

Absalom, Absalom　《押沙龙，押沙龙》，威廉·福克纳的长篇小说

Eugene O'Neill　尤金·奥尼尔（1888—1953），美国戏剧家，对美国戏剧改革运动作出重要贡献，获 1936 年诺贝尔文学奖。

Mourning Becomes Electra　《哀悼》，尤金·奥尼尔的戏剧

The Iceman Cometh　《送冰人来了》，尤金·奥尼尔的戏剧

A Long Day's Journey into Night　《日长路远夜深沉》，尤金·奥尼尔的戏剧

The Waste Land　《荒原》，艾略特的著名诗歌

T. S. Eliot（Thomas Stearns Eliot，1888—1965）艾略特，美国诗人、评论家、戏剧家，1927 年入英国籍，获 1948 年诺贝尔文学奖。

George Bellows　乔治·贝洛斯（1882—1925），美国画家，"八人画派"成员

"Ash Can" school of art　垃圾箱画派，对 20 世纪初起源于美国费城的"八人画派"的蔑称，该画派以描绘大城市风光和日常生活为特点。

Alfred Stieglitz　阿弗雷德·施蒂格利茨（1864—1946），美国摄影家

Pablo Picasso　毕加索（1881—1973），西班牙画家，其作品对西方现代艺术有深远影响。

Georges Braque　布拉克（1882—1963），法国画家，立体主义画派代表之一

overthrow　*v.* 推翻

Charles Demuth　查尔斯·德穆思（1883—1935），美国水彩画家

Joseph Stella　尤瑟夫·斯特拉（1877—1946），美国现代画家

John Marin　约翰·马林（1870—1953），美国画家

Max Weber　马克斯·韦伯（1864—1920），出生于俄国的美国画家

Georgia O'Keefe　乔治娅·奥基夫（1887—1986），美国现代派女画家

Frank Lloyd Wright　弗兰克·洛伊德·赖特（1867—1959），美国著名建筑师，草原式建筑风格的主要代表

Questions for Comprehension and Discussion

1. Why did many of the serious artists have a different and darker view of American society?
2. What did Sinclair Lewis write about in his books?
3. What are the characteristics of Hemingway's writing?
4. Why is *The Great Gatsby* still considered today to be one of the greatest works in the history of American writing?
5. What did Eugene O'Neill do in the theater of the 1920s?
6. What is the "Ash Can" school of art?
7. Why is "the roaring 1920s" considered today as an extremely important period for writers and artists in American history?

44 The Black History of the 1920s

20 世纪 20 年代 的 黑人历史

美国内战后采纳了三条宪法修正案以保障黑人的各项权利：第十三条修正案废止苦役和强迫劳役；第十四条修正案赋予每个出生在美国或归化美国的人以公民的身份，并禁止任何州政府未经适当法律程序制定任何剥夺公民的各项权利或他们的生命、自由和财产的法律；第十五条修正案保证公民的选举权。国会于 1875 年还通过了一项"公民权法案"，该法案禁止在旅馆、公交车辆和剧院等公共场所的种族歧视行为。这时许多白人开始相信，黑人已经完全受法律和宪法的保护，美国的种族歧视可以就此告终。

然而，事实却正好相反。当许多白人因以上这些保证黑人权利的措施而感到心满意足的时候，黑人却仍然处于极度贫困和文盲的状况。从 19 世纪 80 年代起，南方一些州就不断以法律的形式把种族隔离合法化。臭名昭著的"吉姆·克罗法"（Jim Crow laws），就是美国历史上对这一时期的种族歧视和隔离法律的专门名称（Jim Crow 是源自一首流行歌曲中的人物）。美国最高法院在 1883 年和 1896 年的两次重要判决中都宣称，公共场所的种族歧视现象与宪法并不矛盾。这样，宪法修正案在南方成了一纸空文，种族歧视和种族隔离在各地愈演愈烈。此政策一直持续到 1954 年最高法院在"布朗状告教育局"（Brown vs. Board of Education）一案中判决种族隔离违宪时才告终止。

但是，开历史倒车的种族隔离和歧视政策并没有能够阻挡黑人在 20 世纪 20 年代中的觉醒，没有能够阻挡他们在"爵士时代"中为丰富美国文化而作出的骄人成绩。

威廉·杜波伊斯是这个时代最有影响的黑人知识分子。作为全国有色人种进步协会的创建者之一，杜波伊斯从 1910 年至 1934 年一直担任《危机》（The Crisis）杂志的主编。在其最著名的著作《黑人的灵魂》中，杜波伊斯准确地预言到："二十世纪的问题是种族歧视下的肤色界线问题。"

20 世纪 20 年代，美国纽约市黑人聚居区哈莱姆发生了一场重要的黑人文化运动。在这场运动中，黑人作家们第一次有意识地把反映黑人生活与振兴黑人文化视为己任，这就是美国文坛著名的"哈莱姆文艺复兴"（Harlem Renaissance）。在这个黑人文化运动中涌现出以兰斯顿·休斯为领袖的一批试图通过文学创作为黑人创造新的价值观的黑人作家，他们的作品为 20 世纪美国文学的繁荣作出了很大贡献。

在"爵士时代"的黄金十年里，路易斯·阿姆斯特朗和埃林顿公爵是正在崛起的爵士乐领域中的两个巨人。他们通过爵士乐创造的革命性音乐语言，如今已经渗透到美国文化的各个层面，对美国甚至世界人民的精神生活，都产生了重大而深远的影响。

The early years of the 20th century were a time of movement for many black Americans. Traditionally, most blacks lived in the Southeastern states. But in the 1920s, many blacks moved to cities in the North. Black Americans moved because living conditions were so poor in the rural areas of the Southeast. But many of them discovered that life was also hard in the colder Northern cities. Jobs often were hard to find. Housing was poor. And whites sometimes acted brutally against them. The life of black Americans forms a special piece of the history of the 1920s.

The years just before and after 1920 were difficult for blacks. It was a time of racial hatred. Many whites joined the **Ku Klux Klan** organization. The Klan often terrorized blacks. Klan members sometimes burned fiery crosses in front of the houses of black families. And they sometimes beat and murdered blacks. The Ku Klux Klan also acted against Roman Catholics, Jews, and foreigners. But it hated blacks most of all.

The United States also suffered a series of race riots in a number of cities during this period. White and black Americans fought each other in Omaha, Philadelphia, and other cities. The worst riot was in Chicago. A swimming incident started the violence. A black boy sailing a small boat entered a part of the beach used by white swimmers. Some white persons threw stones at the boy. He fell into the water and drowned. Black citizens heard about the incident and became extremely angry. Soon, black and white mobs were fighting each other in the streets. The violence lasted for two weeks. Thirty-eight persons died. More than five hundred were wounded. The homes of hundreds of families were burned. The violence in Chicago and other cities did not stop black Americans from moving north or west. They felt that life had to be better than in the South.

Black Americans left the South because life was hard, economic chances few, and white hatred common. But many blacks arrived in other parts of the country only to learn that life was no easier. Some blacks wrote later that they had only traded the open racism of the rural Southeast for the more secret racism of Northern cities.

Blacks responded to these conditions in different ways. Some blacks followed the ideas of **Booker T. Washington**, the popular black leader of the early 1900s. Washington believed that blacks had to educate and prepare themselves to survive in American society. He helped form a number of training schools where blacks could learn skills for better jobs. And he urged blacks to establish businesses and improve themselves without causing trouble with whites. Other blacks liked the stronger ideas of **William Du Bois**. Du Bois felt that blacks had to take firm actions to protest murders and other illegal actions. He published a magazine and spoke actively for new laws and policies to protect black rights. Du Bois also helped form a group that later became the **National Association for the Advancement of Colored People**. The NAACP became one of the nation's leading black rights organizations in the 20th century.

William Du Bois

Probably the most important leader for black Americans in the 1920s did not come from the United States. He was **Marcus Garvey** from the Caribbean island of Jamaica. Garvey moved to New York City in 1916. He quickly began organizing groups in black areas. His message was simple. He said blacks should not trust whites. Instead, they should be proud of being black and should help each other. Garvey urged blacks to leave the United States, move to Africa, and start their own nation. Marcus Garvey organized several plans to help blacks become economically independent of whites. His biggest effort was a shipping company to trade goods among black people all over the world. Many American blacks gave small amounts of money each week to help Garvey start the shipping company. However, the idea failed. Government officials arrested Garvey for collecting the money unlawfully. They sent him to prison in 1925. And two years later, President Coolidge ordered Garvey out of the country. Marcus Garvey's group was the first major black organization in the United States to gain active support from a large number of people. The organization failed. But it did show the anger and lack of hope that many blacks felt about their place in American society.

Blacks also showed their feelings through writing, art, and music. The 1920s were one of the most imaginative periods in the history of American black art. **Claude McKay**, **Langston Hughes**, and **Countee Cullen** were three of the leading black poets during this time. McKay was best known for his poems of social protest. Hughes produced poems about black life that experts now say are among the greatest American poems ever written. Black writers also produced longer works. Among the leading black novelists were **Jessie Faucet**, **Jean Toomer**, and **Rudolph Fisher**.

The 1920s also were an exciting time for black music. Black musicians playing the piano developed the ragtime style of music. Singers and musicians produced a sad, emotional style of playing that became known as the "blues." And most important, music lovers began to play and enjoy a new style that was becoming known as "jazz." Jazz advanced greatly as a true American

Blacks began to show their music talent in the 1920s (Duke Ellington was playing the piano).

kind of music in the 1920s. Musicians **Louis Armstrong**, **Duke Ellington**, and **Eubie Blake** played in gathering places and small theaters. White musicians and music experts from universities came to listen. Soon the music became popular among Americans of all kinds and around the world.

Blacks began to recognize in the 1920s their own deep roots in the United States. They began to see just how much black men and women already had done to help form American history and traditions. The person who did the most to help blacks understand this was black historian **Carter G. Woodson**. Woodson received his training at two leading universities: Harvard in Massachusetts and the **Sorbonne** in France. He launched a new publication, *The Journal of Negro History*, in which he and other experts wrote about black life and history. Historians today call Woodson the father of the scientific study of black history.

The 1920s also were a period in which a number of blacks experimented with new political ideas and parties. The difficult social conditions of the period led many blacks to search for new political solutions. Two leftist parties—the Socialists and the Communists—urged blacks to leave the traditional political system and work for more extreme change. Two leading black Socialists, **Chandler Owen** and **A. Philip Randolph**, urged blacks to support Socialist candidates. However, they gained little popular support from blacks. Communists also tried to organize black workers. But generally, black voters showed little interest in communist ideas. The most important change in black political thinking during the 1920s came within the traditional two-party system itself. Blacks usually had voted for Republicans since the days of Abraham Lincoln. But the conservative Republican policies of the 1920s caused many blacks to become Democrats. By 1932, blacks would vote by a large majority for the Democratic presidential candidate, **Franklin Roosevelt**. And blacks continue to be a major force in the Democratic Party.

Words, Expressions and Notes

Ku Klux Klan 三K党，主要活动于美国南方的白人秘密组织，从事迫害黑人等少数民族的勾当。

Booker T. Washington 布克尔·华盛顿（1856—1915），美国黑人教育家

William Du Bois 威廉·杜波伊斯（1868—1963），美国激进派黑人领袖、作家

National Association for the Advancement of Colored People 全国有色人种进步协会

Marcus Garvey 马可斯·贾维（1887—1940），美国黑人领袖

Claude McKay 克洛德·默克（1889—1948），美国黑人作家、诗人，哈莱姆文艺复兴时期代表人物之一

Langston Hughes 兰斯顿·休斯（1902—1967），美国黑人作家、诗人，哈莱姆文艺复兴时期代表人物之一

Countee Cullen 康提·卡伦（1903—1946），美国黑人诗人，哈莱姆文艺复兴时期优秀诗人之一

Jessie Faucet 杰西·佛塞特（1882—1961），美国黑人小说家、编辑

Jean Toomer 吉恩·图默尔（1894—1967），美国作家，其1923年出版的描写南方生活的实验性长篇小说 *Cane*（《甘蔗》）对20世纪黑人作家影响巨大。

Rudolph Fisher 鲁道夫·费希尔（1897—1934），美国黑人作家、音乐家

Louis Armstrong 路易斯·阿姆斯特朗（1901—1971），美国黑人爵士音乐家、小号手，"爵士乐之王"

Duke Ellington 埃林顿公爵（1899—1974），美国黑人爵士音乐家、乐队指挥，对美国爵士乐的发展贡献巨大。

Eubie Blake 布雷克（1887—1983），美国黑人爵士音乐家

Carter G. Woodson 卡特·伍德森（1875—1950），美国黑人历史学家

Sorbonne 巴黎大学文理学院

The Journal of Negro History 《黑人历史期刊》

Chandler Owen 钱德勒·欧文（1889—1967），杂志编辑，黑人社会主义积极分子

A. Philip Randolph 兰道夫（1889—1979），美国黑人劳工领导人

Franklin Roosevelt 富兰克林·罗斯福（1882—1945），美国第三十二任总统

Questions for Comprehension and Discussion

1. Why were the years before and after 1920 difficult for black people?
2. What did the Ku Klux Klan do?
3. Why did migration to the cities often not change the black people's status as second-class citizens?
4. How did Booker T. Washington's ideas about Negro advancement differ from those of William Du Bois?
5. Why were the 1920s regarded as one of the most imaginative periods in the history of American black art?
6. What advancement had black musicians gained in the 1920s?

Unit 12 A Nation Crippled and Desperate

45 The Stock Market Crash of 1929

1929 年股票市场崩溃

"美国人的事业就是做生意"（The business of America is business.），这是 20 世纪 20 年代美国全国上下喊得最响亮的口号。这个时期美国正处于空前的繁荣之中，国家信奉和实施的是一种自由放任的政策，反对政府对经济进行任何干预。

乐观的情绪弥漫全国。在浪多人看来，繁荣的景象似乎会永远持续下去。在 1928 年的选举中，总统候选人赫伯特·胡佛就曾自豪地宣称，"贫困从我国消失将指日可待"。这位乐观的美国总统万万没有料到的是，国家表面的一片繁荣浪快就要演变成一场漫长的噩梦。

从 1900 年到 1920 年，美国农业普遍呈现出繁荣景象，农产品的价格涂涂上升，战争对美国农产品的需求大大刺激了农业生产。农场主们乘此机会把休耕多年的贫瘠土地或荒地都开垦出来。由于美国农业的产值大大增加，农场主们开始有能力购买过去买不起的物品和机械了。但是，到 20 年代末，战争时期的需求戛然而止，对主要农产品的需求急剧下降，农业开始呈现出不景气的状况。另外，由于美国实施进口高关税，在美国不向其购买货物的国家和地区，美国农场主注注也不能销售他们的产品，国外市场对美国的大门正在慢慢关闭。

这一时期，美国股票市场投机风盛行，也给社会造成一种虚假的繁荣。从 1928 年初起，证券市场就不断出现哄抬股票行情的情况。进入 1929 年后，这种趋势有增无减。1929 年 10 月 24 日，纽约证券交易所股票价格崩溃，史称"黑色星期四"。一场酝酿已久、席卷全国的经济风暴终于来临。

The election of Republican presidential candidate **Herbert Hoover** in 1928 made Americans more hopeful than ever about their future. In March 1929, Hoover rode down Pennsylvania Avenue in Washington in the rain to become the new president. "I have no fears for the future of our country," he told the cheering crowd. "It is bright with hope."

Herbert Hoover seemed to have just the right experience to lead the nation to new economic progress. He had training in engineering, business, and national leadership. He understood economics and had faith in the future of private business.

The clearest evidence of the public's faith in the economy is the stock market. And the **New York Stock Exchange** reacted to the new president with a wild increase in prices. During the months after Hoover's election, prices generally rose like a rocket. Stocks valued at 100 dollars climbed to 200, then 300, 400. Men and women made huge amounts of money overnight. Publications and economic experts advised Americans to

President Herbert Hoover

buy stocks before prices went even higher. Time and again, people heard how rich they could become if they found and bought stocks for companies growing into industrial giants. "Never sell the United States **short**," said one publication. Another just said, "Everybody ought to be rich."

A number of economic experts worried about the sharp increase in stock prices that followed Hoover's election. The President himself urged stock market officials to make trading more honest and safe. And he approved a move by the **Federal Reserve Board** to **increase the interest charged to banks**.

However, both efforts failed to stop the growing number of Americans who were spending their money wildly on stocks. Some experts pointed to danger signs in the economy during the summer of 1929. The number of houses being built was dropping. Industries were reducing the amount of products that they held in their factories. The **rate of growth in spending** by average Americans was falling sharply. And industrial production, employment, and prices were down. These experts warned that the American economy was just not strong enough to support such rapid growth in stock prices. They said there was no real value behind many of the high prices. They said a stock price could not increase four times while a company's sales stayed the same. They said the high prices were built on foolish dreams of wealth, not real value.

But the prices went still higher. Buyers fought with each other to pay more and more for company stocks. The average price of all stocks almost doubled in just one year. It seemed everybody was buying stocks, even people with little money or economic training. A clothing salesman got advice from a stock trader visiting his store and made 200,000 dollars. A nurse learned of a good company from someone in the hospital. She made 30,000 dollars. There were thousands of such stories.

By early September, the stock market reached its high point of the past 18 months. Shares of the **Westinghouse company** had climbed from 91 dollars to 313. The **Anaconda Copper company** had risen from 54 dollars to 162. **Union Carbide** jumped from 145 to 413. Life was like a dream. But like any dream, it could not last forever.

In September, 1929, stock prices stopped rising. During the next month and a half, stock prices fell, but only slowly. Then suddenly, at the end of October, the market crashed. Prices dropped wildly. Leading stocks fell five, ten, twenty dollars in a single day. Everyone tried to sell their stocks. But no one was buying. Fear washed across the stock market. People were losing money even faster than they had made it.

The stock market collapsed on Thursday, October 24th, 1929. People remember the day as "Black Thursday," the day the dreams ended.

The day began with a wave of selling. People from across the country sent messages to their stock traders in New York. All the messages said the same thing: Sell! Sell the stocks at any price possible! But no one was buying. And so down the prices came. The value of stock for the **Montgomery Ward store** dropped from 83 dollars to 50 in a single day. The **RCA radio corporation** fell from 68 dollars to 44... 24 dollars in just a few hours. Down the stocks fell, lower and lower. Several of the country's leading bankers met to discuss ways to stop the disaster. They agreed to buy stocks in large amounts to stop the wave of selling. The bankers moved quickly. And for two days, prices held steady. But then, like snow falling down the side of a mountain, the stocks dropped again. Prices went to amazingly low levels. One business newspaper said simply: "The present week has witnessed the greatest stock market disaster of all time."

The stock market crash ruined thousands of Americans. In a few short weeks, traders lost 30,000 million dollars, an amount almost as great as all the money the United States had spent in World War I.

Some businessmen could not accept what had happened. They jumped from the tops of buildings and killed themselves. In fact, one popular joke of the time said that hotel owners had to ask people if they wanted rooms for sleeping or jumping.

But the stock market crash was nothing to laugh about. It destroyed much of the money that Americans had saved. Even worse, it caused millions of people to worry and lose faith in the economy. They were not sure what to expect tomorrow. Business owners would not spend money for new factories or business operations. Instead, they decided to wait and see what would happen. This reduced production and caused more workers to lose their jobs. Fewer workers meant fewer people with money to buy goods. And fewer people buying goods meant less need for factories to produce. So it went. In short, economic disaster.

Why did the stock market crash? One reason, people had been paying too much for stocks. Everyone believed that prices would go higher and higher forever. People paid more for stocks than the stocks were worth. They hoped to sell the stocks at even higher prices. It was like a children's balloon that expands with air, blowing bigger and bigger until it bursts.

But there were other important reasons. Industrial profits were too high and wages too low. Five percent of the population

A man who was once a millionaire was trying to earn a few pennies by selling apples in 1931.

owned one-third of all personal income. The average worker simply did not have enough money to buy enough of all the new goods that factories were producing. Another problem was that companies were not investing enough money in new factories and supplies. There were also problems with the rules of the stock market itself. People were allowed to buy stocks when they did not have the money to do so.

Several government economic policies also helped cause the stock market crash of 1929. Government tax policies made the rich richer and the poor poorer. And the government did little to control the national money supply, even when the economy faced disaster. The stock market crash marked the beginning of **the Great Depression**—a long, slow, painful fall to the worst economic crisis in American history.

The Depression would bring suffering to millions of people. It would cause major political changes. And it would be a major force in creating the conditions that led to World War II.

Words, Expressions and Notes

Herbert Hoover 赫伯特·胡佛（1874—1964），美国第三十一任总统（1929—1933）

New York Stock Exchange 纽约证券交易所

short adv.（股票）卖空

Federal Reserve Board 联邦储备委员会

increase the interest charged to banks 向银行征收更高的利率

rate of growth in spending 开支增加率

Westinghouse company 西屋电气公司，由美国著名

发明家、企业家 George Westinghouse 创办。

Anaconda Copper company 阿纳康达铜矿公司，位于蒙大拿州西南部。

Union Carbide 联合卡拜德化工公司

Montgomery Ward store 蒙哥马利·沃德公司，1872 年开业于芝加哥的美国历史上最长的百货连锁店，后因经营不善破产。

RCA radio corporation 美国无线电公司

the Great Depression 大萧条

Questions for Comprehension and Discussion

1. President Hoover said in 1929: "I have no fears for the future of our country. It is bright with hope. " Why was he so optimistic?
2. Why did some people say that the high prices of stock market were built on foolish dreams of wealth, not on real value?
3. How did speculation help to bring on the stock market crash?
4. Why is October 24th, 1929 remembered by people as "Black Thursday"?
5. What were the direct results of the stock market crash?
6. What are the major reasons of the crash?

46 **The Great Depression**

大萧条

胡佛总统领导的政府在股票价格暴跌后，居然天真地对美国经济作出这样的预测："美国主要工商业以及商品的生产和销售，形势很好。"面对美国历史上最大的经济危机，胡佛仍然顽固地相信"自由放任"的经济政策，认为自由经济本身会对运行中出现的偏差加以纠正，因而完全不考虑用政府的力量去干预经济。胡佛失败的反危机政策让美国普通民众异常愤怒，为他在1932年大选中的失败埋下了伏笔。

股票证券价格的迅速下跌立即波及银行，许多金融机构被拖累进而倒闭。金融危机又无可避免地影响到各行各业的公司，使它们的销售、生产和雇工均告削减。到1930年，美国已陷于经济全面大萧条的状况。银行倒闭，千百万投资者和储蓄者的一生积蓄化为乌有；商店关门，工厂停工，千百万失业者踯躅街头。无家可归的失业者在各地用废旧材料搭起的临时居住点"胡佛村"，成为胡佛政府失败的反危机政策与措施的时代象证。

当人们从最初的震惊中清醒过来，探究经济萧条的原因时，他们才看出那些隐伏在20年代表面繁荣下的不良趋势。问题的核心是美国生产力和美国人民消费能力悬殊。战时与战后生产技术的大改革使美国工业产量大大增加，从而超过了美国工人、农场主的购买力。富有阶级和中产阶级存款的增加远远超过了健全投资所能容纳的程度，于是游资流向证券市场和不动产方面用于疯狂的投机。证券市场的崩溃只不过是一系列爆炸中的第一个。在爆炸声中，脆弱的经济崩溃了。

农民的命运在大萧条时期更为悲惨，最典型的例子发生在俄克拉何马州。大萧条年代，这里长期的干旱和不良的耕种方法将大草原变成狂风呼啸的沙漠，春天的大风把沙土抛向天空，形成8公里高的沙墙，绿色的平原顿时变为"尘碗"（Dust Bowl），成千上万的农民被迫背井离乡。获得诺贝尔文学奖的作家约翰·斯坦贝克怀着一颗赤子之心，在他最著名的小说《愤怒的葡萄》（*The Grapes of Wrath*）里，忠实地记录了这些农民破产的真实面貌，深刻地揭示了他们逃荒到加利福尼亚的苦难历程。

The stock market crash of 1929 marked the beginning of the worst economic crisis in American history. Millions of people lost their jobs. Thousands lost their homes. During the next several years, a large part of the richest nation on earth learned what it meant to be poor. Hard times found their way into every area, group, and job. Workers struggled as factories closed. Farmers, hit with falling prices and natural disasters, were forced to give up their farms. Businessmen lost their stores and sometimes their homes. It was a severe economic crisis—a depression.

Nobel Prize winner **John Steinbeck**, one of America's greatest writers, described the Depression this way: "It was a terrible, troubled time. I can't think of any ten years in history when so much happened in so many directions. Violent change took place. Our country was shaped, our lives changed, our government rebuilt." Said John Steinbeck: "When the stock market fell, the factories, mines, and steelworks closed. And then no one could buy anything. Not even food."

An unemployed auto worker in the manufacturing city of **Detroit** described the situation this way: "Before daylight, we were on the way to the **Chevrolet** factory to look for work. The police were already

there, waving us away from the office. They were saying, 'Nothing doing! No jobs! No jobs!' So now we were walking slowly through the falling snow to the employment office for the **Dodge** auto company. A big, well-fed man in a heavy overcoat stood at the door. 'No! No!' he said. There was no work.'' One Texas farmer lost his farm and moved his family to California to look for work. "We can't send the children to school," he said, "because they have no clothes."

The economic crisis began with the stock market crash in October, 1929. For the first year, the economy fell very slowly. But it dropped sharply in 1931 and 1932. And by the end of 1932, the economy collapsed almost completely.

The gross national product is the total of all goods and services produced. During the three years following the stock market crash, the American gross national product dropped by almost half. The wealth of the average American dropped to a level lower than it had been 25 years earlier.

All the gains of the 1920s were washed away. Unemployment rose sharply. The number of workers looking for a job jumped from three percent to more than 25 percent in just four years. One of every three or four workers was looking for a job in 1932.

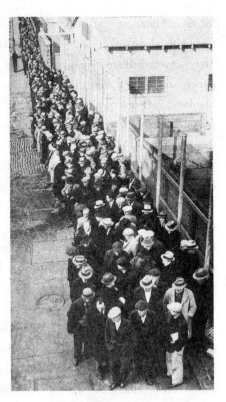

Waiting for a job

Those employment numbers did not include farmers. The men and women who grew the nation's food suffered terribly during the Great Depression. This was especially true in the Southwestern states of Oklahoma and Texas. Farmers there were losing money because of falling prices for their crops. Then natural disaster struck. Year after year, little or no rain fell. The ground dried up. And then the wind blew away the earth in huge clouds of dust.

"All that dust made some of the farmers leave," one Oklahoma farmer remembered later. "But my family stayed. We fought to live. Despite all the dust and the wind, we were planting seeds. But we got no crops. We had five crop failures in five years."

Falling production. Rising unemployment. Men begging in the streets. But there was more to the Great Depression. At that time, the federal government did not guarantee the money that people put in banks. When people could not repay loans, banks began to close. In 1929, 659 banks with total holdings of 200 million dollars went out of business. The next year, two times that number failed. And the year after that, almost twice that number of banks went out of business. Millions of persons lost all their savings. They had no money left.

The Depression caused serious public health problems. Hospitals across the country were filled with sick people whose main illness was a lack of food. The health department in New York City found that one of every five of the city's children did not get enough food. Ninety-nine percent of the children attending a school in a coal-mining area reportedly were underweight. In some places, people died of hunger.

The quality of housing also fell. Families were forced to crowd into small houses or apartments to share costs. Many people had no homes at all. They slept on public streets, buses, or trains. One official in Chicago reported in 1931 that several hundred women without homes were sleeping in city parks. In a number of cities, people without homes built their houses from whatever materials they could find. They used empty boxes or pieces of metal to build shelters in open areas.

People called these areas of little temporary houses "**Hoovervilles**." They blamed President Hoover for their situation. So, too, did the men forced to sleep in public parks at night. They covered themselves with pieces of paper, and they called the paper "Hoover blankets." People without money in their pants called their empty pockets "Hoover flags." People blamed President Hoover because they thought he was not doing enough to help them. Hoover did take several actions to try to improve the economy. But he resisted proposals for the federal government to provide aid in a major way. And he refused to let the government spend more money than it earned.

Hoover told the nation: "Economic depression cannot be cured by legislative action or executive decision." Many conservative Americans agreed with him,

Shantytowns, often bitterly nicknamed Hoovervilles, become common in many American cities.

but not the millions of Americans who were hungry and tired of looking for a job. They accused Hoover of not caring about the common citizen. One congressman from **Alabama** said: "In the White House, we have a man more interested in the money of the rich than in the stomachs of the poor."

On and on the Great Depression continued. Of course, some Americans were lucky. They kept their jobs. And they had enough money to enjoy the lower prices of most goods. Many people shared their earnings with friends in need.

"We joined our money when we had some," remembered John Steinbeck. "It seems strange to say that we rarely had a job," Steinbeck wrote years later. "There just weren't any jobs. But we didn't have to steal much. Farmers and fruit growers in the nearby countryside could not sell their crops. They gave us all the food and fruit we could carry home."

Other Americans reacted to the crisis by leading protests against the economic policies of the Hoover administration. In 1932, a large group of former soldiers gathered in Washington to demand help. More than 8,000 of them built the nation's largest Hooverville near the White House. Federal troops finally removed them by force and burned their little shelters.

For Your Memory

Blowing Down This Old Dusty Road
流浪在尘土飞扬的路上

美国现代民歌运动的奠基人伍迪·格思里（Woody Guthrie）亲身经历了中西部尘暴灾害并与难民一道逃荒。他根据亲身经历创作了一批"尘暴歌曲"，《流浪在尘土飞扬的路上》就是其中的一首。歌曲中流浪者辛酸的叙述，折射出一个令人悲伤的时代侧影。今天，格思里的"尘暴歌曲"与他创作的其他歌曲一道，已经成为一个重要时代的见证，成为美国文化的组成部分。

I'm **blowing down** this old dusty road,

I'm blowing down this old dusty road,

I'm blowing down this old dusty road,

Lord, Lord,

And I ain't gonna be treated this way.

I'm going where the water taste like wine,

I'm going where the water taste like wine,

I'm going where the water taste like wine,

Lord, Lord,

And I ain't gonna be treated this way.

I'm going where the dust storms never blow,

I'm going where the dust storms never blow,

I'm going where the dust storms never blow,

Blow, blow,

And I ain't gonna be treated this way.

They say I'm a **dust bowl refugee,**

Yes, they say I'm a dust bowl refugee,

They say I'm a dust bowl refugee,

Lord, Lord,

But I ain't gonna be treated this way.

I'm looking for a job at honest pay,

I'm looking for a job at honest pay,

I'm looking for a job at honest pay,

Lord, Lord,

And I ain't gonna be treated this way.

My children need **three square meals a day**,

Now, my children need three square meals a day,

My children need three square meals a day,

Lord,

And I ain't gonna be treated this way.

It takes a ten dollar shoe to fit my feet,

It takes a ten dollar shoe to fit my feet,

It takes a ten dollar shoe to fit my feet,

Lord, Lord,

And I ain't gonna be treated this way.

Your two dollar shoe hurts my feet,

Your two dollar shoe hurts my feet,

Yes, your two dollar shoe hurts my feet,

Lord, Lord,

And I ain't gonna be treated this way.

I'm blowing down this old dusty road,

I'm blowing down this old dusty road,

I'm blowing down this old dusty road,

Lord, Lord,

And I ain't gonna be treated this way.

Words, Expressions and Notes

John Steinbeck 约翰·斯坦贝克（1902—1968），美
国小说家，获 1962 年诺贝尔文学奖。

Detroit 底特律，美国汽车工业基地

Chevrolet （美国）雪佛兰牌汽车

Dodge （美国）道奇牌卡车

Hoovervilles 胡佛村。大萧条时期失业者在各地用废
旧材料搭起的临时居住点，并取名"胡佛村"以
表示对总统的不满和抗议。

Alabama 阿拉巴马州

blowing down 流浪

dust bowl refugee 尘暴灾害的难民

three square meals a day 食物充足的一日三餐

Questions for Comprehension and Discussion

1. Why did the depression affect nearly all of the people in the United States?
2. What happened in the early 1930s in the United States?
3. Why did the Depression cause many serious public health problems?
4. Why did people call the little temporary houses they built "Hoovervilles"?
5. Why did Hoover not want the Federal government to actively intervene to end the depression?

47 The Hundred Days of Franklin Roosevelt's Administration

罗斯福当政 100 天

1921 年，年富力强的富兰克林·罗斯福因患骨髓灰质炎而全身瘫痪，他周围的每一个人都认为他的政治前途已经完结。然而，凭借坚强的意志和持续不断的锻炼，罗斯福最终恢复了手和背部的功能。尽管只能以轮椅代步，他仍然感到自己有能力重返政坛。

1932 年，担任纽约州州长的罗斯福以他百折不挠的勇气和乐观向上的精神战胜了胡佛而赢得总统大选。他在就职演说中的话语，"我们唯一恐惧的就是恐惧本身"（The only thing we have to fear is fear itself.），成为一个时代的格言。

新总统为信心低落的国家带来重振旗鼓的信心，人民很快集合在他的旗帜之下。不久，一套被称为"新政"（New Deal）的改革措施出台。罗斯福大刀阔斧、迅速果断地处理国家面临的种种危机。其实，新政在某种意义上，只不过是把英国人、德国人、斯堪的纳维亚半岛人司空见惯的各种改革应用于美国罢了。但它的非同寻常之处是它的推行速度。罗斯福政府以上台后的第一个 100 天为起点，高速度完成了美国过去可能需要几代人的时间才能完成的工作。

在政府出台的各种措施当中，对普通百姓的日常生活最有影响的莫过于取消《禁酒法》。取消禁酒这天，全国人民像过节一样开怀畅饮，持续多年的沉闷气氛一扫而光。

在实施新政的整个时期，公开批评与讨论从未中断，但新政使公民很快重新关心政府事务。有些批评新政的人认为，政府职能的无限制扩大，最终将损害人民的自由。面对批评，罗斯福总统坚持认为，凡有助于经济福利的措施，将会加强自由和民主。在辩论新政策对国家政治与经济生活的影响的过程中，美国人的传统观念开始发生变化，渐渐地赞成政府在为人民谋福利方面负起更大的责任。

Americans voted for Democratic candidate Franklin Delano Roosevelt in large numbers in the presidential election of 1932. They were tired of the policies of Republican President Herbert Hoover. They thought Hoover had done too little to fight the terrible economic depression. And they welcomed Roosevelt's call that the federal government should become more active in helping the common man.

The inauguration speech of President Franklin Roosevelt in March, 1933, gave hope to millions of Americans. The new president promised to fight the terrible economic crisis: the Great Depression. Roosevelt kept his promise. His administration **launched into action** even before the inauguration ceremonies were finished. As Roosevelt and his wife, **Eleanor**, watched the traditional inauguration parade, his assistants began working. The lights of Washington's federal office buildings burned late that night. And not just on inauguration night, but the next night and the next night, too. The

Franklin Delano Roosevelt

nation was in crisis. There was much work to do.

The first three months of Franklin Roosevelt's administration were an exciting time. Roosevelt led the Congress to pass more important legislation during this short period than most presidents pass during their entire term. These three months are remembered today as "the Hundred Days." Sunday, March 5th, was the day after the inauguration. Roosevelt told Congress to begin a special meeting on Thursday. And he ordered all the nation's banks to close until the economy improved. Roosevelt also banned the export of gold. Congress met on Thursday, as Roosevelt had asked. It passed everything that Roosevelt wanted. Both the House and Senate approved Roosevelt's strong new banking laws in less than eight hours. Roosevelt signed the bills into law the same day.

The next day, Friday, Roosevelt called on Congress to cut federal spending. Once again, Congress met and approved Roosevelt's request immediately. Two nights later, Roosevelt spoke to the nation in a radio speech. His warm, powerful voice traveled to millions of homes. He gave listeners hope that they could once again trust their banks and political leaders. On Monday, Roosevelt called on Congress to pass laws making it legal to drink wine or beer. And once again, Congress agreed. Roosevelt's success in passing these important and difficult laws excited the nation. People across the country watched in wonder as the new president fought and won battle after battle.

Washington was filled with activity. The air was full of energy, like a country sky during an electric storm. People from around the country rushed to the capital to urge the administration to support their ideas. Bankers came by the thousands to win favorable legislation. Experts of all kinds offered new ideas on how to rescue the economy. Ambassadors came from Britain, France, **Brazil**, **Chile**, China, and many other countries to speak with Roosevelt on economic and diplomatic issues. And members of the Democratic Party arrived by the thousands to seek jobs in the new administration. Americans watched closely what was happening in Washington. And they liked what they saw. They had voted for action. Now, Roosevelt was giving them action.

One of the most important areas of action for the new administration was agriculture. American farmers had been hurt more than any other group by the economic depression. The average income of American farmers had dropped in three years from 162 dollars a year to just 48 dollars. Farm prices had fallen 55 percent. The buying power of the average farmer had dropped by more than half. Many farmers could not even earn enough money to pay for their tools and seeds. The main cause of the farmers' problem was that they produced too much. There was too much grain, too much meat, too much cotton. As a result, prices stayed low. The situation was good for people in cities who bought farm products. But it was a disaster for the farmers themselves.

Roosevelt attacked the problem by limiting production. His administration put a new tax on grain products, increasing their price and reducing demand. The administration paid cotton farmers to destroy some of their crops. And it bought and killed five-million pigs to reduce the amount of meat on the market. It was a strange situation. Some Americans had trouble understanding the economic reason why food had to be destroyed so people could have enough to eat. But more officials agreed that this was the only way to limit supply, raise prices, and save farmers. The plan worked. Production fell rapidly. Hot weather and bad harvests in 1933 and 1934 reduced the amount of grain even more. As a result, prices rose. Farm income increased 50 percent in four years.

The administration also attacked the problem of falling industrial production. At the time of Roosevelt's inauguration, American industry was producing less than half the goods that it had just four years before. Business owners reacted by cutting costs: lowering wages and reducing the number of workers. This only reduced the number of people with enough money to buy goods. And so production went down further and further. The administration created a national recovery administration to allow companies to cooperate to increase production. Business owners agreed to follow certain rules, such as limiting the number of hours people could work. They also agreed to raise wages and to stop hiring children. They agreed to improve working conditions and to cooperate with labor unions. At the same time, Roosevelt created a public works administration to provide jobs to unemployed workers. The federal government put people to work building dams, bridges, water systems, and other major projects.

On money policy, Roosevelt and the Congress decided that the **dollar should no longer be tied to the price of gold**. They passed a home owner's bill that helped many Americans borrow new money to protect their homes. And a bank insurance bill guaranteed the safety of money that Americans placed in banks, greatly increasing public faith in the banks. Roosevelt and the Congress created a new **civilian conservation corps** to put young men to work in rural areas to protect the nation's natural resources. These young men planted trees, improved parks, and protected natural water supplies. They also worked with farmers to develop crops and farming methods to protect soil from wind and rain.

One of Roosevelt's most creative projects was a plan to improve the area around the state of Tennessee in the southeastern part of the country. The Tennessee River Valley area was very poor. Forests were thin, floods common, and income low. Few farms had electricity. Roosevelt and Congress decided to attack all these problems with a single project. The new Tennessee Valley administration built dams, cleared rivers, expanded forests, and provided electricity. It succeeded in helping farmers throughout the area, creating new life and hope.

"The Hundred Days"—the first three months of the Roosevelt administration—were a great success. One reporter for the *New York Times* newspaper observed that the change from President Hoover to President Roosevelt was like a man moving from a slow horse to an airplane. Suddenly, the nation was moving again. There was action everywhere. Newsman **Frederick Allen** described the situation this way: "The difference between Roosevelt's program and the Hoover program was sharp," Allen wrote. "Roosevelt's was not a program of defense, but of attack. In most of the laws, there was a new push for the good of the common man. There was a new effort to **build wealth from the bottom up, rather than from the top down**." Said Allen: "There was a new willingness to **expand the limits of government**."

Words, Expressions and Notes

launched into action　投入到行动中去

Eleanor（Eleanor Roosevelt）　埃莉诺·罗斯福（1884—1962），罗斯福总统的夫人，社会活动家，在罗斯福总统去世后仍积极投身国内外各种活动，曾担任美国驻联合国代表等重要职务，享有"世界第一夫人"的美誉（First Lady of the World）。

Brazil　巴西

Chile　智利

dollar should no longer be tied to the price of gold　不再实行美元与黄金挂钩的政策

civilian conservation corps　民间环境保护团体

Frederick Allen　弗雷德里克·阿伦（1890—1954），美国著名记者、杂志编辑

build wealth from the bottom up, rather than from the top down　由下而上积累财富，而不是从上到下。意指首先要让普通百姓富起来。

expand the limits of government　扩大政府所能发挥的作用

Questions for Comprehension and Discussion

1. How did Roosevelt's and Hoover's views on the role of the Federal government during the depression differ?

2. Why did the American farmers suffer most in the economic depression? What was the main problem?

3. What did the Roosevelt administration do to help the American industry?

4. Why was the first three months of the Roosevelt administration considered a great success?

5. Do you favor or disapprove of massive government involvement in the economic system?

6. What do you think of the idea that to build wealth from the bottom up, rather than from the top down?

48 The Development of Arts and Popular Culture During the Great Depression

大萧条时期艺术与流行文化的发展

20世纪初期，美国的经济发展达到前所未有的高度；第一次世界大战后，美国又迎来一个空前繁荣的时期。这种繁荣并不只是局限在经济领域，同样也在文学、音乐、电影等领域反映出来。

在传统艺术和文化领域，欧洲具有美国根本无法与之相比的历史和优势。但是，美国也有欧洲国家不具备的特点：一个由世界不同民族和文化组建的一个充满活力的社会，而这样的社会必然会给艺术和文化的发展提供广阔的空间。

在传统文学领域，从第一次世界大战到20世纪30年代末，美国文学出现了一个高峰期，以海明威和菲茨杰拉德为代表的"迷惘的一代"（The Lost Generation）称雄文坛。这批作家的作品之多，接触的生活面之广，题材和内容之丰富，是同时代其他国家的文学远不能企及的。从20年代末起，美国社会的种种弊端日益显露，严酷的现实给予敏感而又富有正义感的作家们以巨大的推动力量，使他们写出不少揭露黑暗、控诉邪恶的有力作品。这也为世界文学的中心从欧洲国家转移到美国奠定了基础。

在流行文化的发展上，美国依靠强大的经济和先进的科学技术，从一开始就走在世界的前列。在20世纪到来之前，处于萌芽期的"流行文化"，无论是在美国还是在其他国家，由于只能依靠传统的途径传播，其实很难真正流行开来。一个典型的例子是，美国19世纪中期著名的音乐家斯蒂芬·福斯特（Stephen Foster）创作有大量脍炙人口的歌曲，被公认为是美国第一位专业流行歌曲作家，但是他的收入却如此微薄，以致不能养家糊口，年仅37岁便在贫困中死去。

19世纪末的两项重要技术发明为20世纪流行文化的高速发展铺平了道路，这就是美国科学家爱迪生发明的录音技术和意大利物理学家马可尼发明的无线电技术。这两项技术率先在美国运用并普及，使过去只能由王公贵族和富人阶层独自享用的音乐步入普罗大众的生活中，而音乐平民化的最直接和最重要的结果就是当代流行音乐的兴起。另外，美国电影工业的快速发展也使流行文化对社会的影响提升到一个新阶段。至少从这两方面来看，美国流行文化的发展从一开始就占得先机，成为20世纪世界流行文化的主流。

Hard economic times and social conflict have always offered a rich source of material for artists and writers. A painter's colors can show the drying of dreams or the flight of human spirits. A musician can express the tensions and uncertainty of a people in struggle. The pressures of hard times can be the force to lift a writer's imagination to new heights. So it was during the 1930s in the United States. The severe economic crisis—the Great Depression—created an atmosphere for artistic imagination and creative expression. The common feeling of struggle also led millions of Americans to look together to films, radio, and other new art forms for relief from their day-to-day cares.

The most popular sound of the 1930s was a new kind of music: **swing music**. And the "King of Swing" was a clarinet player named **Benny Goodman**.

Benny Goodman and other musicians made swing music extremely popular during the 1930s. Swing music was a new form of jazz. Many of its first players were black musicians in small, unknown groups. It was only when more well-known white musicians started playing swing music in the middle 1930s that the new music became wildly popular.

One reason for the popularity of swing music was the growing power of radio during the 1930s. Radio had already proven in earlier years that it could be an important force in both politics and popular culture. Millions of Americans bought radios during the 1920s. But radio grew up in the 1930s. Producers became more skillful in creating programs. And actors and actresses began to understand the special needs and power of this new electronic art form.

Benny Goodman

Swing music was not the only kind of music that radio helped make popular. The 1930s also saw increasing popularity for traditional, classical music by **Beethoven**, **Bach**, and other great musicians. In 1930, the **Columbia Broadcasting System** began a series of concerts by the **New York Philharmonic Orchestra** on Sunday afternoons. The next year, the **National Broadcasting Company**, NBC, began weekly opera concerts.

In 1937, NBC asked **Arturo Toscanini** of Italy to lead an orchestra on American radio. Toscanini was the greatest orchestra leader of his day. Millions of Americans listened at Christmas time as Toscanini and the NBC Orchestra began playing the first of ten special radio concerts. It was a great moment for both music and radio. For the first time, millions of average Americans were able to hear classical music by great musicians as it was being played.

Music was an important reason why millions of Americans gathered to listen to the radio during the 1930s. But even more popular were a series of weekly programs with exciting or funny new actors. Families would come home from school or work and laugh at the foolish experiences of such actors as **Jack Benny**, **Fred Allen**, **George Burns**, **Edgar Bergen**, and **W. C. Fields**. Radio helped people forget the hard conditions of the Great Depression. And it helped to bring Americans together and share experiences.

Swing music. Classical music. Great comedy programs. The 1930s truly were a golden period for radio and mass communications. But it was also during this period that **Hollywood** and the American film industry became much more skilled and influential. In previous years, films were silent. But the "**talkies**" arrived in the 1930s. Directors could produce films in which actors could talk. Americans reacted by attending film theaters by the millions. It was a great time for Hollywood.

The films had exciting new actors. **Spencer Tracy**. **Bette Davis**. **Katharine Hepburn**. The young **Shirley Temple**. The most famous film of the period was *Gone with the Wind* with actor **Clark Gable** and actress **Vivien Leigh**. Directors in the 1930s also produced such great films as *It Happened One Night*, *Mutiny on the Bounty*, and *The Life of Emile Zola*.

The success of radio and films, as well as the depression itself, caused problems for many American newspapers during the 1930s. The trouble was not so much that readers stopped buying newspapers. It was that companies talked about their products through advertisements on radio instead of buying advertising space in newspapers. Nearly half of the nation's independently-published newspapers either stopped publishing or joined larger companies during the 1930s. By World War II, only 120 cities had competing newspapers.

Weekly and monthly publications faced the same problem as daily newspapers—increased competition from radio and films. Many magazines failed. The two big successes of the period were *Life* magazine and the *Reader's Digest*. *Life* magazine had stories for everyone about film actors, news events, or just daily life in the home or on the farm. Its photographs were the greatest anywhere. *Reader's Digest* published shorter forms of stories from other magazines and sources.

Most popular books of the period were like the films coming from Hollywood. Writers cared more about helping people forget their troubles than about facing serious social issues. They made more money that way, too. But a number of writers in the 1930s did produce books that were both profitable and of high quality. One was Sinclair Lewis. His book, ***It Can't Happen Here***, warned of the coming dangers of fascism. John Steinbeck's great book, *The Grapes of Wrath*, helped millions understand and feel in their hearts the troubles faced by poor farmers. **Erskine Caldwell** wrote about the cruelty of life among poor people in the Southeastern United States, and **James T. Farrell** about life in Chicago.

The same social concern and desire to present life as it really existed also were clear in the work of many American artists during the 1930s. **Thomas Benton** painted workers and others with strong, tough bodies. **Edward Hopper** showed the sad streets of American cities. **Reginald Marsh** painted picture after picture of poor parts of New York City. The federal government created a program that gave jobs to artists. They painted their pictures on the walls of airports, post offices, and schools. The program brought their ideas and creativity to millions of people. At the same time, photography became more important as cameras improved in quality and became more moveable. Some photographers like **Margaret Bourke-White** and **Walker Evans** used their cameras to report the hard conditions of the Depression.

All this activity in the arts and popular culture played an important part in the lives of Americans during the 1930s. It not only provided relief from their troubles, but expanded their minds and pushed their imaginations. The tensions and troubles of the Great Depression provided a rich atmosphere for artists and others to produce works that were serious, foolish, or just plain fun. And those works, in turn, helped make life a little better as Americans waited, worked, and hoped for times to improve.

Words, Expressions and Notes

swing music 摇摆音乐，一种具有即兴特点的音乐形式，其风格已成为爵士乐和现代流行音乐最重要的要素之一。

Benny Goodman 本尼·古德曼（1909—1986），美国爵士乐音乐家、乐队领导人，善于演奏单簧管，被称为"摇摆乐之王"。

Beethoven 贝多芬（1770—1827），德国古典音乐家

Bach 巴赫（1685—1750），德国古典音乐家

Columbia Broadcasting System 哥伦比亚广播公司，美国三大广播公司之一

New York Philharmonic Orchestra 纽约爱乐乐团，美国最负盛名的交响乐团之一

National Broadcasting Company 国家广播公司，美国三大广播公司之一

Arturo Toscanini 托斯卡尼尼（1867—1957），享誉世界的意大利指挥家，从1908年起到美国担任交响乐团指挥，取得非凡成功。

Jack Benny 杰克·本尼（1894—1974），喜剧演员

Fred Allen 弗雷德·阿伦（1894—1956），喜剧演员

George Burns 乔治·伯恩斯（1896—1996），喜剧演员

Edgar Bergen 艾德加·伯根（1903—1978），口技演员（通过表演假装与木偶对话引听众发笑）

W. C. Fields 费尔茨（1880—1946），喜剧演员

Hollywood 好莱坞，位于加州的美国电影制作基地，现已成为美国电影工业的代名词。

talkies *n.* 有声电影

Spencer Tracy 斯宾塞·特雷西（1900—1967），美国早期著名电影演员

Bette Davis 贝蒂·戴维斯（1908—1989），著名电影女演员

Katharine Hepburn 凯瑟琳·赫本（1907—2003），著名电影女演员

Shirley Temple 雪莉·邓波尔（1928—），美国著名电影女童星

Gone with the Wind 《乱世佳人》，根据同名小说改编的电影

Clark Gable 克拉克·盖博（1901—1960），美国著名电影演员

Vivien Leigh 费雯丽（1913—1967），印度出生的英

国演员

It Happened One Night　（电影）《一夜风流》

Mutiny on the Bounty　（电影）《叛舰喋血记》

The Life of Emile Zola　（电影）《艾米莉·左拉的生活》

Life　《生活》杂志

Reader's Digest　《读者文摘》杂志

It Can't Happen Here　《事情不会发生在这里》，辛克莱·刘易斯关于法西斯可能控制美国的小说

Erskine Caldwell　厄尔斯金·考德威尔（1903—1987），美国小说家，其最有影响的作品是长篇小说《烟草路》（*Tobacco Road*）。

James T. Farrell　詹姆斯·法雷尔（1904—1979），

美国小说家

Thomas Benton　托马斯·本顿（1889—1975），美国画家，擅长表现美国乡土生活。

Edward Hopper　爱德华·霍珀（1882—1967），美国画家，擅长表现都市生活。

Reginald Marsh　雷吉诺德·马什（1898—1954），美国画家，作品多以纽约都市生活为题材。

Margaret Bourke-White　马格莉特·伯克－怀特（1904—1971），美国女摄影家

Walker Evans　沃尔克·伊文思（1903—1975），美国摄影家，作品以记录南方的穷困而闻名。

Questions for Comprehension and Discussion

1. Why can hard economic times and social conflict offer a rich source of material to artists and writers?

2. Why did radio become an important force in both politics and popular culture?

3. Why was the 1930s a great time for Hollywood?

4. What kind of problems did many American newspapers and magazines have during the 1930s?

5. Why is it said that arts and popular culture played an important part in the lives of Americans during the 1930s?

Unit 13 Fighting in World War II

49 The Road to Pearl Harbor

通往珍珠港之路

罗斯福总统在大刀阔斧解决国内经济问题的同时，注意到世界局势正朝着危险的方向发展。在 1938 年的一次广播演说中，他提醒美国人民：“民主制度已在其他几个大国中消失，其原因绝非是这些国家的人民嫌弃民主，而是由于他们的政府领导无方，造成管理混乱、软弱。面对失业与不稳定的生活，面对子女啼饥号寒，人民束手无策，身心俱疲。他们在绝望中决定牺牲自由，以换取果腹的东西。我们美国人都了解：我们的民主体制能够保持下去并发挥作用。但是为了保持民主，我们必须证明民主政府的实际运转是与保障人民安全的任务同样重要的。美国人民都愿意不惜任何代价保卫自己的自由，而自由的第一道防线，便是保障经济安全。”

1936 年罗斯福连任总统后不久，新的危机就笼罩着他的国内政策，这就是日本、意大利和德国极权主义政权的扩张野心，而当时普通美国人极少注意到这一点。1931 年，日本首先采取行动侵略中国东北，一年后建立“满洲”傀儡政权。受法西斯主义驱使的意大利则在利比亚边境进行领土扩张，并于 1935 至 1936 年征服了埃塞俄比亚。阿道夫·希特勒在德国组织的纳粹党夺取了政权，他进而重占莱茵河地区，并开始大规模重整军备。

这个时期的美国因对第一次世界大战后的局势深感失望，从 1935 年至 1937 年间陆续制定各种中立法律，禁止美国和任何交战国贸易，或向其发放贷款。目的是几乎不惜任何代价，避免使美国卷入一场美洲以外的战争。

当极权主义的真面目日见明显，德、意、日三国继续在世界各地侵略的时候，美国人民的担忧转成愤怒。当希特勒对波兰、丹麦、挪威、荷兰、比利时、法国发动闪电战后，美国的态度逐步转向强硬。虽然美国最初的反应仍然是想置身于欧洲战争之外，但法国的沦陷和 1940 年夏天英国首次遭受空袭使大多数抱中立态度的美国人转变了立场。他们不仅意识到纳粹军事机器的强大，也确信欧洲面临的危险迟早也会威胁美国的安全。

1940 年，罗斯福成为美国历史上第一个三度入主白宫的总统。1941 年 12 月 7 日，正当美国人忧心忡忡地注视着欧洲战局的进展情况，对究竟参不参战举棋不定时，一记重拳突然落到这个力图置身于战事之外的国家。令所有人都万万意想不到的是，这一记重拳不是来自欧洲的德国，而是来自亚洲的日本。

Germany's attack on Poland and the start of World War II presented a serious problem to Americans in September 1939. The United States—by law—was neutral. And few Americans had any desire to fight in another world war. But Americans did not like Germany's **Nazi leader, Adolf Hitler**. They hoped for victory for Britain, France, and the other **Allied Powers**. President Franklin Roosevelt made this clear in a radio talk to Americans soon after the war began. "The peace of all countries everywhere is in danger," Roosevelt said. He added, "I cannot ask that every American remain neutral in thought." He praised the British and other allies. Finally, the President called on Congress to change the neutrality laws that prevented him from sending arms to the Allies to help them fight the Nazis. Congress agreed to change the laws so foreign nations could buy American arms.

In the months that followed, Hitler and his allies won one victory after another. German and Soviet troops captured Poland quickly in September 1939. Then Soviet forces invaded the small **Baltic nations** of **Latvia**, **Estonia**, and **Lithuania**. In late November, they attacked **Finland**. Fighting between Finland and the **Soviet Union** continued through the winter, until Finland accepted Russia's demands.

Fighting grew even more fierce the following spring, in early 1940. Germany attacked **Denmark** and **Norway**, defeating them easily. In May, Nazi forces struck like lightning through Belgium and Holland. Within one day, they were in France. British and French forces were unable to stop the Germans from moving deep into northern France. The British forces finally were forced to flee from the European continent in small boats. They sailed from the French town of **Dunkerque** back to Britain. German soldiers marched through France. And Italian forces joined them by invading France from the South. Soon, Paris fell. A German supporter, **Marshal Petain**, took control of the French government. And France, beaten and crushed, was forced to sign a peace treaty with Hitler.

Now it was just Britain alone against Hitler and his allies. Only the **English Channel** separated the British people from a German army that seemed unbeatable. British Prime Minister **Neville Chamberlain** was forced to resign. The British people turned to a new leader, **Winston Churchill**. Churchill would prove to be strong and brave in the long months ahead. The British would need strong leadership. Hitler wasted no time in launching a fierce air attack on Britain. Throughout the summer, German and British planes fought above the English Channel.

All this military action had an important effect on American popular opinion. War and neutrality were no longer just ideas to be discussed in a classroom or political debate. Now they were real concerns, real events. Fascist troops led by a dictator in **Berlin** were defeating one friendly democracy after another. And Soviet forces were on the march, too. Most Americans still desired neutrality. But how long could America remain at peace? And was peace worth the cost of just sitting by and watching friends like France and Britain be bombed and invaded?

Other issues melted away as Americans began to consider what to do about the darkening world situation. Some Americans, led by newspaper publisher **William Allen White**, called for the United States to help Britain immediately. But other groups, like the America First Committee, demanded that the United States stay out of another bloody European conflict.

The struggle between those who wanted to help Britain, and those who wanted to remain neutral, did not follow traditional party lines. Some of the closest supporters of Roosevelt's foreign policies were Republicans. And some members of his own Democratic Party opposed his policies. Even so, foreign policy was one of the main issues in the presidential election campaign of 1940. The Democrats, once again, nominated Franklin Roosevelt for president. The Republicans had several popular candidates who were interested in campaigning against Roosevelt. At first, it seemed that these candidates would fight it out in a bitter nominating convention in Philadelphia. But to everyone's surprise, a little-known candidate named **Wendell Willkie** suddenly gained a great deal of support and won the nomination.

Wendell Willkie was a tough candidate. He was friendly, a good businessman, and a strong speaker. He seemed honest. And he seemed to understand foreign policy. Most important, Willkie had a progressive record on many social issues. He was not the kind of traditional conservative Republican that Roosevelt had defeated so easily in his first two campaigns. Instead, Willkie could claim to represent the common man just as well as Roosevelt. And he offered the excitement of a change in leadership. While Willkie and Roosevelt began campaign battles with words, German and British planes were fighting real battles with bullets over the English Channel. Winston Churchill sent a desperate message to Roosevelt.

The British prime minister said Britain could not fight alone much longer. It needed help immediately.

Roosevelt did not want to take steps toward war just before an election. But neither could he refuse such an urgent appeal from the British. Roosevelt and Willkie discussed the situation. Willkie agreed not to criticize Roosevelt when the president sent fifty ships to the British navy. He also supported Roosevelt's order for American young men to give their names to army officials so they could be called if fighting began. In this way, Roosevelt and Willkie tried to keep America's growing involvement in the war from becoming a major political issue in the election.

President Roosevelt won the election of 1940. Roosevelt won 27 million votes to 22 million for Willkie. This made Roosevelt the first and only man in American history to win a third term in the White House.

Soon after the election, President Roosevelt received a letter from Winston Churchill. The British Prime Minister wrote that Britain urgently needed more arms and planes to fight Germany. Roosevelt agreed. He went to the Congress to plead for more aid to Britain. He said the United States should change its neutral policy, because Britain was fighting a common enemy of democracy. Roosevelt also said the United States could avoid war if Britain was strong enough to defeat Germany by herself.

Congress agreed, after a fierce debate, to increase aid to London. And in the weeks and months that followed, the United States moved closer and closer to open war with Germany. In March 1941, Roosevelt allowed British ships to come to American ports to be fixed. In June, the United States seized ships under German control. It also took over German and Italian funds in American banks.

Open fighting could not be prevented with this increase in tension between Germany and the United States. In September 1941, a German submarine fired at an American ship. The ship was not damaged. But a number of American troops were killed in other naval incidents that followed.

By the end of 1941, the United States and Germany were almost at war. Even so, most Americans continued to hope for peace. In fact, few Americans could guess that war was just days away. The first blow would come, not from Germany, but from Japan.

American warship *Arizona* is going down in Pearl Harbor.

For Your Memory

Remember Pearl Harbor
牢记珍珠港

凡亲身经历过重大历史突发事件的人，几乎无一例外对自己当时所处的地点和精神上受到的冲击都记忆犹新。对于美国人来说，整个20世纪中给他们带来最大冲击的事件莫过于日本偷袭珍珠港。当罗斯福总统在电台上宣布，美军由于日本"卑鄙无耻"的袭击而遭受到重大伤亡时，美国人的态度由难以置信迅速转为愤怒。12月8日，国会宣布对日进入战争状态；三天后，德、意两国对美国宣战，美国国会应战。此刻，轴心国德国、意大利和日本最强劲的对手终于"被迫"登场。

Where were you on the afternoon of December 7, 1941? If your name is Michelle Piastrol, you are in **Carnegie Hall** tightening the strings of your violin for the Sunday afternoon performance. If your name is **Saburo Kurusu**, your are waiting in the outer office of **Cordell Hull**. If you are a sailor named Polis, at a place called **Pearl Harbor**, you and 2116 of your buddies will be dead, **when the day is done**.

We interrupted this program to bring you a special **news bulletin**. The Japanese have attacked Pearl Harbor at **Hawaii** by air, President Roosevelt has just announced. The attack also was made on all naval and military activities on the principal island of **Oahu**.

Franklin D. Roosevelt's "Infamy Speech" (excerpts)

(The President of the United States.)

Yesterday, December 7th, 1941, a date which will live in **infamy**, the United States of America was suddenly and **deliberately** attacked by naval and air forces of the **Empire of Japan** . . . .

The attack yesterday on the Hawaiian Islands has caused severe damage to American naval and military forces. I regret to tell you that very many American lives have been lost. . . .

With confidence in our armed forces, with the **unbounded** determination of our people, we will gain the inevitable triumph. So help us God!

Let's remember Pearl Harbor   We will always remember
As we go to meet the foe.   How they died for liberty.
Let's remember Pearl Harbor   Let's remember Pearl Harbor
As we did the Alamo.   And go on to victory!

Words, Expressions and Notes

Nazi leader, Adolf Hitler　德国纳粹领导人阿道夫·希特勒（1889—1945）

Allied Powers　（第二次世界大战时期的）同盟国

Baltic nations　波罗的海国家

Latvia　拉脱维亚

Estonia　爱沙尼亚

Lithuania　立陶宛

Finland　芬兰

Soviet Union　苏联

Denmark　丹麦

Norway　挪威

Dunkerque　敦刻尔克，法国北部港口，1940 年英军在欧洲大陆被德国军队打败，经由此港口仓促撤回英国。

Marshal Petain　贝当（1856—1951），法国元帅，第二次世界大战期间法国沦陷后任亲纳粹政权的元首，战后被判处死刑，后改判无期徒刑。

English Channel　英吉利海峡

Neville Chamberlain　张伯伦（1869—1940），英国首相（1937—1940），实行纵容法西斯侵略的绥靖政策。

Winston Churchill　温斯顿·丘吉尔（1874—1965），英国著名政治家、首相、作家，第二次世界大战期间领导英国对德作战，获 1953 年诺贝尔文学奖。

Berlin　柏林，德国首都

William Allen White　威廉·怀特（1868—1944），著名新闻工作者、作家

Wendell Willkie　温德尔·威尔基（1892—1944），共和党总统候选人（1940）

Carnegie Hall　卡内基音乐厅，以美国钢铁大王卡内基名字命名，是世界最著名的音乐殿堂。

Saburo Kurusu　野村吉三郎（1888—1954），日本驻美国大使。当日本正在准备偷袭珍珠港之际，野村前往华盛顿与美国进行和平谈判。此举被认为是日本麻痹美国的阴谋。

Cordell Hull　科德尔·哈尔（1871—1955），美国国务活动家，罗斯福政府国务卿，联合国顾问，获 1945 年诺贝尔和平奖。

Pearl Harbor　珍珠港

when the day is done　当这一天结束时

news bulletin　新闻简报

Hawaii　夏威夷

Oahu　瓦胡岛，夏威夷群岛的主岛

infamy　*n.* 臭名昭著

deliberately　*adv.* 蓄意地

Empire of Japan　日本帝国

unbounded　*a.* 无限的，极大的

As we did the Alamo.　正像我们当年在阿拉莫做的那样。

Questions for Comprehension and Discussion

1. Why was so little action taken to stop aggression by the United States in the 1930s?
2. Why did Hitler and his allies win one victory after another in 1939 and 1940?
3. Why did many Americans want their country to stay out of the war?
4. How did Great Britain do in the war under the leadership of Winston Churchill?
5. How did the United States change its neutral policy?

50 **From Pearl Harbor to Europe**

从珍珠港到欧洲

1940 年，日本似有南下夺取英属马来亚和荷属东印度群岛的石油、锡矿、橡胶的趋势。1941 年 7 月，美国冻结了日本在美国的资产，并对日本实施战略物资禁运。日本的东条英机组阁后，在同年 11 月 9 日派特使到美国，声称将与美国谋求和好。12 月 6 日，罗斯福总统作出反应，亲自向日本天皇发出和平呼吁。12 月 7 日凌晨，日本偷袭珍珠港，美国舰队和防御设施在日本飞机的狂轰滥炸中损失惨重。幸运的是，当天有 6 艘航空母舰没有停泊在港内。这 6 艘逃脱劫难的航空母舰在后来的阻击太平洋日军的攻势中发挥了至关重要的作用。

美国迅速准备动员其庞大的人力和工业生产力。1942 年 1 月 6 日，罗斯福总统宣布了惊人的年度生产指标：飞机 6 万架，坦克 4.5 万辆，高射炮 2 万门，商船 1 800 万吨（载重量）。全国的一切活动，从农业、制造业、采矿、贸易、劳工、投资、交通到教育和文化事业，都被置于政府某种形式的管制之下。在一次又一次的兵役法令征召之下，美国武装部队增至 1 510 万人，到 1943 年底，约有 6 500 万男女穿上军服或从事与战争有关的工作。

美国参战后不久，西方盟国决定把太平洋战区列为次要目标，而把主要军事力量集中于欧洲，这主要是因为轴心国的核心力量在欧洲。此外，罗斯福总统还有一个担心，这就是原子武器。物理学家爱因斯坦在 1939 年给罗斯福总统的一封信中指出，一种新的元素铀可能成为一种新的能源，而且有可能用来制造出威力巨大的新式武器，而德国科学家已经在这方面取得突破。罗斯福担心的是，如果原子武器首先被德国研制出来并用于战争，那将会是什么局面？为赶在希特勒前面，从 1941 年起，美国、英国、加拿大的天才科学家被美国政府搜罗殆尽。1942 年，耗资 20 亿美元的"曼哈顿计划"在美国上马，这是当时全世界最昂贵的一项武器研制计划。同年 12 月 2 日，第一次原子链式反应实验在芝加哥成功进行，一种彻底改变世界政治和军事格局的武器已经处于襁褓之中。

Japan's attack on Pearl Harbor in December 1941 was one of the most successful surprise attacks in the history of modern warfare. Japanese warships, including several aircraft carriers, crossed the western Pacific to Hawaii without being seen. They launched their warplanes on Sunday morning to attack the huge American naval and air base. Many of the American sailors were asleep or at church. They were completely surprised. In fact, some Americans outside the base thought the Japanese planes must be American airmen making training flights in new airplanes. The sounds of guns and bombs soon showed how wrong they were.

The Japanese planes sank or seriously damaged six powerful American battleships in just a few minutes. They killed more than 3,000 sailors. They destroyed or damaged half the American airplanes in Hawaii. American forces were so surprised that they were unable to offer much of a fight. Japanese losses were very light. Japan's destruction at Pearl Harbor was so complete that officials in Washington did not tell the full details immediately to the American people. They were afraid the nation might panic if it learned the truth about the loss of so much American military power.

The following day, President Roosevelt went to the Capitol building to ask Congress for a declaration

of war against Japan. The Senate approved his request without opposition. In the House of Representatives, only one congressman objected. Three days later, Germany and Italy declared war on the United States. Congress reacted by declaring war on those two countries. The Japanese attack on Pearl Harbor ended the long American debate about whether to become involved in the Second World War. American politicians and citizens had argued for years about whether to remain neutral or fight to help Britain and France and other friends. Japan's aggressive attack at Pearl Harbor united Americans in a common desire for military victory. It made Americans willing to do whatever was necessary to win the war. And it pushed America into a kind of world leadership that its people had never known before.

President Franklin Roosevelt and his advisers had to make an important decision about how to fight the war. Would the United States fight Japan first, or Germany, or both enemies at the same

...we here highly resolve that these dead shall not have died in vain...

REMEMBER DEC. 7th!

"Remember Pearl Harbor" becomes a national battle cry like "Remember the Alamo."

time? Japan's attack had brought America into the war. And it had severely damaged American military power. But Roosevelt decided not to strike back at Japan immediately. He would use most of his forces to fight Germany. There were several reasons for Roosevelt's decision. First, Germany already controlled much of Europe, as well as much of the Atlantic Ocean. Roosevelt considered this a direct threat. And he worried about possible German intervention in Latin America. Second, Germany was an advanced industrial nation. It had many scientists and engineers. Its factories were modern. Roosevelt was concerned that Germany might be able to develop deadly new weapons, such as an atomic bomb, if it was not stopped quickly. Third, Britain historically was one of America's closest allies. And the British people were united and fighting for their lives against Germany.

Hitler's decision to break his treaty with **Josef Stalin** and attack the Soviet Union made Roosevelt's choice final. The American leader recognized that the Germans would have to fight on two fronts: in the west against Britain and in the east against Russia. He decided it was best to attack Germany while its forces were divided. So Washington sent most of its troops and supplies to Britain to join the fight against Germany. American military leaders hoped to attack Germany quickly by launching an attack across the English Channel. Stalin also supported this plan. Soviet forces were suffering terrible losses from the Nazi attack and wanted the British and Americans to fight the Germans on the west. However, British Prime Minister Winston Churchill and other leaders opposed launching an invasion across the English Channel too quickly. They worried that such an invasion might fail, while the Germans were still so strong. And they knew this would mean disaster.

For this reason, British and American forces decided instead to attack the Italian and German occupation troops in north Africa. British forces had been fighting the Italians and Germans in north Africa since late in 1940. They fought the Italians first in **Egypt** and **Libya**. British forces had successfully pushed the Italians across Libya. They killed more than 10,000 Italian troops and captured more than 130,000 prisoners. But the British success did not last long. Hitler sent one of his best commanders,

General Erwin Rommel, to take command of the Italians. Rommel was brave and smart. He pushed the British back from Libya to the border with Egypt. And in a giant battle at **Tobruk**, he destroyed or captured more than 800 of Britain's 900 tanks.

Rommel's progress threatened Egypt and the **Suez Canal**. So Britain and the United States moved quickly to send more troops and supplies to stop him. Slowly, British forces led by General **Bernard Montgomery** pushed Rommel and the Germans back to **Tripoli** in Libya. In November, 1942, American and British forces commanded by general **Dwight Eisenhower** landed in Northwest Africa. They planned to attack Rommel from the west, while Montgomery attacked him from the east. But Rommel knew Eisenhower's troops had done little fighting before. So he attacked them quickly before they could launch their own attack.

A terrible battle took place at **Kasserine** in western **Tunisia**. Rommel's attack failed. The American troops held their ground. And three months later, they joined with Montgomery's British troops to force the Germans in North Africa to surrender. The battle of North Africa was over. The allied forces of Britain and the United States had regained control of the Southern Mediterranean Sea. They could now attack Hitler's forces in Europe from the South.

The Allies wasted no time. They landed on the Italian island of **Sicily** in July of 1943. German tanks fought back. But the British and American forces moved ahead. Soon they captured Sicily's capital, Palermo. And within weeks, they forced the German forces to leave Sicily for the Italian mainland. In late July, Italy's dictator, **Benito Mussolini**, was overthrown and placed in prison. The Germans rescued him and helped him establish a new government, protected by German troops. But still the Allies attacked. They crossed to the Italian mainland. The Germans fought hard, returning bullet for bullet. And for some time, they prevented the allied troops from breaking out of the coastal areas.

The fighting grew bloodier. A fierce battle took place at **Monte Cassino**. Thousands and thousands of soldiers lost their lives. But slowly the Allies advanced north through Italy. They captured Rome in June of 1944. And they forced the Germans back into the mountains of Northern Italy. The Allies would not gain complete control of Italy until the end of the war. But they had succeeded in increasing their control of the Mediterranean and pushing back the Germans. One reason Hitler's forces were not stronger in Africa and Italy was because German armies also were fighting in Russia.

Words, Expressions and Notes

Josef Stalin 约瑟夫·斯大林（1879—1953），苏联国家最高领导人

Egypt 埃及

Libya 利比亚

Erwin Rommel 欧文·隆美尔（1891—1944），纳粹德国元帅

Tobruk 托布鲁克，利比亚东北部港市

Suez Canal 苏伊士运河

Bernard Montgomery 伯纳德·蒙哥马利（1887—1976），英国第二次世界大战期间最杰出的将军

Tripoli 的黎波里，利比亚首都

Dwight Eisenhower 德怀特·艾森豪威尔（1890—1969），第二次世界大战时期欧洲盟军最高司令，后任美国第三十四任总统（1953—1961）。

Kasserine 卡塞林，突尼斯城市

Tunisia 突尼斯

Sicily 西西里岛（意大利南部）

Benito Mussolini 墨索里尼（1883—1945），意大利法西斯头子

Monte Cassino 蒙特卡西洛，意大利城市卡西洛附近山上的一座天主教修道院。"二战"中德国把修道院作为一座军事堡垒，遭到盟军围攻。

Questions for Comprehension and Discussion

1. How did the Japanese attack Pearl Harbor?
2. Why did Washington not tell the full details of the losses immediately to the American people?
3. How did Japan's attack at Pearl Harbor change the attitude of American people toward the war?
4. Why would President Franklin Roosevelt and his advisers use most of American forces to fight Germany?
5. Why did British and American forces decide to first attack the Italian and German occupation troops in north Africa?
6. Why were Hitler's forces defeated in north Africa and Italy?

51 The War in Europe

欧洲战事

1944 年，美国同其盟国经过长时间讨论后，决定开辟西欧战场，艾森豪威尔将军被任命为盟军最高统帅。其实，这个代号为"霸王行动"（Operation Overlord）的军事计划的准备工作从 1943 年就开始进行。美英联军从 1944 年 2 月开始对德军占领区的工厂、铁路、海上运输设施以及沿海防御工事实施猛烈轰炸。到 1944 年春季，一支多达 250 万人的大军在英国集结和训练，为即将到来的人类历史上最大规模的跨海军事入侵作最后的准备。与此同时，德国军队也急于在法国北部加固他们的"大西洋城墙"（Atlantic Wall）——一个由射击掩体、机枪和炮火网、地雷及水下障碍物构成的防御体系。

1944 年 6 月 6 日，是一个代号为"D-Day"的计划注定要载入史册的一天。艾森豪威尔将军一声令下，由 700 艘军舰和 4 000 艘商船组成的"无敌舰队"在空军的强力掩护下，开始实施诺曼底海滩登陆。仅仅在这场史无前例的军事行动的第一天，美英联军就有 32.6 万人和 2 万多辆装甲车辆越过英吉利海峡。在巩固滩头阵地后，更多的登陆部队蜂拥而至。从 6 月到 8 月下旬，盟军的钳形攻势使德守军纷纷陷入包围圈。接着盟军开始横穿法国，进入德国，不顾德军顽抗，奋力挺进。

当年 8 月 25 日，巴黎解放。盟军虽然在德国大门口遭到德军猛烈反攻而受阻，但到 1945 年二三月间，美英军队从西面、苏联军队从东面分别向德国本土挺进，德军溃退。4 月 28 日，柏林合围；4 月 30 日，希特勒自杀；5 月 8 日，第三帝国的陆海空残余部队宣布投降。

On June 5th, 1944, a huge Allied force waited for the order to invade German-occupied France. The invasion had been planned for the day before. But a storm forced a delay. At 3:30 in the morning, the Allied commander, General Dwight Eisenhower, was meeting with his assistants. The storm still blew outside the building. General Eisenhower and his generals were discussing whether they should attack the next day.

A weatherman entered the room. He reported that the weather soon would improve. All eyes turned to Eisenhower. The decision was his. His face was serious. And for a long time he was silent. Finally he spoke. "Ok," he said. "We will go." And so the greatest military invasion in the history of the world, **D-Day**, took place on June 6th, 1944.

The German leader, Adolph Hitler, had known the invasion was coming. But he did not know where the Allied force would strike. Most Germans expected the Allies would attack at **Calais**, in France. But they were wrong. Eisenhower planned to strike at the French coast of **Normandy**, across the English Channel. The Second World War was then almost five years old. The Germans had won the early battles and gained control of most of Europe. But in 1942 and '43, the Allies slowly

General Dwight Eisenhower

began to gain back land from the Germans in Northern Africa, Italy, and Russia. And now, finally, the British, American, Canadian, and other Allied forces felt strong enough to attack across the English Channel.

Eisenhower had 150,000 men, 12,000 airplanes and many supplies for the attack. But most important, **he had surprise on his side**. Even after the invasion began, General Erwin Rommel and other top German military experts could not believe that the Allies had really attacked at Normandy. But attack they did. On the night of June 5th, airplanes dropped thousands of Allied **parachute soldiers** behind German lines. Then Allied planes began dropping bombs on German defenses. And in the morning, thousands of ships approached the beaches, carrying men and supplies.

The battle quickly became fierce and bloody. The Germans had strong defenses. They were better protected than the Allied troops on the beaches. But the Allied soldiers had greater numbers. Slowly they moved forward on one part of the beach, then another.

The Allies continued to build up their forces in France. They brought nearly 90,000 vehicles and 600,000 men into France within one week. And they pushed ahead. Hitler was furious. He screamed at his generals for not blocking the invasion. And he ordered his troops from nearby areas to join the fight and stop the Allied force. But the Allies would not be stopped.

In late August, the Allied forces captured Paris. The French people cheered wildly as **General Charles de Gaulle** and free French forces marched into the center of the city. The Allies then moved east into Belgium. They captured the great Belgian port of **Antwerp**. This made it easier for them to send supplies and fuel to their troops. Only when Allied troops tried to move into the Netherlands did the Germans succeed in stopping them. American parachute soldiers won battles at **Eindhoven** and **Nijmegen**. But German forces defeated British "**Red Devil**" troops in a terrible fight at **Arnhem**. Germany's brief victory stopped the Allied invasion for the moment. But in less than four months, General Eisenhower and the Allied forces had regained almost all of France.

At the same time, in 1944, the Soviets were attacking Germany from the east. Earlier, Soviet forces had succeeded in breaking German attacks at **Stalingrad**, Moscow, and **Leningrad**. Soviet forces re-captured Russian cities and farms one by one. They entered Finland, Poland, and Romania. By the end of July, Soviet soldiers were just 15 kilometers from the Polish capital, Warsaw.

Adolf Hitler was in serious trouble. Allied forces were attacking from the west. Soviet troops were passing through Poland and moving in from the east. And at home, several German military officials tried to assassinate him. The German leader **narrowly escaped death** when a bomb exploded in a meeting room. But Hitler refused to surrender. Instead, he planned a surprise attack in December 1944. He ordered his forces to move quietly through the **Ardennes Forest** and attack the center of the Allied line. He hoped to break through the line, separate the Allied forces, and regain control of the war.

The Germans attacked American troops tired from recent fighting in another battle. It was winter. The weather was so bad that Allied planes could not drop bombs on the German forces. The Germans quickly broke through the American line. But the German success did not last long. Allied forces from nearby areas raced to the battle-front to help. And good weather allowed Allied planes to begin attacking the Germans. The battle ended by the middle of the following month in a great defeat for Hitler and the Germans. The German army lost more than 100,000 men and great amounts of supplies.

The end of the war in Europe was now in sight. By late February, 1945, the Germans were forced to retreat across the **Rhine River**. American forces led by **General Patton** drove deep into the German heartland. To the east, Soviet forces also were marching into Germany. It did not take long for the American and Soviet forces to meet in victory. The war in Europe was ended.

Adolf Hitler waited until Russian troops were destroying Berlin. Bombs and shells were falling everywhere. Hitler took his own life by shooting himself in the head. One week later, the German army surrendered officially to Eisenhower and the Allies.

The defeat of Germany was cause for great celebration in Britain, the United States, and other Allied nations. But two facts made the celebrations less joyful than they might have been. One was the discovery by Allied troops of the terrible German **death camps**. Only at the end of the war did most of the world learn that the Nazis had murdered millions of innocent Jews and other people. The second fact was that the Pacific War had not ended. Japanese and American forces were still fighting bitterly.

For Your Memory

The Rangers
突击队

1984 年 6 月 6 日，为纪念 "D-Day" 40 周年，美国总统罗纳德·里根来到法国诺曼底海滩，出席为当年一支美军突击队建立纪念碑的揭幕式。站在纪念碑旁，面对当年在此地浴血奋战后幸存下来但如今已两鬓斑白的英雄们，心潮澎湃的里根总统发表了以下演讲。

We stand on a lonely, **windswept point** on the Northern shore of France. The air is soft, but forty years ago at this moment, the air was dense with smoke and the cries of men, and the air was filled with the crack of rifle fire and the roar of cannon. At dawn, on the morning of the 6th of June, 1944, 225 **Rangers** jumped off the British landing craft and ran to the bottom of these cliffs.

Their mission was one of the most difficult and daring of the invasion: to climb these **sheer and desolate cliffs** and take out the enemy guns. The Allies had been told that some of the mightiest of these guns were here, and they would be trained on the beaches to stop the Allied advance.

The Rangers looked up and saw the enemy soldiers at the edge of the cliffs, shooting down at them with machine guns and throwing grenades. And the American Rangers began to climb. They **shot rope ladders** over the face of these cliffs and began to pull themselves up. When one Ranger fell, another would take his place. When one rope was cut, a Ranger would grab another and begin his climb again. They climbed, shot back, and **held their footing**. Soon, one by one, the Rangers pulled themselves over the top, and in seizing the firm land at the top of these cliffs, they began to seize back the continent of Europe. Two hundred and twenty-five came here. After two days of fighting, only ninety could still **bear arms**.

And behind me is a **memorial** that symbolizes the Ranger **daggers that were thrust into the top of these cliffs**. And before me are the men who put them there. These are the boys of **Pointe Du Hoc**. These are the men who took the cliffs. These are the champions who helped free a continent. And these are the heroes who helped end a war.

Words, Expressions and Notes

D-Day 第二次世界大战盟军在法国北部的开始进攻日（1944 年 6 月 6 日）

Calais 加来，法国北部港市

Normandy 诺曼底，法国北部地区，面临英吉利海峡。

he had surprise on his side （在战争中）实施突袭的

parachute soldiers　伞兵

General Charles de Gaulle　戴高乐将军（1890—1970），第二次世界大战时期领导法国抗击德国法西斯的领导人，法国解放后任临时政府首脑，后任总统（1959—1969）。

Antwerp　安特卫普，比利时港市

Eindhoven　艾恩德霍芬，荷兰地名

Nijmegen　奈梅亨，荷兰地名

Red Devil　红魔，一支英国部队的绰号

Arnhem　阿纳姆，荷兰东部城市

Stalingrad　斯大林格勒，前苏联城市，现称伏尔加格勒。

Leningrad　列宁格勒，前苏联港市，现称圣彼得堡。

narrowly escaped death　勉强逃过一死

Ardennes Forest　阿登高地森林，位于比利时、法国、卢森堡交界处。

Rhine River　莱茵河

General Patton　巴顿将军（George Smith Patton, 1885—1945），美国陆军上将，率部队在第二次世界大战中屡建奇功，死于车祸。

death camps　（德国法西斯政权关押犯人和犹太人的）死亡集中营

windswept point　受到大风吹袭的地点

Rangers　*n.* 突击队员

sheer and desolate cliffs　陡峭而荒凉的悬崖

shot rope ladders　抛出绳梯

held their footing　站稳脚跟

bear arms　扛起武器

memorial　*n.* 纪念碑

daggers that were thrust into the top of these cliffs　刺向悬崖的匕首

Pointe Du Hoc　杜霍克海角

Questions for Comprehension and Discussion

1. What was D-Day? When was it?

2. Why was the invasion of Normandy a most difficult military feat? What made it a success?

3. Why were people in Britain, the United States, and other Allied nations not very joyful when Germany was defeated?

4. What was the worst example of genocide in the war?

5. What factors were chiefly responsible for Germany's defeat?

6. Why did President Reagan call the Rangers "the champions who helped free a continent" and "the heroes who helped end a war"?

52 The War in the Pacific

太平洋地区战事

日本入侵中国后,其主宰亚洲的狼子野心昭然若揭。当美国人忧虑地注视着欧洲战局进展情况时,日本趁机进一步改善其战略地位,企图对整个太平洋地区实行霸权。

珍珠港事件后,日本在最初的6个月内取得了辉煌的战绩:把美国赶出菲津宾群岛,南下夺取英属马来亚和荷属东印度群岛,攻占新加坡,横扫泰国和缅甸,切断了中国与其他国家之间的陆上交通,使中国与外国的联系仅剩下越过喜马拉雅山脉的一条极其危险的空中走廊。面对如此惨败,美军太平洋战区司令麦克阿瑟从菲津宾撤出时在一艘鱼雷艇上发出一句著名的誓言:"我会回来的。"(I shall return.)

从1942年起,美国依靠其强大的空军和海军,在与日本的较量中获得若干重大胜利。5月7日和8日,美国航空母舰上的飞机在珊瑚海空战中同日本的舰载飞机激战并取得胜利,日本海军不得不放弃进攻澳大利亚的念头。6月,在中途岛战役的两天激战中,美国舰载飞机重创日本舰队,击沉4艘航空母舰,击落飞机350架。这一决定性战役成为太平洋战争的转折点,也是日本战败的预兆。

从1943年初起,麦克阿瑟将军率领部队在太平洋地区反攻。尽管强大的美国海军切断了日军的供应线,但是,美军在推进路线上的每个据点都遭到日军的疯狂抵抗,几乎每攻克一个岛屿都要付出沉重的伤亡代价。在1943年11月攻打塔拉瓦岛的战役中,5 600名进攻的美国海军陆战队士兵中,991人牺牲,2 311人受伤。日军守岛军人共4 500人,活着出来的仅有11人。该岛因此而得名"恐怖的塔拉瓦"(Terrible Tarawa)。

1944年10月,美国海军在菲津宾海大捷。1945年1月,麦克阿瑟将军实现了当初他撤退时的誓言,重返菲津宾。日本虽然大势已去,但日本军队的最后疯狂却丝毫没有减弱的迹象。在4月到6月的琉球战役中,美军阵亡12 500人,负伤36 500人,这是太平洋战争中美国军队损失最惨重的战役。

究竟是付出沉重代价占领日本,还是使用美国在1945年7月16日刚刚试验成功的核武器,成为新总统杜鲁门面临的首要问题。他选择了后者。8月6日,美国飞机在广岛投下第一颗原子弹;三天后,又在长崎投下第二颗。原子弹造成的破坏和死亡震惊了全世界。8月14日,日本天皇宣布无条件投降诏书。9月2日,在东京湾美国军舰"密苏里"号上,日本正式签署投降文件,第二次世界大战终于结束。

American military planners had to make an important decision when the United States entered the Second World War in late 1941. They could not fight effectively at the same time in Asia and Europe. They decided to use most of their forces to defeat the German troops of Adolf Hitler. Only after victory was clear in Europe would they use all of America's strength to fight against Japan in Asia and the Pacific. This decision had important results. Japan was able to win many of the early battles of the war in Asia.

Japanese planes. Out of the sky they came, suddenly, secretly, bombing the American military base at Pearl Harbor, Hawaii, in a deadly attack. The Japanese raid in December 1941 marked the beginning of several major victories for Tokyo. The Japanese destroyed Pearl Harbor. They attacked American bases

in the Philippines and destroyed those, too. Within days, Japan captured the American island of Guam. Japanese troops landed in **Thailand**, marched into **Malaya**, and seized Hong Kong. The Japanese moved into Indonesia and **Burma**. Even Hitler's troops in Europe had not moved so quickly or successfully. As one American historian wrote later: "The Pacific Ocean looked like a Japanese lake."

Washington tried to fight back. A group of American planes successfully bombed Tokyo in a surprise raid. However, Japan knew it was winning the war. Its leaders believed no army could stop them. So they expanded their goals and launched new campaigns. This was Japan's mistake. It **stretched its forces too thin**, too quickly. The military leaders in Tokyo believed that the United States could not resist because it was busy fighting the war in Europe. But not even Japan could extend its communications and fighting power over such a great distance and continue to win.

The **turning point** came in June 1942 in the central Pacific in the great battle of **Midway Island**. Japanese Admiral **Isoroku Yamamoto** launched the battle. He wanted to meet and destroy the remaining ships of the American fleet before Washington had time to rebuild them. Yamamoto had 162 ships. The American Admiral, **Chester Nimitz**, had just 76. But the United States had learned how to understand the secret messages of the Japanese forces. For this reason, Nimitz and the Americans knew exactly where the Japanese ships would sail. And they put their own ships in the best places to stop them. The fighting between the two sides was fierce. But when it ended, the Americans had won a great victory. Admiral Yamamoto was forced to call off his attack and sail home. For the first time, the Japanese Navy had been defeated.

The next big battle was at **Guadalcanal**, one of the **Solomon Islands** in the Southwestern Pacific. Guadalcanal's beaches were wide and flat. Japanese officers decided to build a military airbase there. The United States learned of this. It decided it had to prevent Japan from establishing such a base. American marines quickly landed on the island. They were joined by troops from **Australia** and **New Zealand**. But Japanese ships launched a surprise attack and destroyed many of the American ships in the harbor. Allied forces on the island were left without naval support and suffered terrible losses. For six months, the two sides fought for control of the island. Historian Samuel Eliot Morrison later described the action this way:

"For us who were there," Morrison wrote, "Guadalcanal is not a name but an emotion. Remembering terrible fights in the air. Fierce naval battles. Bloody fighting in the jungle. Nights broken by screaming bombs and the loud explosions of naval guns."

The fighting continued, seemingly forever. But finally, in February, 1943, the Japanese were forced to leave Guadalcanal. The battle was an important defeat for Japan. It opened the door for the American and other Allied forces to go on the attack after months of defensive fighting.

American military planners did not agree about the best way to launch such an attack. Admiral Nimitz of the Navy wanted to capture the small groups of Japanese-held islands in the Pacific, then seize Taiwan, and finally attack Japan itself. But General **Douglas MacArthur** of the Army thought it best to attack through **New Guinea** and the Philippines. The American leadership finally decided to launch both attacks at once. Both Nimitz and MacArthur succeeded. Nimitz and his Navy forces moved quickly through the **Marianas** and other islands. General MacArthur attacked through New Guinea and into the Philippines. In the battle for **Leyte Gulf**, American ships completely destroyed Japanese naval power.

Throughout the Pacific Ocean and Eastern Asia, the fighting continued. Many of the fiercest battles were fought on tiny Pacific islands. Japanese troops captured the islands early in the war. And they quickly built strong defenses to prevent Allies from invading. Allied military leaders found a way to defeat the Japanese plan. They simply avoided the islands where the Japanese were strong and attacked other islands. But sometimes the Allies could not avoid battle. They had to land on some islands to seize airfields for American planes.

The names of these islands became well-known to soldiers and families throughout the world. **Tarawa** in the **Gilbert Islands**. **Truk** in the **Marshall Islands**. **Saipan** in the Marianas. And other islands, too, such as Guam and **Tinian**. The two sides fought fiercely in the battle of **Iwo Jima**. And Japanese forces on **Okinawa** resisted for 83 days before finally being defeated by Allied troops.

After the defeat at Okinawa, many Japanese people understood that the war was lost, even if Japan had not yet surrendered. The emperor appointed a new prime minister and ordered him to explore the possibilities of peace. But both sides still expected the Allies to launch a final invasion into Japan itself. And everyone knew that the cost in human life would be terrible for both sides. But the final invasion never came. For years, American scientists had been developing a secret weapon, the atomic bomb. The United States dropped one of the bombs on the Japanese city of **Hiroshima** and another on **Nagasaki**. More than 100,000 persons were killed. Tokyo surrendered within days.

Suddenly, sooner than expected, the war was ended. More than 25 million soldiers and civilians had died during the six years of fighting. Germany and Japan were defeated. The Soviet Union was strong in much of Eastern Europe. And the United States found it had become the world's strongest military, economic, and political power.

"The moment that recorded the soul of a nation"—Flag-raising on the sulfurous island Iwo Jima (This photo is regarded as one of the best pictures taken during the World War II.)

Words, Expressions and Notes

Thailand 泰国

Malaya 马来亚

Burma 缅甸

stretched its forces too thin 兵力过度分散

turning point 转折点

Midway Island 中途岛，位于北太平洋，1867 年被美国占领，第二次世界大战期间美日两国在此激战。

Isoroku Yamamoto 山本五十六（1884—1943），日本海军将领，策划并指挥偷袭珍珠港，后其座机在太平洋上空被击落毙命。

Chester Nimitz 切斯特·尼米兹（1885—1966），美国海军五星上将，第二次世界大战时期任太平洋舰队总司令。

Guadalcanal 瓜达尔卡纳尔岛，所罗门群岛的一部分，位于西南太平洋。

Solomon Islands 所罗门群岛

Australia 澳大利亚

New Zealand 新西兰

Douglas MacArthur 道格拉斯·麦克阿瑟（1880—1964），美国五星上将，第二次世界大战时期任西南太平洋盟军总司令。

New Guinea 新几内亚岛

Marianas 马里亚纳群岛

Leyte Gulf 莱特湾，位于菲律宾中东部

Tarawa 塔拉瓦岛

Gilbert Islands 吉尔伯特群岛

Truk 特鲁克岛

Marshall Islands 马绍尔群岛

Saipan 塞班岛

Tinian 提尼安岛

Iwo Jima 硫磺岛

Okinawa 冲绳群岛

Hiroshima （日本城市）广岛

Nagasaki （日本城市）长崎

Questions for Comprehension and Discussion

1. Why did Japan want to conquer other lands in Asia?
2. Why were the Japanese able to conquer so much territory so quickly?
3. Why was the battle of Midway Island considered the turning point of the war in the Pacific?
4. Why was it difficult and costly for the United States to defeat Japan?
5. Was President Truman's decision to use atomic bombs in the war a wise one? Why or why not?

Unit 14 The Civil Rights Movement

53 The America in the 1950s

20世纪50年代的美国

1945 年 8 月日本投降后，美国人民把大部分注意力集中在国内事务上。当时的第一件事，是要使数百万归国军人重新转入平民生活。在两年内，美国军队人数从 1 200 万减至 150 万。1944 年颁布的《退伍军人就业法》规定，由政府贷款让退伍军人有能力购买房屋、经商或务农，并给他们提供在职训练，从而帮助他们顺利转入平民生活。该法例还资助 200 多万退伍军人上大学。

第二次世界大战结束时，多数美国人乐观地估计，苏联与西方国家在战争期间的合作能继续下去，共同建立一个安全和平的世界。为此，美国积极支持联合国的建立，支持联合国为欧、亚、非各洲战争受害地区开展的经济恢复与救济工作。同时，美国认识到原子武器扩散可能危害到人类的生存，因而谋求控制原子弹的国际协议。1946 年 6 月，美国驻联合国代表向联合国原子能委员会建议，禁止原子武器，对一切原子材料实行国际管制。美国的建议虽然得到联合国原子能委员会 10 个成员国中 9 个成员国的支持，但被苏联所否决。1949 年，苏联成功试验第一颗原子弹。从此，世界进入核武器阴影笼罩下的"冷战"时期。

由于苏联集团的崛起，美国对国外共产主义的担忧在国内引起意想不到的后果。20 世纪 50 年代初，来自威斯康星州的一个默默无闻的参议员约瑟夫·麦卡锡（Senator Joseph McCarthy），利用这种担忧煽起一股全国性反共风潮。此人在所谓的调查美国政府内共产党分子的运动中充当急先锋，肆无忌惮地扩大调查和打击面，对美国社会各阶层许多著名人士提出疯狂而莫须有的指控。一时间，"麦卡锡主义"犹如幽灵一般让人人感到胆寒。直到 1954 年 12 月参议院对麦卡锡的卑劣行径给予公开谴责后，才遏止了他的势头。"麦卡锡主义"三年多的猖獗活动为美国人民提供了一个触目惊心的例子，它使人民认识到，即使在美国这样一个以民主和自由作为立国之本的国度里，法西斯主义也可能变得如此肆无忌惮，民主和自由也可能因而变得极其脆弱。

从 50 年代起，一股强大的政治力量在美利坚大地酝酿，这就是美国黑人的民权运动。一个世纪之前的 1859 年，约翰·布朗用生命的代价呼唤的"黑人问题"，至此仍然没有解决。内战后社会给予黑人均等机会的承诺实际上被忘得一干二净，黑人悲惨的种族隔离生活从城市贫民区一直延伸到铁路、电车、公园、旅馆、学校、医院，甚至坟场。然而，"黑人问题"被压制的时间越久，它的爆发力就越强。一场撼动美国的猛烈风暴即将来临。

In the 1950s, America was a nation that believed it was on the edge of nuclear war. It was a nation where the popular culture of television was gaining strength. It was a nation whose population was growing as never before.

After the terrible suffering of World War II, Americans thought the world would be peaceful for a while. By 1950, however, political tensions were high again. The United States and the Soviet Union, allies in war, had become enemies. The communists had taken control of one East European nation after another. And Soviet leader Josef Stalin made it clear that he wanted communists to rule the world. The

Soviet Union had strengthened its armed forces after the war. The United States had taken many steps to disarm. Yet it still possessed the atomic bomb. America thought it alone had this terrible weapon.

In 1949, a United States Air Force plane discovered strange conditions in the atmosphere. What was causing them? The answer came quickly: the Soviet Union had exploded an atomic bomb. **The race was on.** The two nations competed to build weapons of mass destruction. Would these weapons ever be used? The American publication, *The Bulletin of the Atomic Scientists*, always showed a picture of a clock. By 1949, the time on the clock was three minutes before midnight. That meant the world was on the edge of nuclear destruction. The atomic scientists were afraid of what science had produced. They were even more afraid of what science could produce.

In 1950, the **Korean conflict** increased efforts in the United States to develop a weapon more deadly than an atomic bomb. That was the **hydrogen bomb**. The Soviets were developing such a weapon, too. Many Americans were afraid. Some built what they hoped would be safe rooms in or near their homes. They planned to hide in these bomb shelters during a nuclear attack.

Other Americans, however, grew tired of being afraid. In 1952, the military hero of World War II, Dwight Eisenhower, was elected president. The economy improved. Americans looked to the future with hope. One sign of hope was the **Baby Boom**. This was the big increase in the number of babies born after the war. The number of young children in America jumped from 24 million to 35 million between 1950 and 1960. The bigger families needed houses. In 1950 alone, 1,400,000 houses were built in America. Most new houses were in the suburbs, the areas around cities. People moved to the suburbs because they thought the schools there were better. They also liked having more space for their children to play.

Many Americans remember the 1950s as the fad years. A fad is something that is extremely popular for a very short time. One fad from the 1950s was the **Hula Hoop**. The Hula Hoop was a colorful plastic tube joined to form a big circle. To play with it, you moved your hips in a circular motion. This kept it spinning around your body. The motion was like one used by **Polynesian people** in their native dance, the **hula**. Other **fads** in the 1950s involved clothes or hair. Some women, for example, cut and fixed their hair to look like the fur of a **poodle dog**. Actress Mary Martin made the poodle cut famous when she appeared in the Broadway play, *South Pacific*.

In motion pictures, **Marilyn Monroe** was becoming famous. Not everyone thought she was a great actress. But she had shining golden hair. And she had what was considered a perfect body. Marilyn Monroe's success did not make her happy. She killed herself in the 1960s, when she was 36 years old. Another famous actor of those days was **James Dean**. To many Americans, he was the living representation of the rebellious spirit of the young. In fact, one of his films was called, *Rebel Without a Cause*. James Dean died in a car accident in 1955. He was 24.

The 1950s saw a rebellion in American literature. As part of society lived new lives in the suburbs, another part criticized this life. These were the writers and poets of the **Beat Generation**, including **Gregory Corso**, **Jack Kerouac**, and **Allen Ginsberg**. They said life was empty in 1950s' America. They described the people as dead in brain and spirit. **Jackson Pollock** represented the rebellion in art. Mr. Pollock did not paint things the way they looked. Instead, he dropped paint

James Dean, a cultural icon of the young Americans in the 1950s

onto his pictures in any way he pleased. He was asked again and again: "What do your paintings mean?" He answered: "Do not worry about what they mean. They are just there. . . like flowers."

In music, the rebel was **Elvis Presley**. He was the king of rock-and-roll.

> Well, it's one for the money,
> Two for the show,
> Three to get ready,
> Now go, cat, go.
>
> But don't you step on my blue suede shoes.
> You can do anything but lay off of my blue suede shoes.
>
> Well, you can knock me down,
> Step in my face,
> Slander my name
> All over the place.
>
> Do anything that you want to do, but uh-uh,
> Honey, lay off of my shoes
> Don't you step on my blue suede shoes.
> You can do anything but lay off of my blue suede shoes. . . [1]

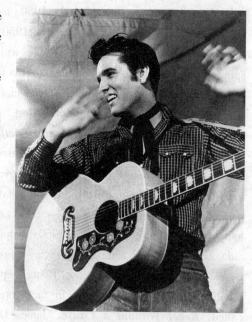

Elvis Presley was a 21-year-old truck driver when he sang on television for the first time. He moved his body to the music in a way that many people thought was too sexual. Parents and religious leaders criticized him. Young people screamed for more. They could not get enough rock-and-roll. They played it on records. They heard it on the radio. And they listened to it on the television program *American Bandstand*.

> We're goin' hoppin'
> We're goin' happin'
> Where things are poppin'
> The philadelphia way
> We're gonna drop in
> On all the music they play
> On the bandstand
>
> We're goin' swingin'
> We're gonna swing in the crowd. . .

Elvis Presley, "king of rock-and-roll"

This program became the most popular dance party in America. Every week, young men and women danced to the latest songs in front of the television cameras.

During the 1940s, there were only a few television receivers in American homes. Some called

---

1   普莱斯利演唱的歌曲《我的蓝色绒面皮鞋》（"My Blue Suede Shoes"）。

television an invention for stupid people to watch. By the end of the 1950s, however, television was here to stay. The average family watched six hours a day. Americans especially liked game shows and funny shows with comedians such as **Milton Berle** and **Lucille Ball**. They also liked shows that offered a mix of entertainment, such as those presented by **Arthur Godfrey** and **Ed Sullivan**.

People from other countries watching American television in the 1950s might have thought that all Americans were white Christians. At that time, television failed to recognize that America was a great mix of races and religions. Few members of racial or religious minorities were represented on television. Those who appeared usually were shown working for white people. A movement for civil rights for black Americans was beginning to gather strength in the 1950s. Many legal battles were fought to end racial separation, especially in America's schools. By the 1960s, the **Civil Rights Movement** would shake the nation.

Dwight Eisenhower was president for most of the 1950s. He faced the problems of communism, the threat of nuclear war, and racial tensions. He had a calm way of speaking. And he always seemed to deal with problems in the same calm way. Some citizens felt he was like a father to the nation. With Mr. Eisenhower in the White House, they believed that even in a dark and dangerous world, everything would be all right.

Words, Expressions and Notes

The race was on. （美苏之间的）核军备竞赛开始了。

The Bulletin of the Atomic Scientists 《原子科学家简报》

Korean conflict = Korean War 朝鲜战争 (1950—1953)

hydrogen bomb 氢弹

Baby Boom 生育高峰

Hula Hoop 呼啦圈，该名称源自商标 Hula-Hoop。

Polynesian people （中太平洋群岛）波利尼西亚人

hula *n.* 草裙舞，一种源于夏威夷岛的舞蹈

fads *n.* 狂热，一时的风尚

poodle dog 鬈毛狗

South Pacific （音乐剧）《南太平洋》，后拍成电影。

Marilyn Monroe 玛丽莲·梦露 (1926—1962)，美国著名女影星

James Dean 詹姆斯·迪恩 (1931—1955)，美国电影演员，因在 20 世纪 50 年代早期饰演反叛青少年形象成为美国一代年轻人的偶像，因车祸去世。

Rebel Without a Cause 《无故反叛》，由詹姆斯·迪恩主演的影片

Beat Generation 垮掉的一代。特指第二次世界大战后美国出现的一批对社会现实不满、蔑视传统观念的作家，泛指持有同样观点的一批年轻人。

Gregory Corso 格利高里·克尔索 (1930—2001)，"垮掉的一代"代表作家

Jack Kerouac 杰克·凯鲁亚克 (1922—1969)，"垮掉的一代"文学流派的代表人物

Allen Ginsberg 阿伦·金斯伯格 (1926—1997)，诗人，"垮掉的一代"文学流派的代表人物

Jackson Pollock 杰克逊·波洛克 (1912—1956)，美国画家，抽象表现派主要代表人物

Elvis Presley 埃尔维斯·普莱斯利 (1935—1977)，美国 20 世纪最著名摇滚乐歌手，被誉为"摇滚乐之王"。

American Bandstand （电视节目）《美国音乐台》

Milton Berle 密尔顿·波尔 (1908—2002)，喜剧演员，美国第一个电视超级明星

Lucille Ball 露西尔·鲍尔 (1911—1989)，美国历史上最持久的电视剧集《我爱露西》的女主角，被誉为美国电视皇后。

Arthur Godfrey 阿瑟·戈弗雷 (1903—1983)，美国 20 世纪 50 年代著名电视节目主持人

Ed Sullivan 艾德·苏利文 (1901—1974)，美国早期著名电视节目主持人

Civil Rights Movement 民权运动，美国黑人争取平等权利的运动。历史学家一般把 1955 年蒙哥马利公共汽车抵制事件作为该运动开始，把 1965 年《选举权法案》的通过作为结束。

Questions for Comprehension and Discussion

1. Why was the world not peaceful after World War II?
2. What was the race between the Soviet Union and the United States from 1950s?
3. What was Baby Boom? Why did it happen?
4. Why are the 1950s remembered as the fad years?
5. What made Elvis Presley famous in the 1950s?
6. What movement was beginning to gather strength in the 1950s?

54 Rosa Parks: The Woman Who Started the American Civil Rights Movement

"美国民权运动之母" 罗莎·帕克斯

尽管开国领袖杰斐逊在《独立宣言》中就提出"人人生而平等"的主张，尽管林肯总统发布的《解放宣言》犹如灯塔的光芒，给千百万受尽煎熬的黑人带来了希望，然而美国现实生活中给予黑人某种形式的平等的努力仅始于 20 世纪 30 年代末期。直到这个时期，才开始有少量的黑人在政府中找到职位，联邦政府才开始拨款为黑人建造娱乐中心、学校和医院。这时，距离《独立宣言》的发表已经有 160 多年，距离《解放宣言》的发表也已过去 3/4 个世纪。

第二次世界大战为改善黑人的境况提供了一个历史机遇。战争本身为黑人争取平等的努力提供了新的动能。罗斯福总统接受黑人劳工领袖的建议，命令和政府订有军工合同的工厂不得歧视黑人。战争期间，黑人不仅大量在陆军和海军中服役，还组建了黑人空军，在打败法西斯的战斗中立下赫赫战功。黑人在战争中显示出来的勇敢和杰出逐步影响到美国社会，使种族主义的观点失去市场。战后，杜鲁门总统设立了民权委员会，下令军队取消种族隔离，使日益增多的黑人在联邦政府任职。同时，两个最重要的职业棒球竞赛联合会和最重要的职业篮球竞赛联合会开始雇用黑人球员。

进入 50 年代后，上大学、参加投票选举、拥有住房和汽车、担任专门性或管理工作、在政府中担任要职的黑人人数超过以注任何时期。但是，与他们在全国总人口中所占的百分比相比，他们的人数仍然是很少的；从地理的角度看，发展也相当不平衡。在美国南方，种族隔离的法律仍然有效，种族歧视的做法仍然普遍而根深蒂固。

1954 年，美国最高法院全体大法官一致裁定，各州或地方规定的黑白分校的法律违反宪法。这一历史性的判决极大地鼓舞了正在酝酿中的黑人民权运动。然而，令所有人都意想不到的是，第一个点燃民权运动熊熊烈火的人，既不是一个著名政治家，也不是一个有着显赫经历的人物，而是一位普通的缝纫女工。她就是随后被人们称为"美国民权运动之母"的罗莎·帕克斯。

We shall overcome

We shall overcome...

Until the 1960s, black people in many parts of the United States did not have the same civil rights as white people. Laws in the American South kept the two races separate. These laws forced black people to attend separate schools, live in separate areas of a city and sit in separate areas on a bus. On December 1st, 1955, in the Southern city of Montgomery, Alabama, a 42-year-old black woman got on a city bus. The law at that time required black people seated in one area of the bus to give up their seats to white people who wanted them. The woman refused to do this and was arrested. This act of peaceful disobedience started protests in Montgomery that led to legal changes in minority rights in the United States. The woman who started it was **Rosa Parks**.

She was born Rosa Louise McCauley in 1913 in Tuskegee, Alabama. She attended local schools until she was eleven years old. Then she was sent to school in Montgomery. She left high school early to care for her sick grandmother, then to care for her mother. She did not finish high school until she was 21. Rosa married Raymond Parks in 1932. He was a barber who cut men's hair. He was also a civil rights activist. Together, they worked for the local group of the National Association for the Advancement of Colored People. In 1943, Missus Parks became an officer in the group and later its youth leader. Rosa Parks was a seamstress in Montgomery. She worked sewing clothes from the 1930s until 1955. Then she became a representation of freedom for millions of African-Americans.

> We are soldiers in the army,
> We have to fight all those we have to fight...

Rosa Parks is fingerprinted by Deputy Sherriff Lackey in Montgomery on February 22nd in 1956, two months after refusing to give up her seat on a bus for a white passenger.

In much of the American South in the 1950s, the first rows of seats on city buses were for white people only. Black people sat in the back of the bus. Both groups could sit in a middle area. However, black people sitting in that part of the bus were expected to leave their seats if a white person wanted to sit there. Rosa Parks and three other black people were seated in the middle area of the bus when a white person got on the bus and wanted a seat. The bus driver demanded that all four black people leave their seats so the white person would not have to sit next to any of them. The three other blacks got up, but Mrs. Parks refused. She was arrested. Some popular stories about that incident include the statement that Rosa Parks refused to leave her seat because her feet were tired. But she herself said in later years that this was false. What she was really tired of, she said, was accepting unequal treatment. She explained later that this seemed to be the place for her to stop being pushed around and to find out what human rights she had, if any.

A group of black activist women in Montgomery was known as the **Women's Political Council**. The group was working to oppose the mistreatment of black bus passengers. Blacks had been arrested and even killed for violating orders from bus drivers. Rosa Parks was not the first black person to refuse to give up a seat on the bus for a white person. But black groups in Montgomery considered her to be the right citizen around whom to build a protest because she was one of the finest citizens of the city. The women's group immediately called for all blacks in the city to refuse to ride on city buses on the day of Mrs. Parks's trial, Monday, December 5th. The result was that 40,000 people walked and used other transportation on that day. That night, at meetings throughout the city, blacks in Montgomery agreed to continue to boycott the city buses until their mistreatment stopped. They also demanded that the city hire black bus drivers and that anyone be permitted to sit in the middle of the bus and not have to get up for anyone else.

The Montgomery bus boycott continued for 381 days. It was led by local black leader E. D. Nixon and a young black minister, **Martin Luther King, Junior**. Similar protests were held in other Southern cities. Finally, the Supreme Court of the United States ruled on Mrs. Parks's case. It made racial separation illegal on city buses. That decision came on November 13th, 1956, almost a year after Mrs. Parks's arrest. The boycott in Montgomery ended the day after the court order arrived, December 20th. Rosa Parks and Martin Luther King, Junior had started a movement of non-violent protest in the South.

That movement changed civil rights in the United States forever. Martin Luther King became its famous spokesman, but he did not live to see many of the results of his work. Rosa Parks did.

Life became increasingly difficult for Rosa Parks and her family after the bus boycott. She was dismissed from her job and could not find another. So the Parks family left Montgomery. They moved first to Virginia, then to Detroit, Michigan. Mrs. Parks worked as a seamstress until 1965. Then, Michigan **Representative John Conyers** gave her a job working in his congressional office in Detroit. She retired from that job in 1988. Through the years, Rosa Parks continued to work for the NAACP and appeared at civil rights events. She was a quiet woman and often seemed uneasy with her fame. But she said that she wanted to help people, especially young people, to make useful lives for themselves and to help others. In 1987, she founded the Rosa and Raymond Parks Institute for Self-Development to improve the lives of black children. Rosa Parks received two of the nation's highest honors for her civil rights activism. In 1996, **President Clinton** honored her with the **Presidential Medal of Freedom**. And in 1999, she received the **Congressional Gold Medal of Honor**.

In her later years, Rosa Parks was often asked how much relations between the races had improved since the civil rights laws were passed in the 1960s. She thought there was still a long way to go. Yet she remained the face of the movement for racial equality in the United States. Rosa Parks died on October 24th, 2005. She was 92 years old. Her body lay in honor in the United States Capitol building in Washington. She was the first American woman to be so honored. Thirty thousand people walked silently past her body to show their respect. Representative Conyers spoke about what this woman of quiet strength meant to the nation. He said: "There are very few people who can say their actions and conduct changed the face of the nation. Rosa Parks is one of those individuals."

Rosa Parks meant a lot to many Americans. Four thousand people attended her funeral in Detroit, Michigan. Among them were former President Bill Clinton, his wife **Senator Hillary Rodham Clinton**, the **Reverend Jesse Jackson**, and Nation of Islam leader **Louis Farrakhan**. President Clinton spoke about remembering the separation of the races on buses in the South when he was a boy. He said that Rosa Parks helped to set all Americans free. He said the world knows of her because of a single act of bravery that **struck a deadly blow to racial hatred**.

Earlier, the religious official of the United States Senate spoke about her at a memorial service in Washington. He said Rosa Parks's bravery serves as an example of the power of small acts. And the Reverend Jesse Jackson commented in a statement about what her small act of bravery meant for African-American people. He said that on that bus in 1955, "She sat down in order that we might stand up, and she opened the doors on the long journey to freedom."

Words, Expressions and Notes

Rosa Parks 罗莎·帕克斯（1913—2005），原是一个黑人缝纫女工、民权活动积极分子，因于 1955 年在公共汽车上拒绝为白人让座的勇敢行为而翻开美国黑人争取平等权利斗争新的一页。

Women's Political Council 妇女政治协商会

Martin Luther King, Junior 小马丁·路德·金（1929—1968），美国 20 世纪最著名的黑人民权运动领袖，1968 年被种族主义分子暗杀。

Representative John Conyers 约翰·康耶斯（1929—），代表密歇根州的国会众议员

President Clinton 克林顿（Bill Clinton, 1946—），美国第四十二任总统（1993—2001）

Presidential Medal of Freedom 总统自由勋章

Congressional Gold Medal of Honor 国会金质荣誉奖章

Senator Hillary Rodham Clinton 参议员希拉里·克林顿（1947—）

Reverend Jesse Jackson 杰西·杰克逊牧师

（1941—），美国黑人民权运动积极分子、政治领导人

Louis Farrakhan 路易斯·法拉汉（1933—），美国

伊斯兰教领导人

struck a deadly blow to racial hatred 对种族仇恨予以致命一击

Questions for Comprehension and Discussion

1. Why was Rosa Parks's refusal of giving up her seat to a white man on a city bus so important in the history of the United States?

2. What was the popular story of Mrs. Parks's not leaving her seat on the bus? What was the real reason?

3. What did the black people do on the day of Mrs. Parks's trial?

4. Who led the bus boycott in Montgomery? Was the protest successful?

5. Why was Rosa Parks so greatly honored by her country and her people?

6. What did President Clinton say about Rosa Parks?

7. Somebody said about Rosa Parks, "She sat down in order that we might stand up, and she opened the doors on the long journey to freedom." What do you think of his words?

55 The Struggle for Racial Equality

为争取种族平等而斗争

第二次世界大战之后，黑人问题逐步成为美国社会问题的焦点。联邦最高法院1954年作出公立学校种族隔离违反宪法的裁决时，美国有多达17个州的公立学校实行种族隔离，另4个州允许学区实行种族隔离。最高法院的裁决不仅推翻了堪萨斯州托皮卡市的种族隔离法，而且推翻了南卡罗来纳、特拉华、弗吉尼亚等州和首都华盛顿的同类法令。位于美国南北交界地带的几个地区立即采取行动终止种族隔离，但是南方的大部分地区却拒不执行裁决。

从此时起到20世纪60年代中期，美国社会废除和维持种族隔离的两大阵营一直冲突不断，而其中最具影响力和戏剧性的事件要数1957年的"小石城事件"。

依照最高法院的判决，公立学校必须"以审慎的速度"向黑人敞开教室的大门。到1957年，阿肯色州的许多学校这样做了，但是阿肯色州小石城的中心中学却迟迟不肯行动。于是联邦法院下令，在9月3日新学期开始的那天，该学校必须执行法院判决。

阿肯色州州长是一个地地道道的种族主义分子，他调动州国民警卫队阻止9名黑人进入学校。开学第一天，黑人学生都没有露面。但是从第二天起直到9月24日，黑人学生都来了。但每一次他们都被国民警卫队和一群疯狂的白人种族主义分子赶了回去。甚至还有人把酸液注黑人学生中的一个女孩子身上泼去。

此事立刻在全美国引发轩然大波。9月23日，艾森豪威尔总统宣称，这种"可耻的"情况不能继续下去，并下令派遣在第二次世界大战中战功赫赫的美国陆军精锐部队101空降师前往小石城。25日，空降兵端着上了刺刀的枪抵达小石城。从那时起一直到学年末，全副武装的士兵们每天护送黑人学生上学放学，并在上课期间持枪从一间教室巡逻到另一间教室，上演了美国历史上反对种族歧视运动中最富有戏剧性的一幕。

最高法院1954年的判决的影响远远超出了公立学校的范围。它为美国黑人争取平等权利的斗争提供了法律基础，把美国黑人运动引入了美国社会的政治进程，从而比以往任何一项最高法院裁决更多地改变了美国人民的日常生活。而1957年发生的"小石城事件"则把黑人民权运动推向一个新的阶段，使这一斗争扩大到学校、公园、餐厅、旅店、影院，并最终导致了1963年8月28日25万人向首都华盛顿的"自由进军"。

The day is August 28th, 1963. More than 250,000 people are gathered in Washington. Black and white, young and old, they demand equal treatment for black Americans. The nation's most famous civil rights leader, Martin Luther King, is speaking.

I am happy to join with you today in what will go down in history as the greatest demonstration for freedom in the history of our nation.

Early in its history, black Africans were brought to America as slaves. They were bought and sold, like animals. By the time of America's Civil War in the 1860s, many had been freed by their owners. Many, however, still worked as slaves on the big farms of the South. By the end of the War, slavery had been declared unconstitutional. But that was only the first step in the struggle for equality.

Most people of color could not get good jobs. They could not get good housing. They had far less chance of a good education than white Americans. For about 100 years, blacks **made slow gains**. **Widespread activism** for civil rights did not really begin until after World War II. During the war, black Americans earned respect as members of the armed forces. When they came home, many demanded that their civil rights be respected, too. An organization, the National Association for the Advancement of Colored People, led the way.

In 1951, the organization sent its lawyers to help a man in the city of Topeka, Kansas. The man, **Oliver Brown**, and twelve others had brought legal action against the city. They wanted to end racial separation in their children's schools. At that time, two of every five public schools in America had all white students or all black students. The law said all public schools must be equal, but they were not. Schools for white children were almost always better than schools for black children. The situation was worst in Southern states.

The case against the city of Topeka—Brown versus the Board of Education—was finally settled by the nation's highest court. In 1954, the Supreme Court ruled that separate schools for black children were not equal to schools for white children. The next year, it said public schools must accept children of all races as quickly as possible.

In September 1957, a black girl tried to enter an all-white school in the city of **Little Rock, Arkansas**. An angry crowd screamed at her. State guards blocked her way. The guards had been sent by the state governor, **Orville Faubus**. After three weeks, a federal court ordered Governor Faubus to remove the guards. The girl, **Elizabeth Eckford**, and seven other black students were able to enter the school. After one day, however, riots forced the black students to leave.

Troops of the U. S. Army's 101st Airborne Division are dispersing a crowd in front of Little Rock's Central High School.

President Dwight Eisenhower ordered federal troops to Little Rock. They helped black students get into the white school safely. However, angry white citizens closed all the city's public schools. The schools stayed closed for two years. In 1962, a black student named **James Meredith** tried to attend the University of Mississippi. School officials refused. John Kennedy, the president at that time, sent federal law officers to help him. James Meredith became the first black person to graduate from the University of Mississippi.

In addition to fighting for equal treatment in education, black Americans fought for equal treatment in housing and transportation. In many cities of the South, blacks were forced to sit in the back of buses. In 1955, a black woman named Rosa Parks got on a bus in the city of Montgomery, Alabama. She sat in the back. The bus became crowded. There were no more seats for white people. So, the bus driver ordered Mrs. Parks to stand and give her seat to a white person. She refused. Her feet were tired after a long day at work. Rosa Parks was arrested.

The Reverend Martin Luther King organized the black citizens of Montgomery. They were the major users of the bus system. They agreed to stop using the buses. The boycott lasted a little more than a year. It seriously affected the earnings of the bus company. In the end, racial separation on the buses in

Montgomery was declared illegal. Rosa Parks's tired feet had helped win black Americans another victory in their struggle for equal rights. And, the victory had been won without violence.

The Reverend King was following the teachings of Indian spiritual leader, **Mohandas Gandhi**. Gandhi urged his followers to reach their political goals without violence. One of the major tools of non-violence in the civil rights struggle in America was the "sit-in." In a sit-in, protesters entered a store or public eating place. They quietly asked to be served. Sometimes, they were arrested. Sometimes, they remained until the business closed. But they were not served. Some went hours without food or water.

Another kind of protest was the "freedom ride." This involved buses that traveled through states from the North to the South. On freedom rides, blacks and whites sat together to make it difficult for officials to enforce racial separation laws on the buses. Many freedom rides—and much violence—took place in the summer of 1964. Sometimes, the freedom riders were arrested. Sometimes, angry crowds of whites beat the freedom riders.

Perhaps the most dangerous part of the Civil Rights Movement was the campaign to win voting rights for black Americans. The Fifteenth Amendment to the Constitution said a citizen could not be denied the right to vote because of race or color. Several Southern states, however, passed laws to try to deny voting rights to blacks for other reasons.

Martin Luther King and his supporters demonstrated to demand new legislation to guarantee the right to vote. They held protests in the state of Alabama. In the city of **Birmingham**, the chief law officer ordered his men to fight the protesters with high-pressure water hoses and fierce dogs. People throughout the country watched the demonstration on television. The sight of children being beaten by policemen and bitten by dogs awakened many citizens to the civil rights struggle. Federal negotiators reached a compromise. The compromise was, in fact, a victory for the protesters. They promised to stop their demonstrations. In exchange, they would be permitted to vote.

President Johnson signed a major **Civil Rights Bill** in 1964. Yet violence continued in some places. Three civil rights workers were murdered in Mississippi. One was murdered in Alabama. Martin Luther King kept working toward the goal of equal rights. He died working. On April 4th, 1968, he was shot to death in **Memphis**, Tennessee. He had gone there to support a strike by waste collection workers. A white man, **James Earl Ray**, was tried and found guilty of the crime.

President Johnson was signing Civil Rights Bill on July 2nd, 1964.

A wave of unrest followed the murder of Martin Luther King. Blacks in more than 100 cities in America rioted. In some cities, areas affected by the riots were not rebuilt for many years. The movement for Civil Rights for black Americans continued. But it became increasingly violent. The struggle produced angry, bitter memories. Yet it also produced some of the greatest words spoken in American history:

When we allow freedom to ring, when we let it ring from every village and every hamlet, from every state and every city, we will be able to speed up that day when all of God's children—black men and white men, Jews and Gentiles, Protestants and Catholics—will be able to join hands and sing in the words of the old Negro spiritual: "Free at last! Free at last! Thank God Almighty, we are free at last!"[1]

For Your Memory

We Shall Overcome
我们必将胜利

第二次世界大战后，美国孤立主义思潮消失，文艺事业迎来发展高峰，各种思潮此起彼伏，日新月异。与此同时，流行音乐也进入一个飞速发展时期，成为人们表达思想感情的重要阵地。从50年代末到60年代中期，一批具有高度音乐修养的民歌手致力于民歌和群众歌曲的挖掘、创作和推广，形成了影响巨大的美国现代民歌复兴运动。这些歌手既是歌曲作家或演唱者，又是社会政治活动的积极参与者。他们把对人类命运的焦虑，对社会底层人民的关怀，对种族主义和侵略战争的控诉，以及对和平的向往和对人权运动的声援，都直接在歌曲中表达出来，成为这个时代一道亮丽的风景线。

《我们必将胜利》是一首由黑人和白人在20世纪30年代共同创作的歌曲，在民歌复兴运动中被挖掘出来重新整理后，成为美国20世纪60年代声势浩大的民权运动的标志性歌曲（它也是1963年8月28日向华盛顿进军的主题歌）。在规模大小不一的各种示威游行和静坐过程中，人们都反复吟唱着这首激励人心、鼓舞斗志的歌曲。本录音的演唱者，正是民歌复兴运动的重要成员、被称为"民谣皇后"的琼·贝兹（Joan Baez）。

We shall overcome,
We shall overcome,
We shall overcome someday.
Oh, deep in my heart I do believe that
We shall overcome someday.

We'll walk hand in hand,
We'll walk hand in hand,
We'll walk hand in hand someday.
Oh, deep in my heart I do believe that
We shall overcome someday.

We are not afraid,
We are not afraid,
We are not afraid today.
Oh, deep in my heart I do believe that
We shall overcome someday.

We shall overcome,
We shall overcome,
We shall overcome someday.
Oh, deep in my heart I do believe that
We shall overcome someday.

Words, Expressions and Notes

made slow gains　　取得缓慢的进展
widespread activism　　广泛的激进行为

Oliver Brown　奥立弗·布朗（1903—1961），在美国最高法院1954年里程碑式的布朗起诉教育委

[1] 当我们让自由之声响起来，让自由之声从每一个大小村庄、每一个州和每一个城市响起来时，我们将能够加速这一天的到来。那时，上帝的所有儿女，黑人和白人，犹太教徒和非犹太教徒，新教徒和天主教徒，都将手携手，合唱一首古老的黑人灵歌："终于自由啦！终于自由啦！感谢全能的上帝，我们终于自由啦！"

员会（Brown v. Board of Education）一案中担任控方律师。

Little Rock, Arkansas　阿肯色州小石城

Orville Faubus　奥维尔·法伯斯（1910—1994），阿肯色州信奉种族主义的州长（1955—1967），但其立场在后来有很大转变。

Elizabeth Eckford　伊丽莎白·埃克福德，小石城事件中的学生之一，她与其他 8 名黑人学生一道被称为 "Little Rock Nine"。

James Meredith　詹姆斯·梅雷迪斯（1933—），美国密西西比州人，高中毕业后就加入空军服役，退役后先在该州的黑人大学读了两年，后申请进入密西西比大学就读遭拒绝。该州州长罗斯·巴尼特（Ross Barnett）甚至宣称："我宁可余生都待在监狱里，也不愿打破校园里的种族隔离政策。"美国最高法院下令该校必须接受梅雷迪斯的入学申请后，该校的白人学生出现暴动倾向。当时的美国总统肯尼迪发表电视演说，要求学生接受法院命令，并派遣 300 名宪兵包围该校行政大楼，保护詹姆斯·梅雷迪斯能顺利注册；该校白人学生拒绝了总统的善意，在演说后大肆暴动，两人在暴动中死亡，48 名士兵和 30 名宪兵受伤。肯尼迪不得已派出 16 000 名国民兵封锁学校，直到梅雷迪斯完成注册，成为该校史上第一位黑人学生。由于此事件的发生地叫牛津镇（Oxford Town），美国当时最著名的流行歌手鲍勃·迪伦（Bob Dylan）创作了一首歌曲，歌名就叫 "Oxford Town"，直接反映了这个被认为是民权运动另一个重大突破的历史事件。

Mohandas Gandhi　穆汉达斯·甘地（1869—1948），印度民族解放领袖，其首倡的"非暴力抵抗"对美国以及世界各国的群众运动有深远影响。

Birmingham　阿拉巴马州伯明翰城。1963 年春天，马丁·路德·金在此领导了一场为黑人争取工作、反对禁止黑人在"白人餐馆"就餐的斗争，史称"伯明翰运动"（Birmingham campaign）。警察使用凶猛的警犬和高压水龙头对付抗议的群众，逮捕了马丁以及许多儿童，并且在拖往监狱的途中对他们进行殴打。这一恶劣行为激起了全国人民的愤怒。在狱中，马丁写了《来自伯明翰监狱的信》。他指出，人们既有遵守正义的法律的义务，又有反对非正义的法律的义务。他引用了罗马天主教圣奥古斯汀的话："非正义的法律实非法律。"他接着说，"和平抗议是必需的，因为我们通过自己惨痛的经验认识到，自由并不是别人自愿给予的，必须靠争取。"《来自伯明翰监狱的信》引起了人们的广泛关注。人权领袖们一致同意为结束黑人二等公民的身份，必须在华盛顿特区举行一次抗议游行，以促使这一联邦法律的生成。他们推举马丁·路德·金牧师为抗议游行后的集会的主要负责人。1963 年 8 月 28 日，25 万人聚集在林肯纪念碑前，在 8 月的烈日下倾听了马丁·路德·金激情四溢的演讲：《我有一个梦想》。

President Johnson　林登·约翰逊总统（Lyndon Johnson, 1908—1973），美国第三十六任总统（1963—1969）

Civil Rights Bill = Civil Rights Act　《人权法案》，1964 年由美国总统林登·约翰逊签署，这一具有里程碑意义的立法宣布在学校、公共场所、工作中的种族隔离为非法。

Memphis　孟菲斯，田纳西州城市

James Earl Ray　詹姆斯·雷，暗杀马丁·路德·金的凶手。该凶手是一个在逃犯人，杀害金后被判处 99 年徒刑；1977 年再次越狱逃跑，三天后又被抓获；1998 年死于监狱中。

Questions for Comprehension and Discussion

1. What problems did black Americans still have to face in the 1950s and 1960s?

2. Why did many black Americans demand that their Civil Rights be respected after World War II?

3. Why was the decision in *Brown v. the Board of Education of Topeka* so important to blacks?

4. What happened when a black girl tried to enter an all-white school in the city of Little Rock, Arkansas in September 1957?

5. How did Martin Luther King become the "soul" of Civil Rights Movement in the United States? What was his major tool in the struggle against racial segregation and prejudice?

6. What was the "sit-in"? And what was the "freedom ride"? How did they help blacks reach their political goals?

7. What happened after Martin Luther King was murdered in 1968?

56 Martin Luther King Jr. : "I Have a Dream"

马丁·路德·金: "我有一个梦想"

马丁·路德·金于 1929 年 1 月 15 日出生于佐治亚州的亚特兰大市。他的父亲是教会牧师，母亲是教师。15 岁时聪颖好学的他以优异成绩进入大学学习，先后获得文学学士学位和神学博士学位。

1954 年，马丁·路德·金成为亚拉巴马州蒙哥马利市一座教堂的牧师。1955 年 12 月 1 日，黑人妇女罗莎·帕克斯在公共汽车上拒绝给白人让座遭到逮捕后，马丁·路德·金立即组织了蒙哥马利罢车运动，号召全市近 5 万名黑人对城市公交系统进行长达一年的抵制，迫使法院判决取消地方运输工具上的座位隔离制度。马丁·路德·金从此成为美国民权运动的灵魂人物。1963 年，马丁·路德·金组织了争取黑人工作机会和自由权利的华盛顿游行，并在集会上发表了历史上最震撼人心的演讲之一：《我有一个梦想》。1964 年 11 月，由于马丁·路德·金对美国反对种族歧视和争取黑人自由平等的斗争所作出的杰出贡献，他获得了该年度的诺贝尔和平奖。1968 年 4 月 4 日，马丁·路德·金被一个白人种族主义分子开枪暗杀，年仅 39 岁。

马丁·路德·金的演讲《我有一个梦想》被公认为是美国历史上最激动人心的演说，其影响力远远超出美国的疆界。从 1963 年 8 月 28 日那天起，这篇演说就成为全世界人民反对种族压迫和剥削的战斗号角，成为 20 世纪人类文明进程的一个里程碑。

在演说中，马丁·路德·金既义正词严，又富有节制。他把《圣经》语言中的铿锵韵津与人们耳熟能详的爱国主义象征熔为一炉，完美阐释了林肯总统和圣雄甘地的伟大思想。他高昂而雄辩的语言表达了一种对理想世界的预言和为种族平等而奋斗不息的理念。

在演说中，马丁·路德·金把正在开展的民权运动比喻为兑现共和国创建者们签署的一张"期票"，这张期票保证每位公民都有生活、自由和追求幸福的不可转让的权利。然而，这个国家给黑人的却是一张空头支票。"但是，我们绝不相信正义的银行已破产，我们绝不相信这个充满机遇的国家的巨大金库已资金不足。所以，我们来此就是要兑现这张期票——这期票将按要求给予我们自由的财富和公正的保障。"

马丁·路德·金扣人心弦的演讲对民权运动的目标作出了精辟阐述，并迅速进入美国语言，成为 20 世纪美国的一种国家意志和全民意识。

I am happy to join with you today in what will **go down in history** as the greatest demonstration for freedom in the history of our nation.

Five score years ago, a great American, in whose symbolic shadow we stand today, signed the Emancipation Proclamation. This **momentous decree** came as a great **beacon** light of hope to millions of Negro slaves, who had been **seared** in the flames of **withering** injustice. It came as a joyous daybreak to end the long night of their **captivity**.

But one hundred years later, the Negro still is not free. One hundred years later, the life of the Negro is still sadly **crippled** by the **manacles** of **segregation** and the chains of discrimination. One hundred years later, the Negro lives on a lonely island of poverty in the midst of a vast ocean of material prosperity. One hundred years later, the Negro is still **languished** in the corners of American society and finds himself an exile in his own land. So we've come here today to **dramatize** a shameful condition.

In a sense we have come to our nation's capital to **cash a check**. When the architects of our republic wrote the magnificent words of the Constitution and the Declaration of Independence, they were signing a **promissory note** to which every American was to **fall heir**. This note was a promise that all men, yes, black men as well as white men, would be guaranteed the **inalienable** rights of life, liberty and the pursuit of happiness.

It is obvious today that America has **defaulted** on this promissory note **insofar as** her citizens of color are concerned. Instead of honoring this sacred obligation, America has given the Negro people a bad check, a check which has come back marked "insufficient funds." But we refuse to believe that the bank of justice is bankrupt. We refuse to believe that there are insufficient funds in the great **vaults** of opportunity of this nation. So we have come to cash this check—a check that will give us upon demand the riches of freedom and the security of justice.

We have also come to this **hallowed spot** to remind America of the fierce urgency of now. This is no time to engage in the luxury of cooling off or to take the **tranquilizing drug** of **gradualism**. Now is the time to make real the promises of democracy. Now is the time to rise from the dark and **desolate** valley of segregation to the sunlit path of racial justice. Now is the time to lift our nation from the **quicksands** of racial injustice to the solid rock of brotherhood. Now is the time to make justice a reality for all of God's children.

It would be fatal for the nation to overlook the urgency of the moment. This **sweltering** summer of the Negro's **legitimate discontent** will not pass until there is an **invigorating** autumn of freedom and equality. 1963 is not an end but a beginning. Those who hope that the Negro needed to **blow off steam** and will now be content will have a **rude awakening** if the nation returns to business as usual. There will be neither rest nor tranquility in America until the Negro is granted his citizenship rights. The **whirlwinds of revolt** will continue to shake the foundations of our nation until the bright day of justice emerges.

But there is something that I must say to my people who stand on the warm **threshold** which leads into the palace of justice. In the process of gaining our rightful place we must not be guilty of **wrongful deeds**. Let us not seek to satisfy our thirst for freedom by drinking from the cup of bitterness and hatred. We must ever conduct our struggle on the high plane of dignity and discipline. We must not allow our creative protest to **degenerate** into physical violence. Again and again we must rise to the majestic heights of **meeting physical force with soul force.**

The marvelous new **militancy** which has **engulfed** the Negro community must not lead us to a distrust of all white people, for many of our white brothers, as evidenced by their presence here today, have come to realize that their destiny is tied up with our destiny. They have come to realize that their freedom is **inextricably** bound to our freedom. We cannot walk alone.

And as we walk, we must make the pledge that we shall always march ahead. We cannot turn back. There are those who are asking the **devotees** of Civil Rights, "When will you be satisfied?"

We can never be satisfied as long as the Negro is the victim of the unspeakable horrors of police brutality.

We can never be satisfied as long as our bodies, heavy with the fatigue of travel, cannot gain **lodging** in the motels of the highways and the hotels of the cities.

We cannot be satisfied as long as the Negro's basic **mobility** is from a smaller **ghetto** to a larger one.

We can never be satisfied as long as our children are **stripped** of their **selfhood** and robbed of their dignity by signs stating "for white only."

We cannot be satisfied as long as a Negro in Mississippi cannot vote and a Negro in New York believes he has nothing for which to vote.

No, no we are not satisfied and we will not be satisfied until justice rolls down like waters and **righteousness** like a mighty stream.

I am not **unmindful** that some of you have come here out of great trials and **tribulations**. Some of you have come fresh from narrow **jail cells**. Some of you have come from areas where your **quest** for freedom left you **battered** by the storms of persecutions and **staggered** by the winds of police brutality. You have been the veterans of creative suffering. Continue to work with the faith that unearned suffering is **redemptive**.

Go back to Mississippi, go back to Alabama, go back to South Carolina, go back to Georgia, go back to Louisiana, go back to the slums and ghettos of our northern cities, knowing that somehow this situation can and will be changed. Let us not **wallow in** the valley of despair.

I say to you today, my friends, so even though we face the difficulties of today and tomorrow. I still have a dream. It is a dream deeply rooted in the American dream.

I have a dream that one day this nation will rise up, **live out** the true meaning of its creed: we hold these truths to be self-evident that all men are created equal.

I have a dream, that one day on the red hills of Georgia the sons of former slaves and the sons of former slave owners will be able to sit down together at the table of brotherhood.

I have a dream, that one day even the state of Mississippi, a state sweltering with the heat of injustice, sweltering with the heat of oppression, will be **transformed** into an **oasis** of freedom and justice.

I have a dream that my four little children will one day live in a nation where they will not be judged by the color of their skin but by the content of their character.

I have a dream today!

I have a dream that one day, down in Alabama, with its vicious racists, with its governor having his lips dripping with the words of **interposition** and **nullification**; one day right down in Alabama little black boys and black girls will be able to join hands with little white boys and white girls as sisters and brothers.

I have a dream today!

I have a dream that one day every valley shall be **exalted**, and every hill and mountain shall be made low, the rough places will be made plain and the **crooked** places will be made straight and the glory of the Lord shall be revealed and **all flesh** shall see it together.

This is our hope. This is the faith that I will go back to the South with. With this faith we will be able to **hew out** of the mountain of despair a stone of hope. With this faith we will be able to transform the **jangling discords** of our nation into a beautiful symphony of brotherhood.

With this faith we will be able to work together, to pray together, to struggle together, to go to jail together, to stand up for freedom together, knowing that we will be free one day.

This will be the day, this will be the day when all of God's children will be able to sing with new meaning, "My country, 'tis of thee, sweet land of liberty, of thee I sing. Land where my fathers died, land of the Pilgrim's pride, from every mountainside, let freedom ring! "

And if America is to be a great nation, this must become true. And so let freedom ring from the **prodigious** hilltops of New Hampshire. Let freedom ring from the mighty mountains of New York. Let freedom ring from the heightening Alleghenies of Pennsylvania!

Let freedom ring from the **snow-capped** Rockies of Colorado. Let freedom ring from the **curvaceous** slopes of California. But not only that; let freedom ring from Stone Mountain of Georgia! Let freedom ring from Lookout Mountain of Tennessee!

Let freedom ring from every hill and **molehill** of Mississippi, from every mountainside, let freedom ring!

And when this happens, when we allow freedom to ring, when we let it ring from every village and every **hamlet**, from every state and every city, we will be able to speed up that day when all of God's children, black men and white men, Jews and **Gentiles**, Protestants and Catholics, will be able to join hands and sing in the words of the old Negro **spiritual**, "Free at last! Free at last! Thank **God Almighty**, we are free at last!"

今天，我高兴地同大家一起，参加这次将载入史册的我国历史上最伟大的争取自由的示威集会。

一百年前，一位伟大的美国人——我们今天就站在他象征性的庇荫下——签署了《解放宣言》。这一重要的法令犹如灯塔一般，把灿烂的希望之光带给千百万在不义之火中饱受煎熬的黑奴。它的到来犹如那欢乐的黎明，结束了他们身陷囹圄的漫漫长夜。

然而一百年后的今天，黑人仍未获得自由；一百年后的今天，黑人的生命仍在遭受种族隔离镣铐和种族歧视枷锁的摧残；一百年后的今天，黑人仍然生活在被物质繁荣的汪洋大海所包围的贫困孤岛上；一百年后的今天，黑人仍然潦倒于美国社会的角落，发现自己是故土家园中的流亡者。因此，我们今天来到这里，就是要把这种可耻的现状公之于众。

在某种意义上，我们来到我们国家的首都是为了兑现一张支票。当我们共和国的缔造者们写下宪法和独立宣言上庄严的词句时，他们也就签署了一张每个美国人都有继承权的期票。这张期票许诺将保证所有的人——是的，既包括白人也包括黑人——都享有生命、自由以及追求幸福的不可剥夺的权利。

就有色公民而言，美国今天显然已经在这张期票上违约。美国没有履行这项神圣义务，只是给黑人开了一张被退回并盖有"资金不足"印戳的空头支票。但是，我们绝不相信正义的银行已经破产，我们绝不相信这个充满机遇的国家的巨大金库已经资金不足。所以，我们来此就是要兑现这张期票——这张期票将按要求给予我们自由的财富和公正的保障。

我们来到这个神圣的地点，也是就当前此事的万分紧迫性提醒美国。现在决非是侈谈冷静下来或是服用渐进主义镇静剂的时候。现在是真正兑现民主诺言的时刻；现在是从黑暗荒凉的种族隔离幽谷中走上种族公平的光明大道的时刻；现在是把我们的国家从种族不平等的流沙中抬起，置于兄弟情谊的磐石上的时刻；现在是对上帝所有的儿女们实现公平正义的时刻。

倘若这个国家忽视此刻的紧迫性，那将造成致命的后果。如果自由平等的清爽秋天不能到来，黑人表达合理不满的酷热夏季就不会过去。1963年不是一个终点，而是一个开端。假如这个国家还想恢复原样，那些原本指望黑人只需要消消气就会满足的人应该猛然醒悟过来。只要黑人不能享受公民的权利，美国就不可能有安宁或平静；只要正义之光一天不到来，反抗的旋风就将继续动摇这个国家的基础。

但是我必需提醒正站在通往正义之殿的温暖入口处的人们，在争取合法地位的奋斗过程中，我们绝不做违法之事，我们切莫端起苦涩和仇恨的杯子来满足我们对自由的渴求。我们进行的斗争必须举止得体，纪律严明。我们不能容许我们创造性的抗议蜕变为暴力行动。我们要不断地升华到用精神力量去对付武力的崇高境界。

现在黑人社会洋溢着的新的战斗精神不应导致我们对一切白人都不信任，因为我们的许多白人兄弟已经认识到，正如他们今天到场所证明的那样，他们的命运与我们的命运紧紧相连，他们的自由与我们的自由息息相关。我们不能单独前行。

当我们前行时，我们立志勇往直前，我们不能倒退。有人质问献身民权运动的志愿者："你们什么时候才能满足？"

只要黑人仍然遭受警察难以形容的野蛮迫害，我们绝不会满足。

只要我们因奔波而疲乏的身躯不能在公路旁的汽车旅馆和城里的旅馆找到住宿之所，我们绝不会满足。

只要黑人的基本迁移活动只是从小贫民区转移到大贫民区，我们绝不会满足。

只要我们孩子们的自我和自尊被"仅对白人开放"的招牌褫夺和抢掠，我们绝不会满足。

只要密西西比州有一个黑人不能参加投票，而纽约州有一个黑人认为没有什么值得他去投票，我们绝不会满足。

是的，我们现在不满足，我们将来也不满足，直到正义如洪水，公正似激流，汹涌澎湃，滚滚而来。

我并非没有注意到，参加今天集会的人中，有些人历尽苦难和折磨；有些人刚刚走出监狱牢笼。为了追求自由，你们中有些人惨遭疯狂迫害而遍体鳞伤，有些人因为警察的野蛮暴行而步履蹒跚。你们是人为苦难的长期受害者。坚持下去吧，并且怀着这样的信念：忍受不应得的痛苦是一种救赎。

回密西西比去，回阿拉巴马去，回南卡罗来纳去，回佐治亚去，回路易斯安那去，回到我们北方城市中的贫民窟和黑人区去，要知道当前的状况可能而且必将发生变化。我们绝不能陷入绝望而不能自拔。

今天我要告诉你们，我的朋友们，尽管我们面对着今天和明日的艰难，我仍有一个梦想。这个梦想深深扎根于美国梦之中。

我梦想有一天，这个国家会站立起来，真正实现其信条的真谛：我们认为这些真理是不言而喻的，即人人生而平等。

我梦见有一天，在佐治亚的红山上，昔日奴隶的儿子将能够和昔日奴隶主的儿子坐在一起，共叙兄弟情谊。

我梦见有一天，连密西西比州这样一个受尽不公和压迫煎熬的酷热之地，也将会变成自由与正义的绿洲。

我梦想有一天，我的四个孩子将在一个不是以他们的肤色，而是以他们的品德来评价他们的国度里生活。

我有一个梦想，就在今天！

我梦想有一天，在阿拉巴马州，尽管那里种族主义者邪恶猖獗，尽管其州长大肆鼓吹"干预"和"废除"，但有朝一日就在阿拉巴马州，黑人男孩和女孩将能与白人男孩和女孩携手并肩，情同手足。

我有一个梦想，就在今天！

我梦想有一天，幽谷上升，高山下降；坎坷曲折，终成坦途；圣光显现，洒满人间。

这就是我们的希望。我怀着这样的信念回到南方。怀着这样的信念，我们将能从绝望之山上劈出一块希望之石。怀着这样的信念，我们将能把我们国家一片嘈杂刺耳的吵闹声变成为一首洋溢着兄弟情谊的美妙交响曲。

怀着这样的信念，我们将能一起工作，一起祈祷，一起斗争，一起入狱，一起为自由挺身而出，因为我们知道，有一天我们终将获得自由。

那将是上帝所有的儿女们以全新的意义放声歌唱的一天："我的祖国，美丽而自由的地方，我为你歌唱。这是父辈们的安息之所，是流离转徙的移民引以为豪的土地，让自由之声响彻每座山冈。"

如果美国要成为一个伟大的国度，这个梦想必须成为现实。让自由之声从新罕布什尔州的山岭上响起来！让自由之声从纽约州的雄伟高山上响起来！让自由之声从宾夕法尼亚州阿勒格尼山的顶峰上响起来！

让自由之声从科罗拉多州白雪皑皑的落基山上响起来！让自由之声从加利福尼亚州蜿蜒的山

坡上响起来！不仅如此，还要让自由之声从佐治亚州的大石山上响起来！让自由之声从田纳西州的眺望山上响起来！

让自由之声从密西西比州的每座山峰、每个土丘上响起来！让自由之声响彻重峦叠嶂！

当自由之声响起，当我们让自由之声传遍每个大小村庄，传遍每个州和每个城市时，我们就可以加速这一天的到来。那时，上帝的所有儿女们，黑人和白人，犹太教徒和非犹太教徒，新教徒和天主教徒，都将手拉着手，同唱那首古老的黑人灵歌："终于自由了！终于自由了！感谢万能的上帝，我们终于自由了！"

Words, Expressions and Notes

go down in history　载入史册

momentous　a. 声势浩大的

decree　n. 法令

beacon　n. 灯塔

seared　v. 煎熬

withering　a. 使枯萎的

captivity　n. 囚禁

crippled　v. 使残废

manacles　n. 手铐

segregation　n. 隔离

languished　v. 使憔悴

dramatize　v. 使戏剧化；使引人注目

cash a check　兑现一张支票

promissory note　期票

fall heir　成为继承人

inalienable　a. 不能转让的

defaulted　v. 违约

insofar as　在…范围内

vaults　n. 库房

hallowed spot　神圣之地

tranquilizing drug　镇静药

gradualism　n. 渐进主义

desolate　a. 荒凉的

quicksands　n. 流沙

sweltering　a. 热得令人发昏的

legitimate　a. 合法的

discontent　n. 不满

invigorating　a. 鼓舞人心的

blow off steam　发泄感情

rude awakening　猛然的醒悟

whirlwinds of revolt　反抗的旋风

threshold　n. 门槛

wrongful deeds　错误的行为

degenerate　v. 退化

meeting physical force with soul force　用精神的力量去对付物质的力量

militancy　n. 战斗精神

engulfed　v. 席卷

inextricably　adv. 无法摆脱地

devotees　n. 奉献者

lodging　n. 住所

mobility　n. 移动性，迁徙

ghetto　n. 黑人或少数民族居住区

stripped (of)　v. 剥夺

selfhood　n. 人格

righteousness　n. 正义

unmindful　a. 漫不经心的

tribulations　n. 艰辛

jail cells　囚室

quest　n. 追求

battered　v. 被猛打

staggered　v. 使摇晃

redemptive　a. 赎罪的

wallow in　沉溺于

live out　实行

transformed　v. 转化

oasis　n. 绿洲

interposition　n. 干涉

nullification　n. 废除

exalted　v. 提升

crooked　a. 扭曲的

all flesh　人类

hew out　凿成

jangling　a. 刺耳的

discords　n. 不协调

prodigious　a. 巨大的

snow-capped　a. 白雪盖顶的

curvaceous　a. 有曲线美的

molehill　n. 小丘

hamlet　n. 小村庄

Gentiles　n. 异教徒

spiritual　n. 黑人灵歌

God Almighty　全能的上帝

Questions for Comprehension and Discussion

1. Martin Luther King mentioned "a great American" at the very beginning of his speech. Who was this great American? Why did he want to mention him?
2. What did King mean when he said that "the Negro lives on a lonely island of poverty in the midst of a vast ocean of material prosperity"?
3. King declared that "we have come to our nation's capital to cash a check." What does the "check" represent here?
4. Why did King and black Americans refuse to believe that the bank of justice was bankrupt?
5. Why did King tell his people not to satisfy their thirst for freedom by drinking from the cup of bitterness and hatred?
6. What was King's faith when he said that "with this faith we will be able to transform the jangling discords of our nation into a beautiful symphony of brotherhood"?

Unit 15　Troubled Waters

57　John Kennedy: A New Beginning

约翰·肯尼迪：新的开端

1960 年 9 月 26 日晚，在芝加哥的哥伦比亚广播公司演播室里，民主党总统候选人约翰·肯尼迪参议员与共和党总统候选人理查德·尼克松副总统进行了美国历史上第一次总统候选人电视直播辩论。面对 7 000 万电视观众（占当时全国成人人口的大约 2/3），43 岁的肯尼迪给人的印象是一位打算更有效地利用国家人力和经济资源的高瞻远瞩的新领袖；而已经在艾森豪威尔内阁中当了 8 年副总统、曾与苏联领导人赫鲁晓夫进行过著名的"厨房辩论"的尼克松则尽量突出自己的从政经验，给选民的印象是试图在一个政敌面前占据上风的人物。尼克松的语言很有节制，但相比于肯尼迪却缺乏政治家应有的风度。当晚大多数通过收音机收听辩论的民众认为尼克松在辩论中占据了上风。但事实恰好相反，所有现场和电视机前的观众都看得出来，肯尼迪占据了上风：他看上去更加轻松，更有自制力；而镜头前的尼克松却显得拘谨胆怯，脸色阴沉憔悴。在浅灰色的舞台背景灯光下，身穿浅灰色西服的尼克松淡化成了一个模糊的人影，而肯尼迪的深色西装却在光线反差中十分引人注目。这次辩论标志着电视这种新媒体在政治中首次成为重要的宣传工具，它使人们直接用眼睛而不仅仅靠耳朵去判断一位总统候选人。经过双方 4 次辩论后，在 11 月 8 日的选举中，肯尼迪以极其微弱的优势战胜尼克松，成为美国历史上最年轻的总统。

人们普遍认为，电视是帮助肯尼迪获胜的关键因素之一。其实，年轻并且信仰天主教的肯尼迪在竞选初期并未获得民主党内领导人的全力支持。但是，肯尼迪通过电视展示出来的自制与活力，正好被选民看做是应付苏联挑战、经济萧条、种族隔离和"杂乱无章的美国生活"的一种优势。而这 4 次里程碑式的总统竞选辩论也被冠以"伟大的辩论"（Great Debates）而载入史册。

1961 年 1 月 20 日，肯尼迪宣誓就任美国第三十五任总统。他的就职演说与富兰克林·德拉诺·罗斯福的第一次就职演说被并列为 20 世纪最令人难忘的两次美国总统就职演说。这篇有 1 355 个单词的演讲成为激励型语言和呼吁公民义务的典范之作。演说中的"不要问你的国家能为你做些什么，而要问一下你能为你的国家做些什么"，更是成为美国总统历次就职演说中最脍炙人口的佳句。

January 20th, 1961. John Kennedy was to be sworn-in that day as president of the United States. It had snowed heavily the night before. Few cars were in the streets of Washington. Yet, somehow, people got to the ceremony at the Capitol building.

The **outgoing** president, Dwight Eisenhower, was seventy years old. John Kennedy was just 43. He was the first American president born in the 20th century. Both Eisenhower and Kennedy served in the military in World War II. Eisenhower served at the top. He was commander of Allied forces in Europe. Kennedy was one of many young navy officers in the pacific battle area. Eisenhower was a hero of the war and was an extremely popular man. Kennedy was extremely popular, too, especially among young people. He was a fresh face in American politics. To millions of Americans, he represented a chance for a new beginning.

Not everyone liked John Kennedy, however. Many people thought he was too young to be president. Many opposed him because he belonged to the Roman Catholic Church. A majority of Christians in America were Protestant. There had never been a Roman Catholic president of the United States. John Kennedy would be the first.

President John F. Kennedy

Dwight Eisenhower served two terms during the 1950s. That was the limit for American presidents. His Vice President, **Richard Nixon**, ran against Kennedy in the election of 1960. Many Americans supported Nixon. They believed he was a stronger opponent of communism than Kennedy. Some also feared that Kennedy might give more consideration to the needs of black Americans than to white Americans. The election of 1960 was one of the closest in American history. Kennedy defeated Nixon by fewer than 120,000 **popular votes**. Now, he would be sworn in as the nation's 35th president.

One of the speakers at the ceremony was **Robert Frost**. He was perhaps America's most popular poet at the time. Robert Frost planned to read from a long work he wrote especially for the ceremony. But he was unable to read much of it. The bright winter sun shone blindingly on the snow. The cold winter wind blew the paper in his old hands.

John Kennedy stood to help him. Still, the poet could not continue. Those in the crowd felt concerned for the 86-year-old man. Suddenly, he stopped trying to say his special poem. Instead, he began to say the words of another one, one he knew from memory. It was called **"The Gift Outright."**

> The land was ours before we were the land's.
> She was our land more than a hundred years before we were her people...
> Something we were **withholding** made us weak
> Until we found out that it was ourselves
> We were withholding from our land of living...
> Such as we were we gave ourselves **outright**.

Soon it was time for the new president to speak. People watching on television could see his icy breath as he stood. He was not wearing a warm coat. His head was uncovered. Kennedy's speech would, one day, be judged to be among the best in American history. The time of his inauguration was a time of tension and fear about nuclear weapons. The United States had nuclear weapons. Its main political enemy, the Soviet Union, had them, too. If hostilities broke out, would such terrible weapons be used?

Kennedy spoke about the issue. He warned of the danger of what he called "the deadly atom." He said the United States and communist nations should make serious proposals for the inspection and control of nuclear weapons. He urged both sides to explore the good in science, instead of its terrors:

> Together let us explore the stars, conquer the deserts, eradicate disease, tap the ocean depths, and encourage the arts and commerce.... Let both sides join in creating a new endeavor, not a new balance of power, but a new world of law, where the strong are just and the weak secure and the peace preserved. [1]

1　让我们联合起来去探索星球，治理沙漠，消除疾病，开发海洋，鼓励艺术和商务活动……让双方携起手来作一次新的努力。这不是建立新的权力均衡，而是创造一个新的法治世界，在这个世界里，强者公正，弱者安全，和平持久。

Kennedy also spoke about a torch—a light of leadership being passed from older Americans to younger Americans. He urged the young to take the torch and accept responsibility for the future. He also urged other countries to work with the United States to create a better world:

> The energy, the faith, the devotion which we bring to this endeavor will light our country and all who serve it—and the glow from that fire can truly light the world. And so, my fellow Americans: ask not what your country can do for you—ask what you can do for your country. My fellow citizens of the world: Ask not what America will do for you, but what together we can do for the freedom of man. [1]

John Kennedy's first 100 days as president were busy ones. He was in office less than two weeks when the Soviet Union freed two American airmen. The Soviets had shot down their spy plane over the Bering Sea. About 60 million people watched as Kennedy announced the airmen's release. It was the first presidential news conference broadcast live on television in the United States. Kennedy welcomed the release as a step toward better relations with the Soviet Union. The next month, Soviet leader **Nikita Khrushchev** made another move toward better relations. He sent Kennedy a message. The message said that **disarmament** would be a great joy for all people on earth.

A few weeks later, President Kennedy announced the creation of the **Peace Corps**. He had talked about this program during the election campaign. The Peace Corps would send thousands of Americans to developing countries to provide technical help. Another program, the **Alliance for Progress**, was announced soon after the Peace Corps was created. The purpose of the Alliance for Progress was to provide economic aid to Latin American nations for ten years.

The space program was another thing Kennedy had talked about during the election campaign. He believed the United States should continue to explore outer space. The Soviet Union had gotten there first. It launched the world's first satellite in 1957. Then, in April, 1961, the Soviet Union sent the first manned spacecraft into **orbit** around the earth.

The worst failure of Kennedy's administration came that same month. On April 17th, more than one thousand Cuban exiles landed on a beach in western Cuba. They had received training and equipment from the United States **Central Intelligence Agency**. They were to lead a revolution to overthrow the communist government of Cuba. The place where they landed was called Bahia de Cochinos—the Bay of Pigs. The plan failed. Most of the exiles were killed or captured by the Cuban army.

It had not been President Kennedy's idea to start a revolution against Cuban leader **Fidel Castro**. Officials in the last administration had planned it. However, most of Kennedy's advisers supported the idea. And he approved it. In public, the President said he was responsible for the failure of the Bay of Pigs invasion. In private, he said, "All my life I have known better than to depend on the experts. How could I have been so stupid."

For Your Memory

The Assassination of John Kennedy
肯尼迪总统遭暗杀

肯尼迪一直被大多数美国民众视为历史上最伟大的总统之一。在他任职期间，美国在国内与

1　我们在这场努力中所献出的精力、信念与虔诚，将照亮我们的国家以及所有为它服务的人，而从这火焰所放射出的光辉将会照亮全世界。所以，我的美国同胞们，不要问你的国家能为你做些什么，而要问你能为你的国家做些什么。全世界的公民们，不要问美国愿为你们做些什么，而应该问我们在一起能为人类的自由做些什么。

国际两条战线上都经历了一系列重大事件，这些事件包括：猪湾入侵、古巴导弹危机、柏林墙的建立、太空竞赛、越南战争的早期活动以及美国民权运动等，而朝气蓬勃的肯尼迪总统应对这些事件的能力也给美国人民和世界其他国家留下深刻印象。

然而，他留给全世界最深刻的记忆，莫过于他自身的悲剧性结局。

1963 年 11 月 22 日中午，肯尼迪在副总统约翰逊陪同下到得克萨斯州的达拉斯市访问。12 时 30 分，他乘坐一辆敞篷汽车游街拜会市民，行至一个拐弯处时，埋伏在一幢楼房中的枪手向他开枪，子弹命中头部。他的妻子惊慌地抱住他，全身都沾满鲜血，总统被送往医院后很快不治而亡。数小时后，一个叫李·

John Kennedy Jr. saluting his father's coffin has become a national memory.

奥斯瓦尔德的人被警方抓获，并被初步认定是刺杀总统的嫌疑犯；但此人仅两天后亦被枪杀，这就使案情趋于复杂化。林登·约翰逊宣誓就任总统后下令组成以最高法院院长沃伦为首的调查组。一年后，调查组提交报告，即著名的《沃伦报告》，认为整个事件全是李·奥斯瓦尔德一人作案。美国民众普遍表示不相信这个结论。此后数年，民间有很多人士尝试调查此案，并出版了相当数量的畅销书。在层出不穷的结论中，古巴政府、中央情报局，甚至副总统约翰逊都曾被列为主要怀疑对象。按照当局的说法，《沃伦报告》将会保密至公元 2047 年。当局表示要等到所有当事人过世后才公开。

肯尼迪遇刺身亡让美国和全世界目瞪口呆，这一事件被视为对美国历史的发展产生重大决定性影响的事件之一，在其后数十年中一直影响着美国政治的发展方向。

下面你将听到记者在肯尼迪总统遭暗杀的现场发回的一段实况报道。

"Something has happened in the **motorcade route**. Stand by, please."

"The presidential car's coming up now. We know it's the presidential car and see Mrs. Kennedy's face. There's a secret service man over the top of the car. Something is terribly wrong."

"I happened to be 50 feet away from the President when the first shot hit him."

"The shots apparently came from the **Texas Bookstore Depository** building."

"Just at that moment we heard a bullet coming in, without... directly to... Hospital and came back with news director Bill Hampden."

"The President of the United States is dead."

"It is a powerful international memory, when, for one weekend in the 20th century, three billion people from all walks of life and different races and cultures joined together in a common expression of grief and pain."

246

Words, Expressions and Notes

outgoing *a.* 即将离职的

Richard Nixon 理查德·尼克松（1913—1994），美国第三十七任总统（1969—1974），任期内访问中国，开辟了中美关系正常化的道路，因水门事件被迫辞职。

popular votes 大众选票。美国的总统选举并不是由选民直接投票选举自己中意的总统候选人，而是基于美国建国初期确立的一种"选举团"（Electoral College）制度。候选人中谁能最后胜出入主白宫，并不由大众选票决定，而是由这种制度中安排的选举人选票（electoral votes）决定。当选民在选举日投票时，他们实际在各州推选一组选举人。这些选举人承诺在选举团投票中支持由本州多数选民支持的候选人，总统和副总统实际上是由选举团这个代表机制选出的。每个州的选举团成员人数同该州在国会的参议员和众议员总人数相等，这样全国的参议员人数100名（每州2名）与全国的众议员人数435名（按人口比例分配于各州）加起来共有535名。另外，哥伦比亚特区——首都华盛顿所在地——在国会中没有正式代表，但有3张选举人票。所以，目前选举团一共有538名成员。总统候选人须获得绝对半数以上的选举人票（至少270张）方能当选。在这种选举制度下，当选总统的候选人不一定是得到大众选票最多的人。这种反常现象产生的原因是，几乎每个州都实行"胜者囊括"（winner-take-all）的制度，即在一个州普选中得票最多的候选人囊括该州在选举团的全部选举人票。但缅因州和内布拉斯加州例外，这两个州分别通过全州普选推选出两名选举人，而其余的选举人则通过州里国会选区的选民投票产生。"选举团"制度是美国历史的产物，它既保障了美国国家最高权力的平稳交接，但同时它也存在着与基本民主原则相悖的缺陷，致使选举人票数不能正确反映实际的选民票数。进入21世纪的今天，美国的选举团制度也面临着需要改革的压力。

Robert Frost 罗伯特·弗罗斯特（1874—1963），美国诗人，4次获普利策奖。

The Gift Outright （罗伯特的爱国主义诗歌）《毫无保留的奉献》

withholding *v.* 抑制；不给予

outright *a. & ad.* 直率的（地）；彻底的（地）

Nikita Khrushchev 尼基塔·赫鲁晓夫（1894—1971），前苏联国家领导人（1953—1964）

disarmament *n.* 解除武装；裁军

Peace Corps 和平队，由美国志愿人员组成的为发展中国家提供技术、医疗和教育等服务的机构，成立于1961年。

Alliance for Progress 进步联盟，一个旨在促进拉丁美洲国家经济发展的计划

orbit *n.* 轨道

Central Intelligence Agency （美国）中央情报局

Fidel Castro 菲德尔·卡斯特罗（1926—），古巴国家领导人

motorcade route 车队行进路线

Texas Bookstore Depository 得克萨斯中学教材仓库，刺杀肯尼迪的凶手就在这座建筑的6楼一个房间里朝总统开枪。

Questions for Comprehension and Discussion

1. Why was John Kennedy extremely popular among young people?
2. Why was Kennedy not liked by everyone in the United States?
3. How has television become an important tool for political candidates?
4. What was American people's major concern when Kennedy was sworn in to be the president?
5. What is the goal of Peace Corps?

约翰·肯尼迪：新的开端

John Kennedy: A New Beginning

247

58 The Space Race

太空竞赛

　　美国与苏联之间的"冷战"从 1945 年开始，至肯尼迪时代达到一个高潮。长久以来，两个政治体系对立的大国都在试图寻找一种不冒任何军事对抗的风险而能够置对方于死地的方法，而太空从 20 世纪 50 年代起便成了两个超级大国进行竞赛的战场。

　　冷战初期，美国与苏联都进行了太空竞赛的准备。早在 1944 年到 1945 年，两个国家就曾争夺过德国 V2 火箭的技术和设计火箭的科学家。从 1953 年到 1954 年，焦点问题是谁将第一个造出能打到敌方领土的洲际导弹。这也是研制运载火箭和进入太空至关重要的一步。1955 年，美苏关系进一步紧张，太空竞赛正式拉开帷幕。

　　1957 年，苏联在太空竞赛的第一仗中打了胜仗，他们于 8 月 21 日发射了第一颗洲际导弹，10 月 4 日又发射了人类的首颗卫星"斯普特尼克 1 号"。苏联的成功给美国一个极大的意外，因为没有人预料到苏联能这么快就发射一颗卫星。凭借首颗人造地球卫星取得的优势，苏联外交部长葛罗米柯在卫星发射后仅一小时要求会见美国国务卿杜勒斯，在会见中葛罗米柯以居高临下的口吻对杜勒斯说："国务卿先生，您的情报机构可能已经向您汇报，苏联科学家已于今天下午发射了第一颗人造卫星。"

　　在随后的一段时间里，月球成为美国与苏联竞争的主要目标，两个超级大国的太空竞赛进入白热化阶段。

　　约翰·肯尼迪总统对载人环月飞行计划有很大热情。他曾向苏联建议，双方在这个项目上进行合作。然而，严峻的事实改变了他的初衷：1961 年 4 月 12 日苏联宇航员加加林首次进入太空。刚从床上被叫醒的美国总统肯尼迪得知消息后十分震惊，认为这让美国的国际形象受到了很大的损伤。1961 年 5 月 25 日，肯尼迪在国会上向世界宣布："美国将在十年之内致力于将人送上月球，并将其安全送返地球。"美国航宇局因此制订了著名的"阿波罗"登月计划。

　　太空竞赛的最高潮发生在 1969 年 7 月 20 日：当天全世界大约有 30 亿人观看了美国"阿波罗11 号"的登月壮举，航天员尼尔·阿姆斯特朗踏上月球时讲的"一个人的一小步，全人类的一大步"立刻成为举世传诵的名言。经过 12 年追赶，美国最终超越了苏联，夺取了太空竞赛的最后胜利。这次科技领域的胜利也为正处在动荡时期的美国社会带来一阵久违的愉悦和安慰。

On a cold October day in 1957, the Soviet Union launched a small satellite into orbit around the Earth. Radio Moscow made the announcement: "The first artificial Earth satellite in the world has now been created. This first satellite was today successfully launched in the **USSR**."

The world's first satellite was called **Sputnik One**. Sputnik was an important **propaganda victory** for the Soviets in its cold war with the United States. Many people believed the nation that controlled the skies could win any war. And the Soviet Union had reached outer space first.

The technology that launched Sputnik probably began in the late 19th century. A Russian teacher of that time, **Konstantin Tsiolkovsky**, decided that a rocket engine could provide power for a space vehicle. In the early 1900s, another teacher—American **Robert Goddard**—tested the idea. He experimented with small rockets to see how high and how far they could travel. In 1923, a Romanian student in Germany,

Hermann Oberth, showed how a spaceship might be built and launched to other planets.

Rocket technology improved during World War II. It was used to produce bombs. Thousands of people in Britain and Belgium died as a result of V-2 rocket attacks. The V-2 rockets were launched from Germany. After the war, it became clear that the United States and the Soviet Union—allies in wartime—would become enemies in peacetime. So, both countries employed German scientists to help them win the race to space.

The Soviets took the first step by creating Sputnik. This satellite was about the size of a basketball. It got its power from a rocket. It orbited Earth for three months. Within weeks, the Soviets launched another satellite into Earth orbit, Sputnik 2. It was much bigger and heavier than Sputnik 1. It also carried a passenger: a dog named Laika. Laika orbited Earth for seven days.

The United States joined the space race about three months later—it launched a satellite from **Cape Canaveral**, in the Southeastern state of Florida. This satellite was called Explorer 1. It weighed about 14 kilograms. Explorer 1 went into a higher orbit than either Sputnik. And its instruments made an important discovery. They found an area of **radiation** about 960 kilometers above Earth.

The next major space victory belonged to the Soviets. They sent the first man into space. In April, 1961, **cosmonaut Yuri Gagarin** was launched in the vehicle known as Vostok. He remained in space for less than two hours. He landed safely by parachute near a village in Russia. Less than a month later, the United States sent its first **astronaut** into space. He was **Alan Shepard**. Shepard remained in space only about 15 minutes. He did not go into Earth orbit. That flight came in February, 1962, with **John Glenn**.

By 1965, the United States and the Soviet Union were experimenting to see if humans could survive outside a spacecraft. In March, Russian cosmonaut **Alexey Leonov** became the first person to do so. A special rope connected him to the spacecraft. It provided him with oxygen to breathe. And it permitted him to float freely at the other end. After about ten minutes, Leonov had to return to the spacecraft. He said he regretted the decision. He was having such a good time! A little more than two months later, an American would walk outside his spacecraft. Astronaut **Edward White** had a kind of rocket gun. This gave him some control of his movements in space. Like Leonov, White was sorry when he had to return to his spacecraft.

Later that year, 1965, the United States tried to have one spacecraft get very close to another spacecraft while in orbit. This was the first step in getting spacecraft to link, or **dock**, together. Docking would be necessary to land men on the moon. The plan called for a **Gemini spacecraft** carrying two astronauts to get close to an **unmanned** satellite. The attempt failed. The target satellite exploded as it separated from its main rocket. America's space agency decided to move forward. It would launch the next in its Gemini series. Then someone had an idea: why not launch both Geminis. The second one could chase the first one, instead of a satellite. Again, things did not go as planned.

It took two tries to launch the second Gemini. By that time, the first one had been in orbit about eleven days. Time was running out. The astronauts on the second Gemini moved their spacecraft into higher orbits. They got closer and closer to the Gemini ahead of them. They needed to get within 600 meters to be considered successful. After all the problems on the ground, the events in space went smoothly. The two spacecraft got within one-third of a meter of each other. The astronauts had made the operation seem easy.

In January, 1959, the Soviets launched a series of unmanned **Luna** rockets. The third of these flights took pictures of the far side of the moon. This was the side no one on Earth had ever seen. The United States planned to explore the moon with its unmanned **Ranger spacecraft**. There were a number of failures before Ranger 7 took pictures of the moon. These pictures were made from a distance. The world did not get pictures from the surface of the moon until the Soviet Luna 9 landed there in February, 1966.

For the next few years, both the United States and Soviet Union continued their exploration of the moon. Yet the question remained: Which one would be the first to put a man there? In December, 1968, the United States launched Apollo 8 with three astronauts. The flight proved that a spacecraft could orbit the moon and return to Earth safely.

The Apollo 9 spacecraft had two vehicles. One was the **Command Module**. It could orbit the moon, but could not land on it. The other was the **Lunar Module**. On a flight to the moon, it would separate from the Command Module and land on the moon's surface. Apollo 10 astronauts unlinked the Lunar Module and flew it close to the moon's surface.

After those flights, everything was ready. On July 16th, 1969, three American astronauts lifted off in Apollo 11. On the 20th, **Neil Armstrong** and **Edwin Aldrin** entered the Lunar Module, called the Eagle. Michael Collins remained in the Command Module, the Columbia. The two vehicles separated. It was a dangerous time. The Eagle could crash. Or it could fall over after it landed. That meant the astronauts would die on the moon.

Millions of people watched on television or listened on the radio. They waited for Armstrong's message: "The

Neil Armstrong walked on the moon on July 20th, 1969.

Eagle has landed." Then they waited again. It took the astronauts more than three hours to complete the preparations needed to leave the Lunar Module. Finally, the door opened. Neil Armstrong climbed down first. He put one foot on the moon. Then the other foot. And then came his words, from so far away: "That's one small step for man, one giant leap for mankind."—That's one small step for man. One giant leap for mankind.

Armstrong walked around. Soon, Aldrin joined him. The two men placed an American flag on the surface of the moon. They also collected moon rocks and soil. When it was time to leave, they returned to the Eagle and guided it safely away. They reunited with the Columbia and headed for home. The United States had won the race to the moon.

Words, Expressions and Notes

USSR 苏联（Union of Soviet Socialist Republics）

Sputnik One 斯普特尼克 1 号，苏联发射的第一颗人造地球卫星

propaganda victory 政治宣传上的胜利

Konstantin Tsiolkovsky 康斯坦丁·齐奥尔科夫斯基（1857—1935），俄罗斯航天科学家，现代航天学的奠基者

Robert Goddard 罗伯特·戈达得（1882—1945），美国火箭发动机发明家，现代火箭技术先驱

Hermann Oberth 赫尔曼·奥伯特（1894—1989），出生于罗马尼亚的德国物理学家，现代航天学先驱

Cape Canaveral 卡纳维拉尔角，美国太空发射基地，位于佛罗里达州。

radiation n. 辐射

cosmonaut n. 宇航员

Yuri Gagarin 尤里·加加林（1934—1968），苏联宇航员，地球上第一个进入太空的人，1968 年 3

月 27 日在一次恶劣气象条件下进行飞行训练时不幸失事而丧生。

astronaut　*n.* 宇航员

Alan Shepard　阿兰·谢泼德（1923—1998），美国宇航员

John Glenn　约翰·格伦（1921—），美国宇航员，退役后当选美国参议员（1974—1999）。

Alexey Leonov　阿列克塞·利奥诺夫（1934—），第一个进行太空行走的苏联宇航员

Edward White　爱德华·怀特（1930—1967），美国宇航员，1967 年在肯尼迪航天中心阿波罗太空船失火事故中身亡。

dock　*v.* （宇宙飞行器）在太空中对接

Gemini spacecraft　（美国的）双子星座航天器

unmanned　*a.* 不载人的

Luna　（希腊神话中的）月神

Ranger spacecraft　徘徊者号探月器

Command Module　指挥舱

Lunar Module　登月舱

Neil Armstrong　尼尔·阿姆斯特朗（1930—），美国宇航员，登上月球第一人

Edwin Aldrin　埃德温·奥尔德林（1930—），美国宇航员，登上月球第二人

Questions for Comprehension and Discussion

1. Why was the world's first satellite Sputnik 1 considered an important propaganda victory for the Soviets in its cold war with the United States?

2. Who were the early important rocket scientists? And what did they do for rocket science?

3. Why did both the United States and Soviet Union want to explore the moon?

4. Stepping onto the moon, Neil Armstrong said: "That's one small step for man, one giant leap for mankind." What do you think of his famous words?

5. What problems have been solved by technology and science? Why have they been unable to solve all our problems?

59 Troubled Times: The 1960s

动荡的20世纪60年代

1961年1月20日，年轻的美国总统肯尼迪在他的就职演说中为他那生气勃勃、富有献身精神的政府定下基调。他说："火炬已经传给了年青一代的美国人。"的确，他的内阁成员和白宫顾问，都是美国有史以来最年轻的一群高级官员，他们虚心接受新思想，愿意采取强有力的行动。然而，1963年11月22日，肯尼迪总统在得克萨斯州达拉斯城遭刺客暗杀，从而使他在国外寻求和平、在国内寻求进步中发挥的有力作用突然告终。

在林登·约翰逊任总统期间，美国在越南战争的泥潭里越陷越深，派驻越南南方的军队人数达到50多万人。战争期间，美国向越南投下了800万吨炸药，远超过第二次世界大战各战场投弹量的总和，造成越南160多万人死亡和整个东南亚国家1 000多万难民流离失所；美国自己也损失惨重，5.7万余人丧生，30多万人受伤。越南战争前后长达12年，是美国历史上最长的海外战争，给美国人民造成了无法估量的心灵创伤，成为他们20世纪最恐怖的记忆。

在越来越多的美国人走上街头参加反战示威游行的1965年，美国数十个城市突然爆发了一连串的黑人暴力骚动。黑人领袖马丁·路德·金博士在1968年遭到暗杀后，人们的愤怒情绪更加失控，甚至出现了在首都华盛顿闹市区焚烧抢掠的事件。两个月后，已故总统肯尼迪的弟弟、参议员罗伯特·肯尼迪在竞选总统候选人提名时又被刺杀。同年夏天，在芝加哥举行的民主党全国代表大会上，又发生了反战的活跃分子和芝加哥警察之间的流血冲突。

这些骚动和暴力冲突表明，美国正在发生深刻的变化：越来越多的美国人对战争，对庞大政府对人民需求表现出来的漠不关心，对因性别、种族背景、民族或者生活习惯而继续存在的歧视感到十分不满。在动荡的20世纪60年代，人们的态度、人与人之间的关系、价值标准，甚至人们的衣着和行为都发生了巨大的变化，而这些变化也使得这一时期成为美国20世纪下半叶最深刻的国家集体记忆。

The 1960s began with the election of the first president born in the 20th century—John Kennedy. For many Americans, the young president was the symbol of a spirit of hope for the nation. When Kennedy was murdered in 1963, many felt that their hopes died, too. This was especially true of young people, and members and supporters of minority groups.

A time of innocence and hope soon began to look like a time of anger and violence. More Americans protested to demand an end to the unfair treatment of black citizens. More protested to demand an end to the war in Vietnam. And more protested to demand full equality for women. By the middle of the 1960s, it had become almost impossible for President Lyndon Johnson to leave the White House without facing protesters against the war in Vietnam. In March of 1968, he announced that he would not run for another term.

In addition to President John Kennedy, two other influential leaders were murdered during the 1960s. Civil Rights leader Martin Luther King was shot in Memphis, Tennessee, in 1968. Several weeks later, **Robert Kennedy**—John Kennedy's brother—was shot in Los Angeles, California. He was campaigning to win his party's nomination for president. Their deaths resulted in riots in cities across the country.

The unrest and violence affected many young Americans. The effect seemed especially bad because of the time in which they had grown up. By the middle 1950s, most of their parents had jobs that paid well. They expressed satisfaction with their lives. They taught their children what were called "middle class" values. These included a belief in God, hard work, and service to their country.

American soldiers were carrying the wounded to helicopters in Vietnam war.

Later, many young Americans began to question these beliefs. They felt that their parents' values were not enough to help them deal with the social and racial difficulties of the 1960s. They rebelled by letting their hair grow long and by wearing strange clothes. Their dissatisfaction was strongly expressed in music.

Rock and roll music had become very popular in America in the 1950s. Some people, however, did not approve of it. They thought it was too sexual. These people disliked the rock and roll of the 1960s even more. They found the words especially unpleasant.

The musicians themselves thought the words were extremely important. As singer and song writer **Bob Dylan** said, "There would be no music without the words." Bob Dylan produced many songs of social protest. He wrote anti-war songs before the war in Vietnam became a violent issue. One was called "Blowin' in the Wind."

> How many roads must a man walk down before you call him a man?
> How many seas must a white dove sail before she sleeps in the sand?
> Yes, 'n' how many times must the cannon ball fly before they're forever banned?
> The answer, my friend, is blowing in the wind, the answer is blowing in the wind.

In addition to songs of social protest, rock and roll music continued to be popular in America during the 1960s. The most popular group, however, was not American. It was British—**the Beatles**—four rock and roll musicians from Liverpool.

> Oh yeah, I'll tell you something
> I think you understand.
> When I'll say that something
> I want to hold your hand,
> I want to hold your hand,
> I want to hold your hand.
> Oh please, say to me...

That was the Beatles' song "I Want to Hold Your Hand." It went on sale in the United States at the end of 1963. Within five weeks, it was the biggest-selling record in America.

Other songs, including some by the Beatles, sounded more revolutionary. They spoke about drugs and sex, although not always openly. "Do your own thing" became a common expression. It meant to do whatever you wanted, without feeling guilty. Five hundred thousand young Americans "did their own thing" at the **Woodstock Music Festival** in 1969. They gathered at a farm in New York State. They listened to musicians such as **Jimi Hendrix** and **Joan Baez**, and to groups such as **The Who** and **Jefferson Airplane**. Woodstock became a symbol of the young peoples' rebellion against traditional values. The young people themselves were called "**hippies**." Hippies believed there should be more love and personal freedom in America.

In 1967, poet Allen Ginsberg helped lead a gathering of hippies in San Francisco. No one knows exactly how many people considered themselves hippies. But 20,000 attended the gathering. Another leader of the event was **Timothy Leary**. He was a former university professor and researcher. Leary urged the crowd in San Francisco to "tune in and drop out." This meant they should use drugs and leave school or their job. One drug that was used in the 1960s was **lysergic acid diethylamide**, or LSD. LSD causes the brain to see strange, colorful images. It also can cause brain damage. Some people say the Beatles' song "Lucy in the Sky with Diamonds" was about LSD.

As many Americans were listening to songs about drugs and sex, many others were watching television programs with traditional family values. These included *The Andy Griffith Show* and *The Beverly Hillbillies*. At the movies, some films captured the rebellious spirit of the times. These included *Doctor Strangelove* and *The Graduate*. Others offered escape through spy adventures, like the **James Bond** films.

Many Americans refused to tune in and drop out in the 1960s. They took no part in the social revolution. Instead, they continued leading normal lives of work, family, and home. Others, the activists of American society, were busy fighting for peace, and racial and social justice. Women's groups, for example, were seeking equality with men. They wanted the same chances as men to get a good education and a good job. They also demanded equal pay for equal work.

A widely popular book on women in modern America was called *The Feminine Mystique*. It was written by **Betty Friedan** and published in 1963. The idea known as the feminine mystique was the traditional idea that women have only one part to play in society. They are to have children and stay at home to raise them. In her book, Ms. Friedan urged women to establish professional lives of their own.

That same year, a committee was appointed to investigate the condition of women. It was led by Eleanor Roosevelt. She was a former first lady. The committee's findings helped lead to new rules and laws. The 1964 Civil Rights Act guaranteed equal treatment for all groups. This included women. After the law went into effect, however, many activists said it was not being enforced. The National Organization for Women—NOW—was started in an effort to correct the problem.

The movement for women's equality was known as the women's liberation movement. Activists were called "women's libbers." They called each other "sisters." Early activists were usually rich, liberal, white women. Later activists included women of all ages, women of color, rich and poor, educated and uneducated. They acted together to win recognition for the work done by all women in America.

For Your Appreciation

Blowing in the Wind
答案在风中飘荡

在风起云涌的20世纪60年代，美国的反战运动与民权运动交织在一起，对传统的美国社会造成强大的冲击。人们用各种不同的艺术形式表达他们的政治态度，表达他们对战争、种族等问题的观点和立场。流行音乐歌手鲍勃·迪伦（Bob Dylan）以其独特的歌曲艺术——更准确地说是歌词艺术——成为这个时期美国抗议运动时代的代言人，他创作的很多歌曲因尖锐地涉及美国社会的敏感问题而常常引发人们的共鸣甚至争论。有评论家指出，鲍勃·迪伦对美国文化最大的贡献就在于"他为音乐注入了语言和思想的力量"。

鲍勃·迪伦创作的歌曲《答案在风中飘荡》被广泛评价为美国 20 世纪 60 年代民权运动和反战运动的非正式颂歌。如今，这首歌曲早已走向世界，成为全世界人民反对侵略战争的最有名的抗议歌曲之一。

How many roads must a man walk down before you call him a man?

Yes, 'n' how many seas must a white dove sail before she sleeps in the sand?

Yes, 'n' how many times must the cannon balls fly before they're forever banned?

The answer, my friend, is blowing in the wind,

The answer is blowing in the wind.

How many times must a man look up before he can see the sky?

Yes, 'n' how many years must one man have before he can hear people cry?

Yes, 'n' how many deaths will it take till he knows that too many people have died?

The answer, my friend, is blowing in the wind,

The answer is blowing in the wind.

How many years can a mountain exist before it is washed to the sea?

Yes, 'n' how many years can some people exist before they're allowed to be free?

Yes, 'n' how many times can a man turn his head pretending he just doesn't see?

The answer, my friend, is blowing in the wind,

The answer is blowing in the wind.

Words, Expressions and Notes

Robert Kennedy　罗伯特·肯尼迪（1925—1968），肯尼迪家族成员，曾任其兄约翰·肯尼迪政府的司法部长，1968 年在总统竞选中遇刺身死。

Rock and roll music　摇滚乐，一种节奏强烈的流行音乐，起源于 20 世纪 50 年代的美国。

Bob Dylan　鲍勃·迪伦（1941—），美国当代最重要的流行歌曲作家之一

the Beatles　披头士乐队（又称甲壳虫乐队），20 世纪 60 年代在全世界范围内最成功、最有影响力的流行音乐组合，对摇滚乐和流行文化的发展做出了非常巨大的贡献。乐队主要由来自英国利物浦的 4 名男青年组成：约翰·列侬（1940—1980），保罗·麦卡特尼（1942—），乔治·哈里森（George Harrison，1943—2001）和林戈·斯塔尔（Ringo Starr，1940—）。

Woodstock Music Festival　伍德斯托克音乐节。这是美国（乃至世界）流行音乐史上的一次重大事件：1969 年 8 月，大约 45 万观众聚集在纽约州的一个牧场上，连续 4 天观看流行音乐表演，并在这里缔造了一个嬉皮士的独立王国。

Jimi Hendrix　吉米·亨德里克斯（1942—1970），美国流行音乐家，摇滚乐史上最伟大的吉他手

Joan Baez　琼·贝兹（1941—），美国 20 世纪 60 年代最著名的歌手之一，被誉为"民谣皇后"。

The Who　英国摇滚乐队，活跃于 20 世纪 60 和 70 年代。

Jefferson Airplane　活跃于 20 世纪 60—70 年代的美国摇滚乐队

hippies　嬉皮士，20 世纪 60 年代出现于美国的青年颓废派成员，对社会现实抱某种不满情绪，实行群居，蓄长发，穿奇装异服，常服用引起幻觉的麻醉品。

Timothy Leary 蒂莫西·利里（1920—1996），作家、心理学家和未来学家，美国 20 世纪 60 年代"反文化"（counterculture）运动的代表人物之一

lysergic acid diethylamide 麦角酸酰二乙胺，一种致幻药物，略作 LSD。

The Andy Griffith Show 《安迪·格里菲思》，美国电视情景喜剧

The Beverly Hillbillies 《贝弗利山人》，美国电视连续剧

Doctor Strangelove （电影）《奇爱博士》

The Graduate （电影）《毕业生》

James Bond 詹姆斯·邦德，007 系列电影中的主角

The Feminine Mystique 《女性的奥秘》

Betty Friedan 贝蒂·弗莱顿（1921—2006），《女性的奥秘》一书的作者

Questions for Comprehension and Discussion

1. Why was John Kennedy regarded by many Americans as the symbol of a spirit of hope for the United States?

2. Why did a time of innocence and hope soon begin to look like a time of anger and violence?

3. Why did many young people rebel against their parents' values in the 1960s?

4. What do you think of "do your own thing"—the common expression in the 1960s?

5. What do you think of the turmoil of American life during the 1960s?

60 Richard Nixon's Achievements and the Watergate Case

理查德·尼克松的成就与水门事件

1969 年 1 月 20 日，理查德·尼克松宣誓就任美国第三十七届总统。早在 1960 年，他和肯尼迪竞选总统，在 6 900 万张选票中，仅以 11.8 万票惜败。两年后，他在加利福尼亚州竞选州长，又告失利。就在大多数政治观察家认为他的政治生涯已经完结时，他去纽约市当律师，在没有政治根基的情况下，尼克松重振旗鼓，实现了美国政坛上百年难得一见的东山再起。

尼克松上任后最紧迫的问题就是结束越南战争。尽管与越南和平谈判的过程艰难曲折，美军最终在 1973 年 3 月全部撤出越南，使因越战而疲惫不堪的美国社会获得一个喘息的机会。

然而，尼克松最大的成就还是在于他改变了 1/4 世纪以来的美国外交政策，决定与中国开展正常的外交往来。中华人民共和国成立后，中美两国关系一直处于不正常状态。进入 20 世纪 70 年代后，国际形势发生了巨大变化，中美两国领导人都认为有必要也有可能改善两国关系，实现两国关系正常化。尼克松就任美国总统后，通过多种方式同中国方面进行接触。1971 年 7 月，美国总统国家安全事务助理基辛格秘密访华。1972 年 2 月，尼克松总统开始了他的"破冰之旅"。

1972 年 2 月 21 日，北京机场，美国总统尼克松从"空军一号"飞机的舷梯上走下，他还没有踏上中国的土地，就把手臂向前来迎接的中国总理周恩来伸了出去，周恩来马上迎上去，尼克松说："我跨越太平洋与中国人民握手。"两人亲切握手的场景被记者永久定格为中美两个大国冰释前嫌的最经典镜头。

尼克松在外交政策上的显著成就使他在 1972 年的大选中轻松获胜。但是，在选举过程中发生的一件并不引人注目的事件却在后来引发轩然大波，最终改变了一个国家的政治方向。

1972 年竞选期间，尼克松总统竞选委员会策划盗窃位于华盛顿商业区的水门大厦的民主党全国总部。事发后，起初只有间接证据牵连到尼克松，但尼克松却矢口否认。最高法院命令他将总统办公室的谈话录音带交出后，事实证明他早已知道水门盗窃案的相关情况。法院调查表明，尼克松政府的上层人物违反了正当的法律程序，企图破坏 1972 年民主党的竞选运动。法院的指控包括争取非法捐款、扣压罪证、侵犯个人自由、非法利用联邦机构，以及向大陪审团、联邦调查局和国会委员会提供伪证等罪行。1974 年 8 月 9 日，面临国会即将启动的弹劾程序，尼克松宣布辞去总统职务，成为美国历史上第一位辞职的总统。

水门事件是美国宪政史上最有影响的事件之一，美国建国以来确立的行政、立法、司法三权分立原则第一次受到一名现任总统的强力挑战。尼克松辞职后，副总统福特在宣誓就任总统时说："我的美国同胞们，我们国家的漫长噩梦结束了。我们的宪法在发挥作用。我们伟大的合众国是法治而不是人治政府。权力属于人民。"

1968 was a presidential election year in the United States. It was also one of the saddest and most difficult years in modern American history. The nation was divided by disputes about Civil Rights and the war in Vietnam.

President Lyndon Johnson had helped win major Civil Rights legislation. Yet he had also greatly expanded American involvement in the war in Vietnam. By early 1968, it was almost impossible for him to leave the white house without facing anti-war protesters.

On April 4th, 1968, the nation's top Civil Rights leader, Martin Luther King, was shot to death in Memphis, Tennessee. Robert Kennedy spoke about King's death to a crowd of black citizens:

> What we need in the United States is not division. What we need in the United States is not hatred. What we need in the United States is not violence and lawlessness, but is love and wisdom. And compassion toward one another. And a feeling of justice toward those who still suffer within our country, whether they be white or whether they be black.

No words, however, could calm the anger of America's black community. Martin Luther King had led the Civil Rights movement with peaceful methods. Yet his death led to violence in almost 130 cities in America. Soldiers were called to crush the riots. Hundreds of people were killed or injured.

It is 1969 in America. Richard Nixon is in the first year of his first term in office. His biggest foreign policy problem is the continuing war in Vietnam. During the election campaign, he had promised to do something to end the war. Some Americans believe the United States should withdraw from Vietnam immediately. Bring the soldiers back home, they say. Others believe the United States should take whatever measures are necessary to win. Expand the ground war, they say, or use nuclear weapons.

The American efforts were both diplomatic and military. The Nixon administration started new, secret peace talks in Paris. The official peace talks were taking place in Paris at the same time. The administration withdrew some troops from Vietnam. Yet it sent other troops into **Cambodia** secretly. And it began dropping bombs on **Laos**. It also started dropping bombs on North Vietnam again.

In late March 1972, North Vietnam launched a major **offensive**. In May, Nixon ordered increased bomb attacks against roads and railways in the North. By the end of August, the Communist offensive had been stopped. Yet many lives had been lost. The pressure to withdraw American forces grew stronger. For the next five months, the Nixon administration continued a policy of official talks, secret meetings, and increased military action. Finally, the president announced that an agreement had been reached at the peace talks in Paris. There would be a ceasefire.

President Nixon made the official announcement from the White House:

> At 12:30 Paris time today, January 23rd, 1973, the agreement on ending the war and **restoring peace** in Vietnam was **initialed** by **Doctor Henry Kissinger** on behalf of the United States and special adviser **Le Duc Tho** on behalf of the Democratic Republic of Vietnam. The agreement will be formally signed by the parties participating in the Paris conference on Vietnam on January 27th, 1973, at the international conference center in Paris.

Another foreign policy problem during the Nixon administration was China. The President had much greater success dealing with this problem than with Vietnam. Communists took power in China in 1949. However, the United States did not recognize the Communist government. Instead, it recognized the **Nationalist government** in Taiwan. In the early 1970s, the Nixon administration began trying to improve relations. It eased restrictions on

President Richard Nixon visited China in 1972.

travel to China. And it supported a visit to China by the United States table tennis team. Then, President Nixon made a surprise announcement. He, too, would visit China.

The historic event took place in February, 1972. Chinese leaders Mao Zedong and Zhou Enlai greeted the American President. Nixon and Zhou held talks that opened new possibilities for trade. The next year, Nixon sent a representative to open a diplomatic office in Beijing. After more than twenty years, the two countries were communicating again. They established official relations in 1979.

Many Americans expressed pleasure that tensions between the two countries had decreased. Many were proud to see their president standing on the Great Wall of China. History experts would later agree that it was the greatest moment in the presidency of Richard Nixon.

On June 17th, 1972, something happened in Washington, D. C. It was a small incident. But it would have a huge effect on the United States. Five men broke into a center of the National Committee of the Democratic Party. The building was called the **Watergate**. That name would become a symbol of political crime in the nation's highest office.

At the time, the incident did not seem important. Police caught the criminals. Later, however, more was learned. The men had carried papers that linked them to top officials in the administration. The question was: Did President Nixon know what was going on? He told reporters he was not involved. In time, though, the Watergate case would lead to a congressional investigation of the President.

Early in 1973, reporters found the evidence that linked the Watergate **break-in** to officials in the White House. The evidence also showed that the officials tried to use government agencies to hide the connection. Pressure grew for a complete investigation. In April, President Nixon ordered the **Justice Department** to do this. A **special prosecutor** was named to lead the government's investigation.

A special Senate committee began its own investigation in May. A former White House lawyer provided the major evidence. By July, it was learned that President Nixon had secretly made tape recordings of some of his discussions and telephone calls. The Senate committee asked him for some of the tapes. Nixon refused. He said the president of the United States has a constitutional right to keep such records private.

A federal judge ordered the President to **surrender** the tapes. Lawyers for the president took the case to the nation's highest court. The Supreme Court supported the decision of the lower court. After that, pressure increased for Nixon to cooperate. In October, he offered to provide written versions of the most important parts of the tape recordings. The special prosecutor rejected the offer. So, Nixon ordered the head of the Justice Department to dismiss him. The **Attorney General** refused to do this, and resigned.

By that time, some members of Congress were talking about removing President Nixon from office. This is possible under American law if Congress finds that a president has done something criminal. Was Richard Nixon covering up important evidence in the case? Was he, in fact, guilty of wrongdoing?

In April, 1974, Nixon surrendered some of his White House tape recordings. However, three important discussions on the tapes were missing. The Nixon administration explained. The tape machine had failed to record two of the discussions, it said. The third discussion had been destroyed accidentally. Many Americans did not believe these explanations. Two months later, the Supreme Court ruled that a president cannot hold back evidence in a criminal case. It said there is no presidential right of privacy in such a case.

A committee of the House of Representatives also reached an historic decision in July, 1974. It proposed that the full House put the President on trial. If Richard Nixon were found guilty of crimes involved in the Watergate case, he would be removed from office. Finally, Nixon surrendered the last of the documents. They appeared to provide proof that the President had ordered evidence in the Watergate case to be covered up.

The rights of citizens, as stated in the Constitution, are the basis of American democracy. Every president promises to protect and defend these Constitutional rights. During the congressional investigation of Watergate, lawmakers said that President Nixon had violated these rights. They said he planned to delay and block the investigation of the Watergate break-in and other unlawful activities. They said he repeatedly mis-used government agencies in an effort to hide wrong-doing and to punish his critics. And they said he refused repeated orders to surrender papers and other materials as part of the investigation.

Richard Nixon's long struggle to remain in office was over. He spoke to the nation on August 8th:

> Throughout the long and difficult period of Watergate, I have felt it was my duty to persevere, to make every possible effort to complete the term of office to which you elected me. In the past few days, however, it has become evident to me that I no longer have a strong enough political base in the Congress to justify continuing that effort. Therefore, I shall resign the presidency effective at noon tomorrow.

Never before had a president of the United States resigned. And never before did the United States have a president who had not been elected. **Gerald Ford** had been appointed to the office of vice president. Now, he would replace Richard Nixon. On August 9th, 1974, he was sworn in as the nation's 38th president.

For Your Memory

American Tune
美国曲调

从 20 世纪 60 年代到 70 年代中期，美国经历了建国以来持续时间最长的社会动荡：国家政治领导人屡遭暗杀、越南战争、民权运动、种族暴乱、妇女解放运动、水门丑闻⋯⋯ 这一系列的事件把一个原本生气勃勃的国家搞得疲惫不堪，全国上下都感到筋疲力尽。随着越南战争和水门事件成为过去，随着民权成为这个国家的法律，美国人民终于在 1976 年深深地吸了一口气，吹灭了国家生日蛋糕上的 200 根蜡烛，安下心来，脚踏实地——而不是高喊抗议口号——去实现他们的梦想。

美国流行音乐家保罗·西蒙（Paul Simon）在他的《美国曲调》里，用歌声表达了整整一代人"美国梦"的破灭和对历史与现实的深刻反思。

> Many's the time I've been mistaken, and many times confused
> Yes and I've often felt forsaken, and certainly misused
> Oh but I'm alright, I'm alright, I'm just weary to my bones
> Still you don't expect to be bright and **bon vivant**
> So far away from home, so far away from home
>
> And I don't know a soul who's not been battered
> I don't have a friend who feels at ease
> I don't know a dream that's not been shattered or driven to its knees
> Oh but it's alright, it's alright, for we live so well, so long

Still, when I think of the road we're traveling on
I wonder what's gone wrong,
I can't help it I wonder what's gone wrong

And I dreamed I was dying,
I dreamed that my soul rose unexpectedly
And looking back down at me, smiled reassuringly
And I dreamed I was flying, and high up above my eyes could clearly see
The Statue of Liberty, sailing away to sea
And I dreamed I was flying

But we come on a ship they called *Mayflower*
We come on a ship that sailed the moon
We come in the age's most uncertain hours and sing an American tune
Oh it's alright, it's alright, it's alright
You can't be forever blessed
Still tomorrow's gonna be another working day
And I'm trying to get some rest
That's all I'm trying, to get some rest

Words, Expressions and Notes

Cambodia 柬埔寨

Laos 老挝

offensive *n.* 进攻

restoring peace 恢复和平

initialed *v.* 草签

Doctor Henry Kissinger 亨利·基辛格博士 (1923—)，美国政治家，曾任国家安全事务顾问、国务卿等职，促进中美建交，致力于中东和平，结束越南战争，获 1973 年诺贝尔和平奖。

Le Duc Tho 黎德寿 (1911—1990)，越南共产党领导人，获 1973 年诺贝尔和平奖，但拒绝接受。

Nationalist government 国民党政府

Watergate 水门，美国华盛顿特区一综合大厦，因水门事件而出名，其后缀 "-gate" 现已成为某种丑闻的代名词。

break-in *n.* 闯入；夜盗

Justice Department 司法部

special prosecutor 特别检察官

surrender *v.* 交出

Attorney General 总检察长

Gerald Ford 杰拉尔德·福特 (1913—2006)，美国政治家，1965 年当选为众议院共和党领袖，1968 年任共和党全国代表大会常任主席；1973 年 10 月 12 日，原副总统阿格纽由于贪污丑闻下台后，他任副总统；1974 年 8 月 9 日尼克松总统由于水门事件被迫辞职后，他出任美国第三十八任总统。福特是美国历史迄今为止唯一一个未经选举就接任副总统和总统的人。

bon vivant （法语）生活舒适讲究吃喝的人

Questions for Comprehension and Discussion

1. Why did the year of 1968 become one of the saddest and most difficult years in modern American history?

2. What was President Richard Nixon's biggest foreign policy problem? And what did he do to solve it?

3. What were the feelings of the American people when they saw their president standing at the Great Wall of China? Why did they have such feelings?

4. How did the Watergate incident develop into a major problem for the Nixon administration?

5. Was Nixon willing to resign the presidency? Why or why not?

Unit 16　Heading for a New Century

61

A Period of Change: The Social and Cultural Issues of the 1970s and '80s

一个改变的时期：20 世纪 70 和 80 年代的美国社会与文化

1982 年，越战纪念碑在美国首都华盛顿落成，这是静静横卧在距离林肯纪念堂几百米的一段黑色大理石石墙。墙的一端，一面巨大的美国国旗飘扬在粗犷的铜柱上，铜柱的底座铭刻着美国陆海空以及海军陆战队的军徽，旁边是三个身着不同军服士兵的铜像，接着就是一段两百多米长的黑墙呈三角形状缓缓展开。在镜面般闪亮的墙面上，密密麻麻铭刻着 5.8 万个在越战中死去的美军士兵和军官的名字。一个小女孩来到墓碑前，她请一位个子高高的军官抱起她，让她去亲吻高处的一个名字，她说那是她从没见过面的爷爷。小姑娘的亲吻深情而持久，抱着她的军官潸然泪下，周围的游客无不为之动容。

大多数美国人都认为，越战是美国历史上最不光彩的战争。当美国军队首次以失败者的身份从战场撤回时，他们首次没有受到国内同胞的夹道欢迎。举国上下都只想尽快忘却这一噩梦，甚至忘掉那些战死沙场而不能生还的军人。

越战纪念碑的落成，不仅表达了美国人民对参加越战士兵的尊敬，而且显示了美国人民经历了痛苦后直面历史和失败的勇气。从 1982 年开始，每年都有上百万的美国人来到纪念碑前，黑色而沉重的墙不仅告诉他们过去的光荣，也记载着他们曾经的苦难。

在经历了十多年风雨飘摇的历史后，美国人民需要改变，美国社会需要改变，美国政府也需要改变。在经历了处于美国历史过渡时期的福特和卡特两届政府后，美国人民终于迎来能够在新时期引领他们作出改变的总统：罗纳德·里根。

An economics professor from the United States was teaching in Britain in the early 1980s. One of his students asked this question: "What is most important to Americans these days?" He said: "Earning money." Clearly, his answer was far too simple. Still, many observers would agree that great numbers of Americans in the 1980s were concerned with money. These people wanted the good life that they believed money could buy.

In some ways, the 1980s were the opposite of the 1960s. The 1960s were years of protest and reform. Young Americans demonstrated against the Vietnam War. African Americans demonstrated for Civil Rights. Women demonstrated for equal treatment. For many, society's hero was the person who helped others. For many in the 1980s, society's hero was the person who helped himself. Success seemed to be measured only by how much money a person made.

The period of change came during the 1970s. For a while, these years remained tied to the social experiments and struggles of the 1960s. Then they showed signs of what America would be like in the 1980s. There were a number of reasons for the change. One reason was that the United States ended its military involvement in Vietnam. Another was that the Civil Rights Movement and women's movements

263

reached many of their goals. A third reason was the economy. During the 1970s, the United States suffered an **economic recession**. **Interest rates** and **inflation** were high. There was a shortage of imported oil.

As the 1970s moved toward the 1980s, Americans became tired of social struggle. They became tired of losing money. They had been working together for common interests. Now, many wanted to spend more time on their own personal interests. This change appeared in many parts of American society. It affected popular culture, education, and politics.

For example, one of the most popular television programs of that time was about serious social issues. It was called *All in the Family*. It was about a factory worker who hates black people and opposes equal rights for women. His family slowly helps him to accept and value different kinds of people. Other television programs, however, were beginning to present an escape from serious issues. These included *Happy Days* and *Three's Company*. Music showed the change, too. In the 1960s, **folk music** was very popular. Many folk songs were about social problems. In the 1970s, groups played **hard rock** and **punk music**, instead.

A man stands before the Vietnam Veterans Memorial.

Self-help books were another sign that Americans were becoming more concerned about their own lives. These books described ways to make people happier with themselves. One of the most popular was called *I'm Okay, You're Okay*. It was published in 1969. It led the way for many similar books throughout the 1970s.

The 1970s also saw a change in education. In the 1960s, many young people expressed little interest in continuing their education after four years of study in college. They were busy working for social reforms. Many believed that more education only created unequal classes of people. By the middle 1970s, however, more young people decided it was acceptable to make a lot of money. Higher education was a way to get the skills to do this. Law schools and medical schools soon had long lists of students waiting to get in.

Politically, the United States went through several changes during the 1970s. There were liberal Democratic administrations for most of the 1960s. Then a conservative Republican, Richard Nixon, was elected. During his second term, President Nixon was forced to resign because of the Watergate case. Vice President Gerald Ford became president after Nixon's resignation. About two years later, he was defeated by Democrat **Jimmy Carter**. The election showed that Americans were angry with the Republican Party because of the Watergate case. But they soon became unhappy with President Carter, too. They blamed him for failing to improve the economy. He lost his campaign for re-election to conservative Republican **Ronald Reagan**.

The 1980s were called the Reagan years, because he was president for eight of them. During his first term, the recession ended. Inflation was controlled. He reduced taxes. Americans felt hopeful that they could make money again. Observers created several expressions to describe some groups of people at that time. One expression was "the 'me' generation." This described Americans who were only concerned about themselves. Another expression was "**yuppie**." It meant "young urban professional." Both these groups seemed as if they lived just to make and spend money, money, and more money.

Entertainment in the 1980s showed the interest society placed on financial success. The characters in a number of television programs, for example, lived in costly homes, wore costly clothes, and drove costly automobiles. They were not at all like average Americans. They lived lives that required huge amounts of money. Two of these television programs became extremely popular in the United States and in other countries. They were called ***Dallas*** and ***Dynasty***.

At the movie theater, a very popular film was called *Wall Street*. It was about a young, wealthy, dishonest, powerful man who traded on the New York Stock Exchange. Power was a popular program idea in action films, too. The most successful action films were about a man called **Rambo**. Rambo was impossibly heroic. Naturally, he always won. The films showed good winning over evil. But Rambo rejected **established rules** and was extremely violent.

Another form of entertainment became popular in the 1980s. It was the television talk show. People appeared on these shows mostly to talk about themselves: their politics, their families, their sexual relations. They talked in public about things that were once considered private. Much of the popular music of the time also showed this new openness. **Heavy metal rock** groups sang about sex and drugs. And then there was the new form of music called "**rap**." In this form, words are spoken, not sung, over a heavy beat. Many Americans found all these kinds of music to be too shocking, too violent, too lawless, and too damaging to the human spirit.

People may have talked and sung openly about sex and drugs in the 1980s. But as the years went by, many became increasingly careful about their own activities. This was because sex and drugs became deadly. A new disease appeared at that time. It was called **AIDS**, Acquired Immune Deficiency Syndrome. The disease spread in several ways. One was through sexual relations. Another was through sharing the needles used to take illegal drugs.

A big change in American life during the 1980s came as a result of the computer. Computers were invented 40 years earlier. They were large machines and were used only at universities, big companies, and in the military. By the 1980s, computers had become much smaller. Anyone could learn how to use them, even children. Millions of Americans soon had a "personal" computer in their home. They could use it to read newspaper stories, buy things, do schoolwork, and play games. Such technological improvement—and a bright economy—filled Americans of the early and middle 1980s with hope. Many felt there were almost no limits on the good life they could lead.

Words, Expressions and Notes

economic recession　经济衰退

interest rates　利率

inflation　通货膨胀

folk music　民歌

hard rock　硬摇滚，20 世纪 60 年代由布鲁斯音乐发展起来的一种摇滚乐风格，具有比较强烈的吉他失真效果。

punk music　朋克音乐，现代摇滚乐的一种形式，其演唱和表演都带有青年人反叛的特点。

Jimmy Carter　吉米·卡特（1924—），美国第三十九任总统（1977—1981）。卡特在位期间，把巴拿马运河的管理权交还给了巴拿马，实现了同中华

人民共和国的关系正常化，并努力推动中东和谈。卡特离开白宫时，被认为是政绩最差的美国总统之一。但是自那以后，他频繁出访世界各地，担任国际和平协调人的角色，2002 年获诺贝尔和平奖。

Ronald Reagan　罗纳德·里根（1911—2004），美国第四十任总统（1981—1989），在美国历任总统之中，他就职年龄最大。他也是历任总统中唯一一位演员出身的总统。里根的总统任期影响了美国 20 世纪 80 年代的文化，80 年代常被称为"里根时代"。

yuppie　*n.* 雅皮士（似乎只喜欢赚钱、买高档物品的

职业青年）
Dallas　《达拉斯》，美国电视剧
Dynasty　《豪门恩怨》，美国电视剧
Rambo　兰博，美国电影《兰博》（又译《第一滴血》）的主人公
established rules　既有的规则
heavy metal rock　重金属摇滚乐

rap　*n.*　说唱音乐，其特征是在机械的节奏声的背景下，快速地诉说一连串押韵的诗句，源于纽约黑人居住区，是美国黑人音乐和街头文化的重要组成部分。
AIDS　艾滋病，即获得性免疫缺损综合征（Acquired Immune Deficiency Syndrome）

Questions for Comprehension and Discussion

1. Why did the American society need a change during the 1970s?
2. Why is it said that the 1980s in the United States were just the opposite of the 1960s?
3. Why did the American people become tired of social struggle in the 1980s?
4. What was the major change in television programs? What was the change in music? What was the change in education?
5. Why did President Jimmy Carter's campaign for re-election fail?
6. Why were the 1980s called the Reagan years?
7. When did computers begin to come into American life?

62 The Reagan Revolution

里根革命

"政府不是解决我们问题的办法；政府是问题所在。我的目标是要抑制联邦政府规模及其影响力。"在 1981 年 1 月 20 日的就职演说中，美国当选总统里根发表的这段讲话吹响了"里根革命"的号角。

美国第四十任总统罗纳德·里根的一生可谓充满了传奇与浪漫。他 1911 年 2 月 6 日出生于美国伊利诺伊州坦皮科城，幼年时期是一个典型的小镇顽童。1932 年，里根从伊利诺伊州尤雷卡学院毕业，获得经济学和社会学学位，但随后他却当上了广播电台的体育节目播音员，然后又步入影坛成为好莱坞的一个二流电影明星。里根一共拍过 54 部电影，并曾任美国电影演员协会主席和电影工业理事会主席。第二次世界大战期间他应征入伍，在空军服役，退役后重返好莱坞。1966 年，里根当选为加利福尼亚州州长，并连任两届。从 1968 年起，里根开始参加总统竞选，最终在 1980 年的大选中战胜谋求连任的卡特总统，登上象征着权力与荣誉的美国总统宝座。

里根是美国历史上上任时年龄最大的总统，也是唯一一位演员出身的总统。他上任刚两个月，就在华盛顿街头遇刺：1981 年 3 月 30 日，里根在希尔顿饭店讲演后走出饭店，一个青年拔出左轮手枪，向他射击了 6 发子弹。受伤的里根被送往附近医院抢救。幸好，子弹并没有直接击中他，而是打在防弹车上反弹进他的胸部，击断了第 7 根肋骨后钻进左肺叶停在离心脏仅 3 厘米的地方。虽然他已 70 高龄，却迅速恢复了健康。

里根是 20 世纪 80 年代世界舞台上的风云人物。他的哲学思想是强调个人主义、自由企业和美国传统的民主制度价值准则。在强调这些要旨的同时，他力图把一种新的乐观精神灌注给这个国家。正是他不倦不息的乐观态度，以及他的鼓舞美国人民争取成就和实现抱负的能力，使他在两届任期内改变了美国社会，重塑了美国的国际形象。尽管世界上不少人对这个来自好莱坞的演员治理国家的能力抱怀疑态度，但在许多美国人的心目中，他却是一个可靠而坚定的人物，体现着美国人所渴望的经济繁荣和社会安定。当里根总统离开白宫时，民众支持率之高创下美国历届总统之最。

1993 年，美国政府授予他总统自由勋章。1994 年 11 月 5 日，里根通过电视向公众宣布，他患上老年痴呆症，并从此淡出美国政坛。2002 年 5 月 16 日，美国国会授予他金质奖章。2004 年 2 月 6 日，美国加利福尼亚州决定将里根的生日定为"里根日"。2004 年 6 月 5 日，里根在洛杉矶去世，享年 93 岁。11 日傍晚，在俯瞰太平洋西岸的里根墓地旁边，"里根"号航空母舰的舰长向前总统遗孀南希敬赠了一面曾飘扬在该舰上的美国国旗。

The president of the United States in 1980 was Jimmy Carter, a Democrat. The months before **Election Day** were difficult for him. Many Americans blamed Carter for high inflation, high unemployment, and the low value of the United States dollar. Many blamed him for not gaining the release of **American hostages in Iran**. About a year earlier, Muslim extremists had taken the Americans prisoner after seizing the United States embassy in **Tehran**. President Carter asked all Americans to support his administration during the crisis. As months went by, however, he made no progress in bringing the hostages home. The Iranians rejected negotiations for their release. Sometimes, they did not communicate with the Carter administration at all. The President appeared powerless.

Carter's political weakness led another Democrat to compete for the party's presidential nomination. It was **Edward Kennedy**, brother of former President John Kennedy. He was a powerful senator from Massachusetts. Carter was re-nominated. So was his Vice President, **Walter Mondale**. Kennedy did not support them very strongly. So the Democratic Party was divided for the general election.

President Ronald Reagan

The Republican Party, however, was united behind a strong candidate. That was Ronald Reagan, a former actor and former governor of California. Reagan's vice presidential candidate was **George Bush**. Bush had served in Congress and as head of the Central Intelligence Agency. He had represented the United States in China and at the United Nations.

The troubles of the Carter administration caused many Americans to feel that their country was no longer strong. Ronald Reagan promised to make it strong again. Several weeks before the election, Carter and Reagan debated each other on television. Some observers said Carter seemed angry and defensive. They said Reagan seemed calm and thoughtful. On Election Day, voters gave Reagan a huge victory. He won by more than eight million popular votes. Republicans called it the "Reagan Revolution."

On Inauguration Day, the new President spoke about the goals of his administration. A major goal was to reduce the size of the federal government. Reagan and other conservatives believed that the nation's economy was suffering because of high taxes and unnecessary laws. In this crisis, he said, government was not the solution to the problem; government was the problem. He urged Americans to join him in what he called a "new beginning." And he expressed hope that the people would work with him:

> The economic ills we suffer have come upon us over several decades. They will not go away in days, weeks, or months. But they will go away. They will go away because we, as Americans, have the capacity now—as we have had in the past—to do whatever needs to be done to preserve this last and greatest **bastion** of freedom.

Soon after Ronald Reagan's presidency began, there was an attempt on his life. A gunman shot him in March, 1981. Doctors removed the bullet. He rested, regained his strength, and returned to the White House in 12 days. The new President's main goal was to reduce the size of the federal government. He and other conservative Republicans wanted less government interference in the daily lives of Americans.

President Reagan won Congressional approval for his plan to reduce taxes on earnings. Many Americans welcomed the plan. Others were concerned about its affect on the national debt. They saw taxes go down while defense spending went up. To save money, the Reagan administration decided to cut spending for some social programs. This pleased conservatives. Liberals, however, said it limited poor peoples' chances for good housing, health care, and education.

President Reagan also had to make decisions about using military force in other countries. In 1983, he sent Marines to **Lebanon**. They joined other **peacekeeping troops** to help stop fighting among several opposing groups. On October 23rd, a Muslim extremist exploded a bomb in the building where the Marines were living. Two hundred forty-one Americans died.

1984 was another presidential election year. It looked like no one could stop President Reagan. His warm way with people had made him hugely popular. He gained support with the military victory in **Grenada**. And, by the time the campaign started, inflation was under control. The Republican Party re-nominated Ronald Reagan for president and George Bush for vice president. On Election Day, he won 59 percent of the popular vote. On Inauguration Day, the weather was not so kind. It was bitterly cold in Washington. All inaugural activities, including the swearing-in ceremony, were held inside.

For years, the United States had accused Libyan leader **Muammar Kaddafi** of supporting international terrorist groups. It said he provided them with weapons and a safe place for their headquarters. In January, 1986, the United States announced economic restrictions against Libya. Then it began military training exercises near the Libyan coast. Libya said the Americans were violating its territory and fired missiles at them. The Americans fired back, sinking two ships.

On April 5th, a bomb destroyed a public dance club in **West Berlin**. Two people died, including an American soldier. The United States said Libya was responsible. President Reagan ordered bomb attacks against the Libyan cities of **Tripoli** and **Benghazi**. Muammar Kaddafi escaped unharmed. But one of his children was killed. Some Americans said the raid was cruel. Others praised it. President Reagan said the United States did what it had to do.

The President also wanted to intervene in **Nicaragua**. About 15,000 rebel troops, called **Contras**, were fighting the communist government there. Reagan asked for military aid for the Contras. Congress rejected the request. It banned all aid to the Contras. At that same time, Muslim terrorists in Lebanon seized several Americans. The Reagan administration looked for ways to gain the hostages' release. It decided to **sell missiles and missile parts to Iran in exchange for Iran's help**. After the sale, Iran told the terrorists in Lebanon to release a few American hostages.

Not long after, serious charges became public. Reports said that money from the sale of arms to Iran was used to aid the Contra rebels in Nicaragua. Several members of the Reagan administration resigned. It appeared that some had violated the law. President Reagan said he regretted what had happened. But he said he had not known about it. Investigations and court trials of those involved continued into the 1990s. Several people were found guilty of illegal activities and of lying to Congress. No one went to jail.

Most Americans did not blame President Reagan for the actions of others in his administration. They still supported him and his policies. They especially supported his efforts to deal with the Soviet Union. To protect the United States against the Soviets, he increased military spending to the highest level in American history. Then, in 1985, **Mikhail Gorbachev** became the leader of the Soviet Union.

The two leaders met in Switzerland, in Iceland, in Washington, and in Moscow. Each agreed to destroy hundreds of nuclear missiles. President Reagan also urged Mr. Gorbachev to become more democratic. He spoke about the wall that communists had built to divide the city of Berlin, Germany:

> No American who sees first-hand can ever again take for granted his or her freedom or the precious gift that is America. That gift of freedom is actually the birthright of all humanity. And that is why, as I stood there, I urged the Soviet leader, Mister Gorbachev, to send a new signal of openness to the world by tearing down that wall.

Ronald Reagan was president as the American economy grew rapidly. He was president as a new sense of openness was beginning in the Soviet Union. Yet, at the end of his presidency, many Americans were concerned by what he left behind. Increased military spending, together with tax cuts, had made the national debt huge. The United States owed thousands of millions of dollars. The debt would be a political issue for presidents to come.

269

Words, Expressions and Notes

Election Day 选举日。美国法律规定，每逢以 4 能除尽的年份的 11 月的第一个星期以后的星期二举行大选，选举总统和副总统，任期 4 年。每逢逢双的年份选举众议员，任期 2 年，并改选 1/3 的参议员，任期 6 年。

American hostages in Iran 扣押在伊朗的美国人质，指"伊朗人质危机"。1979 年，伊朗爆发伊斯兰革命，巴列维国王被推翻。同年 11 月 4 日，激进的伊朗学生占领美国驻伊朗使馆，扣留数十名美国外交官和平民作为人质。卡特政府批准了一项代号为"鹰爪行动"的跨军种联合秘密营救行动，但遭遇沙漠风暴，以一架直升机与一架 C-130 大力神运输机相撞坠毁、8 名美国军人阵亡而告失败。1981 年 1 月 20 日，就在里根的总统就职典礼后几分钟，伊朗宣布释放所有人质，至此他们已被扣押 444 天。伊朗人质危机是 20 世纪国际外交史上最轰动的事件之一。人们普遍认为，总统卡特在这场危机中应对无方是他竞选连任失败的直接原因。

Tehran 德黑兰，伊朗首都

Edward Kennedy 爱德华·肯尼迪（1932—2009），美国资历最长的参议员之一，美国前总统肯尼迪最小的兄弟

Walter Mondale 沃尔特·蒙代尔（1928—），卡特政府时期美国副总统，克林顿总统时期担任美国驻日本大使。

George Bush 乔治·布什（1924—），美国副总统（1981—1989），美国第四十一任总统（1989—1993）

bastion n. 堡垒

Lebanon 黎巴嫩

peacekeeping troops 维和部队

Grenada 格林纳达，加勒比海岛国。美国为防止该国成为第二个古巴，于 1983 年 10 月 25 日凌晨采用突然袭击手段，对岛国格林纳达发动了一场海空联合入侵，这是自越南战争失败以来美国最大的一次军事行动。至 11 月 2 日，美军完全控制了格林纳达，战争遂告结束。战争结果：美军 18 人阵亡，90 人受伤，损失直升机 10 余架；格军死亡 40 余人，被俘 15 人，其余逃散；古巴人死亡 69 人，伤 56 人，被俘者达 642 人。

Muammar Kaddafi 奥马尔·卡扎菲（1942—），阿拉伯利比亚共和国领导人

West Berlin 西柏林

Tripoli 的黎波里，利比亚首都

Benghazi 班加西，利比亚港口

Nicaragua 尼加拉瓜，位于中美洲中部。

Contras 康特拉斯，尼加拉瓜内战时期的反政府组织，曾经受到美国政府的财政援助。

sell missiles and missile parts to Iran in exchange for Iran's help 向伊朗出售导弹和导弹部件以获得伊朗（在释放人质一事上的）帮助。这里指的是美国 20 世纪 80 年代著名的"伊朗门事件"。该事件是指美国向伊朗秘密出售武器一事被揭露后，造成了里根政府严重的政治危机，因人们把它与尼克松水门事件相比，故名"伊朗门事件"。

Mikhail Gorbachev 米哈伊尔·戈尔巴乔夫（1931—），前苏联国家领导人，1990 年获诺贝尔和平奖。

Questions for Comprehension and Discussion

1. What difficulties did President Jimmy Carter have when he was trying to be re-elected in 1980?
2. What was the major goal of Ronald Reagan, the new president of the United States in 1981?
3. What do you think about Ronald Reagan's idea that government was not the solution to the problem of the United States—government itself was the problem?
4. What actions did Reagan administration take against some other countries in the world?
5. What happened during the historic meetings between President Reagan and Mikhail Gorbachev, the leader of the Soviet Union?
6. What was the problem left by the Reagan administration?

63 The 1990s: One of the Best Periods in American History

20世纪90年代：美国历史上最繁荣时期之一

美国在20世纪的最后10年迎来了历史上最繁荣的一段时期。首先，冷战的结束和苏联的解体为美国的发展创造了良好的外部环境；其次，美国在1991年初发动的第一次海湾战争中大获全胜，显示出美军的海空优势和高技术优势，大大提升了国家上下对其军事实力的信心；第三，以电子计算机和互联网为代表的新技术成为国家经济发展的强大推动力。

然而，带给人们最深刻记忆的却是10年间发生的两起轰动全美的惊天大案。

第一桩大案件的主角是美国家喻户晓的黑人体育明星奥伦撒尔·詹姆斯·辛普森。辛普森出身贫寒，幼时双腿畸形，他依靠个人奋斗，从一个普通的黑孩子成为驰骋橄榄球场的明星。告别绿茵场后，又出任电视体育评论员，并出演过影视剧（曾在中国上映的电影《卡桑德拉大桥》中黑人警官的扮演者就是他）。辛普森依靠自己的努力而改变境遇，进入上层社会，还娶了个白人太太，成为美国黑人崇拜的偶像。

1994年6月12日晚，有人发现辛普森的白人前妻和她的白人男友在家中被害，凶杀现场血腥弥漫，惨不忍睹。洛杉矶地方检察官指控辛普森犯有谋杀罪。辛普森从明星到杀人嫌疑犯的戏剧性变化，以及黑白通婚等种族敏感问题使全美各种媒体无一不竞相对此案开始了规模空前的密集报道，辛案因而被称作"世纪审判"（Trial of the Century）。

经过474天的审理，1995年10月3日上午，包括总统克林顿在内的美国1.5亿人都停下工作注视着电视实况转播。由绝大多数黑人组成的陪审团在分析了113位证人的1105份证词后，宣判辛普森无罪。当被监禁9个月的辛普森笑容满面地与他的"梦之队"律师们拥抱时，受害者家属则集体失声痛哭。法庭外，支持辛普森的人大声欢呼，而更多的人却惊诧不已，以至克林顿总统都亲自出面呼吁大家尊重陪审团的判决。

在此案中，警方声称已经掌握了足以证明辛普森杀害前妻及其男友的证据，但他们为使案件更加"铁证如山"，愚蠢地伪造了一双沾有辛普森和他前妻血迹的袜子。而这双袜子，最终被生化学家证明为实验室里的产物。由于有这一伪证，洛杉矶警方获取的大量能证明辛普森有罪的其他证据都不被法庭所采信。

同样令人吃惊的是，辛案结束后，洛杉矶市地区检察官毫不留情，正式立案起诉参与办案的警官。结果是，杀人嫌犯无罪开释，执法警官却因伪证罪被判3年有期徒刑。

这场"世纪审判"无疑是美国建国以来最具影响力的案件之一，案件的结果令全世界所有关注此案的人大跌眼镜，而它传达出的信息更加令人深思。美国宪法和司法制度的核心，是注重保障公民权利和遵循正当程序。在本案中，美国司法制度对程序公正和确凿证据的重视程度，远远超过了寻求案情真相和把罪犯绳之以法的欲望。美国最高法院大法官道格拉斯（William O. Douglas，任期1939—1975）曾经对此作了精辟的说明："权利法案的绝大部分条款都与程序有关，这绝非毫无意义。正是程序决定了法治与随心所欲或反复无常的人治之间的大部分差异。坚定地遵守严格的法律程序，是我们赖以实现法律面前人人平等的主要保证。"

发生在90年代的另一桩重大历史事件就是克林顿弹劾案。

比尔·克林顿出生在美国阿肯色州霍普镇的一个普通人家，他凭借着个人的聪明才智、人格魅力和政治技巧，32岁成为美国历史上最年轻的州长，46岁又击败当时的总统老布什，于1992

年登上了美国政治权力的顶峰。克林顿在两任总统任期内，在美国的经济发展、犯罪控制和医疗保健方面作出了出色的成绩。

1998 年底至 1999 年初，克林顿因与白宫实习生莱温斯基的性丑闻而遭到国会弹劾，并一度成为全球关注的热点。美国国会指责他向联邦大陪审团作伪证和妨碍司法，并启动了弹劾程序。虽然美国参议院最终判定他无罪，但是克林顿还是被冠以美国"第二个在任期内遭弹劾的总统"的头衔。（美国历史上第一次面临总统弹劾程序的是第十七任总统安德鲁·约翰逊。1868 年 2 月 25 日，美国众议院 126 票对 47 票通过"违反官员任职法和阴谋策划反革命武装叛乱"等 11 项弹劾条款，向参议院提出要求弹劾约翰逊。同年 3 月，参议院对约翰逊弹劾案进行缺席审理，投票表决结果是以 35 对 19 票一票之差没有得到弹劾总统需要的 2/3 多数。而尼克松总统则是在 1974 年 8 月 9 日国会启动弹劾程序之前主动辞职。）

2005 年，美国教科书委员会决定将克林顿弹劾案写进中学历史教科书，让数百万中学生可以了解这一历史事件。美国历史专家指出："弹劾案对我们近代历史有着重要的意义，应该写入教科书里。"

Many experts describe the 1990s as one of the best periods in United States history. During almost all that time, America was at peace. The frightening and costly military competition with the Soviet Union had ended. The threat of a nuclear attack seemed greatly reduced, if not gone. Military officials said America's defenses were strong. The economy improved from poor to very good. Inflation was low. So was unemployment. Production was high. Scientists and engineers made major progress in medicine and technology. The Internet computer system created a new world of communications.

America grew by almost 33 million people during the 1990s. This is the most the United States has ever grown during a ten-year period. Some minority groups are growing faster than the white population. For the first time in 70 years, one in ten Americans was born in another country. During the past ten years, there was a huge increase in immigrants from Latin America, the Caribbean and Asia. More than 280 million people lived in the United States by the end of the twentieth century. This population was getting older, however, and needing more costly health

President Bill Clinton

care. And, America had other problems in the 1990s. Some people feared crime in the streets. People were shot and killed in offices and schools. Divisions grew between rich people and poor people. Racial tensions remained high. In 1999, Congress impeached the President of the United States. **President Clinton** was accused of lying to courts about a sexual relationship with a young woman who worked in the White House. Bill Clinton was found not guilty. Still, the trial and the events leading to it caused deep concern among some Americans.

American families changed in the 1990s. More people ended their marriages. The rate of these divorces increased. So did the percentage of children living with only one parent. Children in such families were more likely to be poor or get into trouble. Many American children did not live with their parents at all. The number of children living with grandparents increased greatly. Test scores and national studies during the 1990s showed that many public school students were not learning as they should. The nation needed more and better teachers.

Racial divisions in America were a continuing and serious problem. In 1991, an African-American

man named Rodney King was fleeing from police in Los Angeles, California. The police had chased his speeding car for miles before stopping him. They say he reacted violently when they tried to seize him. Police officers beat and kicked Mr. King as he lay on the ground. A man who lived nearby filmed the beating with a video camera. He took the video to a local television station. Soon people all over the country were watching the police repeatedly striking Rodney King. The four white police officers were arrested for their actions. They were tried outside Los Angeles at their request. A jury in a nearby wealthy, conservative community found them not guilty. Within a short time, angry African-Americans began rioting in the streets of Los Angeles. The unrest lasted three days. Fifty-five people died in the violence. More than 2,000 others were injured. One thousand buildings lay in ruins.

Another major court trial divided black people and white people. **O. J. Simpson** had been a football hero and an actor. In 1994, Simpson was accused of killing his former wife, Nicole Brown Simpson, and a male friend of hers. Simpson is African-American. Nicole Brown Simpson was white. Many legal experts believed the case against him was strong. Still, the mainly African-American jury judged him not guilty. Later, a mainly white jury found him guilty in a civil damage case. Studies showed that white people believed Mr. Simpson had killed his former wife and her friend. Black people thought he was not guilty.

During the 1990s, scientists worked to map the position of all the genes in the human body. Research on this human genome map

O. J. Simpson—His murder case is described as the most publicized criminal trial in history.

progressed slowly at first. Then it speeded up. The goal was to help scientists study human health and disease. The discovery was expected to change the way some diseases are treated. Since 1980, doctors had made important progress in treating diseases like cancer, AIDS and Parkinson's disease. But they still could not cure them. They hoped treatments developed from knowledge of human genes would help. Computer technology also had progressed greatly in the 1980s. During the next ten years computers became even more important in American life. People depended on computers both at work and at home. They used the Internet to send electronic messages, get information and buy all kinds of products. They completed and sent their income tax forms. They read newspapers and books. They even listened to music.

Americans continued to attend classical music concerts and operas. However, many more people enjoyed popular music. One popular music form was called rap. Rap music is spoken quickly rather than sung to the music of recorded rhythms. Some rap songs suggest violent actions. Others contain sexual suggestions that many people found offensive. But rap music was very popular with many young people. So was a form of rock music called "**Grunge**."

During the 1990s, Americans watched traditional television programs as well as new kinds of shows. Millions of people liked weekly dramas like *ER* that takes place in a busy hospital emergency room. A program called *Law and Order* tells about the work of police officers, lawyers and judges. *NYPD Blue* shows the work of police officers in New York City. A show called *Seinfeld* also told about life in New York City. But this program was very funny. *Seinfeld* was the most popular television show of the decade.

Another funny and popular show was the animated series called *The Simpsons*. Cable television programs also grew in popularity. One of the most popular was MTV. It showed music videos and other programs for young people.

At the movies, Americans saw popular films like *Titanic*. It told about the sinking of the famous passenger ship on its first crossing of the Atlantic Ocean in 1912. Two young people are shown falling in love during this tragic event. Another popular film was *Jurassic Park*. It brought ancient, frightening dinosaurs to life.

As usual, Americans enjoyed sports. Public interest in baseball decreased sharply, however, after a players' strike in 1994. The strike cancelled the championship **World Series** games that year. In 1998, interest in baseball increased when two great players competed to hit the most **home runs**. **Sammy Sosa** and **Mark McGwire** helped restore the popularity of baseball. In basketball, experts say **Michael Jordan** became the best player in history. He led the **Chicago Bulls** team to win many championships.

As the 1990s ended, some experts worried about computers making the change to the year 2000. They feared that computer failures might cause serious problems for everyday life. But midnight of December 31st passed with only a few incidents of computer trouble. Millions of people celebrated the beginning of a new century and another one thousand years. Life in the 1990s had been good for many Americans. They hoped for even better days to come.

Words, Expressions and Notes

President Clinton 比尔·克林顿总统 (1946—)，美国第四十二任总统 (1993—2001)

O. J. Simpson 辛普森 (Orenthal James Simpson, 1947—)，美国著名黑人美式足球运动员，1979 年因伤退休后出演过二十多部电影。1994 年卷入杀妻案成为全球知名人物。最后因起诉证据存有漏洞，他得以无罪释放。但死者家属事后提起民事诉讼并获得赔偿。这场"世纪审判"是美国当代最具争议的案件之一。2008 年 9 月 13 日，辛普森伙同他人闯入美国赌城拉斯维加斯一家宾馆，从收集、出售体育纪念品的两个商人手中抢走一些物品，其中包括他当年比赛使用过的一些橄榄球，以及其他橄榄球明星的印刷画及签名的橄榄球等。辛普森声称取回的东西原是自己的私人物品，但警方调查后认为辛普森有违法行为。美国检察机关对辛普森提出 12 项指控，其中包括绑架、攻击他人和使用致命武器实施抢劫等 7 项重罪。2008 年 12 月 5 日，辛普森被判有罪，并处以 33 年徒刑（服刑 9 年后可以获得保释机会）。

Grunge 20 世纪 90 年代发展起来的重金属摇滚乐的一种。"Grunge" 一词是美国俗语，意指"难看难闻，肮脏丑陋的东西"。Grunge 音乐的特点往往是冷漠、怪异和狂躁，但同时又让人感觉耳目一新。

ER （电视剧）《急诊室的故事》

Law and Order （电视剧）《法律与秩序》

NYPD Blue （电视剧）《纽约重案组》

Seinfeld （电视剧）《宋飞正传》

The Simpsons （电视剧）《辛普森一家》

Titanic （电影）《泰坦尼克号》

Jurassic Park （电影）《侏罗纪公园》

World Series 世界职业棒球锦标赛

home runs （棒球比赛中的）本垒打

Sammy Sosa 塞米·索萨，美国职业棒球明星

Mark McGwire 马克·麦奎尔，美国职业棒球明星

Michael Jordan 迈克尔·乔丹，美国职业篮球明星

Chicago Bulls （美国职业篮球）芝加哥公牛队

Questions for Comprehension and Discussion

1. What were the major reasons that made the 1990s one of the best periods in American history?
2. What were the major problems the United States had in the 1990s?

3. Why did African-Americans begin rioting in the streets of Los Angeles in 1991?

4. Why did Congress try to impeach President Clinton in 1999?

5. Why did white people believe Mr. Simpson had killed his former wife and her friend, but black people thought he was not guilty? What is your opinion about the case?

6. What were the major scientific advancements during the 1990s?

64 George W. Bush and the "War on Terror"

乔治·布什与反恐战争

当世界跨入新千年之际，美国经济在持续增长近 10 年后处于巅峰状态；在世界力量对比严重失衡的情况下，美国作为全世界唯一超级大国的地位几乎没有受到来自任何方面的挑战。在这样的形势下，美国迎来了一波三折的 2000 年总统大选。

由民主党候选人、前副总统戈尔和共和党候选人小布什对垒的 2000 年美国总统选举，不仅出现了前所未有的激烈场面，而且爆出了"难产"的世纪大新闻。11 月 7 日大选投票后，本应在第二天宣布大选结果，却因两党总统候选人对决定胜负的佛罗里达州的计票结果发生严重争执，双方由政治竞争发展到对簿公堂，大小官司打了 50 多场，从地方法院、州法院、巡回法院，一直打到联邦最高法院，从而使大选战火四处蔓延，美国上下沸沸扬扬，全世界都在注视佛州关于选票所引起的混乱。一直到联邦最高法院 12 月 12 日对佛州人工重新计票问题作出最后裁决，戈尔 14 日发表声明"退出"竞选之后，大选才有了最终结果。不少政治评论家认为：布什总统不是选出来的，而是由法院"判"出来的。英国《每日电讯报》也指出：由法院判决的大选结果使"美国正在成为全世界的笑柄"。

美国第四十三任总统乔治·布什是继美国第六任总统亚当斯之后第二位踏着父亲的脚印进入白宫的总统。他 1946 年 7 月 6 日生于美国康涅狄格州，在得克萨斯州长大，18 岁进入耶鲁大学主修历史学。毕业后，布什进入得克萨斯州国民警卫队空军，成为一名战斗机驾驶员，直到 1973 年离开空军。此后，布什又在哈佛商学院求学两年。1994 年，他竞选得克萨斯州州长成功，1998 年他再次竞选并成功，成为该州历史上首位得以连任的州长。从竞选州长到入主白宫仅用了 7 年时间，布什的仕途可谓一帆风顺。

然而，上任不到 8 个月的他却遭遇了美国历史上最大的本国受攻击的事件："9·11"恐怖袭击。2001 年 9 月 11 日上午，19 名恐怖分子通过劫持多架民航飞机，对纽约曼哈顿的摩天高楼以及华盛顿五角大楼发动自杀式恐怖袭击。纽约地标性建筑"世界贸易中心"的两幢 110 层摩天大楼在遭到攻击后相继倒塌，美国国防部所在地五角大楼遭到局部破坏。袭击共造成约 3 000 人死亡。这是继日本在第二次世界大战期间偷袭珍珠港之后，美国本土遭遇的最严重的恐怖袭击。

无论是对于美国还是对于全世界，"9·11"事件都是一次历史性的震撼。这次事件以极其猛烈的方式，迫使人们认识到，反恐怖主义活动将是人类社会一项长期、艰苦和复杂的斗争；而美国这个刚以最自信的步伐迈入人类第三个千年的国家，也因此事件而被迫重新审视她的未来。

George W. Bush became the nation's 43rd president on January 20th, 2001. He and his Vice President, **Dick Cheney**, were sworn in on the steps of the Capitol building. George Bush's father, George Herbert Walker Bush, had served as the 41st president. The inauguration marked only the second time in American history that the son of a former president also became president. More than 200 years ago, John Adams was elected the second president of the United States. His son, **John Quincy Adams**, later served as the sixth President.

George W. Bush had been in office for fewer than eight months when the most important event of his first term took place on September 11th, 2001. Americans call the event Nine-Eleven. On that morning,

19 Islamic extremists **hijacked** four American passenger airplanes. The planes were flying from the East Coast to California. The hijackers were from Middle Eastern countries. Each group included a trained pilot. American Airlines Flight 11 had left Boston, Massachusetts, when three terrorists seized control of the plane. Shortly before 9 o'clock in the morning, they crashed the plane into the North Tower of the **World Trade Center** in New York City. Another group seized United Airlines Flight 175 and crashed it into the World Trade Center's South Tower a few minutes later. The two giant skyscrapers stood in the heart of America's financial center. The planes exploded in fireballs that sent clouds of smoke pouring from the skyscrapers. Wreckage and ashes flew into the air. On that morning, each tower held between 5,000 and 7,000 people. Thousands of people were able to escape from the buildings. The

President George W. Bush

South Tower of the World Trade Center fell shortly before 10 o'clock. The North Tower collapsed about 30 minutes later. Within an hour the ruins of the two buildings were being called **Ground Zero**.

Other hijackers on United Airlines Flight 77 crashed the plane into the **Pentagon**, the Department of Defense headquarters near Washington, D. C. The plane exploded against a wall of the huge five-sided building where more than 20,000 people worked. The hijackers also seized United Airlines Flight 93. Some passengers found out about the terrorist attacks in New York and Washington through cell phone calls to their families. Several passengers and crew members tried to retake control of the plane. It crashed near the small town of Shanksville, Pennsylvania. Investigators later said the hijackers probably planned to attack the Capitol building or the White House in Washington.

The terrorist attacks on 9.11 were the most deadly in American history. Almost 3,000 people died. Most of the victims worked in the World Trade Center. They included many citizens of other countries. The victims also included 343 New York City firefighters and 23 city police officers. They died trying to save others.

Search and rescue operations began immediately. Hundreds of rescue workers recovered people and bodies from the wreckage. Aid was organized for victims and their families. President Bush stood in the wreckage of the World Trade Center and promised that the attacks would be answered. It took workers eight months to complete the cleanup of Ground Zero. Every day, thousands of people visited the area to see where the attack took place and to honor those who died there. Near Washington, D. C., people left flowers and messages near the heavily damaged wall of the Defense Department headquarters. One hundred eighty-four military service members and civilians died there.

New York City changed forever on that day. The attack destroyed a major part of the financial center of the city. It had a huge economic effect on the United States and world markets. The New York Stock Exchange was closed until September 17th. When it reopened, American stocks lost more than one trillion dollars in value for the week. For days after the attacks, most planes stopped flying. When normal flights began again, many people were too afraid to travel by air. The airline and travel industries suffered. Thousands of hotel workers and others lost their jobs. Many other businesses suffered as well. When people started flying again, they found it much more difficult because of increased security at airports. People across America experienced great shock, fear, sadness and loss. They could not understand why anyone would attack innocent Americans. They also felt a renewed love for their country. They put American flags on their houses, cars and businesses.

President Bush said **Osama bin Laden** and terrorists linked to his **al-Qaida** group plotted and carried out the attacks on 9.11. On September 20th, the President declared a War on Terror. The goals were to find and punish Osama bin Laden and to use economic and military actions to prevent the spread of terrorism.

Our war on terror begins with al-Qaida, but it does not end there. It will not end until every terrorist group of global reach has been found, stopped and defeated.

American officials said the **Taliban** administration in Afghanistan was sheltering Osama bin Laden. They said al-Qaida terrorists operated a training camp in Afghanistan under Taliban protection. President Bush demanded that the Taliban close the training camp and surrender Osama bin Laden. The Taliban refused. American and British airplanes launched attacks against the Taliban in Afghanistan on October 7th. The goals were to **oust** the Taliban, capture Osama bin Laden and destroy al-Qaida.

The bombers struck in and around the Afghan capital, **Kabul**. Ethnic tribal groups of the Afghan **Northern Alliance** then led a ground attack. By November the Taliban began to collapse in several provinces. Taliban forces fled Kabul and the city of **Kandahar**. The military offensive defeated the

Hijacked airliners were attacking the World Trade Center in New York on September 11th, 2001.

Taliban and ousted them from power. It also captured a number of Taliban fighters and al-Qaida terrorists. But the war in Afghanistan was not over, and the leader of al-Qaida, Osama bin Laden, had not been captured.

Some enemy fighters seized in Afghanistan were sent to a United States **Navy detention center** in **Guantanamo Bay**, Cuba. The United States government did not identify them as prisoners of war. Instead, the detainees were called "**unlawful enemy combatants**. " As such, they lacked some of the rights provided by an international treaty on conditions for war prisoners. The United States government also detained hundreds of foreign citizens. Most of these people had violated immigration laws. No terrorism charges were brought against them. Human rights activists and some legal experts protested the treatment of the prisoners. The activists said holding people in secret without trial violated the United States Constitution.

In October, Congress passed the U. S. A. **Patriot Act**. It provided the government with more power to get information about suspected terrorists in this country. Critics said the legislation invaded citizens' rights to privacy. Civil liberties groups charged that it gave law enforcement and other agencies too much power. After 9. 11, government agencies were criticized for not cooperating to gather intelligence that might have prevented the terrorist attacks. In 2002, a new **Department of Homeland Security** was created to strengthen defenses against terrorism. Twenty-two agencies were combined into a new department of about 200, 000 employees. The Department of Homeland Security was one of the major changes brought about by the attacks of 9. 11. Many Americans believed the attacks had changed their lives, their country, and the world, forever.

Where Were You When the World Stopped Turning
当地球停止转动时你在哪里

无论是对美国还是对世界来说，2001 年的"9·11"事件都是第二次世界大战以来最令人震惊的国际性事件。突如其来的恐怖袭击使两座摩天大楼一下子化为乌有，人才价值的损失更是难以用数字来估量，美国经济也一度处于瘫痪状态。世界各国政府和人民也从这次恐怖袭击中认识到，反恐怖主义活动将是人类社会一项长期、艰苦和复杂的斗争。

美国乡村音乐歌手阿兰·杰克逊（Alan Jackson）为"9·11"事件而感到身心交瘁，他打算写一首歌来表达自己的思想，但他又不愿意写一首表达简单爱国情绪的歌曲或者一首鼓吹复仇的歌曲；他只想要人们不要忘记那可怕而令人震撼的瞬间。2001 年 10 月的一天夜晚，他凌晨 4 时起身，创作了歌曲《当地球停止转动时你在哪里》。这也成为第一件直接以"9·11"事件作为主题的歌曲艺术作品。

Where were you when the world stopped turning that September day

Out in the yard with your wife and children

Working on some stage in **LA**

Did you stand there in shock at the site of

That black smoke rising against that blue sky

Did you shout out in anger

In fear for your neighbor

Or did you just sit down and cry

Did you weep for the children

Who lost their dear loved ones

And pray for the ones who don't know

Did you rejoice for the people who walked from the **rubble**

And sob for the ones left below

Did you burst out in pride

For **the red white and blue**

The heroes who died just doing what they do

Did you look up to heaven for some kind of answer

And look at yourself to what really matters

I'm just a singer of simple songs

I'm not a real political man

I watch CNN but I'm not sure I can tell you

The difference in Iraq and Iran

But I know Jesus and I talk to God

And I remember this from when I was young

Faith hope and love are some good things he gave us

And the greatest is love

Where were you when the world stopped turning that September day
Teaching a class full of innocent children
Driving down some cold **interstate**
Did you feel guilty cause you're a survivor
In a crowded room did you feel alone
Did you call up your mother and tell her you love her
Did you **dust off** that bible at home
Did you open your eyes and hope it never happened
Close your eyes and not go to sleep
Did you notice the sunset the first time in ages
Speak with some stranger on the street
Did you lay down at night and think of tomorrow
Go out and buy you a gun
Did you turn off that violent old movie you're watching
And turn on *I Love Lucy* **reruns**
Did you go to a church and hold hands with some stranger
Stand in line and give your own blood
Did you just stay home and cling tight to your family
Thank God you had somebody to love

I'm just a singer of simple songs
I'm not a real political man
I watch CNN but I'm not sure I can tell you
The difference in Iraq and Iran
But I know Jesus and I talk to God
And I remember this from when I was young
Faith hope and love are some good things he gave us
And the greatest is love

I'm just a singer of simple songs
I'm not a real political man
I watch CNN but I'm not sure I can tell you
The difference in Iraq and Iran
But I know Jesus and I talk to God
And I remember this from when I was young
Faith hope and love are some good things he gave us
And the greatest is love

The greatest is love
The greatest is love

Where were you when the world stopped turning on that September day

Words, Expressions and Notes

Dick Cheney 迪克·切尼（1941—），2000 年作为美国共和党副总统候选人与小布什一起在大选中获胜，出任美国副总统；2004 年再次当选美国副总统。

John Quincy Adams 约翰·昆西·亚当斯（1767—1848），美国第六任总统（1825—1829），美国第二任总统约翰·亚当斯之子

hijacked *v.* 劫持（飞机）

World Trade Center 世界贸易中心，位于纽约市曼哈顿岛，由两座并立的塔式摩天楼及 4 幢 7 层建筑组成，是纽约标志性建筑之一，在 2001 年 9 月 11 日发生的恐怖袭击事件中倒塌。

Ground Zero 原意为炸弹或核弹的爆心投影点，"9·11"事件后又指纽约世贸大厦遗址。

Pentagon 五角大楼，美国国防部所在建筑

Osama bin Laden 奥萨马·本·拉登（1957—），沙特阿拉伯人，世界恐怖组织头目，"9·11"事件的头号嫌疑犯。

al-Qaida 阿尔卡伊达，又称基地组织，是一个从事恐怖活动的团体，其头目是本·拉登。

Taliban 塔利班，阿富汗武装派别，1996 年在阿富汗内战时期攻占首都喀布尔，成立临时政府接管政权。塔利班全面推行伊斯兰法，实行极端宗教统治，禁止电影电视，严控娱乐活动，男人必须蓄须，女人必须蒙面，不允许妇女接受教育和就业，违者受到严厉惩罚。2001 年美国指责塔利班政权庇护恐怖分子而进攻阿富汗，塔利班政权随即垮台，但其抵抗活动一直没有停止。

oust *v.* 驱逐

Kabul 喀布尔，阿富汗首都

Northern Alliance 北方联盟，阿富汗内战时期与塔利班组织对立的武装派别

Kandahar 坎大哈，阿富汗东南部城市

Navy detention center （美国）海军拘留中心

Guantanamo Bay （古巴）关塔那摩湾，有美国军事基地。

unlawful enemy combatants 非法敌军战斗人员

Patriot Act 爱国者法案

Department of Homeland Security 国土安全部

LA = Los Angeles 洛杉矶

rubble *n.* 瓦砾

the red white and blue （此处指）美国国旗

interstate *n.* 州际公路

dust off 拭去灰尘

I Love Lucy 《我爱露茜》，美国 20 世纪 50 年代最受欢迎的电视连续剧

reruns *n.* 重播

Questions for Comprehension and Discussion

1. What happened on September 11th, 2001 in the USA?
2. What happened on the plane of the United Airlines Flight 93 before it crashed to the ground?
3. What did the American people experience in the event of 9. 11? And what did they feel for their country?
4. What were the goals of President George Bush's War on Terror?
5. Is the War on Terror successful? Why or why not?
6. Why is it said that the attacks of 9. 11 have changed America and the world? Do you really think so? Why?

APPENDIX A

Declaration of Independence

When in the Course of human events it becomes necessary for one people to dissolve the political bands which have connected them with another and to assume among the powers of the earth, the separate and equal station to which the Laws of Nature and of Nature's God entitle them, a decent respect to the opinions of mankind requires that they should declare the causes which impel them to the separation.

We hold these truths to be self-evident, that all men are created equal, that they are endowed by their Creator with certain unalienable Rights, that among these are Life, Liberty and the pursuit of Happiness. That to secure these rights, Governments are instituted among Men, deriving their just powers from the consent of the governed, That whenever any Form of Government becomes destructive of these ends, it is the Right of the People to alter or to abolish it, and to institute new Government, laying its foundation on such principles and organizing its powers in such form, as to them shall seem most likely to effect their Safety and Happiness. Prudence, indeed, will dictate that Governments long established should not be changed for light and transient causes; and accordingly all experience hath shown that mankind are more disposed to suffer, while evils are sufferable than to right themselves by abolishing the forms to which they are accustomed. But when a long train of abuses and usurpations, pursuing invariably the same Object evinces a design to reduce them under absolute Despotism, it is their right, it is their duty, to throw off such Government, and to provide new Guards for their future security. —Such has been the patient sufferance of these Colonies; and such is now the necessity which constrains them to alter their former Systems of Government. The history of the present King of Great Britain is a history of repeated injuries and usurpations, all having in direct object the establishment of an absolute Tyranny over these States. To prove this, let Facts be submitted to a candid world.

He has refused his Assent to Laws, the most wholesome and necessary for the public good.

He has forbidden his Governors to pass Laws of immediate and pressing importance, unless suspended in their operation till his Assent should be obtained; and when so suspended, he has utterly neglected to attend to them.

He has refused to pass other Laws for the accommodation of large districts of people, unless those people would relinquish the right of Representation in the Legislature, a right inestimable to them and formidable to tyrants only.

He has called together legislative bodies at places unusual, uncomfortable, and distant from the depository of their Public Records, for the sole purpose of fatiguing them into compliance with his measures.

He has dissolved Representative Houses repeatedly, for opposing with manly firmness his invasions on the rights of the people.

He has refused for a long time, after such dissolutions, to cause others to be elected, whereby the Legislative Powers, incapable of Annihilation, have returned to the People at large for their exercise; the State remaining in the mean time exposed to all the dangers of invasion from without, and convulsions within.

He has endeavoured to prevent the population of these States; for that purpose obstructing the Laws for Naturalization of Foreigners; refusing to pass others to encourage their migrations hither, and raising the conditions of new Appropriations of Lands.

He has obstructed the Administration of Justice by refusing his Assent to Laws for establishing Judiciary Powers.

He has made Judges dependent on his Will alone for the tenure of their offices, and the amount and payment of their salaries.

He has erected a multitude of New Offices, and sent hither swarms of Officers to harass our people and eat out their substance.

He has kept among us, in times of peace, Standing Armies without the Consent of our legislatures.

He has affected to render the Military independent of and superior to the Civil Power.

He has combined with others to subject us to a jurisdiction foreign to our constitution, and unacknowledged by our laws; giving his Assent to their Acts of pretended Legislation:

For quartering large bodies of armed troops among us:

For protecting them, by a mock Trial from punishment for any Murders which they should commit on the Inhabitants of these States:

For cutting off our Trade with all parts of the world:

For imposing Taxes on us without our Consent:

For depriving us in many cases, of the benefit of Trial by Jury:

For transporting us beyond Seas to be tried for pretended offences:

For abolishing the free System of English Laws in a neighbouring Province, establishing therein an Arbitrary government, and enlarging its Boundaries so as to render it at once an example and fit instrument for introducing the same absolute rule into these Colonies:

For taking away our Charters, abolishing our most valuable Laws and altering fundamentally the Forms of our Governments:

For suspending our own Legislatures, and declaring themselves invested with Power to legislate for us in all cases whatsoever.

He has abdicated Government here, by declaring us out of his Protection and waging War against us.

He has plundered our seas, ravaged our coasts, burnt our towns, and destroyed the lives of our people.

He is at this time transporting large Armies of foreign Mercenaries to compleat the works of death, desolation, and tyranny, already begun with circumstances of Cruelty & perfidy scarcely paralleled in the most barbarous ages, and totally unworthy the Head of a civilized nation.

He has constrained our fellow Citizens taken Captive on the high Seas to bear Arms against their Country, to become the executioners of their friends and Brethren, or to fall themselves by their Hands.

He has excited domestic insurrections amongst us, and has endeavoured to bring on the inhabitants of our frontiers, the merciless Indian Savages whose known rule of warfare, is an undistinguished destruction of all ages, sexes and conditions.

In every stage of these Oppressions We have Petitioned for Redress in the most humble terms: Our repeated Petitions have been answered only by repeated injury. A Prince, whose character is thus marked by every act which may define a Tyrant, is unfit to be the ruler of a free people.

Nor have We been wanting in attentions to our British brethren. We have warned them from time to time of attempts by their legislature to extend an unwarrantable jurisdiction over us. We have reminded them of the circumstances of our emigration and settlement here. We have appealed to their native justice and magnanimity, and we have conjured them by the ties of our common kindred to disavow these usurpations, which would inevitably interrupt our connections and correspondence. They too have been deaf to the voice of justice and of consanguinity. We must, therefore, acquiesce in the necessity, which denounces our Separation, and hold them, as we hold the rest of mankind, Enemies in War, in Peace Friends.

We, therefore, the Representatives of the United States of America, in General Congress, Assembled, appealing to the Supreme Judge of the world for the rectitude of our intentions, do, in the Name, and by Authority of the good People of these Colonies, solemnly publish and declare, That these united Colonies are, and of Right ought to be Free and Independent States, that they are Absolved from all Allegiance to the British Crown, and that all political connection between them and the State of Great Britain, is and ought to be totally dissolved; and that as Free and Independent States, they have full Power to levy War, conclude Peace, contract Alliances, establish Commerce, and to do all other Acts and Things which Independent States may of right do. And for the support of this Declaration, with a firm reliance on the protection of Divine Providence, we mutually pledge to each other our Lives, our Fortunes, and our sacred Honor.

APPENDIX B

Constitution of the United States

(Ratified in 1788)

We the People of the United States, in Order to form a more perfect Union, establish Justice, insure domestic Tranquility, provide for the common defence, promote the general Welfare, and secure the Blessings of Liberty to ourselves and our Posterity, do ordain and establish this CONSTITUTION for the United States of America.

Article I

(LEGISLATURE)

Section 1.   All legislative Powers herein granted shall be vested in a Congress of the United States, which shall consist of a Senate and House of Representatives.

(House of Representatives)

Section 2.   The House of Representatives shall be composed of Members chosen every second Year by the People of the several States, and the Electors in each State shall have the Qualifications requisite for Electors of the most numerous Branch of the State Legislature.

(Qualifications for Representatives)

No Person shall be a Representative who shall not have attained to the Age of twenty five Years, and been seven Years a Citizen of the United States, and who shall not, when elected, be an Inhabitant of that State in which he shall be chosen.

(Method of Apportionment)

Representatives and direct Taxes shall be apportioned among the several States which may be included within this Union, according to their respective Numbers, which shall be determined by adding to the whole Number of free Persons, including those bound to Service for a Term of Years, and excluding Indians not taxed, three fifths of all other Persons. The actual Enumeration shall be made within three Years after the first Meeting of the Congress of the United States, and within every subsequent Term of ten Years, in such Manner as they shall by Law direct. The Number of Representatives shall not exceed one for every thirty Thousand, but each State shall have at Least one Representative; and until such enumeration shall be made, the State of New Hampshire shall be entitled to chuse three, Massachusetts eight, Rhode-Island and Providence Plantations one, Connecticut five, New York six, New Jersey four, Pennsylvania eight, Delaware one, Maryland six, Virginia ten, North Carolina five, South Carolina five and Georgia three.

(Vacancies)

When vacancies happen in the Representation from any State, the Executive Authority thereof shall issue Writs of Election to fill such Vacancies.

(Rules of the House, Impeachment)

The House of Representatives shall chuse their Speaker and other Officers; and shall have the sole Power of Impeachment.

(Senators)

Section 3.   The Senate of the United States shall be composed of two Senators from each State, chosen by the

Legislature thereof, for six Years; and each Senator shall have one Vote.

Immediately after they shall be assembled in Consequence of the first Election, they shall be divided as equally as may be into three Classes. The Seats of the Senators of the first Class shall be vacated at the Expiration of the second Year, of the second Class at the Expiration of the fourth Year, and of the third Class at the Expiration of the sixth Year, so that one third may be chosen every second Year; and if Vacancies happen by Resignation, or otherwise, during the Recess of the Legislature of any State, the Executive thereof may make temporary Appointments until the next Meeting of the Legislature, which shall then fill such Vacancies.

(Qualifications of Senators)

No person shall be a Senator who shall not have attained to the Age of thirty Years, and been nine Years a Citizen of the United States, and who shall not, when elected, be an Inhabitant of that State for which he shall be chosen.

(Vice President)

The Vice President of the United States shall be President of the Senate, but shall have no Vote, unless they be equally divided.

The Senate shall chuse their other Officers, and also a President pro tempore, in the absence of the Vice President, or when he shall exercise the Office of President of the United States.

(Impeachments)

The Senate shall have the sole Power to try all Impeachments. When sitting for that Purpose, they shall be on Oath or Affirmation. When the President of the United States is tried, the Chief Justice shall preside: And no Person shall be convicted without the Concurrence of two thirds of the Members present.

Judgment in Cases of Impeachment shall not extend further than to removal from Office, and disqualification to hold and enjoy any Office of honor, Trust or Profit under the United States: but the Party convicted shall nevertheless be liable and subject to Indictment, Trial, Judgment and Punishment, according to Law.

(Elections)

Section 4.   The Times, Places and Manner of holding Elections for Senators and Representatives, shall be prescribed in each State by the Legislature thereof; but the Congress may at any time by Law make or alter such Regulations, except as to the Place of Chusing Senators.

(Sessions)

The Congress shall assemble at least once in every Year, and such Meeting shall be on the first Monday in December, unless they shall by Law appoint a different Day.

(Proceeding of the House and the Senate)

Section 5.   Each House shall be the Judge of the Elections, Returns and Qualifications of its own Members, and a Majority of each shall constitute a Quorum to do Business; but a smaller number may adjourn from day to day, and may be authorized to compel the Attendance of absent Members, in such Manner, and under such Penalties as each House may provide.

Each House may determine the Rules of its Proceedings, punish its Members for disorderly Behavior, and, with the Concurrence of two thirds, expel a Member.

Each House shall keep a Journal of its Proceedings, and from time to time publish the same, excepting such Parts as may in their Judgment require Secrecy; and the Yeas and Nays of the Members of either House on any question shall, at the Desire of one fifth of those Present, be entered on the Journal.

Neither House, during the Session of Congress, shall, without the Consent of the other, adjourn for more than three days, nor to any other Place than that in which the two Houses shall be sitting.

(Members' Compensation and Privileges)

Section 6.   The Senators and Representatives shall receive a Compensation for their Services, to be ascertained by Law, and paid out of the Treasury of the United States. They shall in all Cases, except Treason, Felony and Breach of the Peace, be privileged from Arrest during their Attendance at the Session of their respective Houses, and in going to and returning from the same; and for any Speech or Debate in either House, they shall not be questioned in any other Place.

No Senator or Representative shall, during the Time for which he was elected, be appointed to any civil Office under the Authority of the United States which shall have been created, or the Emoluments whereof shall have been increased during such time; and no Person holding any Office under the United States, shall be a Member of either House during his Continuance in Office.

(Money Bills)

Section 7.   All bills for raising Revenue shall originate in the House of Representatives; but the Senate may propose or concur with Amendments as on other Bills.

(Presidential Veto and Congressional Power to Override)

Every Bill which shall have passed the House of Representatives and the Senate, shall, before it become a Law, be presented to the President of the United States; If he approve he shall sign it, but if not he shall return it, with his Objections to that House in which it shall have originated, who shall enter the Objections at large on their Journal, and proceed to reconsider it. If after such Reconsideration two thirds of that House shall agree to pass the Bill, it shall be sent, together with the Objections, to the other House, by which it shall likewise be reconsidered, and if approved by two thirds of that House, it shall become a Law. But in all such Cases the Votes of both Houses shall be determined by Yeas and Nays, and the Names of the Persons voting for and against the Bill shall be entered on the Journal of each House respectively. If any Bill shall not be returned by the President within ten Days (Sundays excepted) after it shall have been presented to him, the Same shall be a Law, in like Manner as if he had signed it, unless the Congress by their Adjournment prevent its Return, in which Case it shall not be a Law.

Every Order, Resolution, or Vote to which the Concurrence of the Senate and House of Representatives may be necessary (except on a question of Adjournment) shall be presented to the President of the United States; and before the Same shall take Effect, shall be approved by him, or being disapproved by him, shall be repassed by two thirds of the Senate and House of Representatives, according to the Rules and Limitations prescribed in the Case of a Bill.

(Congressional Powers)

Section 8.   The Congress shall have Power To lay and collect Taxes, Duties, Imposts and Excises, to pay the Debts and provide for the common Defence and general Welfare of the United States; but all Duties, Imposts and Excises shall be uniform throughout the United States;

To borrow money on the credit of the United States;

To regulate Commerce with foreign Nations, and among the several States, and with the Indian Tribes;

To establish an uniform Rule of Naturalization, and uniform Laws on the subject of Bankruptcies throughout the United States;

To coin Money, regulate the Value thereof, and of foreign Coin, and fix the Standard of Weights and Measures;

To provide for the Punishment of counterfeiting the Securities and current Coin of the United States;

To establish Post Offices and Post Roads;

To promote the Progress of Science and useful Arts, by securing for limited Times to Authors and Inventors the exclusive Right to their respective Writings and Discoveries;

To constitute Tribunals inferior to the supreme Court;

To define and punish Piracies and Felonies committed on the high Seas, and Offenses against the Law of Nations;

To declare War, grant Letters of Marque and Reprisal, and make Rules concerning Captures on Land and Water;

To raise and support Armies, but no Appropriation of Money to that Use shall be for a longer Term than two Years;

To provide and maintain a Navy;

To make Rules for the Government and Regulation of the land and naval Forces;

To provide for calling forth the Militia to execute the Laws of the Union, suppress Insurrections and repel Invasions;

To provide for organizing, arming, and disciplining the Militia, and for governing such Part of them as may be employed in the Service of the United States, reserving to the States respectively, the Appointment of the Officers, and the Authority of training the Militia according to the discipline prescribed by Congress;

To exercise exclusive Legislation in all Cases whatsoever, over such District (not exceeding ten Miles square) as may, by Cession of particular States, and the acceptance of Congress, become the Seat of the Government of the United States, and to exercise like Authority over all Places purchased by the Consent of the Legislature of the State in which the Same shall be, for the Erection of Forts, Magazines, Arsenals, dock-Yards, and other needful Buildings;—And

To make all Laws which shall be necessary and proper for carrying into Execution the foregoing Powers, and all other Powers vested by this Constitution in the Government of the United States, or in any Department or Officer thereof.

(Limits on Congressional Power)

Section 9.   The Migration or Importation of such Persons as any of the States now existing shall think proper to admit, shall not be prohibited by the Congress prior to the Year one thousand eight hundred and eight, but a tax or duty may be imposed on such Importation, not exceeding ten dollars for each Person.

The privilege of the Writ of Habeas Corpus shall not be suspended, unless when in Cases of Rebellion or Invasion the public Safety may require it.

No Bill of Attainder or ex post facto Law shall be passed.

No capitation, or other direct, Tax shall be laid, unless in Proportion to the Census or Enumeration herein before directed to be taken.

No Tax or Duty shall be laid on Articles exported from any State.

No Preference shall be given by any Regulation of Commerce or Revenue to the Ports of one State over those of another: nor shall Vessels bound to, or from, one State, be obliged to enter, clear, or pay Duties in another.

No Money shall be drawn from the Treasury, but in Consequence of Appropriations made by Law; and a regular Statement and Account of the Receipts and Expenditures of all public Money shall be published from time to time.

No Title of Nobility shall be granted by the United States: And no Person holding any Office of Profit or Trust under them, shall, without the Consent of the Congress, accept of any present, Emolument, Office, or Title, of any kind whatever, from any King, Prince or foreign State.

(Limits on Powers of the States)

Section 10.   No State shall enter into any Treaty, Alliance, or Confederation; grant Letters of Marque and Reprisal; coin Money; emit Bills of Credit; make any Thing but gold and silver Coin a Tender in Payment of Debts; pass any Bill of Attainder, ex post facto Law, or Law impairing the Obligation of Contracts, or grant any Title of Nobility.

No State shall, without the Consent of the Congress, lay any Imposts or Duties on Imports or Exports, except what may be absolutely necessary for executing its inspection Laws: and the net Produce of all Duties and Imposts, laid by any State on Imports or Exports, shall be for the Use of the Treasury of the United States; and all such Laws shall be subject to the Revision and Control of the Congress.

No State shall, without the Consent of Congress, lay any duty of Tonnage, keep Troops, or Ships of War in time of Peace, enter into any Agreement or Compact with another State, or with a foreign Power, or engage in War, unless actually invaded, or in such imminent Danger as will not admit of delay.

Article II   (EXECUTIVE)

(President)

Section 1.   The executive Power shall be vested in a President of the United States of America. He shall hold his Office during the Term of four Years, and, together with the Vice President chosen for the same Term, be elected, as follows:

(Election of President)

Each State shall appoint, in such Manner as the Legislature thereof may direct, a Number of

Electors, equal to the whole Number of Senators and Representatives to which the State may be entitled in the Congress: but no Senator or Representative, or Person holding an Office of Trust or Profit under the United States, shall be appointed an Elector.

(Electors)

The Electors shall meet in their respective States, and vote by Ballot for two persons, of whom one at least shall not lie an Inhabitant of the same State with themselves. And they shall make a List of all the Persons voted for, and of the Number of Votes for each; which List they shall sign and certify, and transmit sealed to the Seat of the Government of the United States, directed to the President of the Senate. The President of the Senate shall, in the Presence of the Senate and House of Representatives, open all the Certificates, and the Votes shall then be counted. The Person having the greatest Number of Votes shall be the President, if such Number be a Majority of the whole Number of Electors appointed; and if there be more than one who have such Majority, and have an equal Number of Votes, then the House of Representatives shall immediately chuse by Ballot one of them for President; and if no Person have a Majority, then from the five highest on the List the said House shall in like Manner chuse the President. But in chusing the President, the Votes shall be taken by States, the Representation from each State having one Vote; a quorum for this Purpose shall consist of a Member or Members from two-thirds of the States, and a Majority of all the States shall be necessary to a Choice. In every Case, after the Choice of the President, the Person having the greatest Number of Votes of the Electors shall be the Vice President. But if there should remain two or more who have equal Votes, the Senate shall chuse from them by Ballot the Vice President.

The Congress may determine the Time of chusing the Electors, and the Day on which they shall give their Votes; which Day shall be the same throughout the United States.

(Qualifications of President)

No person except a natural born Citizen, or a Citizen of the United States, at the time of the Adoption of this Constitution, shall be eligible to the Office of President; neither shall any Person be eligible to that Office who shall not have attained to the Age of thirty-five Years, and been fourteen Years a Resident within the United States.

(Succession to the Presidency)

In Case of the Removal of the President from Office, or of his Death, Resignation, or Inability to discharge the Powers and Duties of the said Office, the same shall devolve on the Vice President, and the Congress may by Law provide for the Case of Removal, Death, Resignation or Inability, both of the President and Vice President, declaring what Officer shall then act as President, and such Officer shall act accordingly, until the Disability be removed, or a President shall be elected.

(Compensation)

The President shall, at stated Times, receive for his Services, a Compensation, which shall neither be increased nor diminished during the Period for which he shall have been elected, and he shall not receive within that Period any other Emolument from the United States, or any of them.

(Oath of Office)

Before he enters on the Execution of his Office, he shall take the following Oath or Affirmation: "I do solemnly swear (or affirm) that I will faithfully execute the Office of President of the United States, and will to the best of my Ability, preserve, protect and defend the Constitution of the United States. "

(Powers of the President)

Section 2. The President shall be Commander in Chief of the Army and Navy of the United States, and of the Militia of the several States, when called into the actual Service of the United States; he may require the Opinion, in writing, of the principal Officer in each of the executive Departments, upon any subject relating to the Duties of their respective Offices, and he shall have Power to Grant Reprieves and Pardons for Offenses against the United States, except in Cases of Impeachment.

(Making of Treaties)

He shall have Power, by and with the Advice and Consent of the Senate, to make Treaties, provided two thirds of the Senators present concur; and he shall nominate, and by and with the Advice and Consent of the Senate, shall appoint Ambassadors, other public Ministers and Consuls, Judges of the supreme Court, and all other Officers of the United States, whose Appointments are not herein otherwise provided for, and which shall be established by Law: but the Congress may by Law vest the Appointment of such inferior Officers, as they think proper, in the President alone, in the Courts of Law, or in the Heads of Departments.

(Vacancies)

The President shall have Power to fill up all Vacancies that may happen during the Recess of the Senate, by granting Commissions which shall expire at the End of their next Session.

(Additional Duties and Powers)

Section 3. He shall from time to time give to the Congress Information of the State of the Union, and recommend to their Consideration such Measures as he shall judge necessary and expedient; he may, on extraordinary Occasions, convene both Houses, or either of them, and in Case of Disagreement between them, with Respect to the Time of Adjournment, he may adjourn them to such Time as he shall think proper; he shall receive Ambassadors and other public Ministers; he shall take Care that the Laws be faithfully executed, and shall Commission all the Officers of the United States.

(Impeachment)

Section 4. The President, Vice President and all civil Officers of the United States, shall be removed from Office on Impeachment for, and Conviction of, Treason, Bribery, or other high Crimes and Misdemeanors.

Article III   (JUDICIARY)

(Courts, Judges, Compensation)

Section 1. The judicial Power of the United States, shall be vested in one supreme Court, and in such inferior Courts as the Congress may from time to time ordain and establish. The Judges, both of the supreme and inferior Courts, shall hold their Offices during good Behavior, and shall, at stated Times, receive for their Services a Compensation which shall not be diminished during their Continuance in Office.

(Jurisdiction)

Section 2. The judicial Power shall extend to all Cases, in Law and Equity, arising under this Constitution, the Laws of the United States, and Treaties made, or which shall be made, under their Authority; to all Cases affecting Ambassadors, other public Ministers and Consuls; to all Cases of admiralty and maritime Jurisdiction; to Controversies to which the United

States shall be a Party; to Controversies between two or more States; between a State and Citizens of another State; between Citizens of different States; between Citizens of the same State claiming Lands under Grants of different States, and between a State, or the Citizens thereof, and foreign States, Citizens or Subjects.

In all Cases affecting Ambassadors, other public Ministers and Consuls, and those in which a State shall be Party, the supreme Court shall have original Jurisdiction. In all the other Cases before mentioned, the supreme Court shall have appellate Jurisdiction, both as to Law and Fact, with such Exceptions, and under such Regulations as the Congress shall make.

(Trial by Jury)

The Trial of all Crimes, except in Cases of Impeachment, shall be by Jury; and such Trial shall be held in the State where the said Crimes shall have been committed; but when not committed within any State, the Trial shall be at such Place or Places as the Congress may by Law have directed.

(Treason)

Section 3.   Treason against the United States, shall consist only in levying War against them, or in adhering to their Enemies, giving them Aid and Comfort. No Person shall be convicted of Treason unless on the Testimony of two Witnesses to the same overt Act, or on Confession in open Court.

The Congress shall have power to declare the Punishment of Treason, but no Attainder of Treason shall work Corruption of Blood, or Forfeiture except during the Life of the Person attainted.

Article IV   (FEDERAL SYSTEM)
Section 1.   Full Faith and Credit shall be given in each State to the public Acts, Records, and judicial Proceedings of every other State. And the Congress may by general Laws prescribe the Manner in which such Acts, Records and Proceedings shall be proved, and the Effect thereof.

(Privileges and Immunities of Citizens)

Section 2.   The Citizens of each State shall be entitled to all Privileges and Immunities of Citizens in the several States.

A Person charged in any State with Treason, Felony, or other Crime, who shall flee from Justice, and be found in another State, shall on demand of the executive Authority of the State from which he fled, be delivered up, to be removed to the State having Jurisdiction of the Crime.

No Person held to Service or Labour in one State, under the Laws thereof, escaping into another, shall, in Consequence of any Law or Regulation therein, be discharged from such Service or Labour, But shall be delivered up on Claim of the Party to whom such Service or Labour may be due.

(Admission and Formation of New States; Governing of Territories)

Section 3.   New States may be admitted by the Congress into this Union; but no new States shall be formed or erected within the Jurisdiction of any other State; nor any State be formed by the Junction of two or more States, or parts of States, without the Consent of the Legislatures of the States concerned as well as of the Congress.

The Congress shall have Power to dispose of and make all needful Rules and Regulations respecting the Territory or other Property belonging to the United States; and nothing in this Constitution shall be so construed as to Prejudice any Claims of the United States, or of any particular State.

(Federal Protection of the States)

Section 4.   The United States shall guarantee to every State in this Union a Republican Form of Government, and shall protect each of them against Invasion; and on Application of the Legislature, or of the Executive (when the Legislature cannot be convened) against domestic Violence.

Article V   (AMENDMENTS)

The Congress, whenever two thirds of both Houses shall deem it necessary, shall propose Amendments to this Constitution, or, on the Application of the Legislatures of two thirds of the several States, shall call a Convention for proposing Amendments, which, in either Case, shall be valid to all Intents and Purposes, as part of this Constitution, when ratified by the Legislatures of three fourths of the several States, or by Conventions in three fourths thereof, as the one or the other Mode of Ratification may be proposed by the Congress; Provided that no Amendment which may be made prior to the Year One thousand eight hundred and eight shall in any Manner affect the first and fourth Clauses in the Ninth Section of the first Article; and that no State, without its Consent, shall be deprived of its equal Suffrage in the Senate.

Article VI   (CONSTITUTION AS SUPREME LAW)

All Debts contracted and Engagements entered into, before the Adoption of this Constitution, shall be as valid against the United States under this Constitution, as under the Confederation.

This Constitution, and the Laws of the United States which shall be made in Pursuance thereof; and all Treaties made, or which shall be made, under the Authority of the United States, shall be the supreme Law of the Land; and the Judges in every State shall be bound thereby, any Thing in the Constitution or Laws of any State to the Contrary notwithstanding.

The Senators and Representatives before mentioned, and the Members of the several State Legislatures, and all executive and judicial Officers, both of the United States and of the several States, shall be bound by Oath or Affirmation, to support this Constitution; but no religious Test shall ever be required as a Qualification to any Office or public Trust under the United States.

Article VII   (RATIFICATION)

The Ratification of the Conventions of nine States, shall be sufficient for the Establishment of this Constitution between the States so ratifying the Same.

(Signatures)

Done in Convention by the Unanimous Consent of the States present the Seventeenth Day of September in the Year of our Lord one thousand seven hundred and Eighty seven and of the Independence of the United States of America the Twelfth. In Witness whereof We have hereunto subscribed our Names.

Amendment I [1791]   (FREEDOMS)

(Speech, Press, Assembly, and Petition)

Congress shall make no law respecting an establishment of religion, or prohibiting the free exercise thereof; or abridging the freedom of speech, or of the press; or the right of the people peaceably to assemble, and to petition the Government for a redress of grievances.

Amendment II [1791]   (RIGHT TO BEAR ARMS)

A well regulated Militia, being necessary to the security of a free State, the right of the people to keep and bear Arms, shall not be infringed.

Amendment III [1791]   (QUARTERING OF SOLDIERS)

No Soldier shall, in time of peace be quartered in any house, without the consent of the Owner, nor in time of war, but in a manner to be prescribed by law.

Amendment IV [1791]   (FREEDOM OF PERSONS)

(Warrants, Searches, and Seizure)

The right of the people to be secure in their persons, houses, papers, and effects, against unreasonable searches and seizures, shall not be violated, and no Warrants shall issue, but upon probable cause, supported by Oath or affirmation, and particularly describing the place to be searched, and the persons or things to be seized.

Amendment V [1791] (CAPITAL CRIMES)

(Protection of the Accused; Compensation)

No person shall be held to answer for a capital, or otherwise infamous crime, unless on a presentment or indictment of a Grand Jury, except in cases arising in the land or naval forces, or in the Militia, when in actual service in time of War or public danger; nor shall any person be subject for the same offense to be twice put in jeopardy of life or limb; nor shall be compelled in any criminal case to be a witness against himself, nor be deprived of life, liberty, or property, without due process of law; nor shall private property be taken for public use, without just compensation.

Amendment VI [1791] (TRIAL BY JURY)

(Accusation, Witnesses, Counsel)

In all criminal prosecutions, the accused shall enjoy the right to a speedy and public trial, by an impartial jury of the State and district wherein the crime shall have been committed, which district shall have been previously ascertained by law, and to be informed of the nature and cause of the accusation; to be confronted with the witnesses against him; to have compulsory process for obtaining witnesses in his favor, and to have the Assistance of Counsel for his defence.

Amendment VII [1791] (CIVIL LAW)

In Suits at common law, where the value in controversy shall exceed twenty dollars, the right of trial by jury shall be preserved, and no fact tried by a jury, shall be otherwise reexamined in any Court of the United States, than according to the rules of the common law.

Amendment VIII [1791] (BAILS, FINES, AND PUNISHMENTS)

Excessive bail shall not be required, nor excessive fines imposed, nor cruel and unusual punishments inflicted.

Amendment IX [1791] (RIGHTS RETAINED BY THE PEOPLE)

The enumeration in the Constitution, of certain rights, shall not be construed to deny or disparage others retained by the people.

Amendment X [1791] (RIGHTS RESERVED TO THE STATES)

The powers not delegated to the United States by the Constitution, nor prohibited by it to the States, are reserved to the States respectively, or to the people.

Amendment XI [1798] (JURISDICTIONAL LIMITS)

The Judicial power of the United States shall not be construed to extend to any suit in law or equity, commenced or prosecuted against one of the United States by Citizens of another State, or by Citizens or Subjects of any Foreign State.

Amendment XII [1804] (ELECTORAL COLLEGE)

The Electors shall meet in their respective states, and vote by ballot for President and Vice President, one of whom, at least, shall not be an inhabitant of the same state with themselves; they shall name in their ballots the person voted for as President, and in distinct ballots the person voted for as Vice President, and they shall make distinct lists of all persons voted for as President, and of all persons voted for as Vice President and of the number of votes for each, which lists they shall sign and certify, and transmit sealed to the seat of the government of the United States, directed to the President of the Senate;—The President of the Senate shall, in the presence of the Senate and House of Representatives, open all the certificates and the votes shall then be counted;—The person having the greatest Number of votes for President, shall be the

President, if such number be a majority of the whole number of Electors appointed; and if no person have such majority, then from the persons having the highest numbers not exceeding three on the list of those voted for as President, the House of Representatives shall choose immediately, by ballot, the President. But in choosing the President, the votes shall be taken by states, the representation from each state having one vote; a quorum for this purpose shall consist of a member or members from two-thirds of the states, and a majority of all the states shall be necessary to a choice. And if the House of Representatives shall not choose a President whenever the right of choice shall devolve upon them, before the fourth day of March next following, then the Vice President shall act as President, as in the case of the death or other constitutional disability of the President. —The person having the greatest number of votes as Vice President, shall be the Vice President, if such number be a majority of the whole number of Electors appointed, and if no person have a majority, then from the two highest numbers on the list, the Senate shall choose the Vice President; a quorum for the purpose shall consist of two-thirds of the whole number of Senators, and a majority of the whole number shall be necessary to a choice. But no person constitutionally ineligible to the office of President shall be eligible to that of Vice President of the United States.

Amendment XIII [1865]   (ABOLITION OF SLAVERY)

Section 1.   Neither slavery nor involuntary servitude, except as a punishment for crime whereof the party shall have been duly convicted, shall exist within the United States, or any place subject to their jurisdiction.

Section 2.   Congress shall have power to enforce this article by appropriate legislation.

Amendment XIV [1868]   (CITIZENSHIP)

(Due Process of Law)

Section 1.   All persons born or naturalized in the United States, and subject to the jurisdiction thereof, are citizens of the United States and of the State wherein they reside. No State shall make or enforce any law which shall abridge the privileges or immunities of citizens of the United States; nor shall any State deprive any person of life, liberty, or property, without due process of law; nor deny to any person within its jurisdiction the equal protection of the laws.

(Apportionment; Right to Vote)

Section 2.   Representatives shall be apportioned among the several States according to their respective numbers, counting the whole number of persons in each State, excluding Indians not taxed. But when the right to vote at any election for the choice of electors for President and Vice President of the United States, Representatives in Congress, the Executive and Judicial officers of a State, or the members of the Legislature thereof, is denied to any of the male inhabitants of such State, being twenty-one years of age, and citizens of the United States, or in any way abridged, except for participation in rebellion, or other crime, the basis of representation therein shall be reduced in the proportion which the number of such male citizens shall bear to the whole number of male citizens twenty-one years of age in such State.

(Disqualification for Office)

Section 3.   No person shall be a Senator or Representative in Congress, or elector of President and Vice President, or hold any office, civil or military, under the United States, or under any State, who, having previously taken an oath, as a member of Congress, or as an officer of the United States, or as a member of any State legislature, or as an executive or judicial officer of any State, to support the Constitution of the United States, shall have engaged in insurrection or rebellion against the same, or given aid or comfort to the enemies thereof. But Congress may by a vote of two-thirds of each House, remove such disability.

(Public Debt)

Section 4.   The validity of the public debt of the United States, authorized by law, including debts incurred for payment of pensions and bounties for services in suppressing insurrection or rebellion, shall not be questioned. But neither the United States nor any State shall assume or pay any debt or obligation incurred in aid of insurrection or rebellion against the United States, or any claim for the loss or emancipation of any slave; but all such debts, obligations and claims shall be held illegal and void.

Section 5.   The Congress shall have power to enforce, by appropriate legislation, the provisions of this article.

Amendment XV [1870]   (RIGHT TO VOTE)

Section 1.   The right of citizens of the United States to vote shall not be denied or abridged by the United States or by any State on account of race, color, or previous condition of servitude.

Section 2.   The Congress shall have power to enforce this article by appropriate legislation.

Amendment XVI [1913]   (INCOME TAX)

The Congress shall have power to lay and collect taxes on incomes, from whatever source derived, without apportionment among the several States, and without regard to any census or enumeration.

Amendment XVII [1913]   (SENATORS)
                                                                         (Election)

The Senate of the United States shall be composed of two Senators from each State, elected by the people thereof, for six years; and each Senator shall have one vote. The electors in each State shall have the qualifications requisite for electors of the most numerous branch of the State legislatures.

(Vacancies)

When vacancies happen in the representation of any State in the Senate, the executive authority of such State shall issue writs of election to fill such vacancies: Provided, That the legislature of any State may empower the executive thereof to make temporary appointments until the people fill the vacancies by election as the legislature may direct.

This amendment shall not be so construed as to affect the election or term of any Senator chosen before it becomes valid as part of the Constitution.

Amendment XVIII [1919]   (PROHIBITION)

Section 1.   After one year from the ratification of this article the manufacture, sale, or transportation of intoxicating liquors within, the importation thereof into, or the exportation thereof from the United States and all territory subject to the jurisdiction thereof for beverage purposes is hereby prohibited.

Section 2.   The Congress and the several States shall have concurrent power to enforce this article by appropriate legislation.

Section 3.   This article shall be inoperative unless it shall have been ratified as an amendment to the Constitution by the legislatures of the several States, as provided in the Constitution, within seven years from the date of the submission hereof to the States by the Congress.

Amendment XIX [1920]   (FEMALE SUFFRAGE)

The right of citizens of the United States to vote shall not be denied or abridged by the United States or by any State on account of sex.

Congress shall have power to enforce this article by appropriate legislation.

Amendment XX [1933]   (TERMS OF OFFICE)

Section 1.   The terms of the President and Vice President shall end at noon on the 20th day of January, and the terms of Senators and Representatives at noon on the 3d day of January, of the years in which such terms would have ended if this article had not been ratified; and the terms of their successors shall then begin.

Section 2.   The Congress shall assemble at least once in every year, and such meeting shall begin at noon on the 3d day of January, unless they shall by law appoint a different day.

Section 3. If, at the time fixed for the beginning of the term of the President, the President elect shall have died, the Vice President elect shall become President. If a President shall not have been chosen before the time fixed for the beginning of his term, or if the President elect shall have failed to qualify, then the Vice President elect shall act as President until a President shall have qualified; and the Congress may by law provide for the case wherein neither a President elect nor a Vice President elect shall have qualified, declaring who shall then act as President, or the manner in which one who is to act shall be selected, and such person shall act accordingly until a President or Vice President shall have qualified.

Section 4. The Congress may by law provide for the case of the death of any of the persons from whom the House of Representatives may choose a President whenever the right of choice shall have devolved upon them, and for the case of the death of any of the persons from whom the Senate may choose a Vice President whenever the right of choice shall have devolved upon them.

Section 5. Sections 1 and 2 shall take effect on the 15th day of October following the ratification of this article.

Section 6. This article shall be inoperative unless it shall have been ratified as an amendment to the Constitution by the legislatures of three-fourths of the several States within seven years from the date of its submission.

Amendment XXI [1933]   (REPEAL OF PROHIBITION)

Section 1. The eighteenth article of amendment to the Constitution of the United States is hereby repealed.

Section 2. The transportation or importation into any State, Territory, or possession of the United States for delivery or use therein of intoxicating liquors, in violation of the laws thereof, is hereby prohibited.

Section 3. The article shall be inoperative unless it shall have been ratified as an amendment to the Constitution by conventions in the several States, as provided in the Constitution, within seven years from the date of the submission hereof to the States by the Congress.

Amendment XXII [1951]   (TERM OF PRESIDENT)

Section 1. No person shall be elected to the office of the President more than twice, and no person who has held the office of President, or acted as President, for more than two years of a term to which some other person was elected President shall be elected to the office of the President more than once. But this Article shall not apply to any person holding the office of President, when this Article was proposed by the Congress, and shall not prevent any person who may be holding the office of President, or acting as President, during the term within which this Article becomes operative from holding the office of President or acting as President during the remainder of such term.

Section 2. This article shall be inoperative unless it shall have been ratified as an amendment to the Constitution by the legislatures of three-fourths of the several States within seven years from the date of its submission to the States by the Congress.

Amendment XXIII [1961]   (WASHINGTON D. C.)

(Enfranchisement of Voters in Federal Elections)

Section 1. The District constituting the seat of Government of the United States shall appoint in such manner as the Congress may direct:

A number of electors of President and Vice President equal to the whole number of Senators and Representatives in Congress to which the District would be entitled if it were a State, but in no event more than the least populous State; they shall be in addition to those appointed by the States, but they shall be considered, for the purposes of the election of President and Vice President, to be electors appointed by a State; and they shall meet in the District and perform such duties as provided by the twelfth article of amendment.

Section 2. The Congress shall have power to enforce this article by appropriate legislation.

Amendment XXIV [1964]   (POLL TAX)

Section 1. The right of citizens of the United States to vote in any primary or other election for President or Vice President, for electors for President or Vice President, or for Senator or Representative in Congress, shall not be denied or abridged by the United States or any State by reason of failure to pay any poll tax or other tax.

Section 2. The Congress shall have power to enforce this article by appropriate legislation.

Amendment XXV [1967]   (SUCCESSION)

Section 1. In case of the removal of the President from office or of his death or resignation, the Vice President shall become President.

Section 2. Whenever there is a vacancy in the office of the Vice President, the President shall nominate a Vice President who shall take office upon confirmation by a majority vote of both Houses of Congress.

Section 3. Whenever the President transmits to the President pro tempore of the Senate and the Speaker of the House of Representatives his written declaration that he is unable to discharge the powers and duties of his office, and until he transmits to them a written declaration to the contrary, such powers and duties shall be discharged by the Vice President as Acting President.

Section 4. Whenever the Vice President and a majority of either the principal officers of the executive departments or of such other body as Congress may by law provide, transmit to the President pro tempore of the Senate and the Speaker of the House of Representatives their written declaration that the President is unable to discharge the powers and duties of his office, the Vice President shall immediately assume the powers and duties of the office as Acting President.

Thereafter, when the President transmits to the President pro tempore of the Senate and the Speaker of the House of Representatives his written declaration that no inability exists, he shall resume the powers and duties of his office unless the Vice President and a majority of either the principal officers of the executive department or of such other body as Congress may by law provide, transmit within four days to the President pro tempore of the Senate and the Speaker of the House of Representatives their written declaration that the President is unable to discharge the powers and duties of his office. Thereupon Congress shall decide the issue, assembling within forty eight hours for that purpose if not in session. If the Congress, within twenty one days after receipt of the latter written declaration, or, if Congress is not in session, within twenty one days after Congress is required to assemble, determines by two thirds vote of both Houses that the President is unable to discharge the powers and duties of his office, the Vice President shall continue to discharge the same as Acting President; otherwise, the President shall resume the powers and duties of his office.

Amendment XXVI [1971]   (VOTING AT AGE 18)

Section 1. The right of citizens of the United States, who are eighteen years of age or older, to vote shall not be denied or abridged by the United States or by any State on account of age.

Section 2. The Congress shall have power to enforce this article by appropriate legislation.

Amendment XXVII [1992]   (LIMITING CONGRESSIONAL PAY INCREASES)

No law, varying the compensation for the services of the Senators and Representatives, shall take effect, until an election of Representatives shall have intervened.

List of Presidents of the United States

Presidency	President	Took office	Left office	Term
1	George Washington (1789—1797)	April, 1789	March, 1797	1
				2
2	John Adams (1797—1801)	March, 1797	March, 1801	3
3	Thomas Jefferson (1801—1809)	March, 1801	March, 1809	4
				5
4	James Madison (1809—1817)	March, 1809	March, 1817	6
				7
5	James Monroe (1817—1825)	March, 1817	March, 1825	8
				9
6	John Quincy Adams (1825—1829)	March, 1825	March, 1829	10
7	Andrew Jackson (1829—1837)	March, 1829	March, 1837	11
				12
8	Martin Van Buren (1837—1841)	March, 1837	March, 1841	13
9	William Henry Harrison (1841—1841)	March, 1841	April, 1841	14
10	John Tyler (1841—1845)	April, 1841	March, 1845	
11	James K. Polk (1845—1849)	March, 1845	March, 1849	15
12	Zachary Taylor (1849—1850)	March, 1849	July, 1850	16
13	Millard Fillmore (1850—1853)	July, 1850	March, 1853	
14	Franklin Pierce (1853—1857)	March, 1853	March, 1857	17
15	James Buchanan (1857—1861)	March, 1857	March, 1861	18

(To be continued)

Presidency	President	Took office	Left office	Term
16	Abraham Lincoln (1861—1865)	March, 1861	April, 1865	19
17	Andrew Johnson (1865—1869)	April, 1865	March, 1869	20
18	Ulysses S. Grant (1869—1877)	March, 1869	March, 1877	21
				22
19	Rutherford B. Hayes (1877—1881)	March, 1877	March, 1881	23
20	James A. Garfield (1881—1881)	March, 1881	September, 1881	24
21	Chester A. Arthur (1881—1885)	September, 1881	March, 1885	
22	Grover Cleveland (1885—1889)	March, 1885	March, 1889	25
23	Benjamin Harrison (1889—1893)	March, 1889	March, 1893	26
24	Grover Cleveland (second term) (1893—1897)	March, 1893	March, 1897	27
25	William McKinley 1897—1901)	March, 1897	September, 1901	28
26	Theodore Roosevelt (1901—1909)	September, 1901	March, 1909	29
				30
27	William Howard Taft (1909—1913)	March, 1909	March, 1913	31
28	Woodrow Wilson (1913—1921)	March, 1913	March, 1921	32
				33
29	Warren G. Harding (1921—1923)	March, 1921	August, 1923	34
30	Calvin Coolidge (1923—1929)	August, 1923	March, 1929	
				35
31	Herbert Hoover (1929—1933)	March, 1929	March, 1933	36

(To be continued)

(Continued)

Presidency	President	Took office	Left office	Term
32	Franklin D. Roosevelt (1933—1945)	March, 1933	April, 1945	37
				38
				39
33	Harry S. Truman (1945—1953)	April, 1945	January, 1953	40
				41
34	Dwight D. Eisenhower (1953—1961)	January, 1953	January, 1961	42
				43
35	John F. Kennedy (1961—1963)	January, 1961	November, 1963	44
36	Lyndon B. Johnson (1963—1969)	November, 1963	January, 1969	
				45
37	Richard Nixon (1969—1974)	January, 1969	August, 1974	46
38	Gerald Ford (1974—1977)	August, 1974	January, 1977	47
39	Jimmy Carter (1977—1981)	January, 1977	January, 1981	48
40	Ronald Reagan (1981—1989)	January, 1981	January, 1989	49
				50
41	George H. W. Bush (1989—1993)	January, 1989	January, 1993	51
42	Bill J. Clinton (1993—2001)	January, 1993	January, 2001	52
				53
43	George W. Bush (2001—2009)	January, 2001	January, 2009	54
				55
44	Barack Obama (2009—)	January, 2009	Incumbent	56